Cities of Gold, Townships of Coal

Essays on South Africa's New Urban Crisis

Patrick Bond

Africa World Press, Inc.

P.O. Box 1892
Trenton, NJ 08607

P.O. Box 48
Asmara, ERITREA

Africa World Press, Inc.

P.O. Box 1892
Trenton, NJ 08607

P.O. Box 48
Asmara, ERITREA

First Printing 2000

Cover design: Debbie Hird

Library of Congress Cataloging-in-Publication Data

Bond, Patrick.
Cities of gold, townships of coal : essays on South Africa's new urban crisis / by Patrick Bond.
p. cm.
Includes bibliographical references.
ISBN 0-86543-611-8 (hb). – ISBN 0-86543-612-6 (pb)
1. Cities and towns--South Africa. 2. Urban policy--South Africa. 3. Housing policy--South Africa. I. Title.
HT169.S6B66 1999
307.76'–0968–dc21 99-24108
CIP

contents

glossary of acronyms

AAC	Alexandra Action Committee
ANC	African National Congress
BESG	Built Environment Support Group
CBOs	Community Based Organisations
COSATU	Congress of SA Trade Unions
CST	colonialism of a special type
DBSA	Development Bank of Southern Africa
DCD	Department of Constitutional Development
GATT	General Agreement on Tariffs and Trade
HWP	*Housing White Paper*
IDASA	Institute for a Democratic Alternative in SA
IDT	Independent Development Trust
IMF	International Monetary Fund
IRI	International Republican Institute
LED	Local Economic Development
LGTA	Local Government Transition Act
LGWP	*Local Government White Paper*
MIF	Mortgage Indemnity Fund
MIIF	Municipal Infrastructure Investment Framework
NBI	National Business Initiative
NEDLAC Council	National Economic Development and Labor
NHF	National Housing Forum
RDP	*Reconstruction and Development Program*
SAMWU	SA Municipal Workers Union
SANCO	SA National Civic Organisation
SBDC	Small Business Development Corporation
UDS	*Urban Development Strategy*
UF	Urban Foundation
UIIF	*Urban Infrastructure Investment Framework*
US AID	US Agency for International Development
WSSA	Water and Sanitation of South Africa

figures

Table 1: Rand/Dollar Values

Year	Avg Rands/US$
1950-80	0.7
1985	2.6
1990	2.6
1991	2.7
1992	3.1
1993	3.4
1994	3.6
1995	3.6
1996	4.7
1997	4.6
1998	5.5
1999	6.1

Figure 1: South Africa

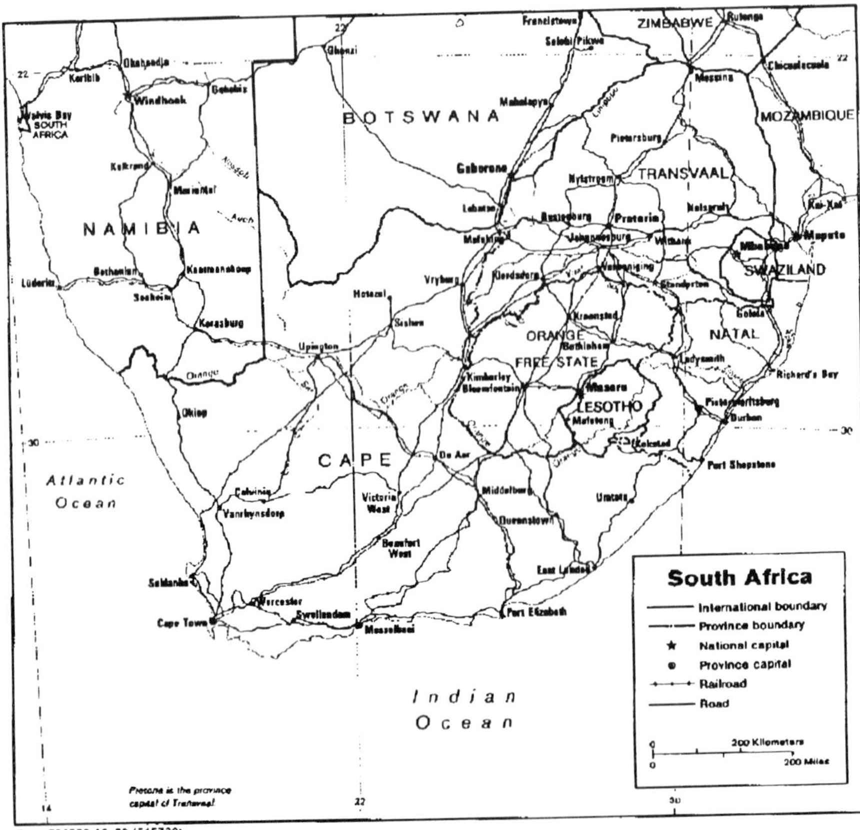

Base 504639 10-80 (545732)

Figure 2: Greater Johannesburg

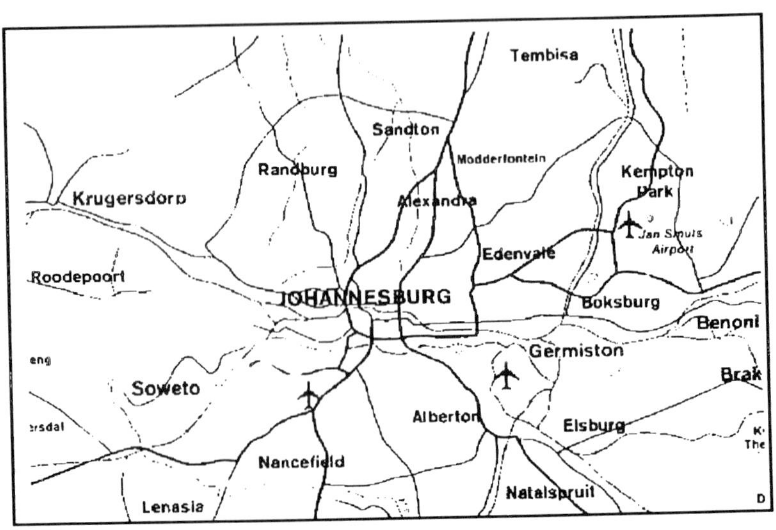

Figure 3: Stutterheim

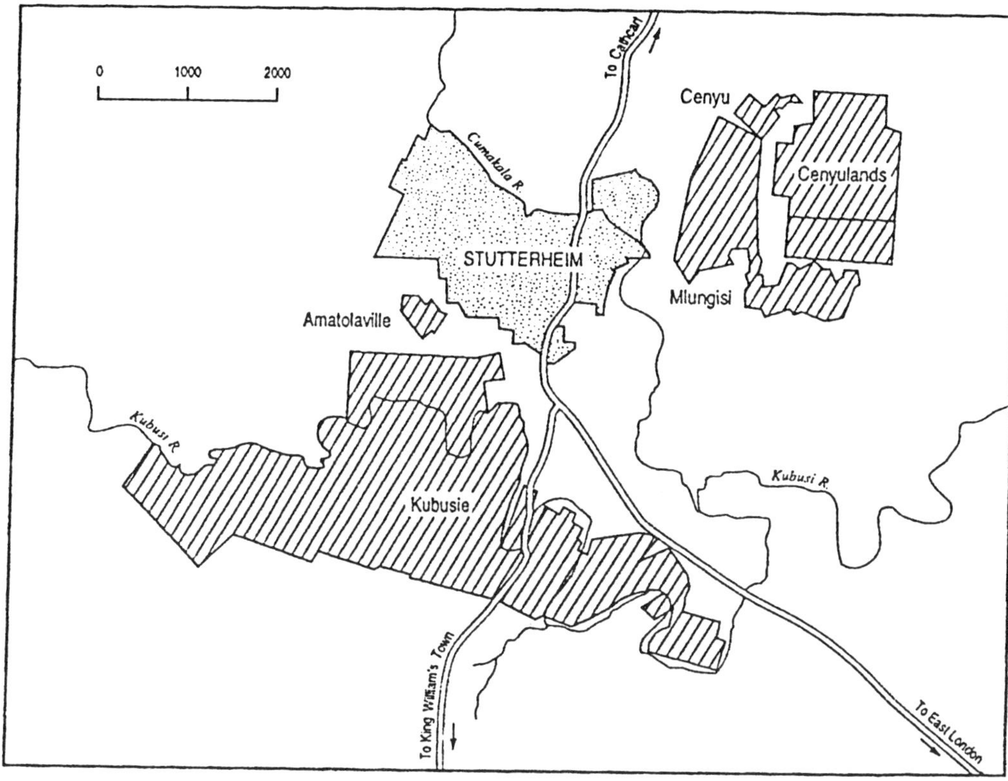

Figure 4: Alexandra Township

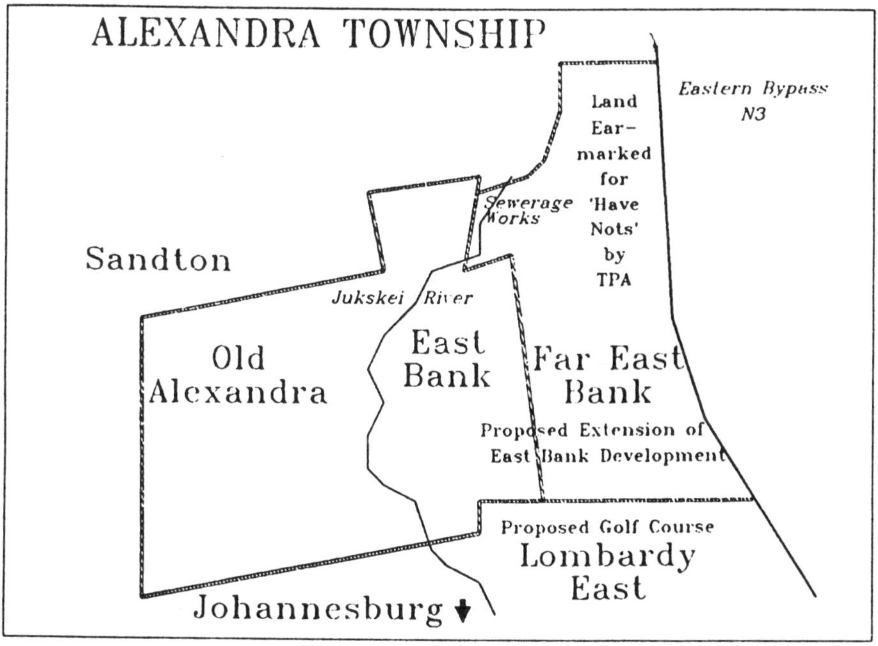

Figure 5: The Johannesburg Central Business District

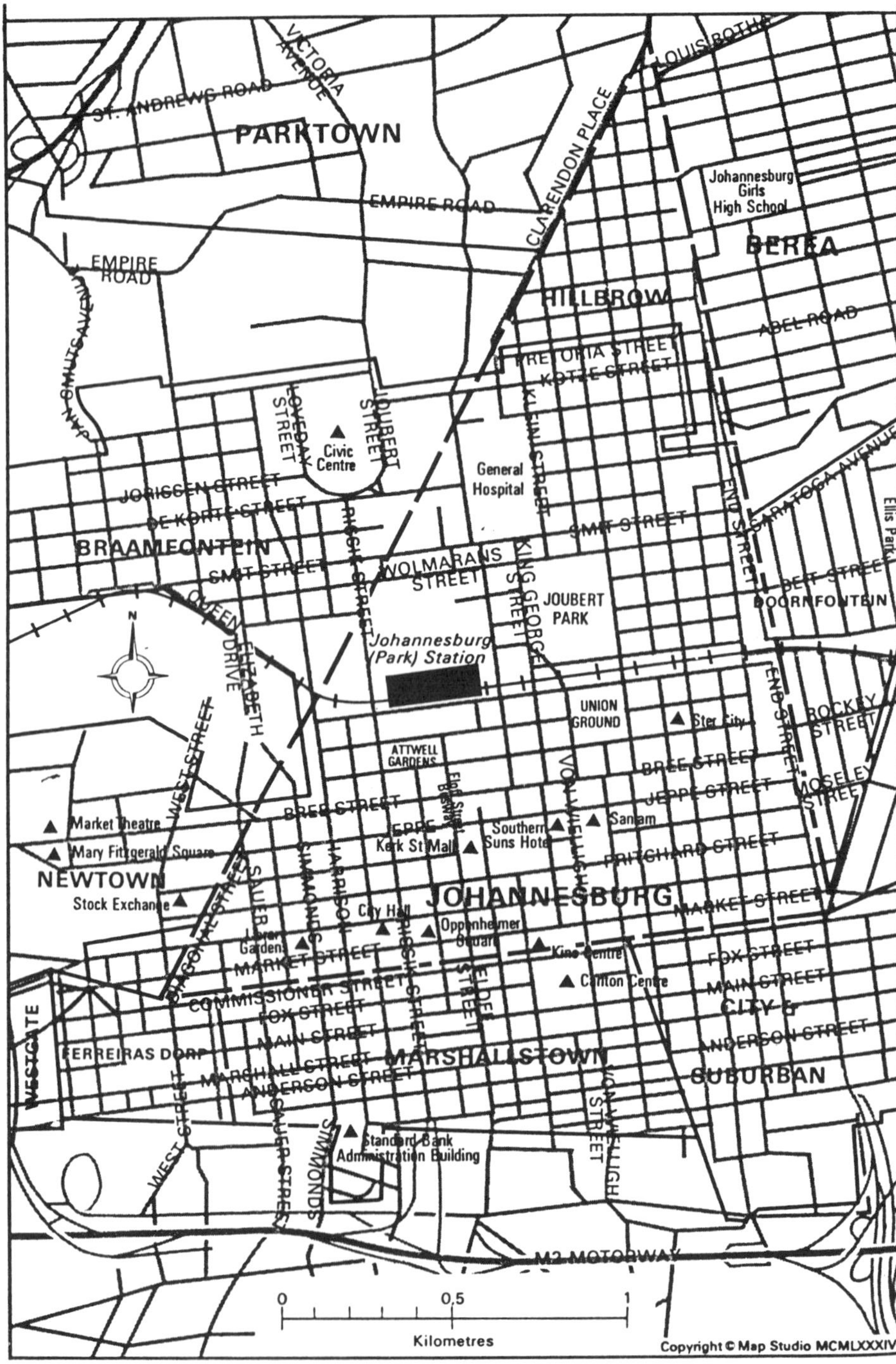

sources

1. "Re-using the Spaces of Confinement: From Urban Apartheid to Post-Apartheid without Postmodernism," *Urban Forum* 3, 1, 1992.
2. "The Changing Scale of Globalisation," *Socialist Studies Bulletin* 47, 1997.
3. "Basic Infrastructure for Socio-Economic Development, Ecological Protection and Geographical Desegregation: South Africa's Unmet Challenge," *Geoforum* 30, 1, 1999.
4. "Privatization, Participation and Protest in the Restructuring of South African Municipal Services: The Basis for Opposing World Bank Promotion of Public-Private Partnerships," *Urban Forum* 9, 1, 1998.
5. "Local Economic Development and Municipal Infrastructure Crisis: The Case of Stutterheim," *Urban Forum* 9, 2, 1998.
6. "Township Housing and South Africa's 'Financial Explosion': The Theory and Practice of Financial Capital in Alexandra," *Urban Forum* 1, 2, 1990.
7. "Contradictions in the Transition from Urban Apartheid: Barriers to Gentrification in Johannesburg" in D.Smith, ed. *The Apartheid City and Beyond: Urbanization and Social Change in South Africa*, Routledge, London, 1992.
8. "Urban Social Movements, the Housing Question and Development Discourse in South Africa," in D.Moore and G.Schmitz, eds. *Debating Development Discourses: Institutional and Popular Perspectives*, London, Macmillan and New York, St.Martin's Press, 1995.
9. "The Housing Question Revisited: 'Blacks like Shacks,' say South Africa's Corporate Liberal Intelligentsia," *debate* 3, 1997.
10. "The Failure of Housing Policy in Post-Apartheid South Africa," *Urban Forum* 8, 1, 1997.
11. "Bank Braves South Africa's Townships," *BankCheck*, February 1994.
12. "The Development Bottleneck," *Southern Africa Report*, April 1996.
13. "Response to Government's Draft *Urban Development Strategy*," *Urban Forum* 7, 1, 1996.
14. "Urban Betrayal: The ANC in the Townships," *Southern Africa Report*, August 1998.

preface

Theory, Analysis, and Practice during Post-Apartheid Urban Crisis

Introduction

My thesis is that the *uneven development* of South Africa's cities and black townships[1] (as well as smaller centers, towns and villages) was generally *amplified* during the 1990s transition to democracy, which was also a transition to "neoliberal,"[2] market-oriented ways of organizing urban policy. Exploring the political-economic roots of this phenomenon, this book brings together articles of various length published during the 1990s. Such an exercise is valuable in that at the very least it forces the author to step back and reconsider arguments, retrospectively, by exploring the analysis for inaccuracies, the political ambitions for miscalculations, and the policy prescriptions for gullible, populist sentiments. Africa World Press has graciously given me the chance to do so in a collection that both reflects a personal journey and captures some of the thinking associated with Left currents in 1990s urban South Africa.

At the outset I want to be forthright about the intellectual and strategic shortcomings associated with writings (and politics) that, at the time, claimed the lofty moral high ground associated with opposition to apartheid and the effects of a profoundly racialized urban capitalism. Alongside similar efforts by several dozen colleagues from non-governmental organizations (NGOs) and academia, and often in step with urban social movements' own praxis, I drafted these articles squarely within the logic of South Africa's deeper liberation struggle (not the triumphant neoliberalism that replaced a few thousand Afrikaners with a new, often terribly opportunistic political and bureaucratic elite, leaving most oppressed South Africans in an objectively worse socio-economic position than before). But it is important to mention that amongst the group most closely associated with these arguments--intellectual-activist-strategists at the Johannesburg NGO Planact--some stalwarts turned 180 degrees away from their moorings (a point I return to later), and in so doing left the legacy of our collective progressive intellectual and professional work in ideological tatters.

With this contradiction-ridden past firmly in mind, I seek to unveil weaknesses of our approach, on the one hand, and on the other, highlight passages or contentions that strike me as relatively more astute. I attempt this partly by providing contextual prefaces to each chapter--in the form of a paragraph that also seeks to update particular issues--and partly by way, here, of offering extended thanks to comrades who guided (or accidentally misguided) me along the way.

To assess what we have collectively and individually learned requires, first, reviewing the structure of the book. Part One contains the more abstract statements about urban processes, although theoretical remarks are to be found scattered across other chapters. My orientation to the South African city depends upon a wider understanding of capitalist crisis formation in urban settings, and tries to simultaneously locate global and national processes that affect space, scale and economic sectors. The overall approach falls within what is known as the theory of uneven development (Bond 1998a, 1998b, 1998c, 1999), which draws upon Marx's *Capital* and upon the work of a contemporary generation of radical geographers with whom I studied. The former gives us the sense of the simultaneous emergence of concentrations of wealth and capital (for capitalists), on the one hand, and poverty and oppression (for workers), on the other. This "general law of capitalist accumulation," as Marx termed it, highlights capital-labor conflict, but is not the only way to ground a theory of uneven development.

In contrast, the contemporary approach, to paraphrase David Harvey (1996:295), is based rather more closely on tracking capital flows, and in particular the differentiated return on investment that creation and/or destruction of entire built environments--and the social structures that accompany them--offer to different kinds of investors with different time horizons. Meanwhile, different places compete endlessly with one another to attract investment. In the course of promoting an interurban entrepreneurialism, they tend to exacerbate unevenness, allowing capital to play one local or regional or national class configuration off against others.

As witnessed in urban South Africa, the outcome is a process of well-structured geographical inequality which (several of the chapters below argue) has become worse during a decade in which embryonic neoliberal policies and practices were cemented, ironically by the very African National Congress politicians and technocrats who led (or gave background advice to) struggles against the late-apartheid regime's creeping neoliberalism. That there is more continuity than change from urban apartheid to post-apartheid is documented at length in the following pages.

Part One, hence, posits that some of the main Marxist statements about urban theory hold up fairly well over time. Indeed both the postmodern, neo-apartheid "spatial fix" (Chapter One) and the shift in control functions from nation-state scale to both the global and the local (Chapter Two)--which I take as the key intermediate reflections of the deeper combination of uneven development and capitalist crisis--are both still very much in progress, sadly enough. As I write, the global financial meltdown intensifies and appears likely to exacerbate the worst tendencies associated with the earlier rise of finance. Can these necessary, theoretically-derived processes of urban unevenness be overcome, so that South Africa reconstructs its cities and townships in a more rational and humane way? At a time when the municipal state is either fiscally hamstrung or ideologically committed to minimalist, neoliberal governance, only the influences of progressive social movements offer that capacity; but around which issues have embryonic progressive movements been struggling, recently?

Part Two reflects the bulk of the urban research in which my colleagues and I have engaged since around 1996, when it was clear that the civic movement and its allies had decisively lost the housing policy advocacy struggles. The retreat, both politically and intellectually, was to defend the extension of basic municipal services. Here, a "toilet-in-the-veld" which was once so readily dismissed as the basis for late-apartheid housing, became something of a revolutionary demand, under a post-apartheid infrastructure policy framework initially authored by the World Bank.

We begin in Chapter Three with a technicist discourse invoking and broadening cost-benefit calculation to fight the Bank's urban neoliberalism. Notwithstanding the attempts to speak truth to power in a language comprehensible to Department of Constitutional Development bureaucrats, this argument did not shift policy by more than a few meters--the distance, indeed, between a community-wide standpipe and a yard connection in urban slums, which, along with an inadequate electricity connection, was the sole victory achieved through the research. The political import of divergent infrastructure discourses is clear in Chapter Four, in which contradictions in World Bank privatization advocacy are exposed. There is no more contradictory a setting for basic infrastructure than Stutterheim, an Eastern Cape town celebrated for its "local economic development" strategies while all around, Chapter Five shows, underdevelopment deepens.

Part Three concerns housing more directly. Chapter Six discusses the early stages of township commodification, particularly the dramatic increase in housing finance penetration during the late 1980s. The case study concerns Alexandra in Johannesburg, a setting that, amidst vibrant politics (Mayekiso 1996), reflected the gamut of contradictions associated with the rush by financial and construction capital into township territory. The search for a site of ameliorated class struggle and capital accumulation was, hence, unsuccessful. Nor, as Chapter Seven documents, did central Johannesburg achieve the modified patterns of gentrification anticipated by late-apartheid planners, again by virtue of the underlying capitalist contradictions that provoke uneven development.

Experiences of this sort, in the wake of decades of social struggles over housing (particularly the rent boycotts of public housing during the 1980s and the early 1990s "bond boycotts" of mortgaged homes), led the Democratic Movement to begin conceptualizing its own policies, even though these would only become relevant in 1993 or so. By then, Chapter Eight explains, the World Bank urban agenda was clear; the late-apartheid regime had definitively closed off public housing options (most municipalities having liquidated their own building capacity); and a National Housing Forum was established to bridge the gaps between these establishment approaches and radical township sentiments. The Urban Foundation--increasingly the institution most responsible for injecting a neoliberal logic into late-apartheid urban policy and practice--positioned itself well to run this Forum; this was permitted by ANC leadership in a manner consistent with the general pattern of popular demobilization associated with negotiations. The disappearance of the Foundation in 1995 did not mean its ideologues had finished their work, for once Minister Joe Slovo's policy sufficiently reflected the neoliberal perspective, renewed efforts would be required (as described in Chapter Nine) to persuade black households that a site-and-service "incremental" housing product would best suit their needs and the national interest. The overall degradation of housing policy was by now complete, as Chapter Ten documents.

In Part Four, we trace the withdrawal of what were once expansive urban imaginations--as set out in the *Reconstruction and Development Programme*--into the neoliberal closet. The policy retreat encompasses the uneven infrastructural and housing development discussed above, but extends into a variety of other realms including local government, geographical processes, transport, environment, gender relations, community participation and the like. Chapter Eleven takes up from the earlier review of World Bank housing discourses to introduce the broader strategy of early 1990s Bank "urban reconnaissance missions." Chapter Twelve traces the early emergence of post-apartheid urban crisis in the form of continued rent and services payments boycotts under conditions of highly-constrained democratic transition. From these early conditions of crisis, state bureaucrats drew all the wrong lessons, as Chapter Thirteen documents. Finally, in 1998, while offering a few minor progressive changes to political power relations--but only at a point at which the traditional progressive forces were either beaten back or despondent or in many cases, simply coopted--the *Local Government White Paper* cemented all the worst socio-economic aspects of urban apartheid.

There are three unifying themes to these chapters: a) the problems caused by neoliberal urban policies and processes; b) the social, ecological, and economic potential of alternative, progressive urban options; and c) the periodic upsurges of resistance and protest by township residents that can help take us from here to there. I should leave the last but most important area of speculation, that concerning community movement regeneration, to those who have most at stake. This is partly a confession of ignorance, for (despite my exposure to the options, strategies, tactics and discourses available to civic associations, in terms of both everyday wars of position and occasional wars of movement) their core dynamics remain a mystery. Byzantine, sometimes egocentric claims to community representation have too often proved a depressing civil society mirror of identical processes within political society. (Witness the petit-bourgeois personality conflicts that lie close to the surface in the ANC and indeed all the political parties.) Of course they also mirror the debates within academia (such as are found in

Chapter Nine), which, as Henry Kissinger once remarked after an administration battle at Harvard, are the most virulent because so little is really at stake.

But in this regard, from the outset I want to confess how consistently wrong I was to argue--as was often enough the rhetoric within the SA National Civic Organization (which I served as a technical advisor) during the militant 1992-93 period--that *the underlying class basis of civics (the combination of working-class and unemployed people) and women's leadership of civics at branch or grassroots level would together place them at the helm of progressive social struggles in South Africa.* At the time, I expected the Congress of SA Trade Unions (COSATU) to opt for decisively corporatist politics favorable only to the leading 30 percent of the working class, leaving the civics to take the broader struggles forward. I was backwards in that assumption and so pay tribute to COSATU for its extraordinarily progressive social and economic policy advocacy since 1994 as well as to the SA Municipal Workers Union for defending its workers' jobs against the privatization juggernaut in a manner that consistently unifies relations with township residents.

That is only one of what readers may consider as a series of egregious errors of judgment that flow from the ideas and interpretations set out in the following pages.[3] Like the opportunity to do policy work--which, at least in terms of infrastructure, distracted us from active grassroots mobilizations occurring around us at the time--I think such misimpressions about resistance reflect the romanticization of social-movement professionalism common to petit-bourgeois intellectual and political voyeurs. Class suicide is no answer. Instead, the reader will soon learn, the route that incessantly stretches ahead is one of critique: critique of state policy and of capitalist practices and of the theories that undergird both. From a first stage of critique to a second stage, based on a formidable grassroots movement for urban reform, perhaps revolution, that shakes the apartheid-capitalist city at its roots, we may not have long to wait around the corner of the 21st century, if the contradictions associated with South Africa's new (i.e., neoliberal) urban crisis continue intensifying.

Acknowledgments

It's been a fantastic privilege to work with excellent comrades in some of the theoretical, political, policy, and applied projects that have flowered over the last decade of South African urban development and underdevelopment. Atop the list are George Dor (Alternative Information and Development Center), Meshack Khosa (Human Sciences Research Council), Mzwanele Mayekiso (Columbia Planning School), Jenny Robinson (Open University), Mark Swilling (Spier Institute), and a group of Johns Hopkins University geography students: Ben Cashdan, Darlene Miller, Greg Ruiters, and Dana Wise. George in particular has served as the primary catalyst for whatever political integrity may have inadvertently been inserted in my writings since 1995; prior to 1995 that debt is owed the township civic movement--Mzwanele and for a time Moses Mayekiso and the Alexandra and national offices of the SA National Civic Organization--and the urban development NGO Planact which, thanks largely to Mark, employed me from April 1990 through October 1994. Meshack's own (Oxford) doctoral study, of the capitalist crisis in the kombi taxi industry, serves as an exemplary model of applied South African intellectual work; likewise, Jenny's pioneering application of Foucault to Port Elizabeth's townships (in a Cambridge thesis) was eye-opening. The doctoral works-in-progress of Ben, Darlene, Greg, and Dana remind me of the strongest traditions of urban political-economic critique (especially when turned, regularly, over a friendly beer, against my own work and practices).

Tracing back to the point where, for the first time, township experiences overwhelmed my middle-class sensibilities and indeed drew me into some of the most stimulating political debates of the 1990s, it is impossible to record the depth of gratitude felt by an expatriate researcher with radical proclivities, finding myself on Rockey Street in Yeoville (Jo'burg's Greenwich Village at that stage) for more than four years in such company, and with the mandate Planact earned from the individual and then national civics. In those continual trips to mass meetings and secretive consultations in Gauteng's far-flung townships, during a period so fraught with repression and violence to be sure, I was taught the cutting-edge insurgent and developmental strategies that somehow the civics managed to synthesize into a unique and organic urban class struggle. The lessons were debated long into the night, during the early 1990s, at seedy Rockey Street pubs and with housemates in Hillbrow and Bertrams, particularly Mzwanele, Dana, Langa Zita, and Dale Mckinley.

For a year, in 1995, I had the fortune of exposure to a quieter but just as rigorous Left education in social policy and politics when Vicente Navarro invited me to join him on the faculty of the Johns Hopkins School of Public Health. Also at Hopkins but beginning a decade earlier, David Harvey and Erica Schoenberger of the Department of Geography and Environmental Engineering provided inspiring doctoral supervision--as did my fellow students Kevin Archer, Michael Johns, Phil Schmandt and Eric Swyngedouw--at a time I was distracted by anti-apartheid activism and a range of community struggles over flows of investment finance in various US cities. David's arguments about the urbanization of capital, and Neil Smith's about the sources of uneven urban development remain the seminal statements of what, in my view, generates cities of gold, townships of coal--here in South Africa, in the US and, as I tried to document in my dissertation, in a very uneven Zimbabwe.

Subsequently, in 1996-97, the National Institute for Economic Policy--a small Johannesburg think-tank of Keynesian repute--proved a frustrating base, for returning to the new South Africa in a consultancy-driven environment was increasingly untenable, intellectually as well as politically. Yet NIEP nevertheless allowed me (assisted by Selby Shezi) to begin some of the detailed work on infrastructure, much in the form of research for government, which constitutes the second part of this book. (Grudging thanks go to the state sponsors and foreign funders--the Reconstruction and Development Ministry, Departments of Constitutional Development, Public Works, Water Affairs and Forestry, and the US Agency for International Development and German and British aid--but alongside many regrets that, our minor efforts notwithstanding, neoliberal forces continually prevailed in virtually all the policy drafting exercises.)

A permanent academic home emerged in mid-1997, which has offered the virtues of stimulating students and colleagues and the freedom of thought essential to a social critic. The University of the Witwatersrand Graduate School of Public and Development Management is widely recognized as the primary South African center of creative (and very often divergent) thinking on urban processes, thanks to Peter Benjamin, Chris Brazell, Ben Cashdan, Graeme Gotz, Kirsten Harrison, Thami Hlekiso, Roland Hunter, Alan Mabin,

Pandelani Mathoma, Thomas Mogale, Kecia Rust, Maliq Simone, Mark Swilling, Richard Tomlinson, Dominique Wooldridge and Horacio Zandamela. Together with critical students too numerous to mention, and other P&DM academics and program managers active in other areas of public policy, collectively and individually my colleagues offer a terrific sounding board. Gavin Cawthra and Keith Yeomans, together with our administrative staff, are due special thanks for making P&DM much much more than a mere professional school.

Wits has also been home to a tendentious group of radical graduate students who edit the journal *debate*, as well as to Departments of Politics and of Geography and Environmental Studies which have been most hospitable. I have taken great encouragement, in pursuing urban problems, from Franco Barchiesi, Lindsay Bremner, Tom Lodge, Rob McCutcheon, Darrell Moellendorf, and Chris Rogerson, as well as the Wits vice-chancellor, Colin Bundy, who envisages the reinsertion of our university into the city in a manner, finally, conducive to social progress.

Colleagues at other universities who regularly correct my misimpressions and urban biases include Angela Tait and Sue Parnell at the University of Cape Town; David Hemson, Brij Maharaj, and Dhieru Soni at the University of Durban-Westville; Steven Hosking at the University of Port Elizabeth; Anne Shlay of Temple University; Martin Murray of the State University of New York; Andrew Nash, David Sanders and John Williams of the University of the Western Cape; Andrew Sessions of the University of Wisconsin; and John Saul of York University.

In the NGO sector, similar service is performed by, among others, Carl Brecker, Brian Ashley and Dot Keet of the Alternative Information and Development Center; Mercia Andrews of Trust for Community Outreach and Education; Becky Himlin of the Development Research Institute; Edgar Pieterse and Firoz Khan of Isandla Institute; Fiona Tregenna of the National Labour and Economic Development Institute; Joel Bolnik of People's Dialogue; and in Washington, Chester Hartman of the Poverty and Race Research Action Center. The strongest thanks for and warmest memories of collaboration, while we worked together on inner-city upgrading and township housing finance, are due Odette Geldenhuys (then of the Legal Resources Center).

None of the intellectual or policy work underway here, however, would make much difference were it not for the heroic struggles against urban neoliberalism waged by South African township residents, aided and abetted by those NGO cadres who have not yet lost their political nerve. Here one can talk with confidence about the underlying rigor of the civics' approach to "working-class civil society" (to borrow Mzwanele's phrase), and honor those who keep the flame burning. Among them are Moses Majola of the Meadowlands 97 Residents; David Letsie, Johnny Mpho and Sam Maredi of Alexandra Civic; Maynard Menu and Simon Mabuza of Soweto Civic; Pressage Nyoni of the Hillbrow Seven Buildings Project; Sandy Singh of the Johannesburg Inner-City Community Forum; Ali Tleane and Tebogo Phadu of the Tembisa Residents Association; and dozens of other hard-core community activists who took part in a series of workshops on Gauteng urban problems, teaching me about concrete issues and feasible political discourses, while keeping a careful eye on their petit-bourgeois technical corps. Many other great leaders of Gauteng townships with whom I had passing contact while at Planact should be added to the list, including several whose sacrifice to the cause included their lives, when their community mobilizing exceeded the tolerance of a late-apartheid state in its most vicious death-throes.

In the more recent period, staff of the South African Municipal Workers Union (Roger Ronnie, Lance Viotti, and Anna Weekes) and their technical backers at the International Labour Research and Information Group in Cape Town (John Pape, Sandra van Niekerk, and Marlea Clark) helped build a progressive ideology of urban services and rooted it in militant campaigns. Linking community and labor struggles throughout the country's poorest province, the Eastern Cape Socio-Economic Consultative Council's cadres--especially Russell Grinker, Nik Hugo, Mcebisi Jonas, and Litha Mcwabeni--regularly explained to me Bisho's often advanced political thinking yet backward development practice. A group of visiting students--Khutso Madubanya (Grinnell), Nikki Reisch (Yale), Jens Buchholz (Technische Universitaet Berlin) and Karen Bakker (Oxford)--proved to be extremely able colleagues. And I thank my coauthors for permission to republish, as well as editors of *Urban Forum, Geoforum, debate, BankCheck, Southern Africa Report* and various books from which chapters are reprinted.

Acknowledgements of a Special Type

Along the way, however, it is important to record the effect on urban South Africa of those who once had, but soon lost, a commitment to radical social change. The civic movement has its share of comrades who were one day vibrant anti-apartheid rent boycotters, the next banal proponents of Operation Masakhane service cut-offs. But other critics (their direct constituents) must be the ones to demand accountability.

From the standpoint of generating technical, professional, theoretical and strategic knowledge about South African cities, there also deserves mention another group whose work was once full of progressive potential but whose reversals had debilitating effects. During the late 1980s and early 1990s, Planact and its fraternal "Urban Sector Network" service organizations in the main South African cities claimed an extraordinary intellectual and political vantagepoint from which, in future, would emerge the vision and political alliances required to restructure the apartheid city. Senior leadership deserted these NGOs during 1993-95, to take up positions in private consultancies first and then bored deep within the state, ultimately designing and implementing policies that in socio-economic respects made things worse not better for their previous community and workplace associates.[4]

An editorial in the journal *debate*--"Intellectuals in Retreat" (1997)--considered this problem insofar as it affected academics:

> Here we refer to an extraordinary social phenomenon, based on what seems to be ceaseless individual meanderings--nearly all by white males in their 40s and 50s--from mid-1980s grassroots to early 1990s "class roots" politics: the lead Marxist critic of the Anglo American Corporation turned to advertizing his consulting services (as a trade union insider) to Anglo and other firms; the two leading Marxist critics of the Urban Foundation (Anglo American's social policy think-tank) became two of its key strategists; numerous academic Marxists did top-secret consulting work for the Urban Foundation, such as regarding land invasions (contemporary and historical) at precisely the time the UF's land speculation strategy was most threatened by the invasion tactic; the two leading Marxist critics of orthodox pension fund management became important exponents and practitioners of orthodox financial packaging through the big institutional investment firms; an energetic Marxist-workerist educator led a high-profile post-apartheid labor commission that rejected a national minimum wage; the lead Marxist critic of export-led growth strategy debuted in the *Financial Mail* by endorsing Taiwan as a model for post-apartheid SA and subsequently co-authored *GEAR*; the most influential Marxist

economist within the trade unions turned from advocating social democracy in the pages of the SACP's *African Communist* to fiscal discipline and free trade within the Finance and Trade/Industry Ministries; and last and possibly least, South Africa's lead Marxist peasant scholar, who was jailed for his SACP ties during the 1960s and later (at the Sussex Institute for Development Studies during the 1970s) supervised the doctoral theses of leading South African neo-Poulantzians, eventually became the strategist of "homegrown" African structural adjustment at the World Bank (and presently serves as the Bank's London representative).

In the process, it has been easy to denigrate the scholarship and pronouncements of erstwhile Leftists, such as the *Independent Group* newspaper columnist who once led the country's premier *Kapital* reading circle but today probably triples his Wits professorial salary by showing Moneybags how to mislead workers into a flexible future. This issue of *debate* is unabashedly full of criticism of patent sell-outs. But we continue a search for explanation--aside from those vulgar Marxists amongst us content to point out the rise of the real interest rate on mortgage bonds from 1986 (-6 percent) to the 1990s (+10 percent) at precisely the time many of our elder brothers turned 35 and bought their first house and fast car. Aficionados of campus fads also know that during the 1980s and 1990s, intellectual life deteriorated. Political theory turned away into Laclauian cul-de-sacs, cultural analysis became grounded--if that's possible--in barren post-structuralist soil, and political economy stagnated as regulation theory distracted attention from classical theory while generating reformist "post-fordist" fantasies.

Are we as intellectuals ready to come home? The answer probably relies most on something else that during the last decade changed perceptibly in South Africa's practical political life: the gradual ebbing of the strategic clarity of progressive forces as all manner of deal-making exercises ensued. The demand upon intellectuals for accountability to the Movement was taken less seriously, as every passing day revealed another profound compromise of principles and "engagement" with the forces of reaction. Under the circumstances, the desire for that elusive ego-boosting quality, relevance, which always motivates political-intellectual work, became overwhelming.

This is not to say that there is anything wrong in turning to public policy, to integrating issues outside the traditional Marxian fold such as gender and environment (which are after all profoundly class-ridden), and to a never-ending search for "agency," for those anti-capitalist challenges by social movements at and beyond the point of production that complement rather than confuse the struggle of the working class for socialism. The problem tended to be the older generation's diminishing rootedness in struggle, added to the self-flattery and opportunism associated with the corridors of power, which continually undermined more durable, and politically radical, analytical approaches to social problems.

Similarly shifting political sands and opportunistic clambering by many erstwhile urban NGO comrades--and their effects upon the next, generally less lively and courageous generation of young NGO managers left behind--deserve more comment because they also give pause for humble reflection. Like the earlier crew, most of the central actors were white upper-middle-class males in their late 30s, and personal positionality is therefore part of the problem.

The new jobs taken by ex-Planact staff (and comparable staff of a couple of closely-related organizations) were formidable: two national directors-general of housing, two national deputy directors-general of local government (at the Department of Constitutional Development), the main advisor to the Minister of Water Affairs, two key national Reconstruction and Development staffmembers and other national officials centrally responsible for land redistribution and community water supply, the treasurer of Gauteng (the country's largest province) and three of Gauteng's leading housing officials, the top planner in the Northern Province, the lead echelon of Johannesburg Metropolitan Council technical staff and several executive managers of Jo'burg and other Gauteng metro substructures, the three most pivotal officials of Cape Town urban management and the Durban housing director, just to mention the highest profile of the group.

Some certainly did what they could, under conditions not of their own choosing, and I honor them. Too many others--here the class, race and gender consistency was striking--shamelessly U-turned from the moral commitments and articulations of social problems and solutions we had worked so hard to generate at Planact. And Planact, meanwhile, faced bankruptcy in 1996 (apparently failing to win any patronage whatsoever from ex-staff), surviving only by becoming a garden-variety local government consultancy, generally uncritical of the neoliberal processes swirling around and about.

My grateful acknowledgement to the NGO radicals-cum-bureaucratic conservatives is the same offered the wayward intellectuals described above: they inspire the Left, especially those of us from a petit-bourgeois class (and white, male) background, to work that much harder now, to overcome not only a devastating material legacy of post-apartheid urban policy and programs, but also the signals they have sent to working-class and poor South Africans of political unreliability. Yet no one from our class background--here I make assumptions of you the reader--is immune to eclecticism and opportunism, and it is worth concluding by restating the humility with which this preface began, so that the people whose lives and livelihoods depend so much upon our professional and even academic urban visions do not conclude--as they might today--that all the intellectuals have to offer is a modification of their inherited urban crisis.

To sum up, then, the chapters were reconstituted here in this form because of my impression that South Africa's new, post-apartheid urban crisis is especially poignant, since neoliberalism requires such an active demobilization of state resources and community struggle. The intellectual activity associated with either defending or attacking that demobilization of social potential has indeed been a spirited exercise, this past decade and more. This activity, and the remobilization of urban social movements, will continue into the next century; in republishing these articles, I hope to help readers avoid spending inordinate amounts of time (needed for organizing and advocacy) bogged down in debates that I genuinely feel were won--though not brought to fruition--during the 1990s.

Notes

1. In the terminology adopted for convenience throughout this book--which is that most often used in South Africa's development industry and amongst policy wonks--the "black" townships are specifically the "African" townships, even though many lower-income "Coloured" and "Indian" people (who are considered "black" in common progressive political terminology) face similar conditions, and have organised urban movements along similar lines to those of the African townships. This terminology is not meant to justify or reify residual apartheid race categories, but rather to most simply and accurately reflect the nature of policy debates. However, in many contexts associated with urban development and social policy, the phrase "black township" also incorporates *low*-income Coloured and Indian communities. As the pace of desegregation remains slow, and as the Zimbabwean deracialized phrase "high-density suburb" (versus the formerly-white "low" and "medium" density suburbs) has not caught on, terminological ambiguity is one unfortunate result.

2. This phrase is commonly used in Europe and the Third World, and unlike the US connotation of the word liberal, implies an extremely conservative, *laissez faire* philosophy based on the notion that free markets best organize societies. The "neo" reflects a revitalization of 19th-century liberalism. Until the economic crisis that began in 1997, neoliberalism had vanquished its macroeconomic opponent, Keynesianism. Similarly, state interventions in urban policy were firmly discouraged by the major neoliberal institutions, including the World Bank, the US Agency for International Development and their South African allies.

3. There were a few other published articles about South African urbanization omitted from this collection for reasons of space or (shallow) depth, but for the sake of transparency and in the event a meticulous reader wants to identify other egregious errors, they are to be found in Bond (1990g-h, 1991c-d, 1992b-g, 1993c-e, 1994b-c, 1995, 1997b-g, 1998d), Bond and Ansell (1992), Bond, Hosking and Robinson (1998), Bond and Pillay (1995), Bond, Pillay and Sanders (1997), and Bond and Swilling (1992).

4. Conventional wisdom surrounding Planact's fate is reflected in this summary by Abbott (1996:202):

> (1992) was the apogee of Planact's power. It employed 36 full-time staff dealing with almost 100 projects and was an integral part of the national consultation process. It was an adviser to the ANC, and World Bank missions could not have credibility unless they had spoken to Planact. It had been the prime mover in the establishment of an Urban Sector NGO Network in South Africa; had extensive contacts internationally with other development NGOs; and was the recognized alternative authority on the urbanization process in South Africa... By 1993, many of its key people had left and its funding base was diminishing rapidly.

Abbott's book does not comprehend nor explain the U-turn by those key people (nor does it discuss Planact's decline adequately), but then again no one else has either, at the time of writing. Planact's ex-staff have been extremely reticent to document reasons for their bizarre trajectories.

PART ONE

URBAN CRISIS AND CRISIS THEORY

chapter one

Liberating Urban Spaces?

This chapter rests on two pillars of political-economic theory: the tendency towards the "overaccumulation of capital," and the geographers' idea of a "spatial fix"--i.e., the systematic displacement (not resolution) of overaccumulation into South Africa's cities and regions since the 1970s. By way of updating, the manufacturing incentives mentioned here--which enjoyed a surprising durability associated with Afrikaans old-boy networks, even as late-apartheid neoliberal opposition mounted--were finally dismantled in the first years of ANC rule, fatally wounding many ANC strongholds (such as riot-torn Butterworth in the Eastern Cape, an industrial ghost town today). As is now more generally the case for rural folk, a double punishment was visited by neoliberalism: once apartheid threw people far afield to hostile bantustans, giving them slight relief in the form of deconcentration points, there emerged during the 1990s a) the ignominy of declining urban migration prospects thanks to the stagnant economy, and b) a reduction in the local circulation of cash (previously associated with decentralization) to a feeble trickle. Even in urban spaces, township housing bonds also virtually dried up during the early 1990s (as explained in Part Three). Other higher-profile spaces that once appeared ripe for at least a non-racial capitalist liberation--Central Business Districts (CBDs) and the gentrification zones that in 1991 held such promise--imploded during the 1990s and are today (for example, in central Johannesburg) characterized by the double urban capitalist process of residential overcrowding with intensifying blight, alongside dramatic levels of vacant office space. Notwithstanding the decision to locate the Constitutional Court in Hillbrow's Fort Prison--an island of pomp within a sea of decay--no amount of postmodern hype or slick marketing of buppie opportunities could hide this betrayal of deracialized capitalism's extravagant promises.

[Following a presentation at a 1991 architects' conference, this chapter appeared as "Re-using the Spaces of Confinement: From Urban Apartheid to Post-apartheid without Postmodernism" in *Urban Forum* 3, 1 (1992).]

Introduction

Invited to comment upon the conference theme, "re-using spaces of confinement," any number of reference points spring to mind. Apartheid, after all, was nothing if not the pinnacle of artificial geographical confinement: mass-organized social control of black populations; all-encompassing restraints on their physical movements, at household, urban, rural and regional scales; bantustan segregation along lines of gender, ethnicity, and culture; and the spatial containment of economic forces. As South Africa transforms geographically, the top priority on most everyone's agenda today boils down to this very question: how to re-use various spaces of confinement? What can stay, what must go, and what new social, cultural, political, and economic practices provide the tools to construct a different built environment that suits particular--and sometimes general--interests?

It is useful to address this issue in as broad a manner as possible, in part in order to appraise theoretical assertions about the political economy of space. As students of the urban process, we have the tendency to confine our perspective on social change to that circumscribed by our disciplinary boundaries. For architects, accordingly, perhaps the challenge offered by a conference like this is most easily and directly dealt with in terms of transforming the functionality of jails and prisons into more aesthetically and morally pleasing uses. The writings of Foucault have been invoked by several participants to lend a certain universality to efforts at re-using the spaces of confinement under post-apartheid conditions.

As one example, Hillbrow's Fort Prison--subject of much of this conference's attention--appears ripe for this sort of transformation, and has received ample attention as a site emblematic of the potential for a new kind of South African urbanism. One obvious danger, of course, is that its role in the revitalization of Johannesburg might fit the typical mold of fleeting, unsuccessful projects designed mainly to enrich developers and politicians, including the Civic Spine, Civic Center, CBD east and west end gentrification, or still-born "heritage industry." In this context it is easy to imagine the Fort Prison--like Robben Island--serving a certain style of re-use of spatial confinement, overwhelmingly oriented to tourism and petit-bourgeois retail development. Whether or not this is liberatory is a matter that should be subject to debate, one involving former prisoners.

But notwithstanding the value of the insights that are to be garnered through a microproject inquiry of this sort, there are also important processes at higher scales--including theory--that shed much brighter light on developments in particular localities. While the tint may be unfamiliar, it is important to shine the light around, decipher the shadows, and stare long and hard at images of change typically relegated to darkness. For just as architects are bound by narrow limitations--site conditions, building materials, financing, parochial aesthetics and political interference, etc.--social scientists likewise often fail to take account of a sufficiently wide set of features of the changing geographical landscape, most particularly the relations between different spatial scales. It is true that national versus local policy issues are now emerging, generating substantial conflict and spawning vigorous discourses on the state and civil society.

However, very few linkages exist, so far, in our South African literature of metropolitan and regional change. Yet at these scales there rests a phenomenal power to restructure other levels of space and society. There is also a fairly coherent logic to spatial restructuring to be found here, following from the logic of geographical flow of capital during periods of accumulation crisis. Therefore in this talk I try to address the issue of spatial confinement in part by jumping scale from the metropolitan to the regional and back, with continual reference to the constraints imposed by South Africa's national economic stagnation, as well as to practices of international capitalism that have come to be known as *postmodern* (sometimes also "post-fordist," in recognition of the decline of mass-production, mass-consumption norms associated with Henry Ford). In material terms, these are expressed by *Marxism Today* (October 1988), a magazine of London's postmodern left, as follows: "Flexibility, diversity, differentiation, mobility, communication, decentralization and internationalization are in the ascendant. In the process our own identities, our sense of self, our own subjectivities are being transformed."

Application of such topics to South Africa is an appropriate digression from our immediate concern with local-level spatial confinement (prison refurbishment). During the 1980s--at a time of rapid shifts in architectural fashion--cities and regions once firmly in the grip of the apartheid order also began breaking free from tradition. Yet what becomes clear is that recent developments at these intermediate scales--i.e., at scales between the easily-comprehended local and the unwieldy national--are being influenced by market forces which are *incapable of ending spatial confinement*, even if they are oriented to changing its form. The point of this presentation, in fact, is that the potential liberatory forces of postmodernity--those features which make the concept as appealing to radical democrats and second-wave feminists as to well-paid urban designers--are generally outweighed by the close association of postmodernity with some of the worst traits of capitalism, both South African and international, in the throes of crisis. We can begin to identify why this is the case by examining what might be termed the *spatial confinement of capital.*

Spatial confinement and the capitalist city

One way to think about the buildings and infrastructure constructed these past few decades in Johannesburg, is as *capital*, set in intractable, immovable, and hence confined, space. This characterization holds true as much for warehouses, retail outlets, office buildings, homes in so-called African townships and white northern suburbs, and all their associated facilities, as it does for the factories, fields and mines where surplus value is extracted from the laborer. Capital confined in the built environment faces even tougher constraints on mobility--in the perpetual search for a rate of return greater than the social average--than does capital confined by nation-states, by social accords, or by outmoded social practices (like apartheid). Our modern and postmodern capitalist cities are, of necessity, the spatial forms that most emphatically support the production and circulation of capital. But in turn, cities are spaces where contradictions in the capitalist mode of production therefore play themselves out most forcefully. Cities are where a society's capacity to reproduce itself--politically, economically, socially, culturally--is on display.

From this perspective, we can address phenomena as diverse as the burgeoning financial districts of CBDs, and the location and the function of such spaces of confinement as apartheid townships. Even the seemingly uncommodified built environment that blacks were confined to (e.g., rental housing, and highly restricted and underdeveloped commerce) respected the most crucial capitalist rules (e.g., the cost structure limitations of low-income housing construction, or the power and capacity of monopoly suppliers of building materials) (Hendler 1987). Moreover, the township as a space within the broader circulation of capital also surrendered to other economic laws of motion (e.g., the regulation and control of labor supplies, the reproduction of labor power, or structuring of gender oppression consistent with long traditions of articulations of modes of production). In the course of reform, therefore, it is no accident that the breakdown of influx controls--which as much as any other instrument regulated labor mobility--was accompanied by a state-sponsored program of deracialized township capital accumulation (Swilling 1990).

On the one hand, urban apartheid's spatial development was restricted, thus, to the limits of what "racial capitalism" (Saul and Gelb 1986)--implemented by coherent race-class ruling local coalitions (McCarthy 1987a)--would support and accept. On the other hand, though, this meant that the confinement of *people* to certain sorts of spatial arrangements provoked some rather important unintended consequences in the form of urban political resistance. The enforced residential union of poor and working-class households, and the segregation of militant black intellectuals within the townships, together formed what is today perhaps the main material basis outside the trade union movement for the highly touted "politics of civil society." However, the successes of resistance thus fomented do not inherently contradict our notion of the built environment primarily *as* and *as for* capital. The accumulation of capital through the built environment remains an overriding principle of the organization of urban space (Harvey 1985a)--no less when channelled by the state for reasons peripheral to the circuitry of landed and financial capital profits (e.g., SA townships prior to the 1980s).

It is in this sense that, as we all know from our daily experience, urban space is itself "confined," in the eyes of its planners, builders, financiers and users, to the *economic rent it can command*. As Ghirardo (1985:190) puts it,

> Contemporary practice shrinks the role of the architect from that of an active agent in the construction of community and its structures to that of an exterior designer or interiors specialist. Leasing agents, developers, commercial loan officers, planning and zoning commissions make the important decisions, leaving the marginated architect the trivial task of selecting finishes and glosses inside and out.

The question of how to re-use the spaces of confinement in cities and regions often boils down to little more than the question of land rent. And that question, while not animating enough to delay us further here, leads directly to all manner of other questions about how urban capitalism works. Land rent reflects the return on capital that can be attributed to locational and spatial attributes. But capital as a social relation is by nature *mobile*, a condition deemed necessary for its reproduction over the ages--in part to maintain the class power of the bourgeoisie against that of labor, hence driving "uneven development" (Smith 1990). And yet there exists simultaneously the condition of *fixity* of physical capital (plant and equipment), which occurs when economic activity is set in the built environment literally in concrete (Harvey 1982:chs.13&14). This emerges as a barrier--indeed as possibly the single most powerful form of confinement--to further capital accumulation.

In turn, the fixity of built environment capital investments generates new tensions for geographical change. What is termed (by the Left) the "crisis" of South African capitalism, has fostered a restructuring of spatial relations, including varied processes now underway in the Witwatersrand metropolis. This reflects the fact that the confinement of capital in a built environment becomes, in effect, a substantial barrier to the circulation of capital, especially under conditions of capitalist crisis. Typical short-term responses to crisis--ranging from the new flexible specialization techniques and technologies, to postmodern cultural and architectural sentiments--are no match for the depth of the problem. (The problem, we argue in the next section, ultimately requires a deeper, more fundamental remedy entailing what Schumpeter called "creative destruction" and what Marxists term "devaluation.")

Nevertheless, the dynamic, if futile, struggle to break this condition of confinement is what *postmodern urban capitalism* is all about. Moreover, the *spatial features* of postmodern capitalism provide an important key to our understanding of changes in the world around us, just as the *postmodern, explicitly capitalist features* of urban geography, design, architecture, are crucial to understanding the dynamics underlying the changing form of these subjects.

Economic crisis and the "spatial fix"

The long-term structural crisis in the South African economy is reflected in persistent overcapacity and overproduction of luxury manufactured goods for the white consumer market side by side with growing surpluses of unemployed black workers. (The mining and agriculture crises are partly exogenous, and don't require extensive integration into our urban spatial analysis, although land ownership and control by mining houses will surely reach the political agenda at some point.) This is not a phenomenon that began with the present recession in 1989. Much more serious is the fact that the rate of reinvestment of capital in new plant and equipment, by for-profit firms, has stagnated badly since the early 1970s, especially in comparison to the skyrocketing share prices of those industrial corporations.

Indeed, dating to the 1960s, "unusually" high capital intensity (World Bank 1991a) led to a declining rate of manufacturing profit (Nattrass 1990), and hence the diminishing return to, and slowdown in, new manufacturing investment, especially machinery. These factors--which are captured by the descriptive phrase "overaccumulation of capital"--represent eternal underlying tendencies of capitalism. In South Africa they emerged to light as a massive glut in inventories of consumer goods in 1967. This forced sufficient liquid capital out of production and into the money and capital markets--hence a massive speculative stock market binge from 1967-69. With the 1969-71 crash, an inordinate amount of capital subsequently flowed into the vast spatial augmentation of South African capitalism, through vehicles like the internationalization of the mining finance houses, or the enormous boom in construction. Hence unprecedented parastatal expansion (Iscor, Eskom, Sasol, SATS); investments such as Richards Bay, Sishen-Saldanha, and the upgrade of SAA; a renewed commitment to transport more generally; infrastructural improvements and wide new electricity grids and water lines; and the extensification of urban sprawl. (There were substantially similar international trends underway, as witnessed by the circulation of overaccumulated Northern financial capital to the South. Of SA's R13 billion in parastatal investments from 1972-78, R3 billion were financed by foreign creditors.)

Capital in a state of overaccumulation, evident from the late 1960s, thus searched and found a short-term *spatial fix* in the 1970s. Space, in other words, came to capital's rescue as the basis for offloading overaccumulated capital. This mainly took the form of the expansion of the geographical boundaries of capitalism, one aspect of which was the upgrading of transport, storage, communications, and other functional components of the built environment. Another aspect, later, was more flexible labor mobility facilitated by taxi deregulation and liberalized urbanization policy. There was, additionally, the formal apartheid antidote to the glut of domestic manufacturing capital: the homelands-inspired regional decentralization policies and subsidies which picked up steam in the 1970s, and turned to specific deconcentration points in the 1980s. Aside from the policy's political purpose (propping up bantustans), decentralization also played a (temporary) role as a form of spatial fix, by promoting a qualitative new degree of "competition in laxity" (dramatically lower wages, tax holidays, and other incentives) which fueled capital mobility. Such mobility reached its peak in the mid- and late-1980s, in attempts to export cheap manufactured goods from deconcentration points resembling low-level export processing zones. Indeed within a few years the percentage of manufacturing employment in the deconcentration points rose from 2 percent to 18 percent of the nation's total, thanks to billions of rands in state subsidies (Urban Foundation 1990a).

In this respect, the spaces in which overaccumulated capital was confined--i.e., the built environments of various regions--were not being *"re-used"* on a wide scale at this stage, but were instead being *stretched* in a frantic search for new ground suitable for capital accumulation. Overaccumulation was being addressed, largely, by further spatially-expansive investment, rather than through the outright *devaluation* of what was by then, in reality (in terms of international competition), economic dead-wood. The concept of devaluation is explained by Harvey (1985b:132):

> Capital can be devalued as money (through inflation or default on debts), as commodities (unsold inventories, sales below cost price, physical wastage), or as productive capacity (idle or underutilized physical plant). The real income of laborers, their standard of living, security, and even life chances (life expectancy, infant mortality, etc.) are seriously diminished, particularly for those thrown into the ranks of the unemployed. The physical and social infrastructures that serve as crucial supports to the circulation of capital and the reproduction of labor power, may also be neglected.

The depth of the irrationality of South Africa's spatial fix, and the need for devaluation prior to a new round of accumulation, are only now becoming fully evident. Partly this reflects the resilience of apartheid and protectionist barriers of confinement, which still permit a certain privileged refuge from the full force of the global law of value (Meth 1990). But by the mid-1980s, recession, sanctions and intense international competition awoke decentralized manufacturing operations (especially those of the ever-flexible Taiwanese) to the dark side of their geographical confinement. They responded to this form of confinement by turning their products inward to the SA market, and thus the decentralization strategy became unpopular amongst certain fractions of capital which had neglected to fully explore the advantages of geographical mobility (Pickles 1991). Fixed urban manufacturing investments were now under even more acute pressure. The response by urban capital's representatives (the Urban Foundation, Johannesburg Chamber of Commerce) included energetic lobbying against this particular state-subsidised form of the spatial fix, an effort that has not yet proven successful due to various entrenched political and ethnic interests (*Financial Mail* 23/5/91).

The extensification of capitalist space was but one response to the overaccumulation crisis, and there were of course others that were, in fact, concerned with the devaluation of capital in space. It is here we can identify more explicit attacks upon spaces of confinement. Consider the vast changes in the role of South Africa's major central cities, traditional home to the mass of industrial and commercial fixed capital. By the beginning of the long-term slump in growth, the phenomenal diversification of the mining houses into manufacturing, finance and commerce had come to fruition, and in the process had virtually eliminated the role of the mid-sized merchant middleman. This *hollowed* that eastern section of the Johannesburg CBD (and similar economic zones elsewhere) formerly devoted to warehousing. On top of this, the decline of various light industries (especially textiles) which had also made the CBD home for decades, was another result of those inexorably tendencies Marx often talked about: ruinous competition, concentration and centralization of capital. A wave of mergers and bankruptcies led to a shakeout of small inner-city producers; this decay of fixed capital hollowed out yet more urban space.

The problem with the approach to devaluation engendered by these processes was that it did not entail the creative destruction of capital required to prepare the ground for a new long-term round of accumulation, since overaccumulated capital was now, in the 1970s and 1980s, simply being moved around. For example, half of the decentralized manufacturing operations are unprofitable without state subsidies (Urban Foundation 1990a). Until a sweeping shake-out is accomplished and a new set of relations of production (e.g., the vigorously-sought social contract) are negotiated, the system will continue to experience excessive capital-intensity (World Bank 1991a), declining real wages and hence limited consumer markets, untenable levels of consumer and corporate debt, rising labor-capital antagonism, and the concomitant political unrest which, almost like clockwork, intensifies under conditions of economic recession (1960, 1976, 1984-86, 1990-91). The Catch-22 is that under such conditions, there would appear no way in which a social contract can be constructed. (South Africa is not alone in this plight. All the above reservations about the endurance of the spatial fix also apply to the global condition of overaccumulation which was firmly established by the mid-1970s. Moreover, other responses to capitalist crisis--expanded credit, massive financial speculation, and rising geopolitical tensions--appear to be reaching their built-in limits to crisis-*resolution* [Armstrong, Glyn and Harrison 1991].)

Ultimately, it is only through the devaluation of capital--and with it, capitalist spaces (e.g., Germany and Japan during World War II)--that geographical confinement of capital, so debilitating under conditions of overaccumulation, can at least temporarily be remedied, and the conditions for a new cycle of accumulation be readied. Notwithstanding the recently-announced continuation of outmoded decentralization policy, precisely this realization is now setting in among capitalists, evidenced by the wave of plant shutdowns, mine closures, and the surprisingly well-advanced debate over redistributing land from overproductive, massively overindebted farmers to dispossessed blacks (warranting even a favorably-inclined DBSA position paper).

Setting aside mining and agriculture, the current epidemic of capacity underutilization in manufacturing generates both sectoral and spatial dilemmas. Hugely overaccumulated subsectors such as automobiles appear doomed not only to lose half the present number of factories, but also to take with them whole cities (Port Elizabeth, Uitenhage, East London) (*Financial Mail* 23/5/91). The spatial restructuring of the textile industry is one of the more advanced, warped examples of spatial confinement, involving, as it does, the highly politicized deconstruction of the industry's traditional vertical integration (*Business Day* 3/5/91). The chemicals industry, too, will experience a fight between hostile brothers, as enormous amounts of overaccumulated capital are destroyed, and as various locations of chemicals production (especially coastal) vie for some form of respite from the swath of devaluation.

The search for a spatial fix for these industries may not be over, but is now widely acknowledged to be an impotent gesture when "restructuring" must first be tackled. This is most emphatically illustrated, ironically, in the need for devaluation of overaccumulated capital in the transport industry (Khosa 1990). Here, the initially successful effort to vanquish spatial confinement through the proliferation of taxis fostered a wholly-inappropriate faith in the potentialities of free enterprise culture for blacks. In reality, there is a severe case of overaccumulation in this industry at present, including epidemic defaults on Wesbank loans and the deterioration of personal entrepreneurial capital, and this has taken the very visible form of taxi-wars and endemic driver speed-up. Only a shake-out along the lines of what was imposed upon the country's biggest bus company, Putco, can begin to resolve the tension (*Sunday Business Times* 26/5/91).

If these examples accurately suggest the extent of the crisis of overaccumulation of capital and the ultimate failure of the spatial fix, we might then consider all these geographical factors as integral to the demise of what Gelb (1987) has called "racial fordism." The applications of French regulation theory in South Africa (e.g., Gelb 1991; Ramos and Cassim 1989) are so far unduly spatially-naive. This is unfortunate given the geographical breadth and diversity of contrasting systems of expropriation, and articulations of modes of production, but there has not yet been a comprehensive spatially-conscious attempt to theorize South African political economy. This means the capability that capital has shown *to move the crisis around* may have encouraged some post-structuralist researchers to conclude that the capitalist system has become self-regulating, capable of reaching a new equilibrium on its own terms if only the right (economically-rational) regional conditions can be imposed.

All these geographical problems certainly apply, as well, to the potential emergence of what is being called a new post-fordist, and perhaps postmodern form of South African capitalism. Some evidence of the untenability of the urban arrangement thus introduced is outlined in the next section. What is important to establish, first, is that the geographic phenomena just reviewed are integral to the current crisis: they represent both *the drive to overcome constraints* imposed by the spatial fixity of capital, and the *contradictions that short-term spatial reorganization presents* to the old order. The spatial fix to capitalist crisis is, in effect, the frantic search for new locations of production, distribution, consumption, administration, etc. But the spatial fix strategy is clearly not succeeding in its stated goals of evening South Africa's absurdly uneven capitalist development. Perhaps only a serious dose of devaluation can permit a restructuring of geographical capital flows, as happened, for example, between international core and periphery during the 1930s. Instead, however, there are emerging a variety of attempts to veil the more destructive processes of spatial restructuring with a post-fordist, postmodern facade.

Re-using urban and regional spaces of confinement

Much of the current discourse on both re-using the spaces of confinement, and economic development more generally, relates to postmodern and post-fordist solutions concentrated in metropolitan settings. The futility of the spatial fix as a response to national and sectoral overaccumulation crisis, as reviewed above, does not annul individual capitalists' efforts to extract profits from the postmodern city. The central question here is whether short-term extraction of profits can contribute to liberating spaces of confinement, or whether such a strategy might not instead exacerbate the crisis by setting up new, more pernicious sorts of barriers? Answers can be found in places as diverse as townships, CBDs and deconcentration points.

Beginning with the built environment of the townships, the most important means of addressing the confinement of capitalist circulation to state-supported housing and infrastructure provision, is the attempt to *commodify* black housing and hence township space. As new public housing construction declined from the 1970s (Lupton 1990), the state reintroduced leasehold and freehold tenure and promoted the Great Sale of housing in the early- and mid-1980s (Mabin and Parnell 1983). There followed the penetration of some R6-8 billion rand (nationally) of for-profit developer capital backed by major financial institutions in the late 1980s. In 1982, black housing development accounted for 13 percent of building plans passed by local authorities, whereas by 1988 the figure had risen to 57 percent (*Financial Mail* 10/11/89).

Add to this all manner of low-income housing and development finance initiatives (Old Mutual's wage-related bond; the Perm's pension-related bond; the Urban Foundation's Loan Guarantee Fund; and the Independent Development Trust's R750 million capital subsidy of R7,500 for site-and-service provision, and R500 million group credit company funding scheme), most of which find extra-economic means of subsidizing for-profit developers and financiers. This should mean that overaccumulated capital is flowing quickly in search of profits towards the one-time spaces of confinement. It is worth looking more closely at the conditions under which this is occurring, however, because that anticipated result is not panning out (see below, Chapter Four). Although mass homeownership can be considered a modernist project (certainly this is the Urban Foundation's rhetoric), simultaneously other factors have intervened. In particular, various postmodern, post-fordist urban characteristics now appear ascendant in townships: impoverishment, informalization, and the intensified search for "symbolic capital."

Intensified impoverishment and informalization derive from the rapid and unplanned process of urbanization underway in South Africa, which is in turn interwoven with other factors: the broader economic crisis; agricultural debt problems which are displacing farmworkers; various regional crises (e.g., Natal); increased mobility stemming from political turmoil; and the demise of influx control laws. But because of the lack of new formal (for-profit) housing available for those households below the 90th income percentile, and exacerbated by rising levels of unemployment, the result is not dissimilar to what Harvey (1987:268) observes in so many advanced capitalist cities: "Social relations within many low income communities have, as a consequence, become much more entrepreneurial, with all of the consequences of excessive and often extraordinary exploitation (particularly of women) in the labor process."

Across the globe, such entrepreneurialism is celebrated by neo-conservatives, "as if that could solve the problems of all the poor rather than those of just a select few," as Harvey puts it. South Africa's townships have certainly become sites of the rhetoric of entrepreneurial self-help (Kane-Berman 1990; Kendall 1991)--and not only with respect to small businesses incubating with SBDC and corporate encouragement. Shack housing (commodified bits of tin and zinc) can also escape the formal circuits of monopoly capital, to the applause of all except its consumers. Even a principal COSATU economic advisor, Kaplinsky (1990:45), joins the chorus of one-sided, insipid support for the "substantial opportunities" micro-enterprises will enjoy in post-apartheid South Africa. (Those taxi wars and Wesbank defaults signal that all is not well with the strategy.)

Also celebrated by postmodernists is the search for and production of what has been termed "symbolic capital." From an architectural standpoint, Callinicos (1989:160) condemns "the packaging needed to differentiate one skyscraper from another in an era when a building's individuality has come to be an important factor in marketing office space." Piet de Beer, editor of *Architecture SA* describes the new breed of decentralized offices in such terms: "Most of the developments are bland, economical sandwich slabs decorated with cliched Po-Mo gables and arches to create corporate prestige and identity" (*ADA* 1992). This is the ideal habitat for those Callinicos (1989) terms "the children of Marx and Coca Cola": the narcissistic, credit-based "new class" (i.e., the mass layer of managers, professionals, new entrepreneurs and rentiers) infatuated with postmodernity in its consumptive forms.

But the implications reach further, as far as black South African townships. Harvey (1987:269) notices that "Producers have begun to explore the realms of differentiated tastes of aesthetic preferences in ways that were not so necessary under a fordist regime of standardized accumulation through mass production." These, Harvey argues, "have become of much greater significance since the early 1970s, in part through their proliferation into layers of the population that were hitherto denied them."

In townships ranging from Alexandra East Bank to Lenasia, symbolic capital is promoted by the developers who offer commodified housing in dozens of different styles. A 1989 Permprop (then Devco) newspaper advertisement expresses the sensation:

> Just positioning a house on a stand in such a way that it is out of alignment with its neighbors is an advantage. Making that home distinctive, different, is yet another advantage. It is a form of expression, a statement that the owners have broken free of the constraints of the past. These emotional factors have to be given due weight by any developer looking at the black market.

The untenability of the whole enterprise, considering the broader economic, political, social and ideological crises still unfolding, is evident. New home construction in townships slowed to a near halt in mid-1990, for reasons mainly relating to the unavailability of financing, those fancy bond initiatives notwithstanding. A *Financial Mail* (31/5/91) survey begins, "The banks and building societies are rapidly closing off the tap on lower-cost housing loans as they see their underlying assets threatened by township violence and their administration costs forced up by constant repayment boycotts."

The bond boycott phenomenon broke in Uitenhage in 1988, where it was tied to a union struggle against Volkswagen. Subsequently the strategy was adopted by civic associations in struggles over the quality of housing in Khayelitsha and Old Crossroads, Botshabelo,

KwaThema, Etwatwa and other townships. In spite of appeals by politicians as diverse as Hernus Kriel and Thabo Mbeki that such actions were irresponsible (Dunstan 1991), they continued, and in several cases resulted in substantial concessions (*Africa South* September/October 1990).

Alongside such resistance to the extraction of short-term banking profits at the expense of human needs exists a set of objective constraints to low-income housing provision, each exacerbated as South Africa entered the 1990s: exorbitant interest rates, land speculation, and the building materials cartel. Under these continuing deep-rooted structural conditions, it will be difficult to accomplish either a modern or a postmodern commodification of townships. As even a major developer (Theuns Kotzee of Group Five) conceded, "We cannot expect to solve the crisis as long as we look for solutions through individual ownership" (*Financial Mail* 31/5/91). Subsidised, community-controlled forms of social housing (community land trusts, housing associations and cooperatives) may prove to be the only viable approach.

There are financial constraints to a postmodern urban solution beyond the townships. In Johannesburg, the inner-city neighborhoods of Joubert Park and Hillbrow are victims of notorious blanket "redlining (geographical lending discrimination) (*Weekly Mail* 25/11/90). Ironically, this in turn may foil ambitious redevelopment visions of both the Urban Foundation and Ampros' "Anglo American Inner-City Property Development Fund." An Ampros brochure labels Hillbrow "undoubtedly one of the primary residential hubs of South Africa, [and] provides the investor with excellent potential in terms of both rentals and sales." Yet the UF concedes that declines of up to a quarter in values of sectional title flats in repossession have been experienced by building societies. Indeed, UF surveys conclude that current black residents are not interested in home ownership in Joubert Park, even though their incomes could support bond repayments. All this throws into question the prospect of a social contract--which in the UF's vision is based on residential redevelopment and a small-scale manufacturing (furniture) strategy (see below, Chapter Seven).

So difficult is it to overcome this underlying contradiction, that the role of housing in the reproduction of labor power may also be threatened by the devaluation of property in an inner-city doughnut ring of ghettoization. According to Perm business development manager Grant Newton: "Hillbrow cannot be allowed to deteriorate further in view of its strategic location as the backbone of the city's workforce" (*Star* 25/5/91). But such a process appears nearly inevitable due to factors beyond the capacity of a formal social contract to remedy. The social contract approach seems to be on the agenda of the two most important financiers--the Perm (Bond and Swilling 1991) and the World Bank (1991a)--now gearing up for re-using confined city spaces. Ideas like the "compact city" are commonplace, and areas like the east end of the CBD may provide experimental turf. One Johannesburg city official established a strategy whereby large corporations would purchase underutilized buildings in this zone of the CBD, restore them, and then sell them through sectional titles to their employees (see below, Chapter Seven).

Contradictions arising elsewhere in the system will very likely negate such an approach to revitalizing urban space. Those contradictions emanate from both intercapitalist competition between land speculators, and the enormous CBD real estate boom which began around 1985. Devaluation of property is occurring, but has not advanced far enough yet for a new surge of land-based capital accumulation. Ampros canceled the forementioned development on grounds that excessive land prices undermined the project's financial viability. Although centered on the west end in the financial district, the rise of CBD land prices has rippled through to the east and up to Joubert Park and Hillbrow, in the process pricing building rehabilitation costs out of synch with the residential market. During a survey conducted in mid-1990, thirty-three east end buildings were being advertised for sale, renovation or offices to let. Common in all was a unilateral move away from residential and industrial usage into office usage. Many landlords gave as a reason for this transformation the role that Actstop is playing in organizing tenants. As in the case of the township, the barriers to adding a social element to a spatial fix may include a combination of structure and struggle. The point in any case is that the spatial fix is capable only of displacement of crisis, not of its resolution (see below, Chapter Seven).

CBD real estate speculation has been the norm in postmodern capitalist cities, although in 1990 from New York to London to Tokyo, the house of cards began to wobble uncontrollably. The speculative bubble in real estate was matched by the rise of finance, rather literally in the form, in Johannesburg, of the JSE building and its Ampros-FNB neighbor at 11 Diagonal Street. These structures date to 1978, when the stock market awoke from the post-1969 malaise. They have been followed by "decadent" mausoleums and monuments like the R700 million Standard Bank superblocks (also owned by Liberty Life) (*Sunday Times* 12/8/90); FNB's up-coming R500 million Bank City; Volkskas' idiosyncratic headquarters which outdazzles the next-door Carlton Center; the intimidating new Anglo headquarters extension; the postmodern refurbishments organized by Ampros in Braamfontein; and several other major developments that testify to the power and urban vision of financial capitalists in Sanlam, Old Mutual, and Liberty Life. Like the explosive JSE, the real estate craze is yet another reflection of flows of investment capital alienated from productive capitalism. Institutional investors appear, simply, incapable of supporting the expansion of productive plant and equipment which, at the end of the day, must extract surplus value so that financial assets can be validated. They know better where the short-term rate of return is highest.

The damage caused by this sort of parasitical investment behavior extends beyond the socio-economic sphere, and into land use planning and even regional development strategies. Unfortunately, because of their control of urban capital flows, it is the financiers who can exert the most profound (market) influence over "growth coalitions" of local ruling elites. "The shape of cities across the world has been much influenced by the activities of growth coalitions, and in the recent period this has taken the form of large, architecturally adventurous consumption spectacles, designed to replace lost industry," reports Robinson (1991:10). Indeed, overlaid on all of this intraurban spatial change and profit-seeking is a broader metropolitan theme now gaining stature in many South African cities: local economic development initiatives.

What this means in practice, according to Robinson (1991:14), is "cheap labor, few regulations, opportunities to export and import without controls, etc.," reminiscent of the conditions for the old deconcentration point strategy. As intrametropolitan and interurban struggles over resources intensify, the competition in laxity that South Africa began experiencing at the regional level via the 1970s and 1980s decentralization initiatives will likely jumped scale to the international level. The result is that "the present package of investment incentives looks like a scene from the Goon Show," in the words of the director of the British Industry Committee on South Africa. "In the last year I have attended 15 separate presentations--from promotions for

Johannesburg and Qwa Qwa, Pietermaritzburg and KwaNdebele or the Cape and Transkei--but nothing which counted as investment in South Africa itself" (*Business Day* 25/2/92).

In this environment, the Urban Foundation (1990a:59) calls for a "'bottom-up' regional development policy, in which functionally-defined regions compete with one another for development funds on the basis of their local and regional comparative advantages." The "winner region" will be Johannesburg, while the likely demise of decentralization incentives also means the demise of household living standards in peripheral areas. Hence overcoming old spaces of confinement in and around homelands will exacerbate classic Third World tendencies towards a primate city effect. Based on Morris and Kaplan's (1987) analysis of post-fordism in South Africa, the UF (1990a:12) celebrates this outcome on grounds that "just-in-time production technology requires spatial compactness and spatial integration of metropolitan areas in order to ensure rapid interactions between complementary firms." As Morris and Kaplan (1987:8,10) warn, however,

> At the very least the wholesale adoption of such technology within the South African economy would have a problematic if not a negative effect on total labor employment.... This is likely to have serious and deleterious differentiating effects on the social productivity of far-flung regions.... The social effects of this are likely to be extremely serious for space is pre-eminently a political question.

But consistent with such economic centralization is the drive towards political decentralization of a rather circumscribed sort. While this is to be expected, in time of transition to a New South Africa, from white suburbs (e.g., Randburg and Sandton, and Bedfordview) attempting to give up as little of their tax base to neighboring townships as possible, the process has even deeper roots. Hendler argues that a "polynucleated megalopolitan structure consisting of several mature cities around Johannesburg as the prime city"--as PW Botha's planning office described the PWV a decade ago--leads inexorably to "the idea that there should be no fusion of these growth poles but rather a separation which would preserve their relative autonomy" (Hendler 1991:18). Such was the apartheid-era Nationalists' premonition of the fragmented logic of intrametropolitan, interurban, interregional and international entrepreneurial competition of what would become a postmodern response to the need to re-use spaces of confinement.

Indeed, David Harvey (1989:66) argues that crucial to urban postmodernism is a break "with the modernist idea that planning and development should focus on large-scale, metropolitan-wide, technologically rational and efficient urban plans, backed by absolutely no-frills architecture." Instead, he suggests,

> Since the metropolis is impossible to command except in bits and pieces, urban design (and note that postmodernists design rather than plan) simply aims to be sensitive to vernacular traditions, local histories, particular wants, needs, and fancies, thus generating specialized, even highly customized architectural forms that may range from intimate, personalized spaces, through traditional monumentality, to the gaiety of spectacle.

The best local example of the application of such ideas is Erky Wood's "Compact City" argument. Wood (1990:15,26) confronts "an environment that requires flexibility in the face of uncertainty, adaptability in the face of change, and responsiveness in the face of unpredictable dynamics" yet emerges with his own postmodern spaces of confinement through "development of intense nodes, urban corridors, local activity strips and selective opportunities to establish compact new towns in town."

The contemporary fascination with customizing space (especially "place") and its potential role in transforming confinement to a "liberatory" (though potentially commercialized) condition disguises, usually rather badly, particular *class interests*. Consider the sorts of sentiments and outlooks that have been identified as bedfellows to postmodernism: the celebration of individualism, desire and nihilism, fragmentation and parochialism (Harvey 1989). A prison-space, the Hillbrow Fort, located at the nexus of many different forms of social control--the corporate-financial power of Liberty Life in Braamfontein; the corporate-oriented intellectual liberalism of Wits; the monumental modernism of the facing municipal buildings; the system of state repression reproduced through the neighboring police and court premises; the racially-tainted hospital (itself originally a twin of the Fort Prison, with the role of sanitizing lumpen prisoners); and the slums-in-formation of Joubert Park and Hillbrow--cautions against leaving the politics of space to the South African state and market, both of which can and do live easily with the outlooks expressed above. Indeed, the question of land rent now returns to the scene, and haunts even those, like the Wits University architecture team, who wish to humanize the Fort Prison, and to create in it an empowering sense of community of victimization, yet of tranquility, of remembrance. But what will the financiers of the helm of the space-economy have to say about these sentiments?

Indeed it is precisely that threat that a pseudo-democratic "deracialized urbanization" poses for those *who cannot afford access to the city* (Swilling 1990). For Callinicos (1989:144), "Capitalism in the 1980s certainly fulfilled Nietzsche's injunction 'to *live dangerously*! Build your cities on the slopes of Vesuvius!'" South Africa in the 1990s is apparently preparing to embark upon the same experiment. Can designers and architects not rather collectively support the *transformation* of cities--not in order merely to re-use spaces of confinement, but to do this in the context of providing the "large-scale, metropolitan-wide, technologically rational and efficient urban plans," thoroughly permeated, however, with *the search for social justice in spatial organization*, so desperately needed in order to move from apartheid to post-apartheid without postmodernism?

chapter two

Globalization and the Neoliberal City

The international context for South African urban problems--and indeed for prospects of urban resistance to neoliberalism across the globe--became increasingly important during the 1990s. Reflecting the fundamental internal contradiction of capitalism, the triple themes of overaccumulation, rising financial speculation and uneven development link together coherently, I believe. But a shortcoming in this chapter was my dereliction in projecting the dynamic as far forward as the late 1990s East Asian and indeed global financial collapse. The structural dimension was, after all, even recognized in an official October 1998 statement issued by South Africa's ruling "Alliance" (including the ANC, COSATU and the SACP): *"The present crisis is, in fact, a global capitalist crisis, rooted in a classical crisis of overaccumulation and declining profitability. Declining profitability has been a general feature of the most developed economies over the last 25 years. It is precisely declining profitability in the most advanced economies that has spurred the last quarter of a century of intensified globalization. These trends have resulted in the greatly increased dominance (and exponential growth in the sheer quantity) of speculative finance capital, ranging uncontrolled over the globe in pursuit of higher returns...."* My own delinquency in pointing out the depth of the coming neoliberal disaster was shared by, without exception, all other globalization commentators. What now becomes important is reconstructing the politics of social and community movements in response to the strains that globalization visits, so that we transcend both anarchic "IMF Riots" and tame urban reformism.

[This chapter was originally presented as a paper--"The Changing Scale of Globalization"--to the Wits University Colloquium on Globalization, September 1996 and to the Human Sciences Research Council Program on Global Change and Social Transformation, November 1996; it drew on material coauthored with Mzwanele Mayekiso in a 1996 *Socialist Register* chapter and on my study of uneven development in Zimbabwe (Bond 1998b); and it was published in *Socialist Studies Bulletin* 47 (1997).]

Introduction

> All old established national industries have been destroyed or are daily being destroyed. They are dislodged by new industries, whose introduction becomes a life and death question for all civilized nations, by industries that no longer work up indigenous raw material, but raw material drawn from the remotest zones; industries whose products are consumed, not only at home, but in every quarter of the globe. In place of the old wants, satisfied by the production of the country, we find new wants, requiring for their satisfaction the products of distant lands and climes. In place of the local and national seclusion and self-sufficiency, we have intercourse in every direction, universal interdependence of nations. And as in material, so also in intellectual production. The intellectual creations of individual nations become common property. National one-sidedness and narrow-mindedness become more and more impossible, and from the numerous national and local literatures, there arises a world literature.
>
> Karl Marx and Friedrich Engels,
> *The Communist Manifesto*, 1848

That Marx and Engels described globalization in much the same way we do today should give us reason to pause. For during the past two centuries or so of world economic development, the ebb and flow of global capital--financial, direct investment, and trade flows--occurred in an extremely uneven way, such that the internationalization of capital posed different sets of problems to ruling elites and subordinate classes at different times and in different places.

This is illustrated nicely in the African National Congress executive's discussion document "The State and Social Transformation" (ANC 1996). It is no accident, I would argue at the outset, that in attempting to persuade its left flank of the necessity of the international neoliberal ideology, the ascendant generation of South Africa's political leadership have turned to an ersatz Leninist discourse. It is important, in this context, to rescue the idea of "dialectics" from its misappropriation in this important document. It is important, in short, to invoke the real dialectical process--entailing contradiction, inter-relationships, and class conflict--as a means of interrogating globalization.

Towards this end, this essay grapples with some conceptual and political problems in the characterization of and response to globalization that have received insufficient attention from the Left in particular. Notwithstanding post-structural fads in the academy, Marx and Engels would probably be quite comfortable in the present circumstances, arguing the old saw of international working-class organization and revolution in the context of capitalist crisis-formation. But they would still have to convince many on the Left and Center that what is happening today is indeed but a variant on the durable processes of capital accumulation initially identified in *Das Kapital*, not an entirely new and different economic epoch. Valiant efforts have indeed been made in recent years to prove contemporary globalization isn't something particularly new and different, but instead reflects traditional problems of crisis and crisis displacement (Gordon 1988; Harvey 1989). This essay, however, isn't quite so ambitious.

Instead, it is concerned with a central intellectual and political dilemma, which is the *scales* at which anyone involved in global change and social transformation must be active. These include local processes; provincial (federalist) policy opportunities; transforming the nation-state and national economy; regional subcontinental relations; and/or the global stage of apparently unchallengeable capital accumulation. But to tackle the issue of scale presumes the relevance of classical conceptual categories such as uneven development, accumulation crisis, and the rise of a simultaneously powerful and vulnerable financial circuit within the world economy. Demonstrating the continuing validity of these old-fashioned tools of the political economy trade would then allow us to pose the problem of scale from the standpoint of its role within the underlying economic dynamic of geographical expansion and contraction, which--notwithstanding the pop thesis that globalization is inevitable and irreversible--still characterizes the world system.

Once such a position has been developed, it is logical to consider modes of resistance to the effects of globalization in terms of the system's primary scalar contradictions, which I take to be manifest most obviously in local--specifically "urban" settings--and in ways that I think are extremely important to the very logic of the "localization of globalization" itself: *the switch in scale in the application of "structural adjustment" from the nation-state to the municipality*. And that argument suggests forms of political organization (beyond traditional "vanguard" parties, social democratic parties, and trade unions) that may be appropriate for today's circumstances. For if we accept--even partially--the proposition that the nation-state (and even a nationally-based working-class political party) is a far weaker instrument to launch policies and programs that improve the well-being of ordinary citizens, workers, the poor, then it behooves us to consider different scales and different forms of agency than have existed to date.

Uneven development of sector, space and scale

"Unevenness" is something often associated with *sectors* of the economy: whether "articulations of modes of production" (defining uneven and combined development in the context of geographically proximate pre-capitalist conditions, such as South Africa's homelands) (Wolpe 1980), or of "fractions of capital" (subject of much debate in South Africa during the 1970s, as to which business elites influenced the state most at which times) (Davies, O'Meara and Dlamini 1986), or of "circuits of capital" (a broader notion that accumulation proceeds not merely on the basis of the institutional appearance of power within business, but through the switch of funds out of some crisis-ridden sectors and into others) (van der Pijl 1984:Appendix).

In contemporary times, intensifying uneven development at the world scale--which is how globalization should really be described--coincides with unevenness between sectors, and in particular *the rise of financial and commercial circuits of capital and the hegemony of the financial fraction of capital* to the detriment of productive capital, workers, and the world's poor (Corbridge, Martin, and Thrift 1994). There is no question but that South Africa has suffered such sectoral unevenness since the early 1980s (Bond 1991a), witnessed in, for example, the dramatic rise of domestic debt and speculation relative to production, the increase in (non-gold) trade as a percentage of GDP, and the consequent hegemony, among South Africa's elites, of neoliberalism as the basis for macroeconomic policy (Department of Finance 1996), no matter how futile this approach appears to be.

But unevenness is also a profoundly *spatial* phenomenon, by which an extremely turbulent "see-saw" of capital (Smith 1990) alternately pushes and pulls national, sub-national, and local economies into either downward slopes or virtuous spirals of capital accumulation. As the "post-Keynesian" school of economics has long noticed, the most basic market processes--supply and demand dynamics, the nature and rate of accumulation, the development of class struggle, etc--do not "equilibrate," but rather *disequilibrate*; that this disequilibration occurs across space is obvious enough.

To illustrate at the global scale, the past decade of intensive world trade integration witnessed nearly half of all developing countries suffering an absolute *decline* in their ratios of trade to GDP, while direct foreign investment has largely been limited to eight developing countries (recipients of two-thirds of all such inflows) in a context of deep-seated debt repayment problems in most Third World countries (with only a few emerging markets--including South Africa--"benefiting," in often disastrous ways, from dramatic flows of speculative financial flows since the late 1980s) (World Bank 1996:1).

At the scale of the continent, it has long been recognized that--as Giovanni Arrighi and John Saul (1973:145) described nearly a quarter-century ago--nation-states have suffered from the

> *uneven development* thrown up by capitalist penetration in Africa. For the underdevelopment of Africa as a whole relative to the industrial centers of the West has been accompanied and mediated by uneven development as between regions, states, tribes, and races *within* Africa itself, and this fact adds important dimensions to the class struggle in Africa and to the character of the resistance of progressive African forces to contemporary imperialism.

Yet in South Africa, aside from specifying "colonialism of a special type" and articulations of modes of production in graphic spatial terms, processes of uneven geographical development within South Africa, and between South Africa and the world economy, require both much more investigation and contemplation for political strategy. However, it is to a different issue that this essay addresses itself, namely the *uneven development of scale*. Because it is only through interrogating how globalization has come to be the dominant notion of economic arbitration that we can ultimately contest it most effectively.

The issue of scale, Neil Smith (1990:134) insists, provides a "crucial window on the uneven development of capital, because it is difficult to comprehend the real meaning of 'dispersal,' 'decentralization,' 'spatial restructuring' and so forth, without a clear understanding of geographical scale." For example, the question often arises as to the relevance of the national scale in a globalizing economy. Smith (1990:144) argues that the "historical stability" of the nation-state scale should be seen with respect to "political control over the working class. As economically obsolete as it is, the nation-state remains highly functional politically." David Harvey's (1989:194) position is more measured: "The nation-state, though seriously weakened as an autonomous power, nevertheless retains important powers of labor disciplining as well as of intervention in financial flows and markets, while becoming itself much more vulnerable to fiscal crisis and the discipline of international money."

But while the nation-state ultimately acts to facilitate capital accumulation--through carrying out a variety of other "functions" such as "guaranteeing property and contracts; standardizing currency, wights and measures; ensuring the availability of key inputs of labor, land, finance, technology and infrastructure; general macro-economic orchestration; regulation of conditions of work, consumption and external diseconomies such as pollution; and provision of ideological, educational and communications conditions for production and trade" (Panitch 1994)--such "political" functionality assumes vastly different forms under a system in which national accumulation is oriented to (domestic) production as opposed to (international) finance. As Robert Cox (1992:30-31) describes it,

> The structural impact on national governments of this centralization of influence over policy can be called the internationalizing of the state. Its common feature is to convert the state into an agency for adjusting national economic practices and policies to the perceived exigencies of the global economy. The state becomes a transmission belt from the global to the national economy, where heretofore it had acted as the bulwark defending domestic welfare from external disturbances. Power within the state becomes concentrated in those agencies in closest touch with the global economy--the offices of presidents and prime ministers, treasuries, central banks. The agencies that are more closely tied with domestic clients--ministries of industries, labor ministries, etc--become subordinated.

Somewhere intermediate between national and global determinations are super-regional currency blocs, such as those of the 1920s and 1930s, as well as what appear to be their 1990s revival in the form, initially, of hemispheric trade blocs. Just such variability — whether in the past (such as the 1930s-60s reign of import-substitution industrialization at a time when production was served, not ruled, by finance) or, as Samir Amin (1990) advocates, through the future "delinking" of the Third World from global circuits of trade, investment and finance — reminds us of the need for concrete investigation. My hypothesis is that while jumping scales to higher levels of determination occurs under conditions of ascendant financial power, the subsequent collapse of finance allows the issue of development strategy to be broached, again, at lower levels.

In short, *uneven hierarchies of scale are exacerbated during times of relative economic stagnation (capitalist crisis) and financial ascendance,* such as the past two decades, at the same time unevenness in sectoral and spatial patterns of development is being generated. While the national scale of economic development usually occupies financial economists to the neglect of the sub-national, it is the international scale of financial power which turns the heads and quickens the pulse of analysts and practitioners alike. Enormous evidence has accumulated to support the vivid claim of Hillel Ticktin (1986:37) that, as of the late 1970s, international financiers "have knowledge, global forms of action and speed on their side. Against them social democracy appears as clumsy peasants attached to one nation and with the horizon of village idiots." The power of international money over development strategies at the national scale is today reflected across the Third World, as well as in many advanced capitalist countries.

Sub-nationally, the ramifications of international financial power are increasingly evident. For smaller, home-bound manufacturing industries not well-located near air or shipping lanes to serve global markets, the fluctuating interest rates and national currency values dictated from Washington, New York, London, Tokyo, Frankfurt, and other sites of international financial control can be debilitating. The size of the national market--which was typically the key consideration in the expansion and contraction of production--now appears nearly irrelevant in the context of trade liberalization enforced by the major financial institutions (hence the SA Department of Trade and Industry adopts Reagan-style "supply-side measures," including tax cuts, while completely neglecting the demand-side stimulation characteristic of traditional industrial policy).

Not just nation-states, but cities and regions are also increasingly caught up in the vortex of the international law of value, as more direct--often municipal-level--strategies of restructuring production and reproduction are brought into play, often at the behest of global financiers and aid agencies. In effect, as argued in more detail later in this chapter, the nation-state gives way to the city as a new unit of analysis, implementation, and control and as a means of enhancing the international competitiveness of production, via structural adjustment policies.

Indeed it sometimes appears that at its peak, financial power has the capacity to level differences of scale altogether. As Dick Bryan (1995:41) insists, "the money form of capital most readily converts distinct and spatially diverse activities into a common unit of measurement" which in turn means that financial power can assert "the primacy of an internationally-determined rate of return on economic activity.... This calculation therefore operates as a limiting factor--dictating what class relations and what industrial organization are not sustainable, and specifying the criterion to which they must adapt."

Yet contradictions are manifest, particularly in relating financial capital to underlying processes of production, and this means that the levelling process could as well represent a tendency to breakdown, not to renewed accumulation (Grossmann 1992). This is understood not only by Michel Camdessus and George Soros--who in early 1995 cited the fragility of international finance when advocating the $50-billion bailout of Mexico (and its Wall Street backers)--but by most observers of contemporary financial power and vulnerability. This lethal combination has taken the form of periodic bursting of financial bubbles; extremely high real interest rates (in relation to the historical record and in relation to the return on fixed capital investment); an explosion in stock market share values (now at their highest in recorded history) and real estate prices; an increase in the outstanding debt of consumers, corporations and governments in relation to most measures of economic activity; and the qualitative increase in the political clout of financiers. Behind this, at national and global scales, there is also evidence of a deepening global structural crisis, now two decades old, that in the spirit of Marx can be characterized as "the overaccumulation of capital" (Clarke 1988:279-360; Harvey 1989:180-197; Mandel 1989:30-58; Armstrong, Glyn, and Harrison 1991:169-260).

The patterns that connect economic crisis, uneven development, rising finance and globalization are hence comprehensible in contemporary terms, and seem to also emerge in the historical evidence, particularly at times when South Africa's insertion into the global economy coincided with financial ascendance.

The historical unevenness of globalization

Historical evidence of financial ascendance during the accumulation cycle--particularly at the high-points of globalization--is impressive, and can be reviewed briefly at this stage in the argument. For example, the existence of "Kondratieff"-style long-waves of capital accumulation is securely established, with global crises occurring roughly from 1825-45, 1872-92, 1929-48, and 1973-present (Kondratieff 1979; Goldstein 1988).

We can also verify the rise and fall of finance during the course of these accumulation cycles, especially at the global level. During four particular periods--the late 1820s, 1870s, 1930s, and 1980s--at least one-third of all nation-states fell into effective default on their external debt following an unsustainable upswing of borrowing at a time of declining foreign-sourced productive sector investment. With the exception of the 1980s (in which there was a significant lag), the onset of global debt crisis was the precursor for the onset of decades-long downswings in the Kondratieff cycles. Drawing on the world-systems perspective pioneered by Immanuel Wallerstein (1979), Christian Suter (1992) explains the "global debt cycle" by way of stages in the long wave, beginning with technological innovation and utilizing international product-cycle theory.

At the upswing of a Kondratieff cycle, as basic technological innovations are introduced in a labor-intensive and unstandardized manner, both the demand for and supply of external financing are typically low, and in any case the residue of financial crisis in the previous long cycle does not permit rapid expansion of credit or other financial assets into high-risk investments. As innovations gradually spread, however, peripheral geographical areas become more tightly integrated into the world economy, supported by international financial networks. As the power of innovation-led growth subsides, and as the consumer markets of the advanced capitalist countries become saturated, profit rates decline in the core. This in turn pushes waves of financial capital into peripheral areas where, instead of achieving balanced accumulation and growth, low returns on investment plus a variety of other political and economic constraints inexorably lead to sovereign default. In sum, at the global scale there is a three-stage process characterized by, as Suter (1992:41) puts it, "first, intense core capital exports and corresponding booms in credit raising activity of peripheries; second, the occurrence of debt service incapacity among peripheral countries; and third, the negotiation of debt settlement agreements between debtors and creditors."

Looking at booms and busts in the history of South (and Southern) Africa, Suter's theory appears to work well (Schumann 1938; Bond 1991a). For example, Ian Phimister (1992:7) contends that increasing geopolitical turbulence across Africa during the nation-forming era emanated from "capitalism's uneven development during the last third of the nineteenth century, particularly the City of London's crucial role in mediating the development of a world economic system." As Britain faced industrial decline during the 1870s in both relative and absolute terms, manufacturers unable to compete in European markets joined ascendant London financial and commercial interests in promoting Free Trade philosophy (in contrast to the protectionism of other Europeans and the United States). Cain and Hopkins (1980:484-485) report that as London financial power increased and as the prospects for domestic tariff protection waned, "industrial interests in Britain shifted, around 1880, into decisive support for the acquisition of new markets in Asia and Africa." Indeed, it is here, and in a parallel crisis of French merchant capital in West Africa, that Phimister locates the well-spring of the "Scramble for Africa" which had such an important role in the Southern African region's subsequent development.

No matter how Africa was partitioned, the funding flows also reflected the last great speculative financial splurge of the 1870s-90s global economic crisis. Some 35 percent of all nation-states had overborrowed during the 1870s and were in default by 1880. This figure dropped to 10 percent by 1890 thanks to British international financial coordination, and the 1890s were characterized by unprecedented numbers of debt settlements on defaulted foreign bonds. Nevertheless, speculative surges continued during the decade, since the conditions for a new round of accumulation were not yet in place in most of the world. As a result, the percentage of nation-states in default rose again to 20 percent in the late 1890s (Suter 1992:64,87,90). It was in this global context that the City of London witnessed a "combination of sentiment, patriotism and opportunities for gain," as economic historian Sally Herbert Frankel (1938:20) put it. "Only against such a background can the almost incredible financial exploits of a Rhodes be understood, or the spasmodic, and at times exaggerated, bursts of capital investment which created the mineral industries of Africa be explained." We can observe, again, that globalization, rising finance, and uneven development all reinforced each other, at least temporarily.

The next uptick of globalization occurred during the 1920s, after fifteen years of war-related chaos in global circuits of capital. External overindebtedness again characterized this period, with £64 million of outstanding government bonds floated overseas on behalf of African colonies in 1925. By 1935, Africa's external debt had risen to £99 million--nearly all of the increase having occurred during the late 1920s--

but the burden was distributed unevenly. External debt as a percentage of export earnings remained under 10 percent in South Africa and Southern Rhodesia, while in Kenya the debt-servicing ratio soared from 12 percent in 1927 to 54 percent in 1934; in the Belgian Congo, the ratio exploded from 8 percent in 1927 to 45 percent in 1933. Nigeria and Tanganyika were similarly affected. Across the African continent, repayment problems were aggravated by a shattering 55 percent decline in the value of exports (from £179 million in 1929 to £117 million in 1931, which was barely above the nominal 1913 value) (Frankel 1938:173-193).

If conditions appeared similar to those that have prevailed over the past fifteen years, the outcome should be no surprise. Many beleaguered Third World countries simply defaulted on their debts, and then during the Great Depression and World War II--when globalization ebbed dramatically--acquired the space to begin the fruitful exercise of inward industrialization. For South Africa, the crash of international financial power allowed strong, relatively balanced growth during the relatively autarchic period of the 1930s-1940s (Martin 1990). As South Africa delinked from the world economy--in terms of foreign direct investment, foreign loans, and manufacturing trade, which were all disrupted by the Great Depression and World War II--its secondary manufacturing industry (beyond the traditionally strong mining equipment sector) burgeoned. Moreover, the rate of growth of the black wage share rose more than 50 percent during this period (from 11 percent to 17 percent; the black share had reached only 21 percent by 1970). And the overall GDP growth rate (8 percent) was the fastest recorded in modern times (Nattrass 1981:Appendix 1). Indeed, as a corollary, it was the post-war reintegration of South Africa into international economic circuits that fostered the crisis conditions that are so overwhelming today: a near-exhausted raw materials export sector; an overproductive luxury goods sector hosting overprotected local monopoly capital and multinational corporations; an inadequate capital goods sector; and a hopelessly under-resourced basic needs sector. As in many semi-peripheral countries, import-substitution industrialization was geared to the desires of the local bourgeoisie and ended up generating serious balance-of-payments tensions. Under such structural conditions as rising levels of class struggle combined with local processes of uneven development, an accumulation crisis surfaced during the 1970s and became acute during the late 1980s.

The subsequent decision by South African capitalists to ditch apartheid and seek export-led growth strategies needs no review (Gelb 1991). What may be of interest is the degree to which this strategy appears to be undermined by virtue of South Africa's national-scale uncompetitiveness--invariably near worst among the leading fifty or so nations in the annual World Economic Forum surveys--and the impressive power of its labor movement, in a context, as a World Bank report (Hinds 1990:15-17) specifies, in which "the overall model chosen to integrate the economy into the international markets.... should aim at avoiding the appropriation of rents by suppliers of nontradables and workers. That is, they should maintain the real wage low, so that excess profits accrue to capital.... In carrying out all these activities, a close alliance between Government and private agents must be developed." Such an alliance is not yet in place, it should be clear. But an even more foreboding possibility awaits, namely, the possibility that the insertion of South African capital into the global economy could also occur through attempts to transform the *city* into, primarily, a site of international production.

Globalization's contemporary scale shift: From nation-state to city-state

The contestation of urbanization is a central component of social struggles against inequality and underdevelopment (Castells 1983; Schuurman and van Naerssen 1989). Such struggles are becoming increasingly difficult for people of Third World cities as a result of what seems to be a shift in the scalar strategy of international capital and aid agencies. In contrast to traditional modernizationists (like Pye 1965:8) who argued for, "above all else, acceptance in the political realm of belief that the prime unit of the polity should be the nation-state," it appears now that the mega-city is becoming a new unit of analysis, implementation, and control for the purpose of more efficiently imposing structural adjustment policies (especially in the wake of the destruction of many nation-state capacities).

To illustrate, one senior advisor to the United Nations Conference on Human Settlements, Shlomo Angel (1995:4), insisted that the 1996 Habitat conference in Istanbul should be about "creating a level playing field for competition among cities, particularly across national borders; on understanding how cities get ahead in this competition; on global capital transfers, the new economic order and the weakening of the nation-state...." This is only one of the more vulgar articulations of an increasingly familiar theme (as expressed again by Angel): "The city is not a community, but a conglomerate of firms, institutions, organizations and individuals with contractual agreements among them."

From such foundations, an entire neoliberal edifice is being constructed. The World Bank's efforts to do so have spanned two decades but have taken on far greater energy since the 1986 launch of the New Urban Management Program, which was further articulated in an important 1991 policy paper (for a critique see Jones and Ward 1994). Meanwhile, the UN's Development Program and Habitat housing division have also been thoroughly co-opted, and the US Agency for International Development, British ODA, Canadian CIDA, the Japanese and other official donor agencies now strictly reinforce urban neoliberalism through cross-conditionality on grants and loans. The overall orientation is nearly identical to the austerity policies at the macro-economic scale, with US AID consultants spelling out the

> ....important change in policy thinking in the developing world closely linked to the acceptance of market-oriented economies: the growing acceptance of rapid urbanization.... An emphasis on national economic growth and export-led development will usually mean that new investment resources must be directed to already successful regions and cities.... Governments have considerable control over the entire cost structure of urban areas. Public policy should be directed to lowering these costs. (Urban Institute 1990)

This, perhaps, comes closest to the point. Lowering these costs--especially by lowering the social wage--is integral to a more direct insertion of "competitive" cities into the world economy. The focus here is not merely on limiting public financing of social services to those deemed to add value (though this is one of the more obvious effects of structural adjustment, and the catalyst for many an IMF Riot). Just as importantly, the New Urban Management Program also highlights the *productivity* of urban capital as it flows through urban land markets (now enhanced by titles and registration), through housing finance systems (featuring solely private sector delivery and an end to state subsidies), through the much-celebrated (but extremely exploitative) informal economy, through (often newly-privatized) urban services such as transport, sewage, water and even primary health care services (via intensified cost-recovery), and the like. The Government of South

Africa's own articulation of this sensibility, in its draft *Urban Development Strategy*, is familiar: "Seen through the prism of the global economy, our urban areas are single economic units that either rise, or stagnate and fall together.... South Africa's cities are more than ever strategic sites in a transnationalized production system" (Ministry of Reconstruction and Development 1995:17,41).

Likewise, however, it is here that urban unevenness spawned by the rule of capital and the intensification of commodification is most vigorously contested by popular movements, which are agitating both around conjunctural social policy decisions (typically, cutbacks in subsidies for food, transport, or other services) and also against the structural conditions through which the political life of cities is reproduced. The movements have, in the process, begun to transcend the traditional dichotomy between an inward-looking territorial identity and the rhetoric of a broader emancipation (Schuurman 1989:43). They have begun exploring a broader set of urban class practices, which in the Latin American case--according to Petras and Morley (1990:53,54)--entail new alliances that traverse the spheres of production and collective consumption, under conditions of persistent capitalist crisis:

> The power of these new social movements comes from the fact that they draw on the vast heterogeneous labor force that populates the main thoroughfares and the alleyways; the marketplaces and street corners; the interstices of the economy and the nerve centers of production; the exchange and finance centers; the university plazas, railway stations and the wharves--all are brought together in complex localized structures which feed into tumultuous homogenizing national movements.

The main structural factor forging the unity of the urban poor and the formal working class, Petras and Morley continue, is economic crisis itself. "The great flows of capital disintegrate the immobile isolated household units, driving millions into the vortex of production and circulation of commodities; this moment of wrenching dislocation and relocation is silently, individually experienced by the mass of people, who struggle to find their place, disciplined by the struggle for basic needs and by the absolute reign of ascending capital." Under such conditions, the social base for urban movements is continually recreated at the point that the limits to both commodity production and consumption become evident.

With respect to production, Petras and Morley on the one hand view the rise of militant urban social movements as a consequence of the sudden increase in mass unemployment since the 1980s debt crisis began, which "lifted the control and discipline of capital over labor--making the latter available for, and receptive to, a new kind of discipline: that associated with the structure and action of mass social movements." On the other hand, a complementary explanation--not grounded in the formal sector labor market (unemployment)--also presents itself. "It comes down to this. Capital transformed an inert mass of atomized producers into a concentrated army; and the market that it created could not sustain it. The impersonal ties--the cash nexus--are the only link in that anonymous urban labor market. The rupture of that tie sets the stage for the eruption of uprooted people."

By considering unevenness in both production and consumption, particularly in so many contexts characterized by market failure, this stylized theory breaks free of many of the constraints associated with previous neo-Marxist approaches to development and underdevelopment. It also highlights the scope for alliance-formation between oppressed classes and across borders. And it brings us back to the self-identity of social movements as a theoretically relevant factor for ultimately moving beyond uneven urban development.

It is not always feasible to specify the construction of social movement identity in urban settings, where conjunctural features are legion, but where overt market processes have torn asunder land relations, rural ties, indigenous culture, and many forms of pre-existing authority and social control. The identity of social movements can be traced, at least to some extent, through their implicit or explicit strategic orientations in contesting uneven development. From experiences with urban movements in Santiago, Tironi (1987) conceptualized two fields of strategic polarization: 1) that between a sense of exploitation or exclusion, and 2) that between the goals of participation within or breaking from the wider political, economic, and cultural system. Four categories--and prototypical modes of political organization--result across this matrix of characteristics (Table 1).

Table 1. Identities of Social Movement Constituents

status:	excluded	exploited
objectives:		
participation	1	2
revolution	4	3

First, those who feel excluded and are anxious to participate more are often supporters of traditional populism (*pobladores*). Second, those who felt both exploited and anxious to participate more in the system included traditional trade unionists. Third, those who feel exploited by the system and who are interested in its formal rupture include traditional revolutionaries. Fourth, there are those alienated social forces which are excluded from the system and which also desire its rupture--and which are also, in many cases, engaged in collective subsistence activities that aim towards the construction of an alternative life-style based, at least to some extent, on the economy of solidarity. It is in this latter category that most progress seems to be occurring by way of mass mobilizing and sustained challenges to neoliberal policies.

If we accept such typologies, South African urban social movements (the civics and other community groups) and their cadre can be seen to have multiple identities. They include both insiders (exploited) and outsiders (excluded), as well as revolutionaries and reformers. Civics may have had a primary identity as traditional anti-apartheid revolutionaries at one stage (Category Three). But at other times, and depending upon local conditions, there are also civics and community structures which represent a profoundly alienated social force (Four); some place today's black youth and some youth-led civics here. In other categories, some civics and their leaderships are today vulnerable to being captured and denuded via corporatist social contracts (Two). And a good many outsiders who feel excluded are anxious to gain access to state resources, even on essentially neoliberal terms dictated by foreign (and some local) development agencies (One).

Yet at other times--particularly the mid-1980s in places like Alexandra township (Mayekiso 1996), for example--the combination of national anti-apartheid politics (Two) and local-level "dual power" (Three) was extraordinarily successful. Not only was the apartheid system shaken and the international progressive community conscientized and mobilized through the urban uprisings of 1984-86. In addition, local people's courts, advice offices, local media, clinics and other institutions were established.

Carter (1991) has compared this latter experience to the Paris Commune (though the lessons are tenuous); and, after all, as Marx understood, it was the *process* of self-emancipation from the dictates of capital, not the outcome, that was most important.

> The working class did not expect miracles from the Commune. They have no ready-made utopias to introduce par secret du peuple. They know that in order to work out their own emancipation, and along with it that higher form to which present society is irresistibly tending by its own economical agencies, they will have to pass through long struggles, through a series of historic processes, transforming circumstances and men. They have no ideals to realize, but to set free the elements of the new society with which old collapsing bourgeois society itself is pregnant (*The Civil War in France*).

In this spirit, we might next consider the more formal challenge of characterizing popular resistance to uneven globalization, for in part because of the tremendous success of the Zapatista movement in Chiapas, the concept of "Thinking Globally, Acting Locally" and now "Acting Globally" can begin to become a reality. Although the Zapatista base is rural, the importance of its "civil society" orientation for urban movement strategy--in Mexico and elsewhere--should be evident.

Urban social movements and resistance to globalization

Much recent resistance to uneven urban development has been defensive, ephemeral, even destructive. Peru, Bolivia, Brazil, and Argentina each witnessed a dozen major anti-austerity urban protests during the 1980s; repeated uprisings were experienced in the cities of Chile, Ecuador, the Philippines, Zaire, Jamaica, Morocco, Sudan, and the Dominican Republic; in Venezuela in 1989, security forces killed more than 600 people involved in a single IMF Riot; and there were isolated incidents in dozens of other countries (Walton and Seddon 1994). In the 1990s, these countries were joined by India, Albania, Nepal, Iran, Ivory Coast, Niger, and Zimbabwe, where large-scale IMF Riots broke out. Do or can these uprisings reflect--or perhaps stimulate--the existence of more visionary, creative, and empowering urban social movements? Are they irredeemably populist in nature? And can they avoid being captured by neoliberal conceptions of civil society, the informal economy, self-help, and the like?

The leading scholars of the IMF Riot, John Walton and David Seddon (1994:336), have contemplated the transition from the chaos intrinsic in most urban uprisings to the more durable mobilizations required for movement-scale democratic transformation. Given that the most decisive factor in the reproduction of everyday life in many Third World urban settings is the shrinkage of the state under conditions of structural adjustment, "the broader trend is toward the decline of clientism and, conversely, the growing autonomy of urban low-income groups." As states lose their patronage capacity to channel social surpluses to supporters, social movements can cast off the worst influences of corporatism and corruption associated with urban civil society under populist regimes. As this becomes a more generalised political process, the urban poor consequently transcend spontaneous and unsustainable reactions to economic crisis such as the IMF Riot.

The loss of patronage power deserves a moment's further reflection, for it undermines the local state as a target of mobilization by a progressive political party. Problems regarding municipal-scale politics in South Africa are too extensive to discuss here (see Part Four of this book). In Brazil, left municipal strategies in cities like Porto Alegre, Diadema, Vitoria, Santos, and Itabuna have been, as Workers Party (PT) leader Lula remarks, "very successful" (Porto Alegre for its model forms of citizen participation in budgets, and Diadema for eliminating slums). Yet the challenge of both governing Sao Paolo (and its surrounding industrial belt, once the PT's stronghold) and nourishing the progressive base proved virtually impossible, given nationally-imposed structural constraints, as reflected in the PT's subsequent electoral losses in the Sao Paolo region. Indeed, at one point in the early 1990s the PT's entire local electoral strategy appeared doomed, as half the PT mayors of three dozen major municipalities either resigned or changed their party affiliation. For Lula, the lesson was to concentrate on running the key municipalities (with 400 out of the country's 5,000 cities and towns as future PT electoral targets), but this too will become increasingly difficult under conditions of all-encompassing neoliberalism imposed by President Cardoso (Branford and Kucinski 1995; Kowarick 1995).

To transcend both the IMF Riot and neoliberal municipal electoralism, it would seem, the form of urban organization, the style of mobilization, and the durability of the democratic process within the movement must all be carefully considered. South Africa demonstrates important impediments to the maturation of urban social movements as forces for broader socio-economic transformation. Consider the trajectory of an urban movement which has its deepest origins in the form of community cooperation and networking via mutual aid systems (especially among women). As local grievances become the basis for political mobilization, the group solidifies as a community-based organization (with or more often without technical NGO involvement, though often taking up unfortunate patriarchal structures and styles). Along the way, it may consciously or subconsciously experiment with decommodified, destratified (and environmentally- and gender-sensitive) forms of what we now loosely term people-centered development to meet basic needs. It experiences repeated conflicts with state bureaucrats over resources and local-level capitalists over investment decisions. And eventually it evolves as an important social force in contesting national economic policy, even linking up to discuss common strategies and tactics with similar forces in other societies.

Impediments along the way are increasingly to be found embedded within the neoliberal version of civil society ideology, particularly the premise that the citizenry must not make demands for state services as entitlements. In South Africa and across the world, therefore, it is now crucial to recognize the ideological lacunae and diversions represented within the many new development organizations that have emerged in response to the broader failure of modernization and of the state. In dozens of wretched Third World cities (including now Los Angeles) where organization and democratic traditions of struggle are simply lacking, matters quickly degenerate into desperate IMF Riots. In many other situations, the opposite--petit-bourgeois professionalization--has taken hold. Given the class groundings, the often patriarchal form and the occasionally imperialist sponsorship of some Third World (and many First World) organizations engaged in development work, it should not be surprising that upon closer examination their progressive rhetoric is merely rhetoric and their practices quite consistent with neoliberalism. Drawing out their relationships to establishment actors (foundations, aid agencies, development banks, consultants and lawyers, construction and civil engineering capital, etc) becomes more and more important at levels of both micro-implementation and macro-policy advocacy.

The ideology of "neoliberal populism," as Vivian (1993:29) puts it, assumes "that if diverse interest groups and social structures are able to compete within a strong and open social 'market,' efficient--and by implication equitable--social institutions will result." Vivian (1993:40-41) also criticizes the radical populist belief in "mass-based, grassroots activity" because its advocates "tend to stress the moral dimensions of their activities and to express faith in the essential altruism and moral integrity of people (or at least of the people with whom they work)," and because "Little attempt has been made to directly confront or refute the 'iron law' ['of oligarchy' of German political theorist Robert Michels: 'Political organization leads to power but power is always conservative'], even by those on the political Left."

This may have been true with regard to some important urban organizing traditions (for example, Alinskyite or Liberation Theology), but in contrast the argument above rests upon economic crisis--market failure at both macro and micro levels--as the primary motivating force for the recent rise of radical social movements, and suggests that "power" is the power of the movements to carve out their own space for people-centered development not necessarily by capturing the (neoliberally-hamstrung) state, but instead through demanding access to the resources it mobilizes in a manner that refutes orthodox developmental logic.

Nevertheless, it must be conceded that across the world, pliant NGOs are now considered to be an integral component of the modernization process for the sake of their efficiency and flexibility (even if results to date have been uniformly disappointing even on their own terms), corresponding with the desire of the international agencies to shrink Third World states as part of the overall effort to lower the social wage. Even indigenous NGOs and some Community-Based Organizations (CBOs) are being drawn into the process, which serves to localize long-standing distinctions between technicist, apolitical development interventions and the people-centered strategies (and militant tactics) of either small-scale CBOs or mass-based social movements of the oppressed.

Thus by the early 1990s, two out of five World Bank projects involved NGOs (including well over half in Africa), and in projects involving population, nutrition, primary health care, and small enterprise, the ratio rose to more than four out of five. During the 1970s and 1980s, more than six percent of Bank operations included some NGO participation, but Paul Nelson (1995) found that NGOs were "primarily implementors of project components designed by World Bank and government officials." Moreover, especially since an upsurge in such participation began in 1988, NGOs have often been used to "deliver compensatory services to soften the effects of an adjustment plan"; in some cases the NGOs were not even pre-existing but were "custom-built for projects" and hence could "neither sustain themselves nor represent poor people's interests effectively."

South Africa remains a case in point, for the regularization and professionalization of development, even among the better CBOs and social movements, was invariably oriented toward the deradicalization of the grassroots. Too often, civic association strategies became more negotiations-centered than people-centered, and time and energy were wasted on arcane details of technical agreements rather than popular, democratic mobilization for the planning and implementation of people-centered development. The role of NGOs--which during the early 1990s were largely guided by white, middle-class staff (mainly with very strong student anti-apartheid credentials)--was ostensibly to iron out the technical details, but disagreements between NGOs and civics about strategy also flowed from professional arrogance and community vulnerability.

This dichotomy is amplified and complicated when we move to the international scale. Here, not only are a variety of Northern NGOs serving as transmission belts for neoliberalism (Sogge 1996), but (as something of a counterweight) efforts are underway among diverse progressive forces to link up and amplify existing grassroots social movement challenges to GATT and the World Bank. In the latter case, an important obstacle has emerged in the form of surprisingly durable reformist (not non-reformist) reformism within the radical petit-bourgeois intelligentsia (the primary consumer, perhaps along with intelligence agencies, of the bulk of the analysis of such movements). This class (the author included) has more than its share of dilettantes, is sometimes politically capricious, and often wavers at key conjunctures which can be crucial for progress towards a broader internationalism. One significant result is that for reasons relating largely to its own "insider" technocratic positionality, many intellectual and strategic campaigners within these international movements argue for reform, not defunding, of the World Bank.

Over the past two decades, the radical petit-bourgeoisie has constructed a critical discourse based largely on the gender, environment, community participation, and transparency shortcomings of orthodox "development" (particularly structural adjustment programs, to which a few "human face" alternatives also emerged). Armed with such weapons, many leading development NGOs, environmental organizations, and churches have engaged in sustained battle with the World Bank, often meeting with a surprising degree of success. Reform advocates point to the inclusion of gender-sensitivity in more than a quarter of all projects and programs, the recent rescission of funds for the Narmada and Arun dams in India and Nepal, the full-blown programs to incorporate NGOs and even CBOs and social movements in Bank projects, and the Bank's more open stance regarding public access to information. (The primary reason for progress, it would seem, has been the looming shrinkage of Northern governments' fiscal support for international development and hence the desire of the Bank, US AID, and others not to have to fight their funding battle on too many fronts.)

Nevertheless, when even the better "inside-the-(Washington, DC) beltway" groups like Friends of the Earth call for the Bank to "shift from large-scale engineering projects into social sector development," it strikes us that there are some reforms that are better off not winning: even low-interest loans for social programs can become extremely expensive once currency devaluation hits; some large infrastructure projects such as urban sewage systems remain desperately needed; and there is great folly in borrowing hard currency funds for projects that can be funded from local currency, that will not earn export revenues, and that come with the "market-oriented" conditions of cost-recovery the Bank insists upon even for social sector development (Friends of the Earth/Center of Concern and other signatories 1995).

Meanwhile, increasing numbers of other organizations are coming to the conclusion that the Bank should instead be shut down, and that a vigorous and potentially decisive campaign along these lines--for example, through divestment (of Bank securities purchased by government, pension, and university funds) in the North and popular boycotts in the South--is eminently feasible (Korten 1995).

It remains to be seen whether in coming months and years, the "50 Years Is Enough" network comprising Northern groups and dozens of excellent grassroots social movements which have fought and sometimes won struggles against the Bank (from Haiti, India, Mexico, Nepal, Nicaragua, Papua New Guinea, the Philippines, Southern Africa, to name a few sites of intense recent activism) can come up with a consensus and cohere as an international movement. If this does occur--if, in other words, those local and national social movements with a more explicitly anti-capitalist development ideology do begin thinking globally and acting globally--it will be, ironically, because of opportunities provided through the technological (transport and communication) fruits of globalization to discuss and debate the roles of movements and of political parties.

To illustrate, Wainwright's (1994:239-240) survey of post-1968 social movements in Europe highlights their "socialization of practical and theoretical knowledge," specifically "the high priority they give to collective development of individual skills for political change (flowing in part from their emphasis on direct action for change in daily life), the way they gather knowledge otherwise ignored, expose knowledge otherwise kept secret, share knowledge otherwise dispersed and under-utilized." The best legacy of these European movements seems to entail both attacks on global-scale power as well as forging new relations of (the) production (of ideas and of understanding--no small undertaking when competing with Murdoch, Time-Warner, Disney, and GE). These lessons are entirely appropriate for new international mobilizations geared to resisting neoliberalism.

We may ultimately agree with Navarro (1980:12) and so many other traditional socialists that "The mass struggle carried out in its many different forms needs to be carried out in the area of representative politics as well as by instruments such as political parties which need to present and articulate the demands made by these movements." But until the terrain is better prepared for representative politics to emerge at the world scale (Wagar 1992), and until wider cracks open in the present hegemony that neoliberal institutions maintain over nation-states, it is our sense that broad-based social movement activism grounded in struggles against both capitalist production and reproduction is where the most portentous political challenges to the international system lie.

From the South African experience, it should be clear that social movements are capable of being tightly networked, and that their immediate territorial base can be expanded regionally, nationally, or even internationally. As this happens, movements cement their common norms, practices, and collective strategies and tactics, in order to advance both local agendas and larger political campaigns. This experience is still ahead, of course, but not too far off if the World Bank remains such an inviting target. In this, the international anti-apartheid movement provides inspiration, but also important lessons about the dangers of demobilization.

It is hence our hope that comrades around the world will gain most inspiration from the South African struggle, and will most effectively contribute to its deepening over the coming difficult period, by recognizing the parallels through which urban (and so many other) social movements have contested uneven development. If we can make progress in the intellectual sphere in this respect, it will be because the movements themselves begin to demand the global analysis which helps draw out the similar conditions and processes, and assess which strategies and tactics work. It will also be because the movements that are emerging in the present conjuncture continue to ward off any and all tendencies to sink into neoliberal civil society, and instead move towards international forms of organization that can one day replace globalization-from-above with globalization-from-below.

PART TWO

THE BASICS--
WATER, ENERGY,
AND MUNICIPAL SERVICES

chapter three

Rationales for Basic Infrastructure

The post-apartheid demise of housing policy and output, as explained in Part Three, gave rise to research and later advocacy around basic municipal services. It is easy to document, technically, the merits of replacing coal-fired township energy--with its (strongly gender-differentiated) inefficiencies and pollutants--with electricity, and of providing a free lifeline water supply, both of which should be paid for by redistribution from the bourgeois suburbs and national industries. Indeed, at the time (late 1996), we perceived an opening within the State, for after being embarrassed a bit in the media, Department of Constitutional Development officials displayed a modicum of coerced (ultimately make-believe) interest in hearing alternative views. Here we were too quickly lured into the policy-making loop. Prospects for improving municipal services standards and subsidies in more substantial ways, via mass action and public denunciation (as was working nicely in the welfare sector in the wake of dramatic child maintenance cuts), were deemphasized. When the National Economic Development and Labor Council contemplated only minor reforms to the neoliberal municipal tariff policy in 1996-97, it proved, as usual, to be a site of debilitating compromise, reflecting the end of the SA National Civic Movement as a viable progressive watchdog (and, as well, a lapse in the judgement of Congress of SA Trade Union leaders). Rather than contributing to robust public debate, my colleagues and I were essentially coopted during this period, and when East Rand rioting over service cutoffs took on a more serious tone in 1997-98 (see Chapter Fourteen), it occurred with no technical backup (as Planact would have provided previously) and hence weak programmatic alternatives. These pages--clean, technicist, and disconnected from praxis--are one result.

[A version of this chapter was published as "Basic Infrastructure for Socio-Economic Development, Ecological Protection and Geographical Desegregation: South Africa's Unmet Challenge" in *Geoforum* 30, 1 (1999).]

Introduction

This chapter considers some of the main concepts that should--but, in South Africa at present, do not fully--inform official policy decisions (as well as academic research) on infrastructure and service delivery. The focus is on how, through *national* programs and cross-subsidies, the new government's socio-economic, ecological, and spatial responsibilities can be met in the course of expanding the quality and quantity of basic services to low-income residents. The style of argumentation combines what David Harvey (1996:ch.13) refers to as "ecological modernization" and "environmental justice" discourses: respectively, expanded cost-benefit analyses and concern for the human "brown" (not just ecological "green") character of development. In this respect, the arguments presented relate directly to South African policy debates but are of a more general character.

The chapter, next, cites the new Constitution as the key juridical reference, and the *Reconstruction and Development Program* as the primary political mandate; then considers shortcomings in the government's new municipal infrastructure policy; reviews economic multipliers associated with infrastructure and services; reviews benefits to women associated with infrastructure and services; reviews environmental issues associated with infrastructure and services; reviews public health benefits associated with infrastructure and services; reviews geographical issues associated with infrastructure and services; and offers remarks on subsidies and tariffs. The conclusion draws together the material in the chapter and suggests ways in which a different set of policy-makers--with social-democratic and socialist rather than neoliberal proclivities--might, in future, offer developmental rewards for expanding infrastructure and service delivery.

By way of background, because of apartheid and the extremely skewed legacy of economic development, South Africa is the second most unequal large country in the world (after Brazil). The wealthiest 2.4 million South Africans account for over 40 percent of all consumption, while the poorest 21 million account for under 10 percent; the ratios for consumption of basic necessities such as water and energy are even more skewed. The poorest 20 percent of the population earns only 3 percent of the national income, while the income share of the top 20 percent of the population exceeds 60 percent. In short, there is limited or non-existent access to infrastructure, education, primary health care and socio-economic opportunities for the majority of people (especially rural women). At present, only 38 percent of "African" households have access to electricity for cooking, heating or lighting (while nearly all "coloured," "Indian," and "white" households have access to electricity). Only 27 percent of African households have running tap water inside their residences, only 34 percent have access to flush toilets, and only 37 percent have their refuse removed by a local authority. Using orthodox cost-recovery techniques to sell water and electricity to low-income households, these figures will only improve at the margins (Department of Public Works 1997).

The context in which this chapter was drafted in 1997-98 included not only the formidable backlogs, but a tightening of fiscal constraints associated with a homegrown structural adjustment policy, cut-offs of services to residential users due to non-payment of increased municipal service charges, and an upsurge in township social unrest in many of South Africa's major urban centers (Barchiesi 1998). This unrest has the potential to spread and intensify, and reminds us of the urgency, at national level, to provide a decisive policy on infrastructure/services which combines Constitutional responsibilities with an effective, redistributive system that can adequately subsidize low-income residents, in part by recognizing the myriad developmental benefits that flow from infrastructure and services.

Constitutional and political mandates

Unique amongst modern states, South Africa's new Constitution (Republic of South Africa 1996) contains guarantees of socio-economic rights in addition to general municipal "developmental duties": the municipality must "give priority to the basic needs of the community, and to promote the social and economic development of the community, and to participate in national and provincial development programs" (RSA 1996:153.) All spheres of government have a duty to champion the Constitution's overall approach, in the Bill of Rights, to equality of access to services:

> Equality includes the full and equal enjoyment of all rights and freedoms. To promote the achievement of equality, legislative and other measures designed to protect or advance persons, or categories of persons, disadvantaged by unfair discrimination, may be taken. (RSA 1996:9.2)

In an expansive reading, municipalities should seek to ensure that citizens receive access to services that have been historically denied them, so as to achieve equal levels of service delivery standards across residential areas. The goal, as spelled out in the Bill of Rights (RSA 1996:ch.2), is to ensure that citizens can exercise their rights of access to water, healthcare, a clean environment, housing and, more generally, dignity, by calling on the state to provide appropriate services.

These Constitutional obligations parallel the political promises made by the African National Congress (ANC) in its *Reconstruction and Development Program* (*RDP*). This 157-page document became the policy platform upon which the ANC won the 1994 campaign, and initially represented a crucial political mandate. The *RDP* was ambitious about meeting basic needs, arguing that on grounds of its upper middle income status, "South Africa can afford to feed, house, educate and provide health care for all its citizens" (ANC 1994:2.1.3).

The amount of social resources to be allocated to meeting basic needs is a central concern. For example, the budgetary goal for housing expenditure in the *RDP* was 5 percent of the entire national budget (ANC 1994:2.5.5); this goal was repeated in the *Housing White Paper* in late 1994. However, due to policy design failure--a market-oriented, bank-centered, developer-driven strategy was adopted, providing tiny, poorly-serviced structures often without walls, that required "self-help," generally by women, to complete--fully 80 percent of state funds allocated to housing from 1994-96 were unspent, leading to dramatic budget cuts in housing and an average spending/budget ratio of probably less than 1.5 percent over the ANC's first (1994-99) term in office (see Chapter Ten).

Likewise, as specified in the *RDP*, the rural land reform "program must include the provision of services to beneficiaries of land reform so that they can use their land as productively as possible" and "must aim to redistribute 30 percent of agricultural land within the first five years of the program" (ANC 1994:sections 2.4.12, 2.4.14). Yet budgetary resources for the Department of Land Affairs have not been sufficient, and again a weak (market-oriented, willing-seller, willing-buyer) policy--designed largely by the World Bank--was adopted. Instead of the 30 percent target, the national land reform program is likely to achieve perhaps 1-2 percent redistribution (Greenberg 1998).

The *RDP* also commented in some detail on how to finance urban and rural infrastructure and services. The *RDP* specified the need for tariff restructuring, cross-subsidies and lifeline services to the poor, with respect to both water (including sanitation) and electricity (ANC 1994:sections 2.6.10, 2.7.8). The rationale for such a system--national tariff reform emphasizing cross-subsidies (using national and provincial resources, not just local) and lifeline tariffs for low-income consumers, based upon a more appropriate use of housing and land subsidies to finance deeper levels of capital infrastructure than actually implemented--is not only to meet Constitutional responsibilities, but also to gain additional public health, environmental, and economic benefits to all of society (particularly women and children).

In the wake of the ANC's dramatic 63 percent electoral victory in 1994, however, under circumstances of financial panic associated with a 20 percent drop in the currency during February-May 1996, the South African government adopted the *Growth, Employment and Redistribution* (*GEAR*) macroeconomic strategy in mid-1996. Most notably, *GEAR* promised reduction of the state's annual budget deficit to 3 percent of Gross Domestic Product. Ironically, however, at least in rhetoric, *GEAR* did not intend to cut back on infrastructure expenditure, but on the contrary was committed to its increase:

> This strategy envisages a substantial acceleration in government investment spending, together with improved maintenance and operation of public assets.... The provision of basic household infrastructure, in particular, is a relatively low cost and effective form of public intervention in favor of the poor and consistent with the reduction of income inequalities. (Department of Finance 1996:7.1)

Thus the South African government retained, in rhetoric at least, an overarching commitment to dramatic increases in infrastructure spending. Yet the detailed infrastructural policies adopted since 1994 bear little relation to the promises made. Like the housing and land policies mentioned above, infrastructure policy also relies excessively on market-oriented, cost-recovery provisions (in each case World Bank advisory teams and conservative consultants recommended contrary policy approaches to those of the *RDP*, and given the balance of forces in society, such advice prevailed).

Post-apartheid infrastructure policy

The Department of Constitutional Development's *Municipal Infrastructure Investment Framework* ("*MIIF*"; DCD 1997a)--the ten-year plan for infrastructure and service delivery released in 1997 but originally drafted in late 1994 by a World Bank team working with local consultants--has been criticized at a detailed level (Bond, Mogale, and Moellendorf 1997), in part based on a legacy of concern about neoliberal World Bank urban policy advice to South Africa (Bond and Swilling 1992; and below, Chapter Eleven). Critiques usually focus on the *MIIF*'s low services standards; their implications for neo-apartheid class segregation; the larger-than-anticipated number of people likely to be adversely affected; the *MIIF*'s failure to factor in positive externalities when designing service standards and subsidies; the implications of such failure for understanding returns on investment; *MIIF*'s insufficient cross-subsidy provisions; and *MIIF*'s dismissal of the main means of resolving many of these problems, namely a system of lifeline tariffs and progressive block tariff cross-subsidization. Each aspect is briefly considered next, with some developed extensively in the rest of the chapter.

Excessively low standards

The "basic" standards advocated in the *MIIF* as the lowest common denominator for municipal investment--such as pit latrines (not waterborne sanitation), yard taps (not inside the house), 5-8 Amp electricity supply (not 20 or 60 Amp, as exists in formerly white areas), untarred roads, no stormwater drainage, etc--will be on offer to the estimated 20 percent of urban residents who have anticipated real monthly incomes of R800--US$160 in 1998--and below, and to 90 percent of rural residents. These are considered excessively low given South Africa's "upper middle-income" standard of living (of roughly US$3,000 per capita annual income in purchasing power parity terms).

Relatively permanent segregation policy

The basic service levels contemplated in the *MIIF* are not merely emergency services (piped water or portable toilets in slum settlements that are without water or hygienic facilities at present), but represent, more fundamentally, development policy that will be in place for at least a decade. It is extremely difficult to incrementally upgrade infrastructure--particularly sanitation systems--from pit latrines to waterborne sewage, resulting in permanently segregated low-income ghettoes (from which households that raise their real earnings to above

R800 per month will have to emigrate in order to gain access to improved infrastructure services).

Inaccurate calculation of the low-income population

The *MIIF* is considered extremely optimistic--by at least a factor of 100 percent--to project that (in real terms) only around 20 percent of urban households will earn less than R800 per month within ten years, given the worsening unemployment situation and failure of the *GEAR* policy to meet most major economic performance targets. The actual percentage is likely to be far higher.

What the MIIF overlooked

Aside from the question of political acceptability, there are several other important problems associated with *MIIF*'s low standards for such a large proportion of the population:

- implications of the infrastructure policy for microeconomic linkages and for macroeconomic policy have not been adequately addressed or factored in as a means of overcoming affordability constraints;
- the implications of infrastructure standards for women are not adequately considered and factored in;
- public health benefits associated with increased access to services have not been adequately factored in;
- environmental problems associated with the proposed standards have not been adequately addressed or factored in;
- the spatial implications of class segregation implicit in the program--with all the consequent economic inefficiencies--lend themselves to creation of new, post-apartheid racial ghettos where it will be physically impossible or excessively costly to upgrade from "basic" to full services (while recognizing this problem, *MIIF* does nothing to counteract it in part because the costs associated with neo-apartheid geography have not been calculated nor factored in); and
- a national tariff structure has not been developed consistent with cross-subsidization and lifeline tariff provisions mandated in the *RDP*.

Implications for calculating "economic returns" to infrastructure investment

Each of these issues will be considered in the following pages. The main investment implications are important to note at this stage, namely that the "net economic return" on infrastructure investments should incorporate not only the immediate financial return--the amount of cost recovery as a ratio of the amount invested--but also other social benefits, costs, externalities and multipliers. Having failed to do so in the areas noted above, the *MIIF* provides for low standards of infrastructure on grounds that these standards are the most that low-income South Africans can afford to pay.

The basis for low infrastructure standards

Specifically, in light of the failure to consider the broader economic returns to infrastructure investment, the main reason that "basic" levels of service are being imposed upon the vast majority of the poor is the allegedly high recurrent costs of water and electricity. In the absence of generous cross-subsidies, these costs prohibit low-income households from paying full cost-recovery rates for even a minimal monthly amount of these services. Such an amount could cover sufficient services--according to the *RDP*, for example, "an on-site supply of 50-60 liters per capita per day of clean water" (ANC 1994:2.6.7), and sufficient electricity to cover the minimal energy requirements associated with essential lighting, heating and cooking (approximately 20 kilowatt hours per person per month)--such that all South Africans attain a relatively decent standard of living regardless of their ability to pay. Instead, *MIIF* emphasizes cost recovery and "limited" local-level cross-subsidies (in the case of "indigent" households who must pass a means test to get access to the Intergovernmental Grant mechanism, funding which has declined in real terms by 85 percent since 1991) (Financial and Fiscal Commission 1997).

The need for more comprehensive "block tariff" subsidies

South Africa's majority is so poor--especially in relation to the minority of luxury consumers who have never had to worry about access to full services--that "limited cross-subsidies" are insufficient and the exercise of recovering costs on collectively consumed services (a communal tap, for example) is often futile or too administratively expensive. Indeed, the reason that the phrase "limited" is used in this context is because of government's explicit refusal to consider (even as an policy option exercise) restructuring national tariffs so that substantial cross-subsidies can be obtained. If such a proposal--as noted, consistent with the *RDP*--had been considered and adopted, it would have been relatively easy to cross-subsidize from national-scale industrial, service-sector, mining and agricultural bulk users of water and electricity, to low-income residential consumers. The vast difference in use patterns--commercial farmers consume 52 percent of water, for instance, while black domestic use is less than 2 percent--would allow a small marginal increase in tariffs for the large users to pay for a lifeline service at no cost to all other consumers. Such a progressive block tariff system, essentially providing an entitlement to all citizens, would also penalize excessive usage, thereby contributing to conservation goals.

By exploring in more detail various developmental characteristics of infrastructure and services, this chapter indicates the extensive benefits of higher standards of infrastructure investment and service delivery; how externalities and multipliers can be calculated and incorporated into full economic (not merely financial rate-of-return) costing; and how infrastructure/services markets sometimes fail to deliver infrastructure of a sufficient standard and affordable price to meet basic human needs--hence requiring extensive state intervention. All such arguments justify a different approach than that ultimately adopted in the *MIIF.*

Economic multipliers

There are four main types of economic multipliers to be considered: construction-related job creation; literacy and productivity enhancement; small business promotion; and water infrastructure for small-scale irrigation purposes.

Job creation through infrastructure construction

Research on potential employment creation in infrastructure and housing are based upon formal sector jobs alone (Merrifield 1996) and upon hypotheses about informal sector activity (Building Industries Federation of South Africa 1995). Formal sector construction employment includes residential (high and low-income groups), non-residential (commercial, industrial and civic amenities) as well as civil engineering construction (for infrastructure, bulk infrastructure and earth works). The formal construction industry is defined as those firms in the sector registered with the Industrial Council or the Registrar of Companies.

According to most accounts, formal employment varies between 7 construction jobs for every million rand (US$200,000) spent in the civil engineering sector, to 12 jobs per million rand in non-residential new construction, to 23 jobs per million rand in public housing construction (Merrifield 1996). But by adding employment creation in the informal sector--specifically, an estimate of 50 jobs per million rand for informally constructed housing--the average for all housing construction is raised to as high as 30 jobs for every million rand spent, a figure competitive with labor-intensive manufacturing.

The Building Industry Federation's (BIFSA's) estimates for employment creation through construction are nearly as optimistic: 28 jobs for every million rand spent. The method used to arrive at this figure is--using Receiver of Revenue statistics of total turnover in the construction industry (R18 billion)--to extrapolate based on assumptions regarding the ratio of materials to labor (at specified levels of wages). Although the informal sector is not explicitly included in this methodology, total turnover does include building materials purchased from formal sector suppliers, which in turn lends itself to some measure of informal building activity, albeit indirect.

Based on differing assumptions about ratio of materials to labor, BIFSA (1995) generated scenarios about the components of construction that relate to differential skills. Drawn from industry data, the most common scenario for the components of construction work is the following: 26 percent semi-skilled workers at R72 per day; 19 percent skilled workers at R120 per day; 50 percent unskilled workers at R45 per day; and 5 percent supervisory staff at R160 per day. The apparently low daily wage for un- and semi-skilled workers takes into account the irregular nature of employment for workers in this industry, especially those in the informal sector who are usually laid off between contracts. By weighting skills in this way, BIFSA conclude that 28 jobs are created for every million rand spent in the construction industry on housing and infrastructure using labor-intensive methods. Such high rates of job creation, in a context of more than 30 percent official unemployment, warrant a large increase in state expenditure in both the construction of infrastructure and in the cross-subsidization of services to enhance basic consumption.

Literacy and productivity improvement

There are several means of considering economic benefits that flow from enhanced literacy and productivity of citizens (World Bank 1993a). Electrification reduces reproductive rates through altering social relationships and generating economic opportunities and, as a result, women in electrified areas place more emphasis on children's education than on children as productive agents. Electrification provides some of the essential prerequisites for education, such as lighting and opportunities for efficient administration. In addition it generates the potential for longer schooldays, opening of night schools, and access to audio visual aids. It enables children and adults to study at home and offers the opportunity for health, promotion through the broadcast media such as television and radio.

Education has been shown to impact directly on a range of variables which, taken together, contribute to the health status of domestic units and ultimately of the nation. There is a high rate of social return through investment in education and this rate of return is substantially higher for women than men. Female education has been shown to impact upon reproductive rates, child-rearing practices, and child-mortality rates. Higher levels of maternal education have a significant impact on nutrition of children, improved child health and reduction in diarrhoea morbidity.

The use of electricity in a household can have several effects on the productivity of inhabitants. Firstly, improved lighting, as well as access to television, bring about considerable improvements to the quality of the working environment of students and scholars. The ability to study at home, although also dependent on other factors such as the number of people in the household and the number of rooms available, is certainly enhanced through electrification. Improved lighting and air quality (to the extent that the latter occurs) can also increase the quality of life of inhabitants and this has a positive effect on their productivity in places of employment or income generation.

Good health results in fewer days lost to illness, increased productivity, greater opportunities to obtain better paying jobs and longer working lives. Healthier workers earn more because they are more productive and can get better paying jobs. Environmentally caused diseases have been shown to impair productive work and lead to heavy loss of income and malnutrition in family members. When illness occurs the loss of income is borne by the household and healthier members have to work harder and longer to make up for the loss in income. With a healthy workforce employers can reduce the cost of building slack into their production schedules, invest more in staff training, and exploit the benefits of specialization.

SMME expansion

Small, medium and micro enterprise (SMME) expansion is crucial to South Africa because all other aspects of orthodox macroeconomic policy have led to massive job loss, not employment creation (instead of 126,000 new jobs in 1996, 71,000 were lost; instead of 252,000 new jobs in 1997, an estimated 116,000 were lost). Yet the hoped-for burgeoning of SMMEs may be hampered at the outset if access to water and electricity is not ensured. Such access comes initially through home-based activities, so a full supply of services to residences (not limited, for example, to a single yard tap or small-voltage electricity meter) should also be seen as an investment in micro enterprises and Local Economic Development.

The benefits of electrification, for example, are obvious, in terms of both SMMEs and the additional R800 million per year that will be spent on appliances from electrification (at existing rates of expansion). Recent Eskom experience suggests that for every 100 households which are connected to an electricity supply, between 10 and 20 new economic activities are started. Electrical fridges are often acquired by small traders to store drinks and perishable goods; in one rural Kwazulu-Natal town, of 23 enterprises 21 required electrical refrigerators to store produce, meat, and drinks for sale. The benefits of moving from very low electricity supplies (the basic 5-8 Amps for urban areas) to an intermediate 20 Amp supply are particularly large given the need to operate appliances such as refrigerators and small motors. For enterprises involved in welding or carpentry, higher levels of service (up to 30 Amps) are required (van Horen 1996a and 1996b) (Bond, Mogale, and Moellendorf 1997). The special case of water for small-scale farming enterprises is considered next.

Small-scale irrigation

Water for small-scale farmers should also be considered an infrastructure/service priority. Particularly in cases where municipalities have a responsibility to such farmers in their hinterlands, or where rural municipalities have authority and resources to supply (unpurified) water through irrigation systems, the economic relationships are important to understand. Here we consider smallholder farmers from historically-oppressed racial and ethnic groups who at present generally work drylands. Their activities--unlike those of large commercial farmers--do not significantly reduce water run-off. They are presently being considered for subsidy by the national Department of Water Affairs and Forestry, but in the context of moving from riparian rights-based allocations of water to a neoliberal economic water pricing system.

A key reason for developing the capacity for municipal intervention in small-scale irrigation systems, where this is geographically appropriate, is that small farmers have been particularly vulnerable to drought. The 1992 Consultative Forum on Drought assessed inequities prevailing in the rural areas during the prolonged drought of the early 1990s, when large-scale irrigation schemes continued to use water inefficiently (approximately half of commercial farm water is wasted), while drying up streams and dams that black farmers depended on for subsistence.

Upgraded irrigation infrastructure would enable smallholders to increase production and improve food security and household income. It is worth observing, however, that many previous attempts to provide irrigation to emerging farmers were unsuccessful. Subsidies were provided selectively in the former "homelands" of South Africa, but were generally failures from financial and institutional standpoints, for reasons attributable in large part to their top-down, unaccountable management by a bureaucratic system which disempowered the black farmers. More than 200 small-scale farmer irrigation schemes were implemented in recent decades, involving about 37,000 participants, with only around 25 percent of farmers able to make a profit. About 47,500 hectares were involved, a very small proportion of the total irrigated land of 1.3 million hectares. Farmers were not allowed to own the land and had no security of tenure, were generally told what to grow and how to do it (without adequate training), suffered from improper management of the irrigation scheme and thus unreliable water supplies, but bore all of the financial risk, including excessive debt burdens (Backeburg 1996).

The context is important, for the system of migrant labor deprived many of these smallholdings of the workers needed to run them effectively, and rural women bore the burden of trying to eke out a living and care for children and a household (and indeed of reproducing urban labor power more generally). Lack of infrastructure inhibited marketing of produce, and still does in these areas. The subsidies provided during the apartheid era did not result in sustainable access to agricultural markets, though they may have slightly enhanced food security and produced a limited number of viable enterprises.

Yet while irrigation has the potential to add enormous value to crop production, there exists little potential in South Africa to introduce new large irrigation schemes given environmental considerations. It therefore makes sense to make optimum use of existing schemes (Hollingworth and Muller 1991). In order to reform such schemes and make them efficient, the issue of tenure must first be resolved and there must be a new regime of participatory management and decision-making.

The modernization framework for drawing small farmers into agricultural markets must also be reconsidered. There are very few independent black farmers who consistently market agricultural produce for profit, due to the historical disadvantages mentioned. Thus far the land reform program has been largely limited to small-scale pilot projects. But there are probably in excess of a million rural black farmers who presently rely on rainfall or low-tech irrigation from local streams or boreholes. Women are in the majority, so not only are there equity considerations based on race and poverty, but also gender. Improving access to water supply to these farmers is therefore important even if it cannot be sustained during the short-term on purely economic, cost-recovery grounds. Economic water pricing could only address inequity if the water savings and revenue achieved from large users were available in part to provide a reliable supply to smallholders. A great deal of potential exists to augment income through agriculture by more secure access to water in the rural (and urban) areas.

One type of smallholder irrigation scheme that deserves attention is small and micro-scale vegetable farming through community gardening. An estimated 150,000 people in South Africa participate in such arrangements, growing for surplus production as an income source.

Participants are usually responsible for their own plot, but cooperate to irrigate the garden, employing techniques such as controlled short-furrow irrigation from hand-dug canals or reservoirs, or bucket watering. A secure source of water of only five liters per person per day may be enough to grow a modest supply of vegetables effectively. Relatively small amounts of reliable water could stimulate other income-generating enterprises, such as ceramics and brick-making, or food preparation and processing. In such cases, and more generally, women tend to be important beneficiaries of infrastructural investments.

Benefits to women

In South Africa, as elsewhere in the developing world, women are the primary care-givers and homemakers, and hence the benefits of infrastructure and service delivery are disproportionately felt by women, and likewise the burden of inadequate standards of infrastructure also fall upon women (Bassett *et al* 1992; Esrey 1996). There are several aspects to women's utilization of time that can be enhanced by infrastructure investments and service delivery, relating to time spent in water queues, time spent gathering fuelwood and making fires, time spent walking from place to place because road conditions are not amenable for public or private transport, and time spent on other tasks that could otherwise be directed elsewhere if proper infrastructure was in place.

To take one example, time savings due to the nearness and availability of an improved water source has been reported to lead to more time for child care, including breastfeeding and better food preparation. Time saved could be used for agricultural or income-generation activities which could result in better family health. In addition, women's savings in energy expenditure from bringing water closer to households results in reduced incidence of low-birth-weight babies born as well as a corresponding reduction in energy intake which could be transferred to children. Similarly, time savings due to the use of electricity for cooking and heating could be utilized in ways more beneficial to health. The time spent by rural households in South Africa (usually women) collecting wood for fires falls within the range of 5.2 to 18.6 hours per week (average 11.9). In aggregate each year, 1.2 million travel hours could be saved (nearly entirely by women), along with 12 million tons of firewood (Bond, Mogale, and Moellendorf 1997).

Environmental implications

A variety of themes have emerged in infrastructure research related to South Africa's fragile ecology (see Himlin 1997 for a more comprehensive overview). Water-related issues are considered first, including sewage-service levels, the negative environmental consequences associated with increased water supply, the importance of water-drainage systems, and issues surrounding water-quality treatment. This is followed by a survey of environmental issues related to electrification.

Water supply, sewage service levels, water drainage, and water treatment

To begin, it is true that there are negative environmental consequences of increased water supply and indeed of the relatively high infrastructure and service levels associated with the *RDP*, particularly with respect to dam construction, the most prevalent method for supplying water in South Africa. An assessment must therefore be made as to how much additional water would be needed to service all additional households with water and water-borne sanitation. According to one study, in the absence of conservation measures, in 1990 the total water supply would only have had to increase by 1.5 percent if all those not yet receiving water-borne sanitation were to receive it, and the additional households that are expected to be provided with new direct water supply would increase household water demand--which itself is responsible for only 15 percent of all water use--by just 12 percent (Palmer Development Group 1993a).

There are very strong possibilities for reducing water demand amongst society as a whole, through the new water pricing policy, catchment area management, fixing leaky supplies--approximately 25 percent before it reaches the household (Rencken and Kerdachi 1991)--and other demand-side management measures. One study found that the cost of detecting and fixing leaks to the system were minimal compared to the savings in the cost of the recovered water over only seven months (Johannesburg City Engineer's Department 1989). Other conservation techniques include more efficient appliances, for toilets that flush with 4.5 liters as opposed to the 9-13 liters common in South Africa can reduce household water consumption by 18-23 percent (Imiesa 1993). A 6-liter flush, common in Europe, could still reduce consumption dramatically. The installation of internal household water meters (rather than solely outside, disguised near the mains) is another common and effective way to raise consumer (including company) consciousness and reduce water demand. By all accounts, conservation makes more sense than constantly building more dams to increase the supply of water, especially given limits to the viability of further dam construction.

In sum, provisions for supplying water to the poor will increase total domestic use to just 17 percent of the water supply by 2010, which means that currently under-served households will not place any substantial burden on South Africa's water supply (Palmer and Eberhard 1994). Moreover, the particularly water-scarce urban conglomeration in Gauteng (Johannesburg, Pretoria, and the Vaal) now enjoys increased supplies (from the first phase of the Lesotho Highlands Water Project). Further dam construction is unnecessary over the medium term (Mayekiso and Menu 1998).

Under such conditions, government's intention to deny water access--in the form of water-borne sanitation--to low-income urban residents is short-sighted. At present it is envisioned that, based on national resources allocated (regarding both capital and recurrent expenses), lowest-income households will receive a minimum "basic" package of a Ventilated Improved Pit (VIP) latrine, water supplies in the form of yard standpipes for urban residents and taps only within 200 meters of rural homes, and open urban stormwater drainage (DCD 1997a). Municipalities are then given the responsibility of deriving the additional resources required to improve standards in low-income areas.

There is no conclusive analysis of the environmental costs and benefits associated with particular sewerage and water-service levels in South Africa. But while there exist conceptual problems and data limitations that prohibit an exhaustive analysis, the major environmental hazards associated with low service standards--and the benefits associated with improved standards--can, nevertheless, be explored.

Regarding sewerage, both major systems--VIPs and water-borne sewage--produce pollutants. VIPs rely on the soil on the site of the latrine to filter out contaminants from the water system, and treatment works for dealing with sludge off-site. A water-borne system controls treatment of the sewage at a central location off-site. Pollutants can usually be better controlled by using a centralized treatment system, except in cases of sewer breakage. Groundwater and/or surface water contamination from pit latrines is virtually guaranteed, and treatment of this contamination is non-existent.

There are important consequences of sewage pollutants. Contaminants from sewage are of two general types, biological and chemical. Biological contaminants include pathogens in the form of bacteria and viruses, with consequent risks to human health. Chemical contaminants (or nutrients) include nitrates and phosphates, which damage ecosystems through eutrophication, which is the excessive growth of algae and other plants at the expense of other aquatic life. There are also health risks to humans (especially infants) consuming nitrified water. Additionally, other organic material present in waste contaminates water supplies by encouraging the growth of bacteria, which depletes the oxygen in the water (chemical oxygen demand), thereby killing other aquatic life (Palmer Development Group 1993a).

With regard to the concentration of water contamination, advocates of VIPs argue that pollution created is generally contained on-site, whereas leakage due to sewer-system failure is more concentrated and therefore poses more of a threat to the environment (Palmer Development Group 1993b). However, the failures of apartheid-era, resource-deprived, badly-managed township sewer systems should not now be assumed as characteristic of future urban or rural developments. The premise must be that well-managed water-borne systems will be adequately maintained and that leaks will be rapidly identified and patched. In contrast, pit latrine pollutants could in fact be relatively concentrated due to high density levels in low-income urban settlements, with no controlled treatment possible.

There is also a high variability of pollutant release by VIPs, depending upon soil conditions and methods of sludge treatment, and the practice of households adding sullage (washing water waste) into the VIP system. Where the water table is high, such as in Cape Town, groundwater pollution due to pit latrines can be severe. In Winterveld, near Pretoria, the high water table allows boreholes to serve as a reliable source of drinking water, yet the use of pit latrines by most residents has resulted in dangerous groundwater exposure to biological contaminants such as fecal coliform bacteria and salmonella, in turn causing a typhoid epidemic in 1991. Of 59 wells and boreholes tested in Winterveld during the early 1990s, only 12 were free of fecal coliform bacteria (Palmer Development Group 1995). Where soil is non-absorbent, the pits may overflow, exposing populations to direct sewage and polluting surface water. In Botshabelo, where pit overflowing was described as "continuous" during heavy rains, high bacterial counts were found in the river system (Palmer Development Group 1994). Low-lying land in floodplains presents another problem, for again in the case of Botshabelo, flooding caused sewage from the pits in the floodplain to flow directly into the river. Where there is rocky ground and/or fissures, such as fractured bedrock or dolomite (as in much of Gauteng), swift lateral and vertical movement of pollutants from VIPs can be expected, which means that even short-lived pollutants like viruses can leach into drinking water supplies or onto the surface, and will also leach quickly into the groundwater (Fourie and van Ryneveld 1995). Such soil conditions pose problems for all VIP-related contaminants. Finally, on steep inclines, as in many residential areas of Natal, leakage to the surface can be expected, where people are directly exposed to the VIP sewage waste (Palmer Development Group 1993c). Where the soil is excessively granular in character, even most of the bacterial contaminants that are filtered out well by most soils, along with the other contaminants, escape into groundwater.

In all such cases, water-borne sanitation is especially important for protecting the surrounding environment. It should be noted that many negative results observed in cases of pit latrines were not associated with VIPs, but rather with poorly-constructed, conventional pit latrines. Yet it is difficult to expect any differences regarding flooding, overflow, and groundwater leakage of VIPs, although sanitation may be improved due to VIP improvements in fly control and ventilation.

Most groundwater pollutants are exacerbated through VIP systems, compared with water-borne systems. Chemical oxygen demand levels are much lower in the water-borne system, as is the nitrogen load. Where there are denitrifying works in water treatment plants, VIPs can only do as well in removing nitrogen in very good soil conditions, according to the nutrient load model. Yet denitrification does not occur in the aerobic, unsaturated soil above the water table, so groundwater contamination seems almost inevitable from pit latrines. There are cases of significant nitrate contamination that can be attributed to on-site sanitation systems in many different types of soil (Fourie and van Ryneveld 1995).

Well-situated and well-managed sewage systems, whether VIP or water-borne, filter out most viral and bacterial contaminants. Water-borne systems should have maturation ponds for this purpose. On-site sanitation systems do pose significant risks to the spread of disease, if conditions are less than ideal, in cases noted above. Regrettably, the South African government's elevation of the principle of affordability above other considerations in the provision of sanitation runs the risk of ignoring the high costs of pit latrine pollution in inappropriate geological conditions. The overriding issue is that the poor are often forced to locate on inferior and precarious land which makes for difficult provision of services and the risk of extreme environmental pollution. In such cases, policy should not pretend that VIPs are a more cost-effective way to confront what are essentially the geographical implications of differential political power.

Regarding other aspects of water-related infrastructure, good water drainage systems are an important protection against flooding in crowded urban developments, where much of the natural drainage capacity of the land has been inhibited as the land is covered with concrete and as surface vegetation is lost (due to its use as firewood as well as by land development). Flood disasters, experienced periodically in South Africa, result in billions of rands in property damage and a substantial death toll every year. The impervious surfaces of urban areas not only increase flood peaks during storms, but also decrease low flows between storms. Less rainwater seeps into underground aquifers and the area becomes drier when the rains stop (Stephenson 1993). In addition, the soil conditions and topography of urban and rural areas makes a major difference in drainage. Drier, uncovered sections of the urban areas, often found in low-income black townships, contribute sediment to stormwater flows. This can smother aquatic life and clog dams. High pollutant loads--particularly nutrients, salts and chemicals--are products of urban run-off (Allanson 1995).

Environmental destruction can be reduced through converting open drains and gravel roads to tarred roads and closed drains beneath roads (the *MIIF*'s affordability guidelines dictate that low-income communities receive the former). In both cases, water is rapidly channelled to downstream areas, which results in heavy downstream flooding. Open drains are much less desirable, however, in heavily settled areas due to their high potential for being blocked by solid waste (this is somewhat less of a problem with closed drains, but improved solid waste collection is required in either case). Open drains may also carry excessive amounts of sediment into the receiving water body, and have proven to be dangerous for young children who can be swept into rivers. Open drains may also facilitate erosion in the vicinity of the channels and result in property damage to nearby homes.

It is true that tarred roads also involve environmental costs, decreasing the surface area for absorption of water, speeding up the rate of stormwater runoff, and increasing the contamination from oil and other automotive by-products to receiving water bodies. And closed drains speed the water flow, increasing the risk of flash flooding. But innovations in closed stormwater drainage systems have a huge potential for savings in construction costs and in costs to the environment. The main principle of a better-integrated system is to slow down the movement of urban run-off. This involves containment areas for stormwater near the site of impact, which would also allow for water treatment of the polluted urban run-off. The cost of constructing a "single pipe" system is lower than dealing with sewer capacity problems by conventional methods (case studies show cost savings of 50 percent and more). Household rain catchment could be introduced to remove a portion of rain water from the sewer system, water that could then be used by individual households to water yards or use for general washing. A third component of integrated management is the strategic planning of green areas that would absorb stormwater runoff (Andoh 1994).

Regarding water treatment, most local water researchers stress the importance of carefully managing South Africa's limited water resources, warning that water pollution is already a serious problem. Poor water quality not only affects South Africa's ability to continue to provide clean drinking water to a growing population, but the ecosystem as a whole suffers from a lack of biodiversity. Enormous environmental destruction is occurring, disrupting the delicate balance of interdependence among species (Allanson 1995). Some of the foreseen consequences include a reduction in the water body's natural purification systems, and increasing levels of flooding and erosion as the vegetation mediating these processes is depleted.

In the case of surface water, point and non-point source pollution from dense urban settlement and industrial sources has created a serious water quality problem. Many urban streams and rivers do not meet the general effluent standards established by the Department of Water Affairs and Forestry. Problems discussed earlier--bacterial contaminants, organic silt, and nutrients, along with toxins and oil--have killed off aquatic life in urban streams and have polluted the major raw water supply reservoirs which now must be treated to high standards for human consumption. Most conventional water-treatment plants are ill-equipped to adequately purify the increasingly polluted water (Rencken and Kerdachi 1991).

The costs of pollution control are justified by the often greater costs of environmental damage and pollution clean-up. Systems that clean up water pollution or ameliorate its effects are becoming available. One temporary measure to preserve aquatic life in the wake of a pollution event is an aeration system that costs more than R25,000 per week to operate, and other even more elaborate systems have been designed to filter pollution from urban water courses (Imiesa 1993). Yet a great deal of effort is required to deal with the after-effects of the pollutants in reservoirs. Control is more difficult for the non-point sources in agricultural run-off and informal settlements (i.e., VIPs) whose effluent is not centralized through a water-borne sanitation system.

In the case of groundwater resources, prevention of groundwater pollution should receive high priority in water management. Such resources are already used to supply water to towns throughout the country and offer enormous potential to further supplement surface water supply, especially during periods of drought. Groundwater remains three to five times cheaper to develop than surface water sources. However, pollution to aquifers is difficult to clean up. Groundwater moves much more slowly than surface water, and thus the self-cleansing properties evident in surface water are weak. The damages from groundwater pollution to ecosystems is often long-term, and often leads to abandonment of aquifers.

Solid waste dumps, leaking underground storage tanks, fertilizers and pesticides, and the lack of sanitation in informal settlements are all sources of groundwater pollution. Because the clean-up of a contaminated aquifer is both technically difficult and expensive, a pro-active approach of preventing aquifer contamination by complete separation of human waste disposal from groundwater is recommended. Such principles also apply to contamination from pit latrines, especially through constant use in a concentrated area over time.

While it is impossible to put a price tag on a clean environment, one of the ways that researchers model environmental costs is by assuming financial costs associated with our use of the environment. For example, if fisheries are damaged by pollution, the revenue that could have been attained through the sale of the lost fish could be considered an environmental cost of the pollution. Likewise, the most direct environmental cost of pollution to the water is the cost of the clean-up of contamination. Preliminary calculations by the Development Research Institute in Johannesburg confirm that if only a 10 percent reduction in water purification costs were achieved by moving all under-served households to water-borne sanitation instead of providing pit latrines, these savings would outweigh the costs for sewage treatment and greater water demand from the additional households served, by roughly R117 million per annum (Himlin 1997).

Other elements that could be included in a more comprehensive environmental cost-benefit analysis that in turn would justify (on economic grounds) higher infrastructural service standards include purification of sewage effluent to required standards, which would generate an increased quality water supply; purification of drinking water reservoirs, which would have commercial fishing potential; removal of silt from dams, which has potential recreational benefits; restoring surface water to required standards, which would generate health care savings; cleaning of groundwater aquifers, which would add to property values; restoration of estuaries, replacing river vegetation and rehabilitation of aquatic life/fish, which would add to the intrinsic value of the ecosystem (Himlin 1997).

Environmental costs and benefits related to electrification

As with water, it is true that increased electricity service levels may cause additional social and ecological costs due to the generation of electricity to meet additional demand, but as in the case of water this demand would represent a tiny fraction of existing consumption (no more than 3 percent additional demand, if all South African households received electricity). Environmental benefits associated with increased access to electricity--certainly beyond the small supplies envisaged in the *MIIF*, which are a 5-Amp supply, compared to the 20 Amps required to run several small appliances and the 60-Amp supply available in most middle- and upper-income white households--include diminished air pollution from coal and wood fires and diminished fuelwood collection. Some of these costs (such as indoor air pollution) are limited to households, while others (deforestation, pollution caused by burning coal in urban neighborhoods) are externalities that society as a whole pays for.

Based on the experience since Soweto was electrified in the 1980s, and in the first five years of the accelerated electrification program, *under conditions that did not include RDP-style lifeline tariffs*, it has been observed that electricity generates a substitution effect for higher-value services such as powering lights, radios, televisions, and small appliances. Without a lifeline tariff, energy-intensive applications such as cooking, space heating, and water heating are more expensive if electricity is used rather than coal, wood, and paraffin (Thorne 1996).

The incremental effects of moving from one service level to the next depends substantially upon the levels of standards and whether a lifeline tariff exists (as well as whether the retail price of small, domestically-produced appliances can be subsidized). At the low infrastructure levels envisaged in the *MIIF*, access to small volumes of electricity may replace the use of candles and paraffin for lighting, and batteries for small appliances, but there will generally be no cooking or space heating.

It is possible to make some monetary estimates of the incremental benefits of improving service levels beyond *MIIF* standards, based on recent doctoral research about the positive and negative externalities (van Horen 1996b) and on a range of studies undertaken of newly-electrified households around the country (Simmonds and Mammon 1996). Some of the costs noted are associated with public health, but are included here due to the fact that disaggregation has not yet been completed. The cost of air pollution due to coal is R307 per household per year, 25 percent of which would be abated if higher supplies than those envisaged through the *MIIF* are provided, even in the absence of a lifeline tariff. The respective estimates for air pollution due to wood usage are R944 per household per year, of which an estimated 5 percent is abated at higher levels of electricity than *MIIF* envisages, but again in the absence of a lifeline tariff. The costs of fuelwood collection are presently estimated at R291 per household per year, and again 5 percent of these costs are abated with higher electricity standards (also without a lifeline tariff). It is only possible to guess what the abatement levels would rise to if both higher standards and a lifeline supply--to provide sufficient free electricity to ensure cooking, a limited supply of refrigeration, water heating, and space heating--were offered. The use of coal and wood for fires would then be largely limited to social purposes.

The main benefits of electrification are with respect to health, as noted below, but there are additional beneficial effects of moving to electricity from coal and wood for the sake of biodiversity, aesthetics, and visibility. Adding health benefits of electrification--i.e., abatement of morbidity costs including medication, lost production, transport costs, and costs of treating in- and out-patients, and mortality costs based on a range of international (and adjusted to take account of South African income levels)--van Horen (1996) found large *net* benefits from increasing electrification standards so as to reduce some of the pollution associated with inefficient energy use. The net effects include not only avoided environmental costs from household consumption, but also an estimate of the additional environmental costs of electricity generation by Eskom to supply these customers. If electrification occurs at intermediate and full levels in urban areas alone, the net benefits begin at roughly R100 million in year one and rise (in present value terms) to R200 million in year two, R400 million in year four and R800 million in year eight. In rural areas, the net environmental benefits of electrification rise more gradually, to R50 million by year eight.

In sum, improvement of infrastructure and service standards should be undertaken in part because of the negative environmental externalities associated with lower standards. It is the environment that pays when pit latrines leak pollutants into groundwater, when sewage systems fail, when improper drainage leads to flooding, erosion, and the washing of human waste into surface water, and when coal and wood are used by households instead of cleaner, healthier electricity. Environmental pollution results in actual costs to health, property, and quality of life. The environment is a public good, and the public as a whole must take responsibility for it. This is not to say, of course, that all individuals do the same environmental damage, have the same capacity to pay, or themselves suffer the same from a polluted environment. Low-income people, especially women and children and the elderly, are typically most affected, and this is especially important when it comes to their health.

Public health promotion

While economic, gender, and ecological benefits of higher levels of infrastructural services are substantial, they do not compare with the large savings to the public health budget that can reasonably be expected. The key component of calculations associated with health and infrastructure is the cost of communicable diseases related to inadequate water supply and sanitation. According to Sanders and Groenewald (1996), such diseases

> may be water-borne (spread through water supply), water-washed (lack of water for personal and food hygiene) or water-based, as well as noncommunicable diseases due to water-borne toxins. In addition, inadequate sanitation can result in the spread of intestinal helminths through contact or ingestion of soil contaminated by human feces. Since the transmission of many of the above diseases depend on access of human wastes to water or people's mouths, the chain of transmission can be broken by safe disposal of excreta, personal and domestic hygiene (washing hands after defecating and before preparing food), improving water quality and preventing recontamination of water supplies.

Diarrhea is the most common such disease, and is generally transmitted through food-borne processes or directly transmitted via fingers, eating utensils, or dirt. Such water-washed transmission can be dramatically curtailed by increasing the quantity, availability, and utilization of water. According to Sanders and Groenewald (1996),

> Here distance to the water source is of the utmost importance as well as the promotion of positive water-use behavior. A recent burden of disease study in developing countries, using the DALY (disability adjusted life year) to measure burden of disease, ranks diarrheal disease as one of the largest causes of disease burden. It is estimated to account for 8.1 percent of total DALY loss in these areas. Infants and children carry the main burden of inadequate water and sanitation-related disease with more than 80 percent of the DALY loss due to diarrhea being the result of infections in children under age 5.

In South Africa, diarrheal disease is responsible for almost 25 percent of deaths amongst black and coloured children between 1 and 4 years of age Africa, and for nutritional deficiency and low weights. The primary risk factors are the absences of an inside tap, a flush toilet in the home, a refuse receptacle, and electricity, as well as low household income and lower than Standard Five maternal education.

Health benefits through water and sanitation services

The impact of improved water and sanitation systems can be decisive, according to Sanders and Groenewald (1996):

> Health benefits of variable magnitude have been reported. Studies have reported 0-81 percent (median 21 percent) lower child mortality rates amongst children with improved water and sanitation facilities than

> those without such facilities. Other studies have reported 40 percent-80 percent reduction in diarrhea mortality in infants and children with the provision of piped water in the house. Several studies analyze the impact of improved water and sanitation on morbidity rates due to diarrheal disease. The expected decrease in morbidity rates associated with access to adequate levels of water and sanitation is regarded to be between 22 percent and 46 percent.
>
> One study shows that a decrease of between 35-50 percent can be expected, if improved water and sanitation are combined with excreta disposal and hygiene education. Another shows that up to 70 percent of diarrheal disease cases can be attributed to inadequate disposal of child feces and garbage and poor caretaker hygiene. A recent review of research into the health benefits of water and sanitation facilities suggests that improved water supply in itself does not necessarily produce significant health improvements, sanitation may be a more important factor than water supply, the greatest benefits seem to be associated with an improvement in both sanitation and water supply, water quantity may be more important than water quality and hygiene education enhances the health benefits of improved water supply and sanitation.
>
> The factors required to achieve maximum impact from improved water and sanitation have not been well researched. Sanitation coverage is slipping behind safe water coverage and if sanitation has a larger impact on health than improving water, this disparity will result in fewer health benefits to the population.

Specifically, based on a review of international evidence of the effects of differential infrastructure and services on disease abatement, Sanders and Groenewald (1996) recommend relatively high standards of infrastructure provision:

> Where water was supplied on site or inside the house and a water-based sanitation system or flush toilet was present diarrhea prevalence was 40 percent lower than with unimproved water and no sanitation. In the same study, improvements in child nutritional status were found with improved water and sanitation. Increases in height ranging from 0.8-1.1 cm were associated with improvements in sanitation to the level of pit latrines, and 1.5-1.9 cm with optimal sanitation improvements (flush toilets) in comparison with no improved sanitation. Another study estimated that provision of in-house water connections would reduce diarrhea morbidity among infants by 12 percent and the provision of private excreta disposal facilities would reduce diarrhea morbidity by 42 percent.

Such estimations allow for rough calculations of cost savings associated simply with abatement of diarrhea, which accrue through improving infrastructure standards beyond the levels set out in the *MIIF*. Assuming a conservative cost estimate of hospitalization of R2,250 per diarrhea case, upgrading from minimal levels to intermediate/full water and sanitation services (to both urban and densely populated rural areas) would yield direct cost savings of more than R750 million to the health sector over a ten-year period, if the 22-percent morbidity decrease is achieved, and more savings if the higher rates are achieved.

Health benefits through electrification

In addition to the positive impact of water on diarrheal disease abatement, University of Cape Town researchers estimate that a universal supply of electricity would curtail more than 3,000 deaths each year due to acute respiratory infection (caused by wood/coal burning), burns, and paraffin poisoning. The direct health sector cost saving due to reduced morbidity associated with electrification is, using even conservative estimates about electricity access and utilization rates, between R343 and R515 million over a ten-year period (van Horen and Davis 1996).

Utilizing a different database that focuses much more on household-level effects (still, however, without lifeline tariff estimation), van Horen and Davis (1996) estimate savings due to the abatement of a broad range of health costs that follow the introduction of additional electricity. In the case of morbidity, costs included transport costs, medication, lost production, and costs of treating in- and out-patients. For mortality, valuation estimates from a range of international studies were used and adjusted to take account of South African income levels.

The implications of reducing household air pollution from coal and wood were noted above. In the case of paraffin poisoning, average per household costs of R90 per year can be abated by an estimated 50 percent due to electricity access *even without a lifeline supply* (and presumably much higher with lifeline), while health costs associated with fires and burns--an estimated R491 per household per year--can be abated by an estimated 75 percent with higher levels of electricity supply.

Health benefits through roads and drainage systems

Municipal investment in the form of higher standards of roads and stormwater drainage will be rewarded by various public health benefits. South African township roads are often unpaved and unlit, with consequent deleterious impact on quality of life. In Soweto, road dust contributed 16 percent on average to particulate pollution, which is linked to respiratory diseases. Improvements in transport infrastructure should promote safe, secure travel. This is not being addressed in most urban areas, where wide roads, a lack of law enforcement, and dangerous rail systems lead to high levels of injury (Sanders and Groenewald 1996).

To illustrate, in the greater Cape Town area from 1981 to 1984, 15 percent of deaths in childhood were due to transport accidents. The majority of transport-related deaths involving pedestrians in Cape Town occurred in peri-urban areas with poor transport infrastructure, substandard roads and poor safety enforcement (Cape Town Metropolitan Non-natural Mortality Study Group and Health Consulting Office 1997). Many pedestrian deaths are preventable if the road network construction is accompanied by speed control, walkways, footbridges, and recreational facilities for children.

There are significant potential health benefits associated with improved drainage of waste and storm water and in the prevention of contaminated ground and surface water and soil by human excreta. With communal standpipes water waste can be high, as there is no individual responsibility to see that the taps are closed. It is also important to point out that in areas where water supplies have been improved without provision of wastewater disposal, the result has been a shift from one set of diseases to another. Many diseases thrive in areas where there is poor drainage and inadequate provision for garbage collection, sanitation, and piped water. Anopheles mosquitos which spread malaria breed in standing water; Culex mosquitos which spread filariasis breed in sewage water (cracked or open septic tanks, pit latrines, and drains); Aedes mosquitos breed in small containers of clean water (tins, tires, water storage containers) and spread yellow fever and dengue. Intestinal parasites are also a major source of morbidity amongst low-income urban settlements (Sanders and Groenewald 1996).

Health benefits from other infrastructural improvements

Broadly, there are seven types of environmental health hazards that are common in urban areas: biological pathogens; chemical pollutants; a shortage or lack of access to particular natural resources; physical hazards; aspects of the built environment with negative consequences on physical or psycho-social health, natural resource degradation, and national/global degradation. The first four directly affect health and the other three influence health indirectly (Sanders and Groenewald 1996). Inadequate water and sanitation service provision result in large numbers of pathogenic micro-organisms and disease vectors in the environment. Air pollutants are produced by biomass or coal combustion as well as road dust. Physical hazards such as burns, scalds, and accidental fires are associated with the use of alternative energy sources to electricity. The risk of fires is further increased in low-income urban settlements because of the proximity of dwellings and flammable materials used for their construction. Flooding is a problem in areas where there is inadequate drainage.

Moreover, many psychosocial disorders are associated with poor quality houses and living environments. The stress of living under these conditions may undermine the immune system and predispose people to diseases. Good quality housing and living environments provided by good quality infrastructure and service delivery can greatly reduce stress and its negative health consequences (Sanders and Groenewald 1996).

Conclusion: Infrastructure and public health

The public health arguments for improving the proposed levels of service provision are numerous. To summarize,

- Incremental improvements in sanitation result in incremental improvements in health, but substantial improvements in both water and sanitation produce much larger impacts than either alone. Health benefits from improved water supplies only appear when improved sanitation is present and only when water is provided on the premises or inside the house. Communal water facilities have been shown to have no or little health impact or in some cases worsen the situation. Water provision without adequate wastewater disposal provision, such as that provided by water-borne sanitation, may be a health hazard in itself. The quantity of water is almost more important than water quality for household health production. For this reason the provision of private household or yard taps is crucial, as distance to the water source is the most important factor affecting the quantity of water used by households. For better health impact, improved water and sanitation and better hygiene behavior are required. The reduction in morbidity due to energy-related diseases is a function of the relationship between electrification and developmental attributes such as housing, safe water, sanitation, education, and health care.

- The direct health sector cost saving that would stem from upgrading the proposed urban infrastructural investment with regard to water and sanitation is R570 million, and almost R450 million with regard to electrification (assuming 80 percent access by 2012). This saving is the direct result of investment in infrastructure, and should be included in any economic evaluation of return on investment. This has implications in the broader debate concerning financing and affordability. The issue of health sector financing is particularly pertinent in the light of the disparity between health expenditures and health outcomes in South Africa. In addition, indirect health benefits will also result in substantial savings due to the release of time, particularly women's time, which can be used for child care and productive activities; improved productivity; and opportunities for education.
- Given the historical disparities between race groups in South Africa, it is not appropriate to provide inferior services to the disadvantaged populations. Countries with the largest gaps in the quality of infrastructure between the wealthy and the poor have the worst overall health status. In addition to the ethical and moral arguments, there are sound public health arguments for improving infrastructure in the poorer areas. Many of the diseases related to poor infrastructure are contagious and, as such, have the potential to threaten the health of higher socio-economic groups in the vicinity, e.g. cholera, malaria, dengue, filariasis, yellow fever, and tuberculosis. It is shortsighted to provide a lower level of infrastructure, given the longer term potential for environmental degradation. In addition, the culture of non-payment is likely to be perpetuated unless good quality services, associated in the minds of the poorer with the advantaged (mainly White) population, are provided. Evidence suggests that people are much more likely to maintain services which are their own than those which are shared.

In short, health is primarily produced at the level of the household and is directly related to the living environment, which includes municipal service provision. There is much evidence, international and local, to demonstrate the significant public health advantages of improved infrastructure. The health gains will be both a direct result of improved water, sanitation, electrification and drainage, as well as indirectly achieved mainly through releasing women's time for caring and productive activities. In sum, equitable development is inextricably connected to the provision of acceptable and vastly improved infrastructure.

Geographical issues

Social, political and economic problems caused by apartheid segregation have been recognized for many decades (e.g., Robinson 1996; Schapera 1928). Deepening South Africa's democratization process will to a large extent depend upon breaking down geographical barriers faced by black (African, Coloured, Indian) people, as well as reducing segregation of people according to their income class. Few citizens would deny that South Africa requires a qualitative shift towards the social integration of society, including residential neighborhoods.

Given that the immediate community is crucial as a shaping force for individuals' values, attitudes, aspirations, expectations, skills, and opportunities, it is important to guard against apartheid-era "insider vs outsider" social divisions emerging in a now-deracialized way along class lines. By tolerating such segregation--and indeed by cementing it through the *MIIF* income test (so that instead of along racial lines, sewage lines become the mark of class-based residential area)--municipal politicians and officials both abdicate their moral responsibility to reunite sharply divided cities and towns, and forego the socio-economic benefits that come from integrated planning.

Economic benefits of desegregation

The economic benefits of community desegregation are important, given how labor-related skills and education are passed along within communities. Studies have shown that education gains are higher within an entire community, and costs are lower, in cases where some families--typically from higher income classes--within the immediate area invest in skills. Using a model that deliberately omits possibly significant differences in abilities, tastes, and endowments between people, Benabou (1993) sought to prove that neighborhood effects by themselves, at least partially, shape the labor force, even the existence of unemployed ghettos. The danger Benabou identified is that individuals who invest in high skills benefit more than those pursuing low skills from the presence of high-skill workers in their community, which leads to bidding more for housing in "high-skill communities" and hence to self-segregation. In short, segregation and stratification drive up the total cost of education, and individuals in the resulting "ghettos" tend to drop out of school.

Likewise, segregation prevents full and fair competition in an efficient and transparent labor market, particularly for low-income job-seekers. Information on job opportunities is not available to all, due to uneven access to door-to-door newspapers. Not all suitable candidates are available to employers, due to travel restrictions. Informal networks are less extended and accessible, through, for example, diminished familiarity with employers and employees in the formal labor-market who in a desegregated community would potentially be neighbors. As Wilson (1987) documents in the case of the United States, living in an integrated residential setting increases opportunities to enter the labor market. Jobs will locally be more available than in segregated ghettos and there is greater access to job-related information directly from neighbors or door-to-door newspapers. Residential segregation has also been cited as a source of employment discrimination by employers (Neckermann and Kirschenmann 1990).

Desegregation and improved housing

Segregated slum housing has a large negative impact on health and welfare, so integrated planning should aim to minimise ghettoes occupied by poor people alone. It is true that South Africa's existing housing stock will be difficult to adapt for residential integration of income-classes. Houses in a geographical community are typically built within the same time-period, by the same contractor, in a very similar manner, aimed at meeting the same sorts of household needs, generally within the same price-category. A block of flats generally contains residential units that are (virtually) identical (if not in size, then in style and quality), as opposed to a mixture of large and small, cheap and dear.

Therefore, without adequate municipal intervention to diversify the housing stock, there tends to be a "natural" (developer-driven) concentration of singles, doubles, large families, etc., each in specific niches, geographically distributed across municipalities. In turn, this often leads to destructive redlining practices by financial institutions in declining areas and the creation of artificial sub-markets in which cash transactions (rather than credit) predominate, hence further lowering the market value of housing.

The implications include inefficiencies in the operation of the housing market, such that homelessness coincides with boarded-up houses and flats (as is now evident in central Johannesburg), relative overinvestment occurs in some areas compared with others, the periodic rise and fall of property markets is amplified, and other undesirable effects go unchecked. By combining the provision of adequate levels of infrastructure and services with attention to the need for residential desegregation, municipalities can partially prevent or at least dampen the impacts of such phenomena.

Enhanced community ecology

A central reason to promote integration through enhanced infrastructure investment and service delivery is to improve community ecology, which in turn has environmental, public health, and social benefits. Middle- and upper-class households usually have larger plots than the average found in a low-income area, and will also have greater political capacity to demand more public open spaces in their communities.

Such open spaces result in more greenery, more light, more fresh air, and physical spacing that in turn helps prevent the spread of fires and certain epidemics. Open spaces also provide more and safer areas for children to play, in contrast to the street with its dangerous litter and traffic. Air pollution caused by the burning of wood or coal fuel will be less concentrated in a mixed residential area, both because of the presence of better stoves and heating systems among wealthier families and through the increased diffusion through open spaces.

Within integrated, efficient communities, financial burdens of maintaining local public facilities can be better carried by higher-income groups. Regarding roads, lower-income residents often don't have cars, but do require roads for rubbish removal and emergency access (ambulance, fire, police). Roads also create opportunities for the development of (semi-) public transport and road-related activities like vending.

Social and cultural integration

Another important social benefit fostered by integration is to limit what some have (controversially) termed a "culture of poverty" that exists within low-income ghettoes (Lewis 1961). As noted, the ecological importance of a community should not be discounted, in part because of the psychological importance of establishing a healthy local milieu.

For example, middle-class communities are usually less littered and have better-maintained houses that are more pleasant to live in, which in turn stimulates others to upkeep and upgrade their own physical environment. From a social standpoint, it has often been suggested that there is a need for role models from different classes to co-exist in the same communities, as opposed to middle-class flight from ghettoes. In South Africa, this new phenomenon has also been cited as a major reason for community dislocation (Tucker and Scott 1992). The main advantage of integration in this respect may be the social connections that higher-income groups have with decision-making structures, based on contacts, skills and influence. These typically lead to stronger community-based organizations and greater attention from local governments.

The biggest gain to low-income residents from integration may therefore lie in the prevention of social disillusionment through provision of more chances for upward mobility. If youths do have opportunities--through access to education, transport, recreation, and the like--it is likely that the benefits will be observed in various areas. Within communities, there is reason to suggest that integration can diminish negative factors such as community distrust and crime, by ensuring that the broader fabric of the community is more tightly-knit (Rakodi 1994).

In sum, developmental municipal planning is required to direct the structure, size, composition, and location of infrastructure and housing so as to promote social and economic residential integration. It is not usually a viable option to try to direct people to migrate into existing lower-income communities. Instead, policies should aim at allowing people to remain within their communities when their (relative or absolute) economic or social conditions improve, rather than move away. The provision of high-quality infrastructure that retains sufficient flexibility to allow upgrading of individual household standards is essential, as is the involvement of many more residents in municipal planning than has ever happened before. But to achieve such flexibility requires a creative and generous approach to the provision of subsidies and the allocation of tariffs.

Subsidies and tariffs

Failure to get the prices right--in this case "wrong" in the neo-classical sense of the word--will mean that the benefits described above cannot be realized. Getting the prices right for basic infrastructure and services provision requires attention to extremely low levels of affordability and a willingness to look beyond the orthodox cost-recovery approach that has dominated policy, programs and projects to date.

For example, most government urban policy documents fail to consider that services in existing middle- and high-income areas (still mainly populated by white South Africans) are still heavily subsidized (and have been for decades) from surpluses generated through business levies (ultimately based on transfers from black workers and consumers whose employers and retail outlets were historically, by law, located in white areas). Redistribution for the sake of social and historical justice is one rationale for dramatic changes in infrastructural service pricing. But there are other reasons why policy-makers should systematically diverge from setting prices based on orthodox marginal cost or other financial-return techniques.

Problems with pure cost recovery on service delivery

A pure cost-recovery model is inappropriate for municipal and other social services. The South African government did not adopt a cost-recovery approach to primary health care, not only because health is a basic human right (guaranteed in the Constitution's Bill of Rights) and because low-income people's spending on health care is typically subtracted from spending on vital food and other components of good health, but also because it is administratively expensive to do so. It often costs more in cost-recovery administration than can be squeezed out of low-income people desperate for treatment. The same is true with respect to other basic government-supplied services.

If we consider the implications of the cost-recovery approach in perhaps the most critical area of services--basic water supply--it is clear that attempting to be thrifty by providing merely collective (not individual on-site) taps, as proposed for most rural water consumption, is penny-wise but pound-foolish. The collection of monies from standpipes poses considerable problems. A flat rate charge is inequitable in that it favors those consuming larger quantities and this has the potential for social conflict. Consumption-related charges entail costly methods of collection which either lead to significant underrecovery of costs or significantly higher prices to consumers.

The lifeline plus block-tariff alternative

In contrast, a block-tariff and lifeline subsidy system would ensure that the basic minimum supply of municipal services could be consumed at no charge by all residents, with progressive increases in prices based on increasing consumption levels. The rationale for a block tariff is partly the long history of resource consumption at inordinately low prices by South Africa's large industrial and agricultural corporations, and extravagant domestic use by the white population. By generating a surplus through slightly higher marginal costs for corporations, free lifeline tariffs can easily be designed for the first block of consumption (e.g., 50 liters of water per person per day). If such lifeline tariffs are to be considered an entitlement, there is no reason that they cannot be structured so that all domestic users receive their first monthly units of water and electricity on a fully subsidized basis, provided that subsequent levels of consumption are priced at increasing rates so as to cover the initial costs.

With respect to financing the capital costs of infrastructure, tariff reform can support the stretching of payment for capital. However at present, an insufficient amount of public sector capital expenditure is occurring, by all accounts. In the case of electricity, Eskom (which in 1995 installed 80 percent of all new connections in South Africa) only spent half of the amount suggested in the *RDP* for the peak annual capital cost of electrification, with no plans to augment its capital expenditure beyond present levels (300,000 units per year) that would decisively diminish the backlog of approximately 4.5 million households.

How much capital investment is required? An "intermediate" service level for urban and rural people--much higher than the proposed

MIIF--would have capital costs of up to R56 billion in urban areas and R59 billion in rural areas over the next decade, amounts feasible within the existing planned housing and land reform budgets. At just over R11 billion per year, this corresponds to the stated desire of government, as noted earlier, to spend 5 percent of its annual resources--in 1998 rand, R10 billion of a R200 billion budget--on housing (of which basic infrastructure is the core component). Additional spending on land reform would support enhancement of rural services (which are more costly to install given geographical friction).

A large part of government's reluctance to expend amounts anywhere near this level--notwithstanding rhetoric to the contrary in even the *GEAR* strategy--stems from the inability of consumers to pay the recurrent operating and maintenance expenses. Because the argument for cross-subsidization and lifeline tariffs is ultimately about recurrent consumption, it is important to show how water and electricity can become self-financing through "ring-fenced" cross-subsidization (requiring no other external subsidies). Other aspects of infrastructure such as roads and water-borne sewage involve relatively minor operating and maintenance costs, which can generally be internalized within the rates base of, and central-fiscal transfers to, local authorities.

To achieve sufficient cross-subsidization in the two most crucial cost-centers, water and electricity, requires moving from local-level tariff determinations (which still often reflect residual apartheid-era distributional arrangements) to a national policy and structure. This could be accomplished while still giving local authorities sufficient autonomy to establish additional levies for other funding purposes, as is provided for in the Constitution (Swilling 1997).

To consider water, there are numerous potential sources of income from within the water sector to cover the operating and maintenance costs of an improved level of service with a basic entitlement provided for free. These include cross-subsidization from rich to poor consumers, from mining and industry to residential users, and from urban to dense settlement and rural. There are sufficient financial surpluses within the water sector at catchment-area and national levels, and some interesting pilot studies of local cross-subsidization (e.g., the Western Cape town of Hermanus), to suggest the feasibility of this approach. Current water pricing policy is indeed to allocate 5 percent of all water in South Africa to a basic needs reserve, for precisely this (abstract) purpose of assuring all basic needs can be met; however, local authorities have generally failed to apply progressive tariff structures, in part due to rising opposition to such block tariffs from the World Bank (Roome 1995; for a rebuttal see below, Chapter Five), DCD and the Department of Finance. (One strong basis for opposition is that it makes privatization of municipal water more difficult, as firms have difficulty matching their marginal cost curves to retail price levels.) With price elasticities of water in the Johannesburg area estimated at 0.3, there will not be a dramatic impact initially on large-scale users (though such an impact would certainly be desired, ultimately, for conservation purposes) (Roome 1995).

Similarly, the electricity sector has historically distorted end-user tariff prices so as to maintain its product artificially inexpensive for many heavy industrial consumers (in part to take up large underutilized capacity due to 1970s-80s overexpansion), hence leading to serious economic distortions. Cheap electricity, according to Fine and Rustomjee (1996), fuelled the corporate "minerals-energy complex" which so dominated other aspects of South African economic development that it can largely be held responsible for many of the country's vast structural economic problems, including the underdevelopment of small-scale business, monopolization, low levels of investment, relative lack of capacity in intermediate and capital goods, poor export performance in manufacturing, low skill levels of the workforce, and inappropriately high capital-intensity in key economic sectors. The problem continues, for between 1987 and 1994, Eskom was able to reduce the real price of electricity by 24 percent, and is aiming to reduce it by a further 15 percent by 2000.

Consumers were not so fortunate (though they are subsidized extensively, given the far higher costs of supplying power at peak morning and evening hours and in relatively small, atomistic volumes). While there has been great variance due to deals favoring particular consumers (such as the giant aluminum exporters), the mean 1994 electricity tariff was R0.05 R/Kwh (40 percent) higher for domestic consumers than for mining or manufacturing consumers (Electricity Working Group 1996). Within domestic consumption, large tariff variances still generally favor residents of well-established areas (not low-income black people) whose predecessors had long ago paid the capital costs of installation.

To replace these distortions with cross-subsidies founded on social justice principles, the cost implications of providing a lifeline subsidy of 20 Kwh per capita per month would be approximately R6 (the average consumption at present by five-six person households with prepayment meters is 80 Kwh per month, which implies that a new system would dramatically increase consumption for lower-income users). As is the case for water pricing, a lifeline tariff is not technically difficult to implement, once either billing systems are adjusted or prepayment meters are fully installed (in the latter case, cards are purchased regularly from outlets and it would be administratively feasible to provide the subsidy to a household representative each month at a given sales point).

With approximately nine million households, the total annual cost internal to the electricity supply sector would eventually reach approximately R3 billion per annum (roughly twice the existing internal cross-subsidy to domestic users), once the entire nation had electricity connections. As noted below, there will be economic consequences of an inclining block tariff, including fuel-switching and conservation. Ideally, fuel-switching would also encourage the development of inexpensive solar and wind systems with much lower life-cycle cost and greater applicability in isolated rural areas (Davis 1996). Data on price elasticities are relatively scarce, although one study indicated a short-run price elasticity of 0.097 and a long-run price elasticity of 1.01 (Pouris 1986).

In short, given South Africa's combination of maldistribution of resources and enormous poverty, there is a crucial need for a systematic approach to cross-subsidies, at national level, but with scope for some degree of municipal variation, thus ensuring a lifeline supply for all.

Conclusion: Expanded developmental infrastructure

To sum up the intellectual and policy argumentation, there is a good case for considering the criteria listed as the basis for

a) generous infrastructure and service subsidies, utilizing national tariff restructuring so as to achieve redistribution, conservation, and other socio-economic objectives;
b) increasing the standards of infrastructure provision, even to the very poor, based on sound socio-economic benefits of higher standards; and

c) much more effective roles for the state and communities in infrastructure investment and services provision, regulation, and pricing.

All of these conclusions from the review of available international and domestic evidence should be considered as minimal justifications for broader state intervention and community participation. The broader cost-benefit analysis supported in this chapter should help shift the terrain of debate surrounding allocation of national budgetary resources so as to allow policy-makers from the national DCD (as well as Finance, Water Affairs, Minerals and Energy Affairs, and related departments), the provinces and municipalities to make a stronger case for infrastructure investment and broader service delivery.

There is, in addition, a growing political imperative associated with aligning infrastructure and service delivery to developmental goals (instead of merely to full cost-recovery principles). This imperative is reflected in the severe tensions, particularly evident during 1997-98, associated with cut-offs of services by municipalities in highly-politicized townships. Some such cut-offs have occurred in a manner that even important community organizations (such as SA National Civic Organization branches) have been unable to mediate or justify, and that have intensified local-level alienation and anger (leading in some cases to firebombings of houses belonging to municipal councilors, even from the ANC, and to violent attacks on municipal officials).

The difficulty of marrying two lines of advocacy--on the one hand, technical, rationalist, and accepting of the broad premises of capital accumulation, and on the other hand grounded in decades of social struggles for both racial and socio-economic justice--is here apparent. For it is quite likely that the "liberal illusion" described by Benton (1993) will now become evident: "In societies governed by deep inequalities of political power, economic wealth, social standing and cultural accomplishment the promise of equal rights is delusory with the consequence that for the majority, rights are merely abstract, formal entitlements with little or no *de facto* purchase on the realities of social life." South Africa appears as such a society, for even in the face of evidence that basic infrastructure for socio-economic development, environmental protection, and geographical desegregation is affordable and pays handsome direct and indirect dividends, the numerous government departments associated with its supply from national to local levels have all, in varying degrees, endorsed a stingy system of low-quality, relatively unsubsidized infrastructure and service provision which will neither capture the bulk of positive externalities described above, nor fulfill popular yearnings for dignity.

Thus far the people (and their organizations) most affected by municipal infrastructure and service delivery policy have been somewhat excluded from the national policy debates, aside from through their political representatives in government and parliament, and an ineffectual tripartite bargaining fora. There is still a chance, however, given the politicized nature of these issues at present and the threat they pose to the popularity of the nationalist government, to change that. An exploration of how, politically, low-income South Africans can reinsert themselves into the decision-making process should become a top priority, prior to any finalization of the policy debates.

chapter four

Municipal Privatization Debates

The most compelling aspect of urban struggle in 1990s South Africa may have been the emergence of progressive leadership within the SA Municipal Workers Union (SAMWU), and its growing resistance to the Department of Constitutional Development's municipal privatization mania. The work my colleagues and I contributed was less at the point of production, where SAMWU's researchers made excellent progress, and more associated with the problems the South African government will cause by selling off what have traditionally been public goods to transnational corporations. The Nelspruit battle, which during the late 1990s reflected the most important stand-off between SAMWU and DCD, is yet to be rigorously documented. But in this chapter the broader community development critique of municipal privatization is established, while in the next we briefly look at a prototype water deal in the town of Stutterheim. Here again, the technicist spirit prevails, and perhaps this chapter suffers from a shortcoming associated with trying to convince conservative policy-makers by resorting to their own reductionist (cost-benefit) language. In this case, the use of extensive World Bank citations also reflects the original presentation of the paper to a dialogue on privatization between the Bank and its critics (organized by Friends of the Earth). Here one discovers that the Bank is not monolithic, for what its (mid-1990s) socio-economic analysis grudgingly conceded in Washington, DC meant very little to the (late 1990s) ideologically-driven army of Bank loan-pushers and equity investors plying their trade in backwaters like Pretoria. The contradictions, amidst the new South African government's impetuous, foolhardy rush to privatize municipal services, are evident.

[This chapter was published as "Privatization, Participation and Protest in the Restructuring of South African Municipal Services: The Basis for Opposing World Bank Promotion of Public-Private Partnerships" in *Urban Forum* 9, 1 (1998).]

Introduction: The World Bank and South African municipal services

The several dozen trade unionists gathered in Port Elizabeth city hall one sleepy, humid Saturday in February 1998, at a workshop on participation in "PPPs" (public-private partnerships), were stunned from the outset. A Department of Constitutional Development (DCD) deputy director-general began by blaming the "failure of the *RDP*" on union opposition to privatization. Following up, the PE city treasurer revealed in a slide-show that, unbeknownst to these leaders of the Eastern Cape region of the Congress of South African Trade Unions (COSATU), World Bank staff had visited PE roughly eighteen months earlier (September 1996) to offer counsel on expanding the city's water system.

The treasurer, inherited from the previous government, had joined the Bank in a week-long model-building exercise that focused entirely on one option: increasing capital expenditure by privatizing the city's water works. Various claims about likely efficiency enhancements were made, some of which--such as the feasible reduction of staff from 6.5 to 3.5 per 1,000 water consumers, and a 1.2 percent interest rate advantage on capital-related borrowing for a private firm in contrast to the PE municipality--were based on highly dubious assumptions. A lose-win bargain stared the trade unionists in the face: if the DCD official, Bank staff and treasurer were right, only the loss of many hundreds of union jobs, the opportunity for huge rates of private profit, and the more thorough commodification of services would allow the city to expand water-related infrastructure to tens of thousands of residents of unserved townships and shack settlements.

Over the next day of deliberations, critical reactions began to gel. Representatives of the SA Municipal Workers Union (SAMWU) recalled their own national slogan--"No to privatization! 50 liters of water per person per day free of charge!"--as a means of disentangling the false division between producers and consumers. Outsiders offered advice. A Johannesburg lawyer from Rand Water--the country's largest intermediate buyer of water--suggested a "public-public" partnership based on a water utility model instead. The Eastern Cape Socio-Economic Consultative Council's Bisho-based specialist on Local Economic Development argued for an approach that combined public ownership, expanded services, much greater cross-subsidization and more explicit economic linkages. A representative of the International Labor Research and Information Group in Cape Town presented options for public sector reform as a means of improving services. COSATU leadership then made the decision to throw down the gauntlet, vowing that PE would replace Nelspruit as South Africa's most vibrant site of struggle over infrastructure privatization.

All of this was reactive, however. Already a year earlier, the PE Municipality's (1997:6) Director for Administration conceded, there had been "pressure for Port Elizabeth to carry the [privatization] investigations further.... from banks and commercial concerns"--Banque Paribas, Rand Merchant Bank, Colechurch International, Development Bank of Southern Africa, Generale des Eaux, Metsi a Sechaba Holdings, Sauer Interantional and Lyonnaise Water had all met with PE officials--as well as from DCD, which allocated R2 million from a R50 million US Agency for International Development grant to fund PE's Public Private Partnership business plan development. (In spite of repeated promises, DCD staff repeatedly refused SAMWU's request for financial support to look into alternative business plan options centered around public sector reform.) The workshop participants found themselves at the end of a chain that began with international capital and that was welded together by Washington agencies and their local state allies.

In this chapter, I argue that to the extent we can trace the involvement of the World Bank--in this instance working closely with senior local authority personnel, more generally with high-ranking DCD officials and local consultants--the subsequent pressure upon politicians to privatize municipal services will be based on incorrect formulations of the problem, an inability or lack of desire by Bank staff to explore options drawn from South Africa's Democratic Movement, and a potential conflict of interest between Bank institutional investment interests and its policy advice. What this boils down to, as reflected in PE and many other settings in the near future, is a decisive failure by privatization advocates--particularly analysts from the Bank and its private sector investment subsidiary, the International Finance Corporation (IFC)--to both respect the core political and developmental aspirations of the local citizenry and demonstrate that privatization assists in meeting such aspirations.

The question that must also be asked, is whether a public participation process--now often seen as a significant ameliorating exercise--would make any difference in all of this. Too often, participation is a euphemism for clever marketing of top-down, market-oriented policies which have to be sold, to enhance public "ownership," because they are essentially unpopular and harmful to either the interests of specific interest groups and/or the people as a whole. This chapter concludes that much of the advocacy work done by the Bank and IFC in South Africa is very much in this spirit and, hence, the more participation, the more informed opposition there will be. This helps explain the secretive nature of the Bank's work in PE. Indeed I argue that the problem lies in the broader attempt to privatize in a context in which democratic design of social and economic policy is demanded (and denied). So long as the Bank's work in South Africa follows the patterns outlined next, privatization itself will be hotly contested.

The politicization of privatization

It has been long recognized in South Africa's democratic movement that basic human needs related to infrastructure--especially basic access to water, sanitation, energy, housing, a clean environment, transport, and communications--are vital to many aspects of everyday life: to women's status (at home and in society), to children's welfare, to personal and public health, to the natural environment, and to a better balanced local and national and indeed international economy. Moreover, it is also axiomatic that there are modes of appropriate technology available in South Africa that do not require the kinds of "megaprojects" (like Lesotho dams) often associated with infrastructure but that nevertheless would meet universal coverage of basic needs--if affordable approaches that entail sufficient subsidies and cross-subsidies could be developed. This possibility is growing increasingly remote, however, in a South African environment characterized by growing poverty (and its "feminization"), unequal distribution of resources, intensifying fiscal discipline and budget cuts, high interest rates, heightened competition between cities and towns, and--in many cases--a lack of respect by the World Bank and even the African National Congress government itself for mass social movements, community-based organizations, and non-governmental organizations.

South African social movements and allied technical resource personnel have long campaigned for infrastructure and services for all. This was reflected in extremely generous promises made to the populace in the *Reconstruction and Development Program* (*RDP*), the African

National Congress campaign platform, in early 1994. But by late 1994, as shown below, World Bank staff and conservative local consultants were actively involved in undermining those promises by developing initial arguments for the South African government about household affordability and funding options related to infrastructure and services. The technical advice was based on faulty information and was explicitly biased towards privatization and high user fees for at least three reasons. First, the Bank's South Africa staff ignored not only the *RDP* but also the Constitutional guarantee of basic services and housing to all citizens. Second, the Bank failed to correctly analyze and incorporate information about relative affordability and the indirect benefits of basic services (e.g., public health, environment, geographical integration, women's time, and micro-/macro-economic multipliers). Third, in their review of funding options Bank staff did not consider utilizing a simple mode of redistribution of resources from national to local level that the ANC had explicitly promised during the 1994 election campaign and that even the World Bank's own *World Development Report 1994* endorsed--namely, cross-subsidization through a progressive block tariff that ensures "lifeline" access to basic services for all. There are other technical and political problems associated with the Bank's South Africa advice and the later decision by the Bank to invest in privatized infrastructure, as discussed below.

Within a few years of the Bank's initial arguments about privatization and funding mechanisms for municipal infrastructure, and just as these arguments were being codified as official policy, progressive resistance emerged. In April 1997, SAMWU initiated a national campaign against the privatization of essential municipal services, which were emerging from minor Eastern Cape pilot towns to the battlefield represented by a small city, Nelspruit. The union later filed (unsuccessful) requests to the DCD to develop alternative local solutions that retained infrastructure-related jobs in municipal government and met the needs of unserved residents. SAMWU's campaign against the high-profile privatization of Nelspruit water services was temporarily successful, as the ANC Youth League, Communist Party and COSATU leaders managed to delay the sale well into 1998. (Of interest, reflecting the increasingly corporatist reorientation of the SA National Civic Organization (SANCO), SANCO Investment Holdings opted instead to support water privatization, by becoming a junior joint venture partner in the ultimately successful bid by the British firm Biwater, although the local SANCO affiliate was persuaded to oppose the privatization.)

Just as SAMWU, NGOs, and social movements began turning their attention to the forthcoming infrastructure policy, the World Bank and South African government were finalizing many of the central details. In May 1997, the South African Cabinet approved in principle two contradictory policies, one (from the Water Minister) stating the aim of supplying a free lifeline water service to all households and the other (from the Minister of Constitutional Development) promoting cost-recovery policies for household water supplies; the contradiction was still not resolved in September, when the *Municipal Infrastructure Investment Framework* (*MIIF*) was released to the public.

Moreover, in May 1997, the International Finance Corporation announced a $25 million investment in the Standard Bank "South Africa Infrastructure Fund" with the aim of providing the foreign currency component required for privatization. That fund, as shown below, anticipates gaining a return on investment of more than 30 percent in 90 percent of its projects. Notably, the IFC makes no explicit effort to invest in a manner that directly broadens ownership to the black majority, but rather promotes an investment fund run by the country's largest bank.

In July-September 1997, as the SA government insisted on using harsh tactics to enforce a cost-recovery approach to infrastructure and services, a series of township protests broke out in Gauteng, Mpumalanga, and Eastern Cape provinces. Grassroots demands included lower service charges, an end to pre-paid (and more expensive) electricity meters, and cut-offs of basic services. The protests turned violent in some areas (KwaThema, Tembisa, Butterworth), and included clashes with the police and municipal councilors (ANC councilors' houses were even burned down in rage) (Barchiesi 1998; Phadu 1998). In addition to organized civic groups, a variety of other community-based organizations became active on the issue.

In the fourth quarter of 1997, nearly all municipalities began widespread cut-offs of basic services to non-payers. In even central Johannesburg, where public health hazards loomed, this entailed shutting off access to water to tenants who *had* paid though their landlords had not paid the city council. DCD's "Project Viability" was expected to declare more than half of all South Africa's municipalities illiquid, which would intensify the now massive pressure to cut services, including water, to those who could not pay the unsubsidized bills (and for whom, generally, little or no safety net existed). In the Eastern Cape town of Stutterheim, for example, often promoted as the ideal-type Local Economic Development success story (Nussbaum 1997), more than 10 percent of the town's households--nearly all in Mlungisi township--suffered water cuts during the last quarter of 1997, and of these only 6 percent found sufficient resources to pay their bills and restore their service.

In short, local democracy had been judged too expensive for South Africa, and the 400 or more municipalities expected to fail would be amalgamated into large district councils. Yet behind this lay no large-scale, formal "rent boycott" (the only one of any significance was by white businesses and residents in Sandton). Instead, the growing municipal fiscal crisis emanated from the Department of Finance, which in real terms cut the crucial "Intergovernmental Grants" (which pay for municipal service subsidies) by 85 percent between 1991 and 1997, according to the Financial and Fiscal Commission (1997:18), lending new meaning to the idea of a "culture of non-payment."

In January 1998, a coalition of community, environmental, consumer, labor and non-governmental advocacy organizations from Gauteng province, Lesotho and other countries joined forces to begin challenging World Bank funding for continued construction of the Lesotho Highlands Water Project, partly because of its negative implications for water conservation and lifeline service provision in Gauteng, and partly because of the dam project's extraordinary ecological and social implications. With vast Lesotho water costs about to be assumed by Rand Water, to be passed on to Gauteng municipalities which were already seriously cash-strapped, the pressure on those municipalities to privatize basic services was sure to increase dramatically. In March 1998, as this chapter was drafted, a formal request was made to the Bank's Inspection Panel by two Gauteng civic associations--which simultaneously split away from SANCO--to investigate a myriad of allegedly flawed procedures, decisions and analysis by Bank staff in relation to the retail implications of tripling the raw cost of water so as to pay for the Lesotho dams (Mayekiso and Menu 1998).

There are many issues that deserve exploration here. To keep matters brief and to understand the role played by the World Bank in the run-up to privatization of municipal services requires, first, considering its back-door route to privatization through the IFC loan, and then the specific debates that distinguished the Bank's South Africa staff not only from local popular movements--on privatization and a variety of related issues--but also from Bank headquarters (as seen in conflicting policy advice offered from the two Bank sources).

The IFC'S Back-Door Route to Privatization

The financial logic behind the IFC's $25 million investment in privatized infrastructure--through the Standard Bank South Africa Infrastructure Fund (SAIF)--is worth examining at the outset, for here is where World Bank conflicts of interest visibly emerge, where the exploitative character of privatization becomes obvious, and where the broader alliance of international and domestic financial capital with international managerial capital is unveiled. According to the IFC,

> The principle objective of SAIF is to invest in infrastructure projects in order to achieve long-term capital appreciation for investors. The Fund will focus on equity investments in the environmental (water, waste, sanitation and sewerage), energy, telecommunications and transport sectors. Although [the Fund] has achieved some success in developing its deal flow, it is constrained by domestic regulation from bidding for privatizations that require foreign funds. The additional financing will satisfy the Fund's need for foreign exchange and help diversify its portfolio. IFC's presence on the board of [the Fund] will help transfer expertise from IFC to the Fund.... This is an environmental review category FI project. The Fund will only invest in projects which meet World Bank environmental policies and host country standards. (IFC announcement, May 1997)

Privatized South African infrastructure is potentially highly profitable, with Internal Rates of Return (IRR) approaching 30 percent. According to an African Development Bank (ADB) study (1997:13, Annex 6), SAIF projection for before-tax IRRs of 26-27 percent "during SAIF's 15-year life in constant US dollar terms" assumes that "10 percent of all investments will fail; 50 percent of all investments will generate an IRR of 30 percent; and 40 percent of all investments will generate an IRR of 35 percent." To earn such high rates of return on infrastructure investments that are often long-term in nature (often forty years before full social and economic returns on investment are realized), and on top of that to compress the high earnings into the early stages of investment (on average 7.5 years, given that the SAIF will shut down after 15 years), and to do so using a wide range of social infrastructure investments, implies an extremely high cost-recovery burden for direct infrastructure recipients, or dramatic cost reductions at the level of the enterprise. Amongst SAIF "potential project pipeline" investments are the hotly debated Nelspruit water treatment, Eskom electricity transmission lines, Empangeni water management, and Telkom's partial privatization, all of which entail infrastructure aimed at bringing low-income people into the economy (ADB 1997:Annex 1).

As it stands, the DCD recognizes the need for a regulatory framework to prevent undesirable practices such as monopoly pricing or "cherry-picking" (limiting access for low-income people) by private firms (unconscionable profiteering is apparently not considered a matter requiring regulation, however). But by 1998 it had still not yet formally established such a framework even though large documents had been generated by Washington-based consultants and though such investments were being made regularly. As a result, low-income people may face a large hurdle: covering both relatively non-subsidized recurrent (operating and maintenance) costs, and paying sufficiently high service charges so as to reward investors with a 32 percent rate of return. As the rand declines against the dollar (inexplicably, something not explicitly foreseen by the African Development Bank in its report), the IRR target will have to be raised much higher, so as to remain competitive with other international investments.

Several questions emerge through this example. How appropriate is it that infrastructure investment for low-income people becomes the basis for this high a rate of return, with relatively short-term private financial commitment in relation to the entire project? Where are the cost-savings anticipated by the private firms in which local and international financial investors will invest? If such cost savings come through large-scale rationalization of public sector workers, what are the implications?

The IFC--a low-profile institution in South Africa--has not publicly addressed these questions, and this author knows of no internal or public IFC document that does. To get a sense of how cost-recovery may be achieved from widespread privatization of municipal services at a time of extreme politicization of services and payment levels requires considering the World Bank's broader policy work on municipal infrastructure and services, the *Urban Infrastructure Investment Framework*, in which the Bank played a decisive role in late 1994 and early 1995. As a precursor, though, it is useful to glance through the document that should have given Bank staff ideas on what kinds of policies to design, the *RDP*.

Government's mandate on municipal services

The contrasts between (on the one hand) infrastructure investments being undertaken at present by the IFC and infrastructure policy design carried out by World Bank staff in South Africa in late 1994 and early 1995, and (on the other hand) that recommended in the *RDP* in early 1994 and later by the Bank's *World Development Report: Infrastructure for Development* (*WDR*) in mid-1994, are striking. To begin with the *RDP*, it is worth recording the status attributed to the document by President Nelson Mandela, in his victory celebration speech on 2 May 1994:

> We have emerged as the majority party on the basis of the program which is contained in the Reconstruction and Development book. That is going to be the cornerstone, the foundation, upon which the Government of National Unity is going to be based. I appeal to all leaders who are going to serve in this government to honor this program. (*Business Day* 5/3/94)

The *RDP* lists a number of specific areas (many related to the International Covenant on Economic, Cultural and Social Rights) in which South Africans can consider themselves *entitled* to an adequate consumption level of goods and services. These were codified in the 1996 Constitution, which commits to the citizens of South Africa that the state will ensure second-generation socio-economic rights (such as water, housing, health care, and other services), along with a general commitment to equality of state service provision.

The *RDP*'s approach is to ensure that essential service needs are met through vast increases in government subsidies and redistributive tariff systems when a cost-recovery approach fails to deliver services to those who need them. For example, the *RDP* suggests the characteristics of a decent residential existence: "As a minimum, all housing must provide protection from weather, a durable structure, and reasonable living space and privacy. A house must include sanitary facilities, storm-water drainage, a household energy supply (whether linked to grid electricity supply or derived from other sources, such as solar energy), and convenient access to clean water" (2.5.7). The budgetary goal for housing expenditure in the *RDP* is 5 percent of the entire national budget; this goal was repeated in the *Housing White Paper*, and if delivery capacity improves there is no reason not to anticipate meeting this target at some stage soon in the course of budget reprioritization.

Perhaps most importantly for municipal services, the *RDP* commented in some detail on how to finance infrastructure and the recurrent costs of services. The *RDP* specifies the need for tariff restructuring, cross-subsidies, and lifeline services to the poor, with respect to both water (including sanitation) and electricity:

> To ensure that every person has an adequate water supply, the national tariff structure must include the following:
>
> - a lifeline tariff to ensure that all South Africans are able to afford water services sufficient for health and hygiene requirements;
> - in urban areas, a progressive block tariff to ensure that the long-term costs of supplying large-volume users are met and that there is a cross-subsidy to promote affordability for the poor, and
> - in rural areas, a tariff that covers operating and maintenance costs of services, and recovery of capital costs from users on the basis of a cross-subsidy from urban areas in cases of limited rural affordability. (2.6.10)
>
> The electrification program will cost around R12 billion with annual investments peaking at R2 billion. This must be financed from within the industry as far as possible via cross-subsidies from other electricity consumers. Where necessary the democratic government will provide concessionary finance for the electrification of poor households in remote rural areas. A national Electrification Fund, underwritten by a government guarantee, must be created to raise bulk finance from lenders and investors for electrification. Such a fund could potentially be linked to a Reconstruction Fund to be utilized for other related infrastructural financing needs. A national domestic tariff structure with low connection fees must be established to promote affordability. (2.7.8)

With national tariff reform emphasizing cross-subsidies (using national and provincial resources, not just local) and lifeline tariffs for low-income consumers, and with a more appropriate use of housing subsidies to finance deeper levels of capital infrastructure--*neither of which should ultimately cost central government anything extra beyond even the (original) urban housing and rural land reform targets*--promises of humane standards of infrastructure and services for all South Africans can be kept and additional public health, environmental, and economic benefits to all of society (particularly women and children) can be gained.

It is possible to translate these broad mandates into a concrete policy directive: a marginal increase in the price of water and electricity should be applied to large corporations and farms (which consume more than 75 percent of water and energy resources, and in a wasteful manner), to pay for a lifeline service to households (the majority of black households together consume less than 2 percent of these resources). It was precisely this funding mechanism that would have obviated the need for privatization of municipal services; it was precisely this mechanism that was ignored by Bank staff in their detailed study of municipal services, even though the same mechanism was endorsed in the 1994 *WDR*.

Contradictory Bank policy advice: The 1994 *WDR* and the SA staff reports

Bank policy advice, which was decisive in shifting the terrain of debate over infrastructure investment away from government's *RDP* mandate, began with several Urban Reconnaissance Missions to South Africa during the early 1990s (for a critique, see Bond and Swilling 1992). It included repeated conservative interpretations, profoundly flawed, of how generous the state should be with respect to housing, concluding in 1994 that subsidy levels should be lower and reliance upon bankers heavier than those envisaged by most South African commentators (see below, Chapter Eight); the resulting *Housing White Paper* was applauded by the Bank's deputy resident representative (who also coordinated the PE privatization research) at a mid-1997 Johannesburg meeting with the South Africa NGO Coalition (personal communication with SANGOCO leaders; also see below, Chapter Ten). For our purposes here, it will be sufficient to analyze the more direct policy advice offered once the ANC government had taken office, particularly two drafts of the *Urban Infrastructure Investment Framework* (*UIIF*), dating from November 1994 and March 1995. The irony implicit in the *UIIF* derives not only from its rejection of the *RDP*'s core arguments on financing, service standards and redistribution, but from the Bank South African staff's rejection of the *WDR: Infrastructure for Development* report issued just a few months earlier. The *WDR* recommended a relatively interventionist approach to policy, program and project design, for several reasons:

- to internalize developmental externalities associated with infrastructure and recognize the public character of infrastructure goods, instead of leaving these to the market;

- to amplify the effect of infrastructure on the reduction of poverty;
- to incorporate economic multipliers as integral to infrastructure investment;
- to incorporate infrastructure's environmental effects;
- to incorporate infrastructure's public health effects;
- to incorporate locational externalities;
- to incorporate infrastructure's role in reducing gender inequality;
- to establish an appropriate tariff pricing system that will accomplish the social as well as economic objectives associated with municipal infrastructure; and
- to learn lessons of infrastructure project failure so they are not repeated.

Yet World Bank staff in South Africa (and government consultants engaged in parallel work) failed to take such lessons seriously. In many cases, the *WDR* guidelines regarding such issues were ignored entirely. As a result, the case for state intervention is much weaker in the *UIIF*, the net economic benefits of infrastructure are suppressed, and recommendations for infrastructure standards are extremely low. The inadequate analysis, failure to engage with the *RDP*, and lack of participation with its advocates led the Bank to adopt a pro-privatization position regarding municipal services.

In the series of brief comments below, in each case starting with the *WDR*, it is clear that the precise language of the *Infrastructure for Development* report was ignored or distorted by the Bank's South African staff and allied local consultants in the *UIIF* documents that were generated in late 1994 and early 1995 (leading to similar problems in the final *MIIF* in drafts from 1995-97, including a short version publicly released in September 1997). In turn, this generally led to lower standards and smaller subsidies for low-income residents than should have been the case.

Identifying public and private infrastructural goods

One of the key issues under debate in the controversy over privatization is whether infrastructural goods are public or private and, if the latter, whether public management is necessary to internalize externalities. While World Bank staff in South Africa have strongly advocated privatization of municipal services, in part or full, a more measured position appears in the *WDR*,

> Because many infrastructure facilities are locationally fixed and their products are non-tradable, users cannot readily obtain substitute services that better suit their needs. Moreover, it is often difficult for users to obtain information about service alternatives or characteristics. They cannot, therefore, "shop around" for the best source of supply and are vulnerable to any abuse of monopoly power.... Roads are not private goods.... Water outside of piped networks is often--in practice and in principle a "common property" resource.... Although most infrastructure goods are private, they produce spillovers or external effects--many of which affect the environment. Ignoring the important negative externality of emissions from fossil fuel power generation could lead to excess power being produced with the wrong mix of fuels. By contrast, some cities have neglected to develop a well-designed public transport system, even though such a system can have positive environmental effects and also promote social equity. To ensure that society obtains positive benefits--such as public health benefits from water and sanitation--the private goods must also be delivered effectively. Thus, although infrastructure services differ from other goods, they also differ among themselves. The characteristics of various infrastructure activities have important implications for how services should be provided. To the extent that specific infrastructure activities entail natural monopoly or depend on a network characterized by natural monopoly, they will not be provided efficiently by an unfettered market (World Bank 1994:23-24)
>
> A number of problems arise for which markets cannot guarantee solutions. Many infrastructure services, especially those that resemble public goods, will be undersupplied if markets alone are left to determine their provision. Market outcomes may allocate fewer infrastructure services to the poor than society desires. (1994:73)
>
> Because markets often fail to reflect these externalities, their management usually falls to government. (1994:82)

The clear message, in short, is that even for those infrastructural services that are private (not public and hence extremely difficult to price) there is compelling evidence to retain state control. *For to effectively internalize the developmental externalities associated with infrastructure will generally require the state--which has the capacity to address the social costs and reap the social benefits--to make calculations about the broader economic cost/benefit analysis associated with infrastructure (whereas private sector suppliers tend to rely upon only narrow financial cost/benefit analysis), and to implement infrastructure and services provision in a manner that captures the benefits and minimizes the costs.* This is particularly obvious with respect to the need for universal access and cross-subsidization from large to small consumers, which are the opposite incentives of what private sector providers react to, as profit-maximizing actors in a market setting.

Thus far in South Africa, there has been very little case material--no conclusive evaluations of public-private partnerships in the handful of locales--to draw upon to contradict such findings, except to add the importance of community-based participation in infrastructure investment and services delivery, a matter taken up in the conclusion of this chapter. The most exhaustive review of the international literature and application to South Africa--by David Hemson (1997)--lists the following likely problems:

> corruption in the tendering and drawing up of contracts, particularly in the US; monopoly in the privatized service; higher user charges; inflated director's fees, share options, and management salaries; widescale retrenchments; and anti-union policies.

Nevertheless, the *UIIF* and *MIIF* are firmly in favor of privatization, although the latter acknowledges the need for a regulatory framework. By and large, the issues discussed above were not taken into consideration in the policy advice offered, and this is one of the reasons why it will be exceedingly difficult to gain a consensus on privatization of basic services.

Incorporating economic multipliers

A key problem was that economic multipliers associated with infrastructure were not adequately conceptualized by the Bank's South Africa staff and were not factored into either financial or socio-economic calculations of the affordability of infrastructure investment. According to the *WDR*:

> Infrastructure represents, if not the engine, then the "wheels" of economic activity.... Users demand infrastructure services not only for direct consumption but also for raising their productivity by, for instance, reducing the time and effort needed to secure safe water, to bring crops to market, or to commute to work. Much research in recent years has been devoted to estimating the productivity of infrastructure investments. Many studies attempting to link aggregate infrastructure spending to growth of GDP show very high returns in a time-series analysis.... What is evident is that a strong association exists between the availability of certain infrastructure--telecommunications (in particular), power, paved roads and access to safe water--and per capita GDP. An analysis of the value of

> infrastructure stocks indicates that their composition changes significantly as incomes rise (1994:14-15).

The original Bank contribution to the *UIIF* included no attempt to incorporate the economic multipliers--job creation, productivity enhancement, creation of SMMEs, irrigation for small farmers, etc.--associated with varying infrastructure levels (see above, Chapter Three); hence extremely low standards were recommended. (An estimate for employment benefits was made but not incorporated in the economic calculation [*UIIF* 16/11/94:54]; later suggestions for incorporating economic multipliers in another draft of the *UIIF* [23/3/95:v.II:25] included only employment but no other multipliers, but the economic appraisal failed to show how incorporation of employment multipliers would affect standards of construction and/or consumption.)

As a result of failing to adequately calculate or incorporate economic multipliers, the case for a strong role for municipalities and state intervention more generally was diluted, as was the importance of providing relatively high levels of standards along with generous cross-subsidies to enhance affordability.

Considering the environmental implications

According to the *WDR*:

> Infrastructure provision results from the efforts of individuals and communities to modify their physical surroundings or habitat in order to improve their comfort, productivity, and protection from the elements and to conquer distance.... Environment-friendly infrastructure services are essential for improving living standards and offering public health protection. With sufficient care, providing the infrastructure necessary for growth and poverty reduction can be consistent with concern for natural resources and the global environment (the "green" agenda). At the same time, well-designed and -managed infrastructure can promote the environmental sustainability of human settlements (the "brown" agenda).... The relationship between each infrastructure sector and the environment is complex. The most positive impacts of infrastructure on the environment concern the removal and disposal of liquid and solid wastes. But much depends on how disposal facilities are planned and executed. Underinvestment in municipal sewerage relative to water supply in densely populated cities such as Jakarta has been found to lead to harmful contamination of water reserves, to exacerbate flooding, and to reduce the health benefits from water investments. Provision of sewerage without wastewater treatment can lead to severe downstream pollution and public health problems where receiving waters are used for drinking-water supply or for recreation, irrigation

> and fisheries, as suggested by the cholera outbreaks in Peru and neighboring countries in recent years. Poor management of solid waste complicates urban street drainage and has been linked with the proliferation of disease-bearing mosquitos in standing water. The growing problem of hazardous and toxic wastes as countries industrialize poses particular concerns about safe disposal.... Power plant and vehicle emissions are important contributors to air pollution, so their air quality impacts deserve careful analysis when facilities are expanded.... A 20 percent improvement in air quality in Bangkok, as a result of a reduction in pollutants related to vehicle or power plant emissions, would produce annual health benefits valued at between $100 and $400 per capita for Bangkok's 6 million residents.... Beyond urban areas, overuse of water for irrigation (which accounts for about 90 percent of water withdrawals in most low-income countries) damages soils and severely restricts water availability for industry and households, which often have a higher willingness to pay for the quantities of water they use. The inefficient burning of biomass fuel (plant and animal waste) for household energy contributes to deforestation and thus to erosion and loss of soil nutrients, as well as to indoor air pollution. (1994:20-22)
>
> Infrastructure often has widespread indirect impacts--frequently, on the environment--which can be beneficial or harmful. Irrigation infrastructure can reduce pressure on land resources by permitting greater intensity of cultivation on existing plots, but it can also promote excessive water usage, resulting in groundwater salinization and land subsidence.... Environmental sustainability involves innovation in technology and organization, as well as improved efficiency in the use of infrastructure services through pricing and regulation. (1994:82)
>
> Environmental regulation and promotion of the efficient use of infrastructure help reduce adverse consequences from *existing* infrastructure, issues that have been explored in more detail by *World Development Report 1992*. More options are available with *new* projects, although investment decisions can be consistent with environmental objectives only if environmental impacts are identified and assessed. (1994:87)

Initially, the *UIIF* apparently failed to incorporate all these (and other) environmental factors in infrastructure costing and hence design. Although an "environmental impact" was acknowledged, the benefits were not estimated, and potential costs (associated with potential expanded water and electricity use) ignored in the statement "There are no major environmental problems anticipated for this project" (*UIIF* 16/11/94:54). Indeed, the *UIIF* (and the final *MIIF*) underplayed the environmental impact of infrastructure, and failed to provide quantitative estimates of costs and benefits that would otherwise justify higher infrastructure standards.

It must be acknowledged that the environmental impact of increased infrastructure and services is complex, for both benefits and costs are associated with higher levels of services and consumption. It is generally accepted that large-scale bulk infrastructure projects (such as major dams or roads through ecologically sensitive areas) are to be avoided. But incorporating the benefits of infrastructure remains crucial.

In comparing pit latrines to water-borne sewage, for example, it is clear from South African research that if installed properly, the latter is potentially a far more environmentally-friendly approach (particularly in the many areas affected by inopportune geological conditions). However, alternative systems for treating effluent should also be considered due to risks associated with leakage from centralized treatment systems.

Similarly, there is likely to be environmental damage that may arise from increased utilization of water by those who presently do not have access. But it should be clear that the additional requirement to meet the *RDP*'s consumption targets--1,5 percent of present capacity, according to one estimate--will not be overwhelming in comparison to other benefits. In addition, there is no doubt that water conservation should be improved, and, as argued below, a progressive block tariff structure is a well-recognized approach to this end.

South African experience with stormwater drainage issues demonstrates that 1) drainage systems must be viewed in a holistic manner, given the wide ranging consequences of inappropriate drainage systems; 2) the approach recommended in the *UIIF* and *MIIF* tends to be narrow, component-based, and does not include innovative stormwater management, and instead provides drainage solely based on community income while ignoring regional environmental costs and benefits; and 3) innovative, holistic systems could be both more cost effective and equitable.

Any consideration of water quality must account for both surface water and groundwater, and emphasizes the case for higher standards of infrastructure and maintenance. In general, environmental costs and benefits related to water are difficult to measure. But in just one water-treatment pricing exercise, substantial net benefits--in excess of R100 million per year--arise from higher standards (water-borne sanitation instead of pit latrines).

Finally, there are also environmental effects of higher electricity service levels, including the benefits, amongst others, of reduced air pollution from coal and wood. On the other hand, increased electricity use will cause additional environmental costs through the generation of electricity by South Africa's coal power stations, although these additional costs are more than offset by the environmental gains occurring in newly-electrified households.

Promoting public health

The *WDR* makes a strong stand in favor of raised infrastructure standards so as to achieve higher levels of public health:

> Worldwide, roughly 1 billion people lack access to clean water and more than 1.7 billion do not have adequate sanitation. Diarrheal disease, often caused by contaminated water, represents one-sixth of the world's burden of disease. The most widespread contaminant of water is disease-bearing human wastes. The environmental benefits of water supply depend not only on delivering safe water for drinking but also on providing enough water to permit good human hygiene.... [In Kathmandu] based on estimates using narrowly defined project appraisal techniques, [net] benefits from the city's new $150 million water distribution system.... [equalled] $5.2 million. Using the more detailed service-level approach to project appraisal, however, it was determined that in some cases health benefits from a reduction in coliform contamination of the water approached $1,000 per unit serviced. An education program that improved water use led to further reductions in health and transport costs. After these indirect benefits were factored in, the project showed a positive net benefit of about $275 million. (1994:82)

The original *UIIF* mentioned but failed to calculate the health benefits of infrastructure (and in the final *MIIF*, such benefits were also mentioned but not calculated). Again, this resulted in a recommendation of lower standards of infrastructure than should otherwise be the case.

Participation with South African public health researchers would have allowed Bank staff the opportunity to learn in local conditions what the *WDR* was able to generalize. The public health arguments for improving the proposed levels of service provision beyond those recommended in the *UIIF* are numerous.

Both the international and the South African literature (as summarized in Bond 1997a) shows that incremental improvements in sanitation result in incremental improvements in health, but that health benefits from improved water supplies only appear when improved sanitation is present and only when water is provided on the premises or inside the house. Communal water facilities, as were recommended for large proportions of even urban populations in the *UIIF*, have been shown to have no or little health impact or in some cases worsen the situation. Water provision without adequate wastewater disposal provision (such as that provided by water-borne sanitation) may be a health hazard in itself, for the quantity of water is almost as important as water quality. For this reason the provision of private household or yard taps is crucial, as distance to the water source is the most important factor affecting the quantity of water used by households. Improvements in both water and sanitation produce larger impacts than either alone. For better health impact, improved water and sanitation and better hygiene behavior are required. The reduction in morbidity due to energy-related diseases is a function of the relationship between electrification and developmental attributes such as housing, safe water, sanitation, education, and health care.

The direct health sector cost saving that would stem from upgrading the proposed urban infrastructural investment with regard to water and sanitation is at least R570 million over a decade, and almost R450 million with regard to electrification (assuming 80 percent access by 2012). This saving is the direct result of investment in urban infrastructure, and should have been included in financial evaluations of urban infrastructure investment. In addition, indirect health benefits would also result in substantial savings due to the release of time, particularly women's time, which can be used for child care and productive activities; improved worker productivity; and opportunities for education, as discussed below.

Given the historical disparities between race groups in South Africa, it is not appropriate to provide inferior services to the disadvantaged populations. Countries with the largest gaps in the quality of infrastructure between the wealthy and the poor have the worst overall health status. In addition to the ethical and moral arguments, there are sound public health arguments for improving infrastructure in the poorer areas. Many of the diseases related to poor infrastructure are contagious and, as such, have the potential to threaten the health of higher socio-economic groups in the vicinity, e.g. cholera, malaria, dengue, filariasis, yellow fever and tuberculosis. It was shortsighted of the Bank staff to advocate a lower level of infrastructure given the longer term potential for environmental degradation. In addition, problems of non-payment for services are likely to be perpetuated unless good quality services, associated in the minds of the poorer with the wealthy (mainly white) population, are provided. There is evidence to show that people are much more likely to maintain services which are their own than those which are shared.

In short, health is primarily produced at the level of the household and is directly related to the living environment, which includes municipal service provision. There is much evidence, international and local, to demonstrate the significant public health advantages of improved infrastructure, beyond the standards and consumption levels envisaged in the *UIIF*.

Accounting for benefits to women

It is conventional wisdom now that infrastructure and services can benefit women disproportionately. According to the *WDR*:

> The poor--women in particular--must commit large shares of their income or time to obtaining water and fuelwood, as well as to carrying crops to market. This time could otherwise be devoted to high-priority domestic duties, such as childcare, or to income-earning activities. Such gender-specific effects need to be considered in the evaluation of proposed projects. (1994:20)
>
> For the poor, easier access to water can free up time that can be used to pursue income-earning activities. In rural Pakistan, women with access to improved water supply spend nearly 1.5 fewer hours a day fetching water than do women without this access. (1994:49)
>
> The beneficial impacts of infrastructure on women can be profound, often extending beyond the commonly cited impacts of water and sanitation infrastructure on household health or women's time allocation. But ensuring such outcomes requires foresight and attention to detail during project planning.... Predicting the impact of infrastructure on women can be difficult and requires a close understanding of the details of their activities, opportunities, and constraints. (1994:85)

The initial *UIIF* infrastructure recommendations mentioned but failed to quantify and incorporate these issues, even though they are widely recognized in South Africa. As elsewhere in the developing world, women are the primary care-givers and homemakers, and hence the benefits of infrastructure and service delivery are disproportionately felt by women; likewise the burden of inadequate standards of infrastructure also fall upon women.

There are several aspects to women's utilization of time that can be enhanced by infrastructure investments and service delivery, relating to time spent in water queues, time spent gathering fuelwood and making fires, time spent walking from place to place because road conditions are not amenable for public or private transport, and time spent on other tasks that could otherwise be directed elsewhere if proper infrastructure was in place (see above, Chapter Three).

Because such benefits were not quantified and incorporated into the *UIIF*, Bank staff recommended far lower levels of infrastructure than were appropriate. By recommending the provision of only communal taps for low-income people, neglecting to promote sufficient energy supplies and failing to calculate an appropriate subsidy system that would allow infrastructural services to be utilized, Bank staff effectively dismissed the actual importance of these services to women, by designing a system that will deny infrastructure to women in practice.

Designing appropriate subsidies and tariff reform

The importance of assuring universal access to basic infrastructural services through "lifeline" and rising block tariffs is well recognized, in part because this is a more efficient way of directing subsidies to those who need infrastructural services most. According to the *WDR*:

> Certain characteristics of infrastructure also create challenges in financing. Where a minimum level of consumption of a particular service (such as water, heating, or power) can be identified as a "lifeline" for some users, society may judge that they should not be excluded if they cannot afford to pay. Financing strategies also have to be designed to take account of the risk that arises because many infrastructure investments are large and long-lived, while the revenue stream is often slow to develop. (1994:24)
>
> Adjustments in the general pricing formula can be used to avoid an operational deficit and minimize the tradeoffs imposed by the need to jointly address equity, efficiency, and financial goals. In general, if financial autonomy is a requirement, the public price has to be revised to cover the cost of providing the service plus a markup, often resulting in multipart tariffs and possible cross-subsidies. Two common options to minimize the distortions (to efficiency and equity) of achieving financial autonomy are increasing-block tariffs and time-of-use rate structures. Under an increasing-block tariff, consumption of services (usually water or power) is priced at a low initial rate up to a specified volume or use (block) and at a higher rate per block thereafter. The number of blocks varies from three to as many as ten. (1994:48)
>
> Subsidized provision of infrastructure is often proposed as a means of redistributing resources from higher-income households to the poor. Yet its effectiveness depends on whether subsidies actually reach the poor, on the administrative costs associated with such targeting, and on

> the scope for allocating budgetary resources to this purpose without sacrificing other socially beneficial public expenditures. Price subsidies to infrastructure almost always benefit the nonpoor disproportionately.... There are, however, ways in which infrastructure subsidies can be structured to improve their effectiveness in reaching the poor. For example, for water, increasing-block tariffs can be used--charging a particularly low "lifeline" rate for the first part of consumption (for example, 25 to 50 liters per person per day) and higher rates for additional "blocks" of water. This block tariff links price to volume, and it is more efficient at reaching the poor than a general subsidy because it limits subsidized consumption. Increasing-block tariffs also encourage water conservation and efficient use by increasing charges at higher use. These tariffs are most effective when access is universal. When the poor lack access, as is frequently the case, they do not receive the lifeline rate and typically end up paying much higher prices for infrastructure services or their substitutes. (1994:80-81)

As noted above, this position was also adopted in the *RDP*. However, in its discussion of funding for infrastructure, the first draft of the *UIIF* notes "various sources including a) the existing fiscal instruments available to local government and the RSCs/JSBs, b) the existing transfer mechanisms between the center/provincial and local tiers, c) additional transfer payments and d) the reallocation of expenditure priorities combined with efficiency improvements. The extra dimension to all of these options is the role of the *RDP* funds in financing a share of the investment program and/or the annual recurrent costs.... Additional options, to be evaluated in the forthcoming months, include a) the impact of incorporating governmental transfers (including alternative assumptions about the running costs of black residential areas), b) revenue sharing of the provincial governments' fuel levy and c) the piggy-backing of a local income tax" (*UIIF* 16/11/94:42,43) This was repeated in the final *UIIF* draft (23/3/95:62).

It would have been extremely easy to establish a national tariff reform that included block tariffs, for Eskom sets national redistributive tariffs for electricity already (low-income households pay 23 cents per kilowatt hour, while large corporations pay less than 6 cents, due to the economies of scale in consumption and their greater bargaining power); this redistribution could have been altered to benefit low-income people, who consume less than 3 percent of all electricity (in contrast to industry, including mining, which consumes more than 50 percent, or to high-income consumers, who consume 12 percent). In the case of water (and hence sanitation), redistributive lifeline supplies and block tariffs were also feasible in view of the decision by the Minister of

Water Affairs and Forestry to assume responsibility for ownership of all South African water resources (hence negating riparian rights). This will allow the minister to establish a national tariff framework that will eventually permit redistribution of water; at present, more than 50 percent of water is consumed by (white) commercial farmers, with domestic consumption only 12 percent and low-income domestic consumption less than 2 percent (Bond 1997a).

In spite of these well-known circumstances and the specific mandates in both the *RDP* and *WDR*, no provision was made by Bank staff for national-level cross-subsidies with progressive block tariffs with a lifeline supply. Once again this had the effect of leading to recommendations of lower standards of infrastructure than should otherwise have been the case.

The reasons for this hostility to block tariffs in the South African case became clear in an October 1995 presentation to Minister of Water Affairs and Forestry Kader Asmal, by John Roome (1995:50-51), who was then the World Bank's task manager of the Lesotho Highlands Water Project. By ignoring the demand-side management and conservation issues associated with progressive block tariffs, Roome argued against sliding tariffs--citing in particular the case of Johannesburg, which has a moderately progressive tariff structure--for six reasons (overhead slide points by Roome are in quotes, and my rebuttals immediately follow in parentheses):

- "poorly targeted--rich and poor alike benefit from subsidy" (a code phrase for Roome's opposition to universal entitlement, which is the preferred system of distribution of goods so as to avoid the class fragmentation, stigmatization, and administrative difficulties associated with means testing) [and] "since measured per household, rich single adult pays only lifeline tariff, while poor large family of 15 or 20 and backyard shacks pays 'luxury' tariff" (not true, since it is technically feasible to credit bills with lifeline entitlements according to the number of individuals in the household, whose i.d. numbers can only be claimed by payers once);
- "financial strain of meeting subsidy rests with 3rd tier--allocation of welfare better done over a large economy" (again not true, since it is possible through both Eskom and the new national water pricing system to establish a free lifeline "reserve" plus additional distribution costs, through cross-

subsidization at *national*-scale, allowing sufficient redistribution of resources such that even impoverished municipalities could offer retail lifeline services);

- "source and meaning of subsidy is not transparent" (again not true, since it is perfectly feasible to engage in public education and transparent billing regarding the lifeline entitlement for the first block and rising charges for additional blocks);
- "asking water boards and utilities to merge service provision and welfare is dangerous" (this critique is illogical since there is no "welfare" task in the case of a universal entitlement);
- "incentive is not to expand services to areas where larger proportion of lifeline customers exist" (this incentive is true for all pricing systems--especially associated with privatized delivery--in which low-income people face economic discrimination, and merely confirms the need to establish a working system for realization of constitutional rights through, for example, penalties to those municipalities which are not extending services at a sufficient rate to meet all residents' basic needs); and
- "may limit options with respect to tertiary providers--in particular private concessions much harder to establish" (no rebuttal).

The last of Roome's critiques of progressive block tariffs is the most telling, and indeed is the only accurate one. For if the World Bank's goal is to privatize water, which it is, and if by encountering an obligation to consider redistribution (the lifeline water supply) when pricing water deters private bidders (since a firm's marginal cost curve will thus necessarily depart from a redistributive water pricing structure), then the Bank has no qualms about advising Minister Asmal to dispense with social-justice pricing. In a context in which, as noted, the majority of African consumers use less than 2 percent of all water, the Bank prioritizes privatization above universal-entitlement access to water.

In Port Elizabeth, a similar line of argument emerged in March 1998, when the City Engineer firmly advocated against adopting a "multiple point stepped water tariff" (as was recommended by the Department of Water Affairs and Forestry's Working for Water program, as part of its "Urban Water Demand Management," and the Council agreed that Port Elizabeth should become a "major role model" by adopting block tariffs and other demand management techniques). But a tender for a full investigation of how to privatize the city's water had just been bid upon, according to the Engineer (Port Elizabeth Municipality 1998:5), "and a change in the water tariff at this stage may pre-empt later tariff proposals to the disadvantage of the Municipality."

Learning from previous project failure

The *UIIF* also suffered from the fact that earlier Bank lessons regarding infrastructure investment were not taken seriously. According to the *WDR*:

> Another approach to assessing the economic returns from infrastructure investment is to examine the rates of return in a large sample of completed World Bank projects.... Returns have been lowest (and declining) for irrigation and drainage, airports (for a very small sample), railways, power water supply, and sewerage. Why should this be so, given the expected benefits of such investments in developing countries? Some of the causes relate to implementation problems.... and others to project identification and design. A common pattern discovered in project completion reviews of water, railway, and power projects is the tendency at the time of appraisal to overestimate the rate of growth in demand for new production capacity and, therefore, of revenues. For the power projects in the sample, demand was overestimated by 20 percent on average over a ten-year operating period. In water projects, overestimation of rates of new connections and per capita consumption also averaged about 20 percent.... One important explanation for the misjudgments during appraisal is inadequate procedures for assessing demand (including the effects of tariff increases). (1994:17)

These issues were apparently not flagged by Bank staff in the original *UIIF* recommendations. The *UIIF* and the final *MIIF* also run the risk of overestimation, given two main factors: estimating annual GDP growth at 3 percent for the next ten years (which although half of what is projected by the Department of Finance in its "Growth, Employment and Redistribution" strategy is probably overoptimistic given flat growth over the previous eight years), and assuming a level of affordability which is not likely to be achieved (given ongoing "jobless growth," income polarization and additional overoptimistic assumptions about the availability of intergovernmental subsidies from the central fiscus). Neither the *UIIF* and *MIIF* conducted analysis of the effects of the tariff increases envisaged (for those who have recently not been paying for services, or who have paid on a flat-rate basis) on household affordability and demand.

Regarding learning from past privatization experience in more general terms, at least one senior Bank official--none other than the chief economist, Joseph Stiglitz (1998:17-18)--has conceded that

> the conditions under which privatization can achieve the public objectives of efficiency and equity are very limited, and are very similar to the conditions under which competitive markets attain Pareto-efficient outcomes. If, for instance, competition is lacking then creating a private, unregulated monopoly will likely result in even higher prices for consumers. And there is some evidence that, insulated from competition, private monopolies may suffer from several forms of inefficiency and may not be highly innovative.... there are strong incentives not only for private rent seeking [i.e., corrupt patronage-related activity] on the part of [privatized firm] management, but for taking actions which increase the scope for such rent seeking.

Stiglitz (18-19) cites the examples of China, which "managed to sustain double-digit growth by extending the scope of competition, without privatizing state-owned enterprises," and Russia, which in contrast "privatized a large fraction of its economy without doing much so far to promote competition. The consequence of this and other factors has been a major economic collapse." The conclusion Stiglitz (19) reaches is that "Privatizing monopolies creates huge rents. It has proved difficult to administer privatization without encouraging corruption and other problems. Entrepreneurs will have the incentive to try to secure privatized enterprises rather than invest in creating their own firms."

In South Africa, most municipal services--water, electricity, roads--represent public goods with monopoly status and large sunk infrastructure costs, and the lessons from past experiences that Stiglitz draws should have been high on the public agenda for debate. Yet it is precisely these services that are today being promoted as privatization prospects (in the process generating private monopolies), most forcefully, by local Bank staff. To do so requires redefining the notion of public participation.

Participation

As expressed in the *RDP* (ANC 1994:2.5.21), "Beneficiary communities should be involved at all levels of decision-making and in the implementation of their projects.... Key to such participation is capacity building, and funds for community-based organizations must be made available." It bears mention, as well, that in two *WDR*s, the World Bank itself has offered conflicting signals on the merits and modalities of participation.

Although the Bank made commitments to participation in the 1994 *WDR*, the 1997 *WDR* indicates a shift towards a more instrumentalist approach. According to Greenfield (in a review of the *World Development Report 1997* on the role of the state), the Bank's conception of participation is now comparable to a national-scale Machiavellian application of workplace (shopfloor) "Total Quality Management" (TQM):

> In the sections [of the *World Development Report*] dealing with NGOs, for example, the Bank includes particular types of NGOs and excludes the mass organizations and associations of farmers, workers and residents--the people. NGOs act like company-based unions under Total Quality Management. Despite the absence of a genuine mandate, they can *claim* to represent the people and advocate their (narrowly defined) interests. More importantly, like company unions, NGOs can implement TQM at the grassroots more effectively than the state (management). This is where the World Bank arrives at a solution to the social unrest and instability that threatens economic growth and the wealth and power of the ruling classes. Just as pro-management unions can "manage" the workers and act as a mechanism for preventing workers' struggles and collective action, the World Bank has discovered that NGOs can act in a similar way. Not only will NGOs take on a lot of the functions and responsibilities of the state (like the delivery of social services, poverty alleviation, and retraining), but they can also redirect people's demands and grievances away from the state. Furthermore, the "participation" of NGOs (not mass-based organizations or social movements) in the workings of an effective state also acts as a substitute for democracy, not its realization.

In South Africa it is not easy to find "company unions" in the form of popular social movements or NGOs willing to promote participation in privatization. A framework for such participation will no doubt fail because it would contradict the basic premises of the democratic movements in both countries.

To illustrate, the World Bank's role in researching the infrastructural needs of urban South Africa was not uncontroversial (Bond and Swilling 1992), and attempts to draw civic associations into a participatory research partnership came to naught. Consider this report by Mark Swilling and Tshepiso Mashinini (reprinted from *BankCheck*, January 1994), which describes a 1992 meeting between a Bank urban mission and Civic Associations of Johannesburg.

> Both delegations left the meeting thoroughly dissatisfied. There was a sense that something had gone wrong, but no-one was quite sure what.

How to interpret the experience? What does it reveal about the different approaches of the civics and the traditional development experts?

The Bank's objective was to compile a "shopping list" of key infrastructural projects (water, sanitation, electricity, roads, waste and drainage). The only way that it can possibly go about this task is to gather data from the existing apartheid local authorities, which is where the bulk of information resides.

However, Bank experts are well aware of the fact that this information is not value-free, but instead is biased by the material interests and planning ideologies of the white local authorities. This poses a serious problem: there is a risk that the future of the city could be determined by projects that reflect what the old order thinks is required, instead of what the new order will actually need.

To avoid this, and to gain wider legitimacy for its own program, the Bank correctly made strenuous efforts to consult with the civics. What happened?

The discussion began with the Bank asking the civics the same set of technical questions that were posed to white local government officials, but obviously in a simpler form: population, level and standard of services, what is expected and what are the priorities. The answers, however, were not forthcoming. Instead, every civic representative emphasized the need for capacity building.

The problem lay in the way Bank staff asked the questions. As technical experts who deal in hard quantitative data every day, they related to the leaders of social movements as if they were local government officials whose every-day activity is the manipulation of organized data captured through established research methods. This is *not* what civic leaders do every day.

No one with community organizing experience would sit down at a first meeting with local leaders and ask: What are your needs? Instead, the questions would be: Comrades, what organizational structures do you have here? What struggles have you embarked upon? What were your demands when you went on the rent boycott? What were the demands in the petition you handed to the administration when you marched? What were your short-, medium- and long-term demands at the negotiations? What compromises did you accept, and why? What research are you doing to back up you demands?

Questions are asked in this way in order to tap *organic* knowledge about socio-economic conditions. Knowledge is inseparable from the rhythms of the daily struggle to transform local and regional conditions. However, civics do not have the resources to transform this practical and usable knowledge into quantitative data which really applies mainly to policy formulation. Even negotiation forums, where civics do have a use for hard data, are structured in a way that conventional quantitative information becomes a site of struggle.

> Information answers certain questions about objective conditions, which in turn leads to certain views of how to change those conditions. The agency which generates information and controls it will be the agency that most effectively acts upon the conditions in a way that suits its particular interests.
>
> Local authorities have huge banks of quantitative data generated from their records and from surveys of various kinds. Civics have an intimate experience-based knowledge of the inner workings of each community, in particular the structure of power, distribution of resources, leadership formations, and--most importantly--the key socio-economic "demands" that have risen up from below via a well-structured process of community organization, grievance expression and mobilization in each community.
>
> To really address community needs, these two sets of knowledge must be married. But how? Will civics be intimidated by the dazzling technical competence of traditional data collection methods and start disregarding what they themselves know from first hand experience? Will the technical experts be intimidated by their complete ignorance of the community knowledge, and give up trying to use traditional research methods?
>
> The point is to avoid reinforcing the knowledge base of technical experts who currently have such a huge influence over policy formulation, whether they are located in the World Bank, local authorities or progressive service organizations.
>
> All this raises even more serious questions about the current Bank mission. By parachuting into complex regional negotiation processes and struggles and focusing mainly on one aspect of the development process--namely financing shopping list infrastructure--the Bank could unintentionally deflect attention away from the central development question: what resources are required to make sure that the development programs of the future really reflect the needs and priorities of the communities?
>
> If this question is *not* answered, the Bank--and every other agency involved in development--will end up supporting a development process that will blow up in their faces. If the Bank thinks that answering this question is outside its mandate, then its mandate must either be changed or the Bank should be asked to leave the country immediately.

Instead of being asked to leave immediately, however, the Bank was offered a deal by the civic associations: to jointly sign a protocol which would regulate the Bank's research work in transitional South Africa (recall that the Bank could not legitimately be seen to be working with the apartheid government, which only left power in May 1994). The components of the protocol were as follows (reprinted from *BankCheck*, January 1994):

Proposed "Protocol" between Johannesburg Civic Associations and the World Bank

Principles:

- Non-racialism
- Non-sexism
- Democratic accountability
- One city — one tax base
- Redistribution
- Guaranteed minimum services accessible to all
- Affordable housing for all
- Economically viable city that promotes growth and employment
- Empowerment of local communities to play a central role in transformation and reconstruction
- Development of human resources through appropriate skills upgrading and training programs
- All central, regional and local government activities must promote development, empowerment and democratic participation

Development guidelines:

1. All information pertaining to potential or actual World Bank involvement in this region must be transparent and made available to community representatives on an on going basis.
2. There should be maximum utilization of internal resources in the public and private sectors for developmental purposes.
3. Finance for development must be controlled by local communities via democratically accountable community based institutions and democratic local governments.
4. All development initiatives must be undertaken in a way that promotes rather than undermines community-based organizations and institutions.
5. Any local government projects for which World Bank finance is provided should have full support of local communities.
6. The World Bank should not enter into discussions about finance for possible development projects with local authorities that refuse to participate in genuine negotiations to achieve a democratic non-racial local government system within a nationally accepted framework (i.e., excluding The Interim Measures Act of 1992).
7. Criteria to select projects for World Bank funding should be negotiated by the relevant stakeholders in this region within appropriate negotiation forum.

The protocol was rejected by the Bank mission (led by Jeff Racki) in July 1992. Nevertheless, it was not long before community participation in projects that affect people's immediate lives became a relatively uncontroversial component of development planning. As recognized in the 1994 *WDR*:

> The importance of participation in effective delivery of local public goods is well recognized, and it is central to community provision of

> service.... Without local participation, projects often either foundered at the implementation stage or were not maintained and failed to produce sustained benefits.... There are risks of exploitation of the poor and of low labor productivity under the banner of self-help and voluntarism.... Participatory processes take time and often require the skills of professional intermediaries who interact with formal sector agencies, explain technology options, and help resolve disputes.... Special interests, local elites, or powerful minorities can capture the process to the exclusion of others. (1994:76,78)
>
> User groups and other interested parties need to be consulted by the public officials and technical specialists who usually lead the process, and mechanisms for conflict resolution are necessary. (1994:84)

Turning to the *UIIF*, there was no community participation in the design of the key financial and institutional components of infrastructural policy in South Africa. This partly reflected the Bank's practice of parachuting in three-week missions whose team members consulted with government officials on overall design, but with community representatives (such as SANCO) only with respect to their participation in future infrastructural projects. The parameters of those projects were designed by technical experts with no sense of the political and social importance of infrastructure, no reference to the *RDP*, and hence no incentive to establish higher standards and more generous subsidy arrangements. (Likewise there was no participation whatsoever by the IFC when contemplating its $25 million investment in privatized infrastructure.)

Participation is not only about drawing all stakeholders in a policy, program, or project together to assure its appropriateness and assist in its implementation. Participation processes must address the differential costs and benefits of privatization, and be prepared to host conflicts over differing interests that are at stake. It is easy to demonstrate that the primary risk associated with municipal infrastructure privatization is that low-income people will receive substandard, unaffordable services. As Hemson (1997) has recently argued in a literature review,

> The effects of privatization bear most radically on the poorest in the community; there is widespread evidence of more cut-offs in service and generally a harsher attitude towards low-income "customers." Water in Britain is a case in point. Water and sewerage bills have increased by an average of 67 percent between 1989/90 and 1994/95, and during roughly the same period the rate of disconnections due to non-payment by 177 percent. The inflexibility and hostility which often characterized public utilities attitude towards non-payment has, over the same period, been replaced by an emphasis on pre-payment

> meters and "*self-disconnection*" as public goods have been commodified. Pre-payment metering is greatly advantageous to companies as the problem of poorer customers is avoided, there is a continuous revenue stream in advance of consumption, less of a "political" problem in confronting disconnections, and better form of debt recovery. Self-disconnection is education of consumption below the level consistent with health, safety and participation in normal community life. Surprisingly high number of self-disconnections for various periods of 49 percent by those using pre-payment devices in a trial period. Self-disconnection is associated with the reduction of consumption below the level consistent with health, safety and participation in normal community life. Studies have shown a surprisingly high number of self-disconnections of water supply for various periods by as much as 49 percent by those using pre-payment devices over a trial period. The most critical feature of privatization, however, has been that cross-subsidies are rooted out after privatization: those who need costly help have to pay for these services *directly* themselves.... Rather than cross-subsidies there has been the introduction of "cost-reflective" pricing (in which prices reflect the particular costs associated with a particular customer) will end with greater differences in regional charges, the poorer paying more, and better off people with cheque accounts paying less with direct debits.

Where the *UIIF* did discuss community participation, it ignored the danger of self-exploitation and the need for capacity-building support (aside from training and "joint ventures with training institutions" in the case of upgrading but none noted in the case of greenfield developments), focusing instead largely on community "involvement" as "the basis for breaking the culture of non-payment" (*UIIF* 23/3/95:5 and VII:27-29,33). The costs of staffing and capacitating the mobilization work of community organizations were neglected. And where the *UIIF* addressed job creation, it assumed that the average cost of each job was R2,290, an exceedingly low amount per annum given prevailing construction wage rates and the *RDP* commitment that public works jobs would not undermine prevailing wages and standards (*UIIF* 16/11/94:54).

In South Africa, the seminal recent statement on participation in development projects remains the 1994 document by the South African National Civic Organization, *Making People-Driven Development Work* (SANCO 1994). Representing mass community group constituencies (called "civics" in South Africa), SANCO reflected on participation-related lessons learned in development projects associated with the Independent Development Trust (IDT), a quango involved in implementing infrastructural development ("site&service") capital subsidies (the loose use of the word "community" here does not mean that democratic systems of establishing community wishes were not conceptualized earlier in the document):

> A still to be completed study of the IDT site&service (capital subsidy) scheme will be a harsh indictment of top-down development. It notes the scheme stressed delivery and pipe in the ground. Site&service was "developer-driven"; consultation and participation were intentionally limited in order to get the job done quickly. But it was more than that. One member of the study said they "gained a consistent impression that IDT was wary of allowing community leadership too much say"; developers, professionals, and local government also resisted community involvement. Consultants' mistrust of civics and their attempts to bypass civics delayed some projects.
>
> This has resulted in badly chosen sites which have not been occupied and the failure to organize maintenance leading to "a high risk" of collapse of roads, outlets and pipes.
>
> The study notes that the single biggest complaint--greater even than the vociferous objection to getting a toilet and not a house--was about the lack of consultation and participation. One team member commented: "This is not just political rhetoric as some would assume. It is a genuine desire on the part of community organizations to be taken seriously and be given due responsibility for implementation."
>
> The "few" instances in which communities were able to force the IDT to give them an active role were the smoother-running projects.
>
> Indeed, the only aspect that worked well was the one where communities were in charge--site allocation. "Community structures proved themselves capable of ensuring that fair, transparent and widely supported mechanisms of allocation were put in place." The IDT could not have done as well on its own, commented the researcher. "More than any other argument, this demonstrates that more could have been achieved in other aspects of the projects had the local organizations been trusted and trained to make critical decisions." (SANCO 1994:ch.4)

Having the power to be in charge of a project is one matter. SANCO also insisted that participation could not occur effectively until communities were empowered, and this required financial support as an entitlement (not charity nor patronage):

> One effect of apartheid has been that many people feel disempowered--that they have no right and no ability to control their own lives and environment. It requires time, organization and money for communities to gain confidence, experience and the capacity to organize. Even well organized communities will require finance to hire a local coordinator and for training in basic skills such as bookkeeping.... Because of the legacy of apartheid, capacity building will not be cheap. For small grants in its drought relief development program, IDT allocated 7.5 percent for capacity building and this was

> insufficient. Capacity building costs will probably be at least 5-10 percent of the cost of the actual physical works of large capital projects, and up to 25 percent of smaller projects.
>
> Capacity building has become a popular part of the jargon of development agencies, but they tend to consider it to be visits by "facilitators" and a few weekend workshops. Capacity building does require this, but it also requires much more. It always requires hiring someone locally as a community organizer. It also means training in management, financial control and bookkeeping skills that cannot be passed on in a weekend; this typically requires one to three month courses. Capacity building demands support and training which continues after the construction is done to ensure that management and maintenance skills are learned. Capacity building support might include vouchers for special training courses, for example for bookkeeping or management.
>
> Finally, capacity-building requires time--for long meetings where people learn to take control, for the initial slowness in all processes as people gain experience, and for the local recognition of what skills are needed and what further training is required.
>
> Capacity building is sometimes just a more sensible use of existing resources. IDT for its site&service scheme allowed 10 hours a month of consultant time for visits, at a cost of more than R2,000 a month. For half that it would have been possible to hire a local person full time in most areas.
>
> So far, capacity building finance has only been available as a donation from an NGO or IDT or DBSA. It was not communities who decided who should be funded, but donors who have their own political agendas. In future, capacity building finance must be seen as essential and as a right. We must curb the power of unelected gatekeepers. The challenge for the new government will be to develop mechanisms which are simple, quick, transparent and efficient, while preventing corruption and ensuring broad participation. In the following chapters, we put forward proposals.
>
> But the key step is to see capacity building finance as an essential right, and not a form of charity. (SANCO 1994:ch.3)

Much the same could be said of trade unions facing privatization. Yet such discussions of the material requirements for community organizations to make participation in infrastructure investment more than a token gesture are uniformly missing from Bank South African staff assessments of participation possibilities.

In sum, when it comes to municipal infrastructure privatization, the South African people (and their organizations) most affected by municipal infrastructure and service delivery policy have been relatively excluded from the national policy debates (aside from through their political representatives in government and parliament, and some opportunity for comment on municipal tariffs through the National Economic Development and Labor Council). Protest resulted (e.g., Nelspruit, not to mention the 1997 East Rand demonstrations over infrastructure installation and services cuts), effectively stalling the privatization process. Would participation have made a decisive difference, a cynic would rightly enquire. From evidence of the negative impact of privatization upon the interests of the mass social movements, it may be just as easy to conclude that *the more participation there is in highly-politicized societies such as South Africa, the less likely it is that privatization will be met with consent--the more likely it is to generate protest.*

Conclusion

In the context of the highly politicized nature of municipal infrastructure privatization and at a time South Africa faces enormous backlogs, the IFC made a large privatization investment with questionable financial calculations. This chapter's review of the *RDP* mandate and of the *WDR*, *UIIF*, and *MIIF* noted that notwithstanding sound policy directives in the first two documents, the Bank's South African staff and some of their local colleagues failed to construct an infrastructure investment framework that could internalize developmental externalities associated with infrastructure; decisively contribute to the reduction of poverty through infrastructure; incorporate economic multipliers in infrastructure investment calculations; incorporate infrastructure's environmental effects; incorporate infrastructure's public health effects; incorporate infrastructure's role in reducing gender inequality; establish an appropriate tariff pricing system that will accomplish the social as well as economic objectives associated with municipal infrastructure; and learn lessons of infrastructure project and privatization failures so they are not repeated.

Not only has much of the policy design work on infrastructure been flawed. Central in the World Bank's and government's thinking has been the privatization of services, even at the cost of local democracy. Hemson (1997) identifies the *MIIF*'s underlying approach to privatization.

> In this document a fundamental distinction is made between service authority and service provider, between *ensuring* that services are

> delivered and *actually* delivering services (paras 16 and 155). This builds on the idea of local government as an "enabler" rather than a provider, setting the context for private sector intervention. The *MIIF* privileges the private sector as the most appropriate vehicle for delivery as it rests on the understanding that local authorities do not have the capacity to deliver. Rather than making a critique of the excessive hierarchies and bloated management systems associated traditionally with local government, the lack of local government capacity in rural areas, and arguing for the revitalization of local government to secure the development of infrastructure and service delivery, it argues that "local governments will need to weigh up political concerns (such as relinquishing direct accountability in a new democracy) against efficient and cost effective service delivery." Here democracy is opposed to delivery and the private sector is given the strategic advantage of being able to deliver. More specifically the document spells out a range of alternative ways of delivering services from public ownership in the form of service departments to private ownership either through "demonopolization" or new entry, or through the sale of public assets (para 186). In assessing the form of service which could be offered, the *MIIF* lists the need for local government to "deliver services in a competitive manner," to provide "an enabling environment for private action" although it also mentions as constraints to the development of PPP the private sector response and trade union attitudes. The various alternative delivery mechanisms put forward in the *MIIF* demonstrate the influence of the commercialization and privatization policy framework (see particularly para 186).

Yet notwithstanding the overall lack of information and the potential problems associated with privatized infrastructure, the Bank's closely-linked IFC staff in South Africa nevertheless invested in an ill-designed infrastructure privatization fund through which they anticipate 90 percent of projects to achieve a rate of return of at least 30 percent. This is particularly short-sighted in a highly politicized country such as South Africa. Here there are many other reasons for additional state intervention (rather than privatization) and for far higher infrastructure standards than Bank staff recommended:

- Unique among modern states, South Africa's new Constitution provides for water and housing (along with health care and environment) as basic rights in the Bill of Rights.
- The South African private sector is unusually concentrated and often exhibits anti-competitive pricing and product behavior, and hence in areas of natural monopoly (such as roads, rail transport, distribution of water and water-borne

sanitation, and energy distribution) the case is stronger for provision of goods and services by the state, not the private sector.

- In addition, the facts that private sector production processes have been extremely capital-intensive in recent years, and that private sector growth has been associated with a loss of jobs (employment has risen in only the public sector and one or two industries such as finance and insurance) also justify a stronger role for state intervention.

In sum, the *WDR* arguments for intervention and for higher standards of infrastructure given many other indirect benefits, must be considered as only the minimal basis for a larger state and community role. Thus it is disturbing that even this minimal basis was largely ignored by Bank staff assigned to South Africa and allied local consultants when detailed recommendations were made to policy-makers beginning in late 1994.

Finally, hard-currency financing of infrastructure by the World Bank and IFC is not required, given a) the high cost of financing once rand depreciation is taken into account; b) the fact that a very small percentage of infrastructure investment requires imports (hence the danger of taking on excessive foreign debt not linked to vital foreign inputs); and c) the enormous liquidity in domestic South African financial markets.

The weight of these arguments leads this author to conclude that the South African government--particularly DCD and local authorities--run great risks by continuing to allow the World Bank such a central role in advice and investment choices surrounding municipal services. Alternative approaches have been set out (in the *RDP*) and are being refined (particularly by SAMWU and some in the civic movement associated with the Development Research Institute). Given the somewhat unfavorable balance of forces faced by progressive organizations in South Africa at present, it may well be that a public participation process will best become a multipronged strategy for posing critical questions to privatization advocates, pointing out the many internal inconsistencies apparent in Bank analysis, and synthesizing the organic insights of community groups and organized labor in order to offer concrete alternatives.

Consider the offer made to those Port Elizabeth trade unionists on that February 1998 weekend: participation in a Bank-designed national infrastructure framework; in which extremely low capital standards and ungenerous recurrent subsidies are offered as a means of avoiding redistribution; as a precursor to considering a sole, highly-constrained privatization option offered by the Bank in conjunction with the (old guard) city treasurer; so as to pave the way for a Bank investment that will require a 30 percent and higher rate of return. Precisely this offer is likely to be made to South African municipalities and their constituents in coming months and years. There Is No Alternative, Tina, say privatization proponents.

"There Must Be an Alternative," Themba (hope), say many in the Democratic Movement: rejection of such a prospect, alongside the intensification of popular demands for local, provincial, and national redistributive programs grounded in the *RDP*, taking advantage of the entire range of socio-economic justifications for greater public investment in municipal infrastructure.

chapter five

Infrastructure and Local Economic Development

with LITHA MCWABENI

Stutterheim, a small Eastern Cape town with a bloody century-and-a-half history of oppression and resistance, is worthy of a lengthy study. Here, the confluence of extraordinary hype over "Local Economic Development" strategies and miserable conditions for consumers of municipal services became sufficiently stark, in 1998, to attract a long-overdue critique. It appeared to my colleagues at the Eastern Cape Socio-Economic Consultative Council that vaunted Stutterheim's fatal flaws included extensive infrastructural backlogs, anti-redistributive municipal services practices, and similar problems in other areas of urban and rural development. The study documented a myriad of ways in which contemporary neoliberal policies assure continuing persecution of those without sufficient economic resources to enter the marketplace on its own terms. Ironically, the "Stutterheim Experience" had been widely praised precisely for extending the terrain of the market, even if just to a few hundred recipients of (unsustainable) job training and entrepreneurial advisory support. Modernization strategies are, indeed, often guilty of simultaneously moving the market slightly downwards along the socio-economic scale, while commodifying more and more goods to the point that they become increasingly unaffordable. (As with the previous two chapters, this analysis of infrastructure provision carried out by researchers of the Left was subsidized by the then definitively neoliberal Department of Constitutional Development, itself supported by the British Department for International Development.)

[An abridged version of this chapter appeared as "Local Economic Development and Municipal Infrastructure Crisis: The Case of Stutterheim" in *Urban Forum* 9, 2 (1998).]

Introduction: Stutterheim's crisis

The town of Stutterheim in the Amatola mountains of the Eastern Cape is South Africa's most celebrated case of Local Economic Development (LED). The town leaders' efforts since 1990 have attracted published commentary in dozens of South African and international newspaper articles (e.g., Lewthwaite 1998), in NGO evaluations (e.g., Tandy 1992), in development training manuals (e.g., Chaturvedi 1996), in consultancy reports (e.g, Dewar 1995), in academic papers (e.g., Nel 1994), in a short book (e.g., Nussbaum 1997), and in a video documentary (South African Broadcasting Corporation 1993). The contemporary policy-paper technique of illustrating the merits of favored strategies through "boxes" has been applied to Stutterheim LED by advocacy groups ranging from the SA National Civic Organization (1995:68-69) to the National Business Initiative and International Republican Institute (1998:5). Without exception, these commentaries have been effusive in their praise for the "Stutterheim experience."

As the driving force behind the publicity, the Stutterheim Development Foundation regularly hosts South African and international visitors and trains officials from dozens of other municipalities on how to "do" LED. Observers such as those who visited Stutterheim in May 1998 for an international conference on LED can be forgiven for concluding that South Africa's overall transition "miracle" is encapsulated in this town, and that Stutterheim should be a role model for similar initiatives by municipalities and local civil societies.

After all, in key demographic and geographic respects, the Stutterheim area has characteristics not unusual for the many dozens of South African agricultural centers tied firmly to impoverished rural hinterlands. Of roughly 55,000 people living in the vicinity of Stutterheim, the African township of Mlungisi is estimated to have approximately 8,000, the traditionally white town of Stutterheim is estimated to have somewhat less than 4,000, and the traditionally coloured Amatolaville township is considered to have around 1,000. There are another 18,000 or so "Greater Stutterheim" residents--though excluded from the Stutterheim Transitional Local Council--in the African townships of Kubusie (8,000), Cenyulands (6,000), and Cenyu (4,000). Another 24,000 or more (Africans) live in surrounding villages within 30 km of the town: Mgwali (12,000), Wartburg (8,000), Isedenge

(3,500), and Heckel (1,000) (Stutterheim Development Foundation unpublished estimates).

Even outstripping national population growth, the number of Stutterheim residents is said to be expanding by 3.5 percent per annum (Makalima Johnston Associates 1997:15). The area's economy is based partly on raw materials--timber and the Lentz and Rance saw mills--but there are two other major employers: Boardmans factory (paint, candles, toiletries) and the Dohne Agricultural Development Institute. Stutterheim also has relatively good tourism prospects and is a potential site for further industrial production based on its location near key transport routes and in the proximity of the provincial capital, Bisho.

Most importantly, at first glance Stutterheim appears to have made the transition to the new South Africa seamlessly. The town, according to Barbara Nussbaum (1997:back cover) of the University of the Witwatersrand Business School, "managed to change its destiny from a town crippled by violence, poverty and racial tension, to one in which black and white created a partnership, working together, meaningfully engaged in social and economic development." Similarly, in the words of Lewthwaite (1998), "It is a dramatic turnaround for a town which, in the 1980s, was an example of the worst of South Africa, characterized by racial conflict, fear and uncertainty. Today it is the epitome of the best, a community that has stolen the lead on the policymakers in Pretoria."

A closer look at Stutterheim, however, reveals a variety of substantial problems that warrant a more critical perspective:

- Stutterheim resegregated itself after an initial movement towards ending the apartheid urban form, and now consists of a mainly "white" area, a mainly "coloured" area, and an "African" township, with at least three other close-by African townships and many other proximate, highly-dependent rural villages--together representing more than three quarters of the Stutterheim community--effectively left out of resource distribution, local democracy, and planning for future development.
- The resegregation of the town of Stutterheim is also well advanced, with early 1990s notions of a "buffer zone" that would separate low-income black people from white residential areas now replaced by class-conscious residential development planning which has the same effect.

- Stutterheim's LED activities--particularly those coordinated by the Stutterheim Development Foundation--have never managed to develop beyond a few discrete projects, many of which proved to be unsustainable, while skills training left people still unemployed or forced to leave the area in search of employment, and indeed the very existence of the Foundation itself was at one point threatened by delivery crisis.
- Privatization of water in Stutterheim was carried out in a manner that a large foreign firm successfully "cherry-picked" the lucrative white and coloured areas, which receive dependable water supplies at present, but which left much of the official Stutterheim township (Mlungisi) unserved and the unofficial neighboring townships (Cenyu, Kubusie, Cenyulands) nearly entirely unreticulated--at the same time the general secretary of the area's civic association won a job at the water company.
- The ability of even the fortunate township residents who are incorporated into Stutterheim to pay their bills, under circumstances in which a redistributive block tariff has not been instituted, is so limited that 61 percent of Mlungisi residents have effectively been declared indigent for the purposes of paying for municipal services. (Moreover, the use of "remissions" for these residents--consistent with national Department of Constitutional Development "indigence policy"--has backfired, according to the Stutterheim Council, in that it has generated a doubling of consumption by those who receive free water, in part, it is alleged, because of "free-riding" by those who were cut off.)
- Water service was cut off to nearly 20 percent of Mlungisi residents during the final three months of 1997 (the latest available information), in a manner that was probably both unconstitutional and illegal, and only 6 percent of this group had their water reconnected during the course of the three-month period.
- The overall ratio of municipal services payments in arrears to payments due, was 112 percent in Mlungisi in January 1998 (due to accumulated arrears), as compared to 15 percent for

the white and coloured areas of Stutterheim and 27 percent nationally.

- There has been no effort, as yet, made by the Stutterheim Council to price basic services in a socially-just manner, to repair water and electricity lines and hence save resources lost to apartheid-era leaks and faults, or to carry out other aspects of demand-side management.
- There has been a general failure, by Stutterheim Council councilors and officials, to link the provision of infrastructure to opportunities for job creation, public health provision, gender equality and geographical desegregation.
- Capital spending has been declining, with virtually no transformation of the municipal budget.

Each of these aspects of Stutterheim's LED crisis is explored in the pages below. To fully comprehend the crisis faced by Stutterheim, however, also requires looking, first, at the roots of this town, so as to understand the extraordinary conflict associated with its very origins and early development. This tragic history--dating back 160 years and suffused with power plays by missionaries and mercenaries, and divide-and-rule tactics successfully deployed against the indigenous African inhabitants by white settler armies--helps to put into context the present set of circumstances. For, as in past times, Stutterheim is a town that today, in the estimate of its supporters in South Africa's development establishment, does everything by the (neoliberal) book, yet nevertheless is failing to bring what we have come to call "sustainable development" to the vast majority of its citizenry.

Stutterheim's legacy of uneven development

Missionary colonialism, 1837-1856

In 1837, the seeds of what is now known as Stutterheim were planted in the nearby establishment of the Berlin Mission Society's Bethel Mission Station by Dr. J.L. Dophne. Colin Bundy (1988:37) describes two central features of such Eastern Cape religious missions: "first, the role of the missionaries as torch-bearers of capitalist social norms and the market economy, as advocates of increased trade and commercial activity, and secondly, their contribution to class formation in African society."

In this latter regard, the cooptation of native African peasants resulted in both the emergence of a favored group of peasants--the Mfengu people (originally from KwaZulu-Natal, drawn to the Eastern Cape by Methodists)--and their service to settlers during the colonial frontier wars of 1846 and 1850-53 (and later, 1877-78). This generated unprecedented social differentiation amongst the African peasantry of the Eastern Cape, in part because land was taken from the Gcaleka, Tembu, Ngqika, and other ethnic groups and awarded to Mfengu collaborators (Bundy 1988:34-35; see also Peires 1981 and Mostert 1992 for historical context).

The main point of the early missionary activity was, as Bundy (1988:37) comments, "to transform social institutions and practices that were alien or incompatible with capitalist society into ones that were compatible, and hence to encourage a total change in the world-view of the people in whose midst they lived." In 1875, the *Kaffir Express* newspaper made just such a linkage by justifying why peasants were being explicitly encouraged to construct square houses:

> With a proper house, then comes a table, then chairs, a clean table-cloth, paper or whitewash for the walls, wife and daughters dressed in clean calico prints, and so forth.... The church-going Kaffirs purchase three times as much clothing, groceries and other articles in the shops as the red Kaffirs; but with a change in their habitations the existing native trade would soon be doubled. (Cited in Bundy 1988:37.) ["Red" was a vulgar reference to Xhosa people who had rejected Christianity and wore red clay.]

In this context, as one of 32 missions in the Eastern Cape--which in turn hosted 16,000 of the province's population of roughly 400,000 Africans in 1850--Bethel required continuing fortification. In 1846 and again in 1850, the Bethel mission's church was burnt by local African people. Dophne's wife and infant son died of illnesses and in 1846 he left, embittered, to become a minister to the Voortrekkers in Natal. Dophne's successor was notable as the first translator of the bible into Xhosa in 1889 and a decade later as having compiled a Xhosa-English dictionary (Stutterheim Historical Society 1984:4-5).

But as Bundy (1988:40) remarks, "Particularly between 1836 and 1857, the mission records are a chronicle of abandoned stations, dispersed congregations, despondency and a fair measure of disillusionment." Aggression from local residents continued, and hence the village of Stutterheim was formally founded in 1857, a short distance from the Dophne settlement, by mercenaries of the British German

Legion. Stutterheim initially took the form of a fort housing roughly 50 men. "In the Stutterheim Caravan Park there is what remains of this, the real beginnings of our village as we know it today," namely, walls of a building that--in the records of the Stutterheim Historical Society (1984:7)--"was likely to have been the 'lock-up' used to discipline offenders against the military regime."

The man whom the town was named after, Major-General Richard von Stutterheim, began building "a large mansion," but left the work unfinished after eight months and departed for Germany, never to return (Stutterheim Historical Society 1984:1). "While some of the mercenaries were mere opportunists out for adventure and soon drifted off to India or other parts of South Africa, many of those who settled with their families became successful farmers...." and were joined in 1858-59 by another 34 German families, according to the Stutterheim Historical Society (1984:2). By 1861 a mill was up and running and within the next twenty years churches were built for white settlers of Lutheran, Catholic and Baptist faiths (Stutterheim Historical Society 1984:9,11).

Meanwhile, at Mgwale, 30 kilometers away, the Church of Scotland established a mission on 5,000 hectares of land, also in 1857. According to the Border Rural Committee (1997:9), "Instead of travelling to the people to evangelize to them, they could now focus on rehabilitating refugees who entered the Colony as a result of famine. People sought refuge in the missions, looking for shelter and provisions."

This was not an unusual story of the origins of towns along the colonial frontier. Bundy (1988:237) has recorded the extent to which, from the early 19th century,

> the merchants of Cape Town and Port Elizabeth sought an expanded market; missionary ideologues equated the spread of Christianity with the spread of metropolitan economic influences and "habits of industry"; administrators sought allies or "buffers" against hostile kingdoms to the north, and they also looked to an increased production in African areas as a means of making the colony pay its way.

Mercenary repression of African resistance, 1857-1878

Indeed, the white settlers' toehold relied enormously upon the expropriation and exploitation of indigenous peoples. The most famous single incident of the Xhosa nation's suffering--the suicidal cattle-killing in 1856-57 which starved an estimated 25,000 people--aided the settlers enormously, according to Bundy (1988:49-50). "Enforced participation in the money economy by pauperized survivors, the diminution of the power of the chiefs, and the closer integration of frontier territories into the colonial orbit [which resulted from the cattle-killing] were precisely those aims" pursued by colonial Governor Sir George Grey beginning in 1853.

Grey's strategy of establishing "civilized communities" on the frontier relied on "undermining chiefs by introducing white magistrates into their areas, by insisting that chiefs accept salaries from government instead of tributes and fines, and by the appointment of paid headmen to serve as a police force. These policies effectively curtailed the judicial, economic and political powers of the chief" (Bundy 1988:50). To illustrate, the Border Rural Committee (1997:9) notes that under Grey's influence the Mgwali mission "focused on securing individualized land ownership," which took the form of a leasehold, "quitrent" tenure on ten-acre lots with rights over use of commonage land, subject to "beneficial" use of the land, payment of a local tax, and family transfer based on male primogeniture succession. In the process, peasants in the area were temporarily granted the possibility of inclusion in the non-racial, male, propertied franchise.

Grey's biographer observed that ultimately, the governor aimed to "break up the larger tribes into smaller, more manageable units, overawe them by a show of military force, remove large numbers of natives out of the province altogether, concentrate the rest in village settlements under European officers, and convey large areas of the best land to European farmers" (cited in Bundy 1988:50). Grey announced that "we can draw very great permanent advantages from the circumstance" of the cattle-killing, initially because, thanks to the weakening of the Xhosa people, "throughout British Kaffraria the native has no recognized right or interest in the soil" and later, in 1858, by permitting several hundred wealthier Africans to buy freehold land or lease land that was formerly communally owned (cited in Bundy 1988:50-51).

To achieve this degree of dominance, divide-and-rule tactics were common, with one colonial official recommending in 1867 that the authorities should "keep up until a fitting time, without actually causing a rupture, the old animosity between Kafir and Fingoe, and this has effectively been done [by the Mfengu emigrations across the Kei River].... For many years, the Kafirs will require a watchful policy, and if they are to fight, it is better that they should do so with the Fingoe first." (Cited in Bundy 1988:84)

Peasant resistance continued, and survival strategies emerged between the periodic conflagrations. One militant leader, Sandile (son of the Paramount Chief Ngqika Gaika, who founded the Ngqika clan), was born around 1820 and by 1835 was recorded as visiting a nearby fort with other Ngqika chiefs (Peires 1981; Mostert 1992). Sandile was defeated in one battle and his followers were moved to "a long strip of unoccupied country.... The greatest part of it was absolutely bare, woodless, and unsheltered" (according to a contemporary account cited in Bundy 1988:47). The peasantry persevered, however, and from 1869-74, as the wool trade expanded dramatically, the number of trading stores in Sandile's area increased from 5 to 25.

Sandile was finally killed in 1878 in the "Ninth Kaffir War"--fighting against a "detachment of Fingo troops under the command of Captain Massey-Hicks"--and was buried 20 kilometers outside Stutterheim. His grave lies between those of two white soldiers killed in the same battle, in order "to convince his followers that his spirit would not roam," according to accounts cited by the Stutterheim Historical Society (1984:14). Yet Sandile was beheaded in the process, and his head is apparently still buried in Cheltenham (*Mail and Guardian* 2/2/97).

That ninth war, notes Bundy (1988:83), "was followed by further land expropriations and the enforced migrations of clans, and in several districts led directly to a reversal of peasant gains of previous years." The white Frontier Armed Mounted Police were "apt to degenerate into desultory or promiscuous cattle lifting," as one soldier conceded (Bundy 1988:84), and the colonists' Mfengu allies were extremely effective at destroying the fields and capturing the cattle and sheep of the Ngqika and Gcaleka people. Bundy (1988:84) described this as

> warfare pursued by the destruction of the economic capacity of the enemy. It was not merely that the "rebels" lost a vastly higher number of men than their mounted and better armed adversaries, that ensured their defeat, but in addition the capture of their cattle, sheep and corn stocks, and the destruction of their standing crops, reduced them to their piteous state in the Pirie forests by the first quarter of 1878.

But the Ngqika and some Thembu people continued to defy colonial domination, and in early 1878 attacked trading stores and food consignments. Repression immediately intensified and in Komgha, not far from Stutterheim, more than 8,000 cattle were confiscated by authorities after a decisive battle. "The defeated rebels, in short, lost not only the war, but also the bulk of their means of subsistence," Bundy (1988:85) observed,

> and the devastated and depressed state of Africans in the Eastern Cape war zone was used by imperial and colonial authorities to serve the interests of would-be employers and settlers.... the shattered Ngqika were driven across the Kei to join a mainly Gcaleka population in the congested districts of Kentani and Willowvale. There they became in later years a byword for conservatism, for "red" and "heathenish" ways and for a resistance to any "improvements" or experiments. Yet before the war and their spoliation, the Ngqika had demonstrated clearly their responsiveness to opportunity: evidence from the early 1870s has already been quoted which told of doubled wool production, the sale of cattle to buy sheep, a much greater volume of trade, and so on.

Municipal development and rural underdevelopment, 1879-1932

The Native Location Act of 1879 codified the emerging rural land tenure relationships that would pose such a challenge in future years, and in Mgwali 152 male households were certified to have quitrent tenure; this also gave them a vote and made them Mgwali's key decision-makers. In 1881, mission stations were allowed to establish formal local administrative structures under Cape Colony rules, but still with the franchise limited to male property owners (Mgwali became a Village Management Board in 1899, again reaffirming the power of quitrent property holders, and reporting to the Native Affairs Commissioner) (Border Rural Committee 1997:10).

With African peasant resistance in the area now conclusively repressed, Stutterheim became a formal municipality in 1879 and a year later the nearby East London-Queenstown railroad was completed, making "a tremendous difference to trade in the area" (Stutterheim Historical Society 1984:2). As Standard Chartered Bank's report for the first half of 1879 confirmed, "At King William's Town and Queenstown Branches we are doing an increased business caused in a great measure by a settlement of the native difficulties and a revival of trade generally in the districts lately devastated by war" (cited in Mabin and Conradie 1987:81).

This was by no means unbroken prosperity, as various financial crises struck the banking system, leading Standard's "branch in King

William's Town to complain [during the early 1860s] that it could make little headway against local competitors [including one savings bank and two friendly societies] if Cape Town continued to levy such a high rate of interest on its overdraft" (Henry 1963:8). Following an "intense boom in banking expansion" of the 1860s, as Schumann (1938:75-80) described it, there came the "inevitable reaction." Another severe banking crash started in Port Elizabeth in 1865, borne of "overintensified speculation which had reached breaking point." In turn, this kicked off one of the century's worst depressions, with widespread agricultural bankruptcies, and as a result of the uneven ebb and flow of financial resources, the well-funded imperial banks--Standard and Oriental (later Bank of Africa and then Barclays)--were ultimately able to buy up nearly all their competitors (Mabin 1985).

The 1870s and 1880s brought renewed booms and busts, in commodities--some of which were peripheral or unrelated to Stutterheim--ranging from diamonds to ostrich feathers to the Stutterheim district's standby, wool (the price of which collapsed in 1884, generating many more rural bankruptcies). Nevertheless, by this stage a more durable but no less repressive relationship between settlers and African peasants had emerged, which meant that, as Marks and Atmore (1980:24-25) put it,

> capitalist development first stimulated the growth of a peasantry by providing the demand for foodstuffs and cash crops--and then helped undermine it in its search for vast quantities of cheap labor, though again the process was far from complete even at the turn of the century.... the "traditionalism" and "stagnation" of contemporary African agriculture in the "reserves" is a consequence not a cause of the way in which the peasantry was integrated into the developing capitalist economy of South Africa in the late nineteenth and early twentieth centuries.

There were enormous difficulties with this process of market penetration and attempts to legislate them away, as reflected in the 1893-94 Cape Labor Commission findings of insufficient African labor on white farms; the 1894 Glen Grey Act aiming at agricultural modernization; other "Location Acts" which displaced peasants in 1892, 1899, and 1909; increased taxes (reaching 20 percent on goods purchased by 1906); greater competition in sales of grain due to transport improvements; the unevenness by which merchant and financial capital affected productive sectors; plagues of locusts and rinderpest; and the disruptions of the Anglo-Boer War--which included a concentration camp in the vicinity (the cemetery of which borders Mlungisi township)

(Bundy 1977). The 1899 Private Locations Act, for example, was the first substantial anti-squatting legislation. By regulating the number of tenant farmers allowed on a given farm, it led to large-scale evictions in the Stutterheim area. This in turn led to regional migrations to those areas such as Mgwali where quitrent owners inherited an influx of labor tenants (Border Rural Committee 1997:10).

Mgwali was named a "native reserve" for exclusive land purchase by African people as a result of the 1913 Land Act. More systematically, according to Bundy (1988:241-243), the Act

> sought not only to suppress successful squatter-peasants and to shield white agriculture from competition by black farmers, but also to "freeze" social relations in the Reserve areas. How does one explain the "incomplete" form of proletarianization in South Africa, or the preservation of certain precapitalist forms and relationships?.... The 1913 Land Act sought to arrest the tendency towards a bipolar stratification (farmers and workers) and to preserve instead an underdeveloped peasantry: a peasantry whose productive capacity had been so inhibited, whose access to land so confined, whose access to markets rendered so unfavorable, that its members must have recourse to labor for white employers even at the very low wage levels prevailing.... While the underdevelopment of the peasant sector ensured a vast reservoir of migrant labor, at the same time the ability of the Reserve inhabitants to supply a portion of their subsistence through peasant production conferred direct benefits upon urban employers--particularly the mines--in the form of low wages, cheap housing, the avoidance of welfare considerations for workers' dependents, and a brake on the growth of an urban proletariat.

This see-saw of development and underdevelopment would characterize Stutterheim's relationship with its own immediate (African) hinterland for many decades to come, as well as its subordinate status as a supplier of wool and later timber to East London and of labor to the Witwatersrand mines and industry. In the process of developing unevenly, Stutterheim's first public works project of record was a furrow that in 1886 augmented the Dophne Fort water supply. Two decades later, piped water was provided through a six-inch main pipe from a forest stream, and in 1922 and 1933 this was augmented by a major dam and weir. In 1924, the Stutterheim Town Hall was built and in 1929 electricity was provided thanks to a municipal investment of 8,000 pounds (of which 75 percent was borrowed). The municipal services were reserved, of course, for white business, industrial, agricultural, and residential consumption.

Apartheid-era development and underdevelopment, 1933-1989

To some extent the municipal development activity recorded above represented the power of the town's white leadership to meet their growing commercial needs during the early 20th century. But the pressure to compete as a location for investment in the world economy--at least until the Great Depression of the 1930s--must have also played a role in upgrading municipal infrastructure. Research on Stutterheim's attempts at attracting investors has not been carried out, but in nearby King William's Town and at East London, a German blanket manufacturer was able to play the two councils off against each other during the early 1930s as each attempted "to outbid each other with offers of various incentives, such as cheap land and reduced electricity tariffs," according to Nel and Rogerson (1996:76).

The extent to which Stutterheim was victimized during the era of early industrialization by serving as East London's dependent hinterland is not yet documented. But certainly by the 1930s, aspects of "the development of underdevelopment" (Frank 1967) in the Stutterheim area, and especially its rural periphery, could be discerned. The previous era of direct rule over Africans--characterized by the emergence of a small property-owning class--was evolving into indirect rule along the lines of the system operative in Natal. The 1927 Native Administration Act reintroduced tribal rule, which "undermined not only the control of the quitrenters in Mgwali, but also their ownership of the commonage," according to the Border Rural Committee (1997:11). The power of the "headman" over local government was cemented in the 1952 Bantu Laws Amendment Act, which in turn led to homelands policy.

Social and economic security was also decaying in the most rural settings around Stutterheim. In much traditional literature, the ecological, social, and economic degradation of African agricultural areas has been blamed upon the victim. In the words of economic historian D. Hobart Houghton (1978:71)--who conducted research in Keiskammahoek, near Stutterheim--"overstocking and bad farming are progressively reducing the future carrying capacity of the land." The 1930 Macmillan study of the Herschel district, the 1932 Native Economic Commission which analyzed the Border area in depth, the Betterment Proclamation of 1939, a 1946 Social and Economic Planning Council study of the reserves, the 1955 Tomlinson Commission, and the hundreds of agricultural demonstrators active in the reserves at any one time during the post-war era all, according to Houghton (1978:72-74),

> were acutely conscious of the inadequacy of tribal farming practice.... In spite of deep thought and heroic effort agricultural conditions continued to deteriorate. Failure to effect a significant change in agricultural methods should not be attributed to lack of zeal on the part of a noble band of dedicated workers, but must be explained in other ways. The explanation would appear to be that the African peasants have failed to adapt their farming practice to modern requirements. General conservatism, the system of land tenure, and certain social customs, like *ukulobolo*, combine to perpetuate obsolete methods of farming in spite of the visual evidence of modern methods applied at agricultural schools in the reserves and by adjacent white farmers.

On the basis of such analysis, the Department of Bantu Administration and Development pursued, during the post-war era, "a policy much on the general lines recommended by the Tomlinson Report. In particular the basic division of the population into full-time farmers and full-time non-agricultural workers appears to have been accepted as the ultimate objective" (Houghton 1978:77). In Mgwali during the 1960s, the Border Rural Committee (1997:11) observes, the results of "betterment" policy were "villagization, the separation of arable land from grazing land, fencing and demarcation and, for all people residing on arable land, allocation of residential sites on some portions of the commonage." Closely following the logic of the quitrent system, approximately 120 sites were allocated through "Permission to Occupy (PTO) Certificates," and soon afterwards--as administrative control over Mgwali was shifted to the Ciskei--a chief was chosen who in turn allocated a further 100 residential sites. Ultimately some 600 PTO sites of 0.1 hectares each were allocated. Much of this formalization came at the expense of commonage land--which was later the basis for a land claim--and "no additional land for grazing was provided" so that PTO residents established informal tenancy arrangements with those Mgwali landowners whose land was arable (Border Rural Committee 1997:12, 25).

Likewise, peasant farming activity outside larger villages like Mgwali was regularized. In the King William's Town district, "full economic units" per household were 5-8 hectares of arable plus grazing for 10-14 cattle units, with an average utilization of 35 hectares per family, according to Houghton (1978:78-79). However, such calculations meant that in 1955, the King William's Town district would have sufficient land for only 3,400 out of 11,400 families, with the rest to be both resettled elsewhere or provided employment in urban centers (Houghton 1978:80). Under the logic of modernization theory, Houghton and likeminded, otherwise liberal economists could self-justify apartheid spatial development policy, including bantustan-hugging decentralization points and resettlement.

For white centers like Stutterheim, however, the decades after 1933 were marked by more sophisticated labor control systems, the accommodation of a "non-permanent" urbanized population, and the emergence of numerous central state planning interventions, in a context of the country's most rapid, sustained economic growth ever before or since. Access to Stutterheim's trade potential improved dramatically in 1942 with the opening of the Stutterheim station on the redirected East London-Queenstown line. There were continued hints of social conflict though, as the white Lutheran community found itself divided between those who supported and those who opposed the Nazis during the early 1940s (St. Paul's Evangelical Lutheran Church 1989:12). (Nearly a half-century later, the same conflict between white *verkramptes* and *verligtes* was won by the latter, as a consumer boycott of white businesses by black residents conclusively shifted power relations, as described below.)

Meanwhile, the vast majority of Stutterheim's black residents were denied services and formal housing in the townships and villages in the vicinity of the white town. By 1977, the *Daily Dispatch* noted that

> Mlungisi location is the shame of Stutterheim. It is a slum and for ten years all development has been frozen in the township while the government decides whether to build a new one. Twenty five taps serve water to 4,000 people of the township and yet Bantu Affairs Administration Board intends to spend only R240 on washing facilities in the coming year. (Cited in Nussbaum 1997:8)

Nussbaum (1997:9) cites the threat of forced removals to the Ciskei as the main reason that the white government's funding on township development was inhibited. This was also a problem in neighboring Mgwali, declared a "black spot" and cited for permanent removal to Frankfort in the Ciskei. The offer of residential and arable plots in the Ciskei may have appealed to some Mgwali residents, but the Mgwali Residents Association was dominated by quitrent tenure holders, who successfully mobilized against the forced removal. In 1985, a court granted Mgwali a reprieve (Border Rural Committee 1997:13).

Regardless of the homeland factor, the 1980s in any case witnessed the withdrawal of the South African state from provision of black urban housing, under the assumption that thanks to liberalized urban residential status (beginning with the 99-year lease), housing and infrastructure supplied by the private sector (bank and developer) and parastatal (SA Housing Trust, Development Bank of Southern Africa) could make up the difference. In 1990, the retreat from housing policy was codified by the establishment of the Independent Development Trust, whose site-and-service schemes represented a decisive shift in policy consistent with international trends that dated to the 1970s.

Internationally, the neoliberal era brought fiscal constraint, high interest rates, deindustrialization (or, at best, jobless growth), and the rapid decline in workers' and poor peoples' standards of living. In the housing field, the World Bank and conservative international aid agencies recommended shifting the state responsibilities to house the poor towards merely providing serviced stands, upon which "self-help" shacks could be constructed, which would have the effect of lowering the amount of money workers would require from employers on a monthly basis to meet housing needs (Burgess 1978, 1985).

Even in upper-middle-income South Africa, neoliberal development policy makers reached the conclusion that decent public housing would be impossible to provide to the citizenry. In the wake of the state's 1980s retreat from public housing construction, several public- and private-sector agencies formally adopted the analysis and language of neoliberal development, gradually growing more sophisticated about the need for social contracts and community consultation, so as to give more credence to policies in which the state would play a smaller role in maintaining the social wage (see Chapter Eight). These included the Urban Foundation (a corporate think-tank and development agency whose origins date directly to the 1976 Soweto uprising), Development Bank of Southern Africa (which although set up to promote bantustan "independence," ultimately attempted to reform during the late 1980s by modeling itself on the World Bank), Independent Development Trust (founded in 1990 and then run by the former chair of the Urban Foundation, with a mandate to promote local negotiations over development), and Small Business Development Corporation (increasingly a vehicle to promote a black free-enterprise ideology, notwithstanding a loan book biased to white entrepreneurs).

The state relied, unwisely, upon a combination of repression and "winning hearts and minds" through the heightened responsibility these agencies bore for kickstarting development at a time Black Local Authorities had lost all credibility. But the highly-constrained form of "development" posited in the neoliberal model, and the assurance that the existing system of capital accumulation would continue virtually unhindered, generated new contradictions which erupted in late 1989 into a major offensive by the black community against the white power structure.

The battle for Stutterheim's future, 1989-1990

In Stutterheim, as across South Africa (Mayekiso 1996), the combination of state socio-economic neglect and repression, augmented by intense racial discrimination by white residents and businesses, generated growing resistance (Tandy 1992; Nussbaum 1997). Although "a new spirit of protest was evident" in Mlungisi township beginning in mid-1989, according to Tandy (1992:7), there had been precedents several years earlier. The mid-1980s witnessed increased protests, stayaways, boycotts, and conflicts with the police. A boycott of local businesses in 1986 compelled white leaders to spend R1.8 million in upgrading Mlungisi and to construct a new school (*Daily Dispatch* 11/1/90).

But it was the students of Mlungisi who catalyzed sustained community resistance in August 1989 by leading a march of 1,000 residents in protest against segregated schooling. Workers at a local saw mill went out on strike. And on 5-6 September, a stayaway against the white parliamentary elections was estimated to be 90-percent effective (Tandy 1992:7).

The security state was still extremely effective, however, as reflected in a series of incidents that infuriated the town's black residents:

- the August student march was broken up by police;
- a progressive priest, Lulama Ntshingwa, was detained two days before the September stayaway;
- more than 250 people--including 23 priests--were beaten by police during a prayer session for the release of Ntshingwa;
- white businesses dismissed workers who joined the September stayaway;

- a smear campaign was launched by shadowy elements against the activist clergy;
- a magistrate then refused permission for township residents to march in protest against conditions;
- on Christmas Day, a meeting to give solidarity to death row prisoners was teargassed by police; and
- on 16 January 1990, 214 residents were arrested in what was purported to be an anti-crime operation (Tandy 1992:8-10).

But the security state could not prevent a combined consumer and rent boycott, which was the tactic upon which township residents embarked on 13 September. Local civic associations from the townships and villages came together as the Stutterheim Coordinating Committee (later known as the Stutterheim Unit of the United Democratic Front), with the following goals (some of which were national in character, some essentially local):

- upgrade conditions in the township;
- improve health services;
- increase wages;
- gain the release of detainees and lifting of detainee restrictions;
- reinstate dismissed workers;
- revise rentals and grazing rights;
- establish non-racial schools; and
- have troops removed from the townships (*Daily Dispatch* 16/1/90).

Specific developmental demands were made for the tarring of the main road in Mlungisi and other potholed, non-navigable roads, the erection of security lights, installation of stormwater drains, provision of low-income housing at "affordable rents," and a better sanitation system. One victory for the Stutterheim Unit was the resignation of the Black Local Authority. Yet ongoing living conditions remained untenable. There were regular complaints that domestic and farmworkers earned as little as R40 per month. Rental rates, meanwhile, had increased from R12.98 to R21.50 per month in July 1989, although many residents lived in mud houses without services.

Racism was rife in local education, and accusations were leveled at the Stutterheim hospital that rejected patients on racial grounds (the mayor, Nico Ferreira, later insisted that "treatment is differential on an economic and not on a racial basis") (*Daily Dispatch* 18/1/90). Economically, the Small Business Development Corporation's hive of industries was "doomed to failure," according to the Committee, because "A man who earns R40 a month does not have money to become involved in a scheme like this" (*Daily Dispatch* 16/1/90). Farmworkers were evicted in February 1990 in another display of white power and insensitivity.

The consumer boycott, initially set for one month but then extended for another six, was aimed in large part at conservative shopowners. The context was the decisive role played by the Afrikaanse Sakekamer, a *verkrampte* business body which actively petitioned the local state to clamp down on dissidents. The Stutterheim Council, however, was controlled by *verligte* elements beginning in 1988 when a group of independents led by Ferreira were elected as councilors, a factor which ultimately allowed for a resolution of the crisis after 14 white businesses went bankrupt (interview, Hamish Scott, 1998).

The May 1990 negotiations between Ferreira and Chris Magwangqana--leader of the township civics--led to a few minor but immediate victories for the Stutterheim Unit, including a commitment by the white council to try to persuade white businesses to rehire dismissed workers (this was only partially successful); the withdrawal of the rental increase and writing off of arrears; and a reward offered for information about the smear campaign against the clergy. It also confirmed the grassroots power of township residents, and forced Stutterheim's elite to come to terms with the leaders of the boycott (Tandy 1992:10-11).

All of this history is important to understanding the changes that began in mid-1990. Barry Erasmus, then Stutterheim's town clerk, explained to a newspaper in 1991 "the origin of distrust and suspicion that had arisen from the land issue--when settlers came into the area and took possession of black ancestral land" (*Daily Dispatch* 11/7/91). Clearly, a great deal of what happened inbetween, including in relation to developmental and political grievances, also shaped the town's culture and race/class/gender relations. As in South Africa as a whole, the old way of doing business had to change, but the change itself could be mediated to suit the interests of elites.

What followed was the ascendance of *verligte* politicians in white Stutterheim politics and the moderation of a few central black leaders. To return to Bundy's description of missionaries, at this crucial stage of Stutterheim's development, leaders emerged as "torch-bearers of capitalist social norms and the market economy, as advocates of increased trade and commercial activity."

Reconciliation and the promise of development, 1990-1998

The change from early 1990 to mid-1991 was remarkable, by all accounts. As one reporter put it (Maclean 1991), "A year and a half ago, Stutterheim was a microcosm of everything wrong in South Africa." A great deal of attention has been paid to the extremely effective conflict-resolution function of the key leaders--amongst them Chris Magwangqana, Nico Ferreira, Loel Ferreira, Nosimo Balindlela, Miniyakhe Balindlela, Hamish Scott, and Max July--who were the founders of the Stutterheim Forum and later the Stutterheim Development Foundation (SDF) and various spin-off initiatives. The Forum was a negotiating platform with numerous subcommittees, and was established following a meeting in May 1990 led by the mayor (Ferreira) and main civic leader (Magwangquana), which also ended the boycott of Stutterheim's white shops and ultimately resulted in the SDF's prominence as the central strategic and implementing agency for LED.

Nussbaum (1997:2) considers the SDF--which had offices in the Stutterheim industrial site and a staff from across racial and class divides--a "Community-Based Organization," although in reality it much more closely resembles the corporate-sponsored Urban Foundation. In this case, similarly, Barlow Rand--itself submerged in a strike and threatened by a national boycott by several unions at the time, in 1990--sponsored much of the SDF's start-up activity and seconded the SDF's director (the former mayor, Ferreira, whose wife's brother was, coincidentally, the main Development Bank of Southern Africa sponsor of the SDF). Barlows was "a trusting, committed, unimposing outside champion," according to Nussbaum (1997:5). (Barlows also sponsored the 1998 NBI/IRI book on LED.)

There were other emblems of reconciliation established nationally and applied in Stutterheim. In 1991, the town Council sponsored five Forum leaders to attend the Old Mutual/Nedcor "Scenario on a New South Africa" in East London, and Council minutes show that copies of the book *The Heart of a Nation*--a neoliberal description of community development by Francis Kendall--were ordered for the Municipality of Stutterheim (hereafter "MoS") (MoS

1991b:5,7). Institutions like the Development Bank of Southern Africa (DBSA) and Independent Development Trust (IDT) became directly involved. Indeed, Ferreira had served as a project manager on a DBSA-sponsored project during the late 1980s and Magwangqana and Scott would later have jobs as IDT communications officer and project manager, respectively.

The Institute for a Democratic Alternative in South Africa held a transition conference in East London in 1991, in which, according to Ferreira (reporting back, as mayor, to his Council), "The Stutterheim model, a product of the Forum and its related committees, was referred to by a number of people, and what was happening locally drew much attention" (MoS 1991a:4). Stutterheim was, after all, "the only town in the country to achieve what it did on such a scale at the time," according to Pumla Kubukeli of the DBSA (Nussbaum 1997:1).

Politics moderated significantly under these circumstances. Magwangqana was quoted in the *Daily Dispatch* (Blacklaws 1991) as saying "the term 'radical' need no longer be applied to the white or black communities, as democratic forces had brought about significant changes in attitudes." According to Lt.Theo Meyer, "Police figures indicate that since 1989, there has been a remarkable decline in marches and political violence," cited by Nussbaum (1997:29) as a lead "indicator of success."

Yet this was not a universal sentiment. Magwangqana noted in a video documentary (SABC 1993) that the township leaders were accused by militant youth of selling out the struggle, a point reiterated by Max July (interview 1998). But although activism was apparent in protest marches in 1992 and 1993 (after the Boipatong and Bisho massacres and the Hani assassination)--Meyer acknowledges "eleven open air gatherings and marches" in 1993 (Nussbaum 1997:29)--there was a marked stagnation of the ANC's own local branch development (Tandy 1992). This led a researcher aligned to the Democratic Movement, Patrick Tandy of the progressive East London service NGO Corplan (1992:21), to worry that "The Stutterheim experience also alerts us to a number of possible pitfalls in engagement in development structures, namely, that there is a danger that communities can be drawn into local development to the exclusion of wider political activity."

The negotiations and reconciliation activities were occurring virtually entirely within the Forum during the early 1990s, while the development resources of local government were mainly denied to black residents. The Stutterheim Council occupied itself with an extremely narrow range of issues. Promotion of pigeon homing, dog licenses, Kruger Day, the German festival and the like took far more of the white councilors' meeting time than even the 1989-90 crisis, and there are no records in the Council minutes of any concrete action being taken--or concern registered--about the devastating consumer boycott.

To the extent development was considered for black residents, the Council resolved in March 1990 that a housing scheme could go ahead in Mlungisi provided that

> a buffer zone be created adjacent to white land owners and that the proposed future extensions be planned towards the airfield to allow for such a buffer zone. After a discussion it was resolved that the report of the Deputy Mayor Cllr P S Rautenbach be noted and that Council agree to a buffer zone being created and the proposed extension be as suggested. That this matter be referred to the town planner Mr Barrow for incorporation in the structure planning. (MoS 1990a:6)

And reflecting the spirit of what can only be described as "disengagement" that permeated municipal offices during the transition period, as early as April 1990 the possibility of privatizing services was officially mooted (MoS 1990b:2). By May 1993, First National Bank had presented a symposium on the issue (MoS 1993b:1). "Delegated management" to the privatized water company, Water and Sanitation of South Africa (WSSA, ultimately controlled by Lyonnais des Eaux), began during the 1994/95 fiscal year, leading to a dramatic increase in waterworks and sewerage spending for virtually the same levels of services, as shown below.

Only in July 1990 did Mayor Ferreira inform the Council about the status of the consumer boycott, referring to a meeting between the Forum's Steering Committee and three DBSA officials (MoS 1990c:1). At the same meeting it was recorded that the 1990 *Stutterheim Structure Plan*, carried out by Parkin, Tomlinson, and Partners, was invoiced at a price 50 percent higher than had been budgeted. (That *Structure Plan* was subsequently dropped and was replaced in 1991 by one funded by the DBSA and drafted by David Dewar, a University of Cape Town planner; a further *Structure Plan* was commissioned from Makalima Johnstone Associates and was due to be presented to the Council in 1998.)

Ferreira reported back again to Council in July 1990 that at the Forum "a lot of discussion hinged around the shortage of houses and the improvement and extension of the education system" (MoS 1990d:1).

But it was only in October 1990 that Council approved an investigation of a purification works and sewage treatment plant for Mlungisi (MoS 1990e:1).

Only occasionally did other local development issues--mainly disputes over paying for grazing land by residents of Cenyu, Cenyulands and Kubusie--arise in Council. As late as March 1993, Cenyulands farmers demanded "grazing land stretching to the mountains," the ability to pay rents for grazing at a later date, to erect a fence to split the municipal land into two sections, and to have more dams were all rejected by Council. The Town Clerk told Council that the 200 protestors who marched to town "were courting trouble as Stutterheim was still a declared unrest area but this fell on deaf ears" (MoS 1993a:7).

The DBSA emerged in early 1991 as the main outside funder of Dewar's new development plan. Yet apartheid segregation considerations were still dominant, for, in June 1991, Council considered whether the Boer War "concentration camp cemetery in the vicinity of [Mlungisi should] be included in the narrowing of the buffer strip" (MoS 1991c:4). And services for the new housing scheme were also of an earlier era, as they did not include electricity. There was also no funding left over for housing. Nevertheless, in August 1991, nearly 900 serviced sites were approved for Mlungisi by the IDT (MoS 1991d:4).

Reconciliation was also tempered by long-standing suspicions. The Stutterheim Council's Constitutional Committee, for example, approved the names of civic representatives for a transitional local authority in November 1991, but the committee "was not happy with the nomination received from the Cenyulands Civics" (MoS 1991e:1).

Finally, in April 1992, the coin dropped on local negotiators that the most durable problem of all--getting low-income residents to pay for municipal services--could not be resolved through an elite-pacting process that was celebrated as a political victory with little attention to development problems. Council minutes show that Mlungisi's

> financial position remains critical as, although a reduced service fee was negotiated with the Civics only a small percentage of the accruals per month are being paid. This is not as agreed to with the Civics who indicated a 100 percent commitment to paying the reduced fee.... This matter be discussed again at a later stage as Council moves towards an integrated community/council where the non-payment of service fees/charges will have to be addressed. (MoS 1992b:2)

This problem was also flagged by Tandy (1992:19), who, in a review of the Stutterheim experience, asked "How do we anticipate communities engaged in local development structures responding to a central government cut to development/municipal funding--e.g., cutting services, increasing service charges, winding down IDT/DBSA support?.... Municipalities normally expect full cost-recovery. This is unrealistic in the short, and even medium, term."

Although it was evidently impossible for the Council to impose the rule of law at this stage, the "integrated" (but only partially) community would indeed have to address municipal services non-payment within a few years. It is easy to hypothesize that within the broader local political settlement, a key understanding on the part of *verligte* whites was that in turning over the local state to black rule, *no real redistribution would take place.* From this unspoken consensus, in turn, a local economic development crisis was assured.

Local economic development crisis

The mythical status of Stutterheim as South Africa's premier LED success story is difficult to comprehend, given the distressing status of low-income people in the town during the late 1990s. An estimated three quarters of economically active people were formally unemployed, and about the same ratio were functionally illiterate (Chaturvedi 1996:4-5). Aside from an unverifiable, highly dubious claim that the area claimed a 15 percent annual economic growth rate, made by a former town clerk (SABC 1993) and repeated often enough elsewhere, the following were typically cited as triumphs: "Since 1992, the [SDF] has raised more than R25 million providing housing, schools, day care centers and more. A local business service center provides extensive consultation and advice supporting local entrepreneurs. Extensive educational and job skills training courses are other important functions of the Foundation" (NBI/IRI 1998:5).

Yet, as discussed below, the sustainability of these activities was soon thrown into question. Indeed there are many ways to understand Stutterheim's late 1990s local development crisis. Since municipal service delivery problems stood out in many South African townships--and indeed generated protest riots in some (Barchiesi 1998; Phadu 1998)--it may be most appropriate to begin with the sudden surge of service cuts that occurred during the last quarter of 1997 (the most recent "Project Viability" records provided by the Department of Constitutional Development for this study), before proceeding to a general examination of missed opportunities in municipal services "demand-side management," budget transformation, housing, small business and land reform--all leading to an uncertain but decidedly pessimistic future.

Municipal services: Tariffs, non-payment, and cut-offs

By year-end 1997, the Stutterheim Municipality's books carried chronic deficits in payments on several municipal accounts (although these were budgeted for surpluses) and an inherited provincial government loan of R3,682,098 was long in arrears, due (according to the acting treasurer) to "non-payment--lack of history supporting individual balances--not financially healthy to afford the cost of interest and redemption" (*sic*) (DCD 1997b:4). Stutterheim's financial problems were most often blamed on low payment levels for municipal services by Mlungisi township's low-income citizens. Of 4,468 Stutterheim households receiving accounts, 45 percent did not pay regularly. Punishment, in the form of cut-offs during late 1997 and early 1998, was severe.

The broader context, to repeat, was a virtually complete lack of household services to the nearly 20,000 residents of Greater Stutterheim who lived nearby--in Cenyu, Cenyulands and Kubusie--but fell outside the Stutterheim, Amatolaville, and Mlungisi boundaries. The situation was particularly dire in Mlungisi, where payment rates of 22 percent were recorded in early 1998 (down marginally from 25 percent during 1997). According to the Stutterheim treasurer, more than three out of five Mlungisi households--those with below R1,050 per month income--received "remissions" or sliding-scale payment subsidies, and 44 percent of Amatolaville households received remissions. A free-rider problem quickly emerged, according to officials, for "It was also discovered that consumers receiving a 100 percent remission have increased their water consumption by more than double!" (Stutterheim TLC 1998:1). As discussed in more detail below, such remissions were a far cry from the lifeline service and progressive block tariff system that could have been adopted. Means testing was unscientific, to put it mildly, in a township--Mlungisi--in which more than half the workers were unemployed.

Before looking at the remission schedule, consider the existing set of service charges. For households with less than a R550 monthly income, the connection fee (which included a 12 percent mark-up for WSSA) amounted to R60.23 (half the amount of the normal domestic connection) plus 14 percent Value Added Tax (VAT). In

Stutterheim/Amatolaville, "all income categories" of domestic residents paid the same monthly fees for refuse removal (R18.62) and sewage services (R39.12)--although business paid R31.46 and R66.30, respectively. For non-water-borne sewage, tanker removal in Mlungisi cost R93.09. The connection fee for water-borne sewage was R264.99 (Stutterheim TLC 1998:43). To the Council's credit, an attempt in June 1997 by commercial farmers within Stutterheim for reductions in rates and levies was rejected (MoS 1997d:8).

As for Mlungisi's recurrent water and electricity costs--the real basis for the arrears problem--there was only a slight concession to affordability and low quality of services. In Mlungisi, the flat rate for water on unmetered stands (before VAT was added) was R21.90; for refuse removal R18.62 (the same as in Stutterheim); and for basic services R21.90. Even the lowest-income residents were expected to pay R62 per month unless they received a remission. For those with metered stands, water was charged at a basic rate of R15.77 plus R1.80 per kiloliter above 11 per month; refuse removal was R18.62; sewerage for "informal dwellings" was R26.06; and basic charges were also R21.90 (Stutterheim TLC 1998:46). In Stutterheim and Amatolaville, the basic rate for water was R19.67 (i.e., R1.80 per liter for a minimum of 11 kiloliters per month) plus R1.80 for each additional kiloliter above 11 per month. In short, there was no tiered block charge for water consumption, so luxury consumption carried the same marginal cost as basic needs consumption.

Electricity, in contrast, was charged at variable rates, but these were, in fact, *regressive*. The two-tier block model charged consumption below 300 Kwh at 31 cents per Kwh and above at just 25 cents. In addition, a basic charge was levied, ranging upwards from R54.17 for single phase connections of below 20 Amps. New connections were charged R1,616.96 in Stutterheim, but as much as R3,419.89 in some outlying rural areas. Reconnection fees were R88.20 (Stutterheim TLC 1998:44). According to treasurer Geoffrey Hill (interview 1998), the National Electricity Regulator--at the time, influenced by cost-recovery principles--wrote to the Council in March 1998 informing them that their tariff schedule was disapproved and that they should not have any block tariff, whether regressive or progressive.

The failure to redistribute income through tariff reform--whether water or electricity--cost Stutterheim dearly, not only in socio-economic terms but because using cost-recovery methods it was impossible to balance the books. All told, while South Africa as a whole witnessed accumulated arrears of debtors reaching 27 percent of the value of municipal accounts in 1997, Mlungisi's had risen to 112 percent by year's end (at R2,149,619--including balances older than three years, which had not yet been written off--compared to charges of R1,917,600). The combined Stutterheim/Amatolaville's ratio was just 15 percent (Stutterheim TLC 1998:3).

These figures hint at the underlying issue, which was the maldistribution of basic infrastructural resources in a context of generalised poverty. They also indicate the potential solution, which was to view the provision of a lifeline service of water and electricity to all Stutterheim's residents--followed by a steep rising block tariff to pay for consumption--as integral to a bottom-up LED strategy. Instead of drawing such obvious lessons, Stutterheim's local officials focused on getting politicians to address the non-payment problem.

Extremely low payment rates in Mlungisi were initially recorded during the 1991/92 fiscal year. At that stage, however, central government's Intergovernmental Grant (IGG) mechanism was providing sufficient subsidy funding that Stutterheim and most other municipalities rarely resorted to service cuts. But the national budget commitment to IGGs fell, in real terms, by 85 percent over the subsequent six years, from R856 million (in 1990 rand) to just R133 million in 1997/98 (Financial and Fiscal Commission 1997:20). This left most South African municipalities to engage in service cuts by late 1997.

A variety of discussions about low payment rates were held in the Stutterheim Council, which with its increased credibility was now expected, by officials and outgoing white councilors, to clamp down on what became generally known as "the culture of non-payment" of service charges. Simultaneously, at national level Operation Masakhane--"let us build together"--was a R30-million campaign founded in February 1995 and largely built on advertizing. By July 1995, the failure of the national housing policy was evident, as Minister Sankie Mthembi-Mahanyele labeled the program she had inherited from her predecessor Joe Slovo "toilets-in-the-veld" and as rates payments in many Gauteng townships fell to below 5 percent (see below, Chapter Eleven). But national pressure on local authorities to cut services intensified.

By early 1996, a few months after the first democratic municipal elections in South Africa's history, the new Stutterheim Council had achieved sufficient legitimacy to consider "drastic steps to be implemented with regard to the recovery of arrear service charges and the commencement with general payment of service charges" (MoS 1996a:9-10). Interestingly, to this end, the engineers Ove Arup developed a video "intended for use as a method to encourage people to pay service charges," but their R40,000 bill was considered so "excessive" that the Council "furthermore questions whether the beneficiaries of the Old Mlungisi Project supported this expenditure" (MoS 1996a:9-10).

Disconnections were clearly now on the agenda, including "cutting off services for certain periods during the day and thereafter monitoring the effects thereof and reaction thereto" (MoS 1996a:10). Disconnection of even water was not limited to Mlungisi, as the new Council agreed that "the Amatola Regional Services Council (ARSC) be advised that unless outstanding amounts in respect of services rendered to Cenyu, Cenyulands and Kubusie by the Transitional Local Council on behalf of the ARSC are settled the services will be discontinued without further notice" (MoS 1996a:10).

Hence, in the three non-municipal townships, the Stutterheim Council was by now prepared to engage in mass cut-offs of the inadequate (communal tap) water supply regardless of individual propensity to pay. The fault for non-payment may not have been with the residents, but with the contractor (ultimately the Amatola District Council), which had no feasible means of directly supplying services to its constituents, locked in as they were to residual apartheid-era patterns of residential segregation. A few weeks later, the Amatola District Council's (ADC's) chief executive formally confirmed receipt of a Stutterheim bill for R49,000 "in respect of water consumed by the residents of Cenyu, Cenyulands, and Kubusie which had been paid by the ADC on behalf of the residents." Yet since the ADC had no means of billing the township residents, the ADC chief executive now expected "a firm proposal" from the Stutterheim Transitional Rural Council (STRC)--which itself had practically no capacity, and which reported to the ADC--"in conjunction with community structures in respect of the payment for services," failing which he "would have no other alternative but to request [Stutterheim] to discontinue with services to the abovementioned areas" (MoS 1996b:13). Although water supplies had reportedly not been cut to the STRC towns by 1998 (interview with STRC chief executive, 1998), other Stutterheim services remained out of reach. Access to the library was effectively denied residents of outlying townships, on economic grounds. The Stutterheim Council refused, in

August 1997, to waive the R50 fee for access to the library, which was payable by residents of Cenyu, Cenyulands and Kubusie (MoS 1997e:10).

Mlungisi, as a formal part of Stutterheim, fared little better, although to its credit the Stutterheim Council beat back an old-guard attempt to restore the apartheid town's geographical inheritance. The Stutterheim treasurer was told by Council at that same January 1996 meeting to "once and for all 'bury' the Old Cumakala Town Council concept and ensure that all financial administration is finalized and integrated with the Stutterheim Transitional Local Council by the end of March 1996" (MoS 1996a:10). Nevertheless, Mlungisi was still subject to far lower-quality standards than in Stutterheim. In February 1996, the treasurer conceded that "intermittent supply problems occurred as a result of existing pipes being damaged which resulted in an irregular supply of water to Mlungisi" and, as a result, disconnections should be postponed until supply was normal (MoS 1996b:13).

A month later, the Council declared April would be "the month for the commencement with the payment of service charges" and threatened that "if by the end of April there was no significant improvement with regard to the payment of services charges, e.g. approximately 60 percent," then

> i) Electricity and water accounts in arrear be cut off with immediate effect and without private arrangements between regular defaulters and officials, however genuine cases who request deferment in payment due to financial reasons be considered on merit, a cut off list be made available one week after due date for payment whereafter water meters be removed and sealed where possible....
> ii) Withdrawal of services to be focused on areas where payment is lowest;
> iii) Employers and employees be consulted in an effort to reach agreement on a voluntary basis whereby the employer may deduct outstanding service charges from the wages/salaries of employees by means of stop order facilities....
> iv) That the use of the traffic vehicle and Traffic Officer be authorized so as to enable the respective ward Councilors to inform residents of the consequences with regard to default....
> v) Switching off of street and high mast lighting from Mondays to Thursdays, whereafter these be switched back on again during week-ends, subject to careful consideration of the implications of such action particularly with regard to the already serious crime rate in certain areas and based on the principle of "with darkness comes crime," however the message and intention to the residents must be loud and clear;

> vi) Discontinuation with the provision of refuse removal services to individuals who were in arrears;
> vii) the utilization of debt collectors and attorneys with regard to the recovery of arrear service charges be considered after all other measures have proved to be unsuccessful....
> viii) The employment of casual labor be scaled down to the minimum with the exception of project based labor....
> ix) A moratorium be placed on the appointment of additional new staff until such time there was a satisfactory improvement of the situation with regard to the payment of service charges;
> x) That the Finance Committee investigate the possibility of introducing an incentive scheme in respect of those consumers who commence with the payment of service charges and who pay before due date or in advance;
> xi) That the determined and approved "flat rate" system be retained until such time that all areas were supplied with individually metered services. (MoS 1996c:14-15)

The eleven measures included three (ii, v, and vi) that constituted collective punishment of a geographical area notwithstanding the possibility that individuals in the area were not themselves personally guilty of non-payment. The temptation to punish labor for community non-payment (viii, ix) was also clearly a divide-and-rule attempt that the SA Municipal Workers Union (SAMWU) was at the same time beginning to contest with its unity slogan, "No to privatization, 50 liters of water per person per day free!" Because of the intensifying financial pressure, however, Stutterheim Council began employing casual laborers for long periods of duration, to which SAMWU later unsuccessfully objected (MoS 1997a:3).

By May 1996, the treasurer testified "that although the payment of service charges had increased to 20 percent in respect of April 1996 this was still far from satisfactory and a marked improvement thereon was essential." But the treasurer also reported that "services such as water and High Mast Lighting would be 100 percent normal by 1 June 1996 which included the repairing of all High Mast Lighting, upgrading power supply to newly erected pump station, and installation of bigger dimension main supply piping" (MoS 1996d:13). In fact, substandard and broken services to Mlungisi continued, leaving the authors of the October 1997 *Stutterheim Draft Structure Plan* to comment, "Losses of [water] pressure also occur as Mlungisi is fed through the central area of town, and the TLC is investigating the possibility of diverting the flow to Mlungisi to avoid the central area of town" (Makalima Johnston Associates 1997:18).

To the Council's credit, it finally came to realize that non-payment wasn't a matter of choice. Councilors requested information in May 1996 about, "as a matter of extreme urgency, ways and means of implementing remission of service charges for those people who genuinely cannot afford to pay" (MoS 1996d:13), a group that quickly became the majority of Mlungisi residents and almost a majority of Amatolaville residents. The remission strategy included a schedule for rebates that ranged from 100 percent for households with less than R300 per month income, to 3 percent for households whose income was between R1,026 and R1,505. For every R25 per month additional income, an additional 3 percent of the municipal service charges had to be paid. The amounts in remission claimed by the 61 percent of Mlungisi households (numbering 1,170) plus the 40 percent of Amatolaville households (numbering 83) who received rebates, rose from R93,762 in September 1997 to R113,848 in February 1998. The average monthly rebate was more than R90 over the period.

Before the remissions system became fully operative, however, service cut-offs remained a potent tool for the Stutterheim Council. The first wedge would, "once the services .... have been restored to 100 percent normality," be "the withdrawal of refuse removal services with effect from 7 June 1996.... as a first step towards implementing punitive measures" (MoS 1996d:13). That services never achieved 100 percent normality did not stop the cut-offs, nor did the cut-offs succeed in increasing the payment levels.

Nor did cut-offs help in providing new connections to those without services. Frustrated by the lack of progress in the Mzamomhle area of Mlungisi, the local civic association zone committee--Mzamomhle SANCO--requested in February 1997 that Eskom be allowed to take responsibility for supplying electricity (in view of the failure of the Council to extend its services to the area). This was a mistake, however, earning a stern--even defensive and arrogant--rebuke from the Council (MoS 1997c:4; 1997b:8):

> i) Council takes exception to the fact that they keep on by-passing Council in matters pertaining to the area, thereby creating the impression that they do not accept the authority of Council.
>
> ii) That as they are part and parcel of the Stutterheim TLC area Council will in future not entertain or pay attention to any requests unless the correct channels of communication are strictly adhered to, i.e. correspondence to be directed to the Town Clerk for presentation to Council.

iii) Council insists that the Mzamomhle Village SANCO attend meetings held by Councilors in Mlungisi as they cannot be treated in isolation of the rest of the area, failing which no attention will be given to any requests made by them.

(The breakaway of a zone of SANCO from ANC loyalty or merely from adherence to established procedures of municipal governance--which was also evident in SANCO-ANC tensions surrounding the SDF--was not unusual in mid-1990s South Africa, particularly given systematic attempts at national level and in many provinces and locales to co-opt SANCO through corporatist deal-making. Attempting to play the dual role of community mobilizers and close allies of the governing political party often proved difficult for SANCO leaders, who faced on the one hand grassroots rebellions and on the other, deals that didn't deliver. Nationally, SANCO's investment arm, headed by Moses Mayekiso, decided to participate in joint municipal infrastructure ventures with the British firm Biwater, which became controversial in Nelspruit when virtually all civil society forces opposed this pilot case of water privatization. In Stutterheim, a parallel phenomenon was the decision by SANCO's general secretary to take a job with WSSA, promoting water privatization.)

When finally the Council agreed to make a request to Eskom on behalf of residents, the parastatal replied in October 1997 that "it was not in a position at the present time to electrify Mzamomhle" and would only be able to evaluate such a proposal when "occupation exceeds 80 percent.... permanent houses are built and occupied; an approved surveyor general layout plan is available; and housing and civil services are completed" (MoS 1997f:6). Notwithstanding the informal character of many of the Mzamomhle dwellings, the Stutterheim Council eventually approved electrical hookups (interview, Councillor Anna-Marie Mayekiso 1998).

In mid-1997, arrears had reached such high levels (more than 100 percent of the recurrent bill) that Council decided to take even more drastic measures. By October, a "think-tank" met to discuss "Credit Policy" and decided that

i) in respect of the nonpayment of electricity (conventional meters) such service to be cut off and not reconnected until all services such as water, sewerage, refuse including electricity have been paid up to date or acceptable arrangements having been made with the Town Treasurer in respect of payment of all arrears;

ii) in case of prepaid electricity meters the issue of "coupons" BE BARRED until such time all other services such as water, sewerage and

> refuse have been paid up to date or acceptable arrangements for payments having been made with the Town Treasurer;
> iii) that in the case of defaulters in respect of non-payment of water, such service to be cut and not reconnected until such time all services such a sewerage and refuse have been paid up to date or acceptable arrangements having been made with the Town Treasurer in respect of payment of arrears service charges and furthermore that a disconnection fee of R50 BE LEVIED to cover costs with regard to disconnection and such levy to be reviewed annually when the budget is prepared;
> iv) should the actions as more fully detailed above still not have the desired impact, Council will have no other alternative in spite of the crime factor to cut off electricity in respect of the high mast lighting. (MoS 1997f:10-11)

Hence, cut-offs commenced that left nearly a fifth of Mlungisi without access to household water. In November 1997, 400 Mlungisi households and 45 Amatolaville households had their water supplies disconnected. Only 35 households subsequently made payments so as to have their water service reconnected (DCD 1997b:4). In interviews, one of the town's councilors and its treasurer surmised, however, that Mlungisi residents whose services were cut were either using their neighbors' water, which was now partially (or in some cases fully) subsidized, or using nearby communal standpipes that were legacies of the old government's provision of infrastructure. The implications, however, of the cut-offs for sanitation, sewerage, and public health were not known, nor had they been considered.

In addition, electricity disconnections numbered 70 during the fourth quarter, with 34 paying to be reconnected (DCD 1997b:4). The number increased dramatically in the town of Stutterheim, from average monthly levels of 25 during 1997, to 112 in February and March 1998. In Amatolaville, average electricity cut-offs of 1 per month during 1997 soared to 48 during March 1998. The Council's policy was to cut off electricity services to all people whose accounts showed any indebtedness (even if not on the electricity account). Of electricity cuts, only 50 percent of households cut off later reconnected.

The October 1997 think-tank was followed, the next day, by a frightening letter from the Eastern Cape Member of the Executive Committee responsible for local government, which cited Project Viability estimates that only 10 percent of South Africa's municipalities were financially viable. The letter notified town treasurers that their books would be looked at by an accounting firm to identify whether their municipalities were part of the problem. At the subsequent

Council meeting, one councilor "voiced his dissatisfaction regarding the short-notice 'Walk through Audit' to be carried out on instruction from MEC for Local Government and Housing.... stating that such action has caused considerable delay in implementing Councils' Credit Policy" (MoS 1997f:12). This was not to be the case in Stutterheim, as November witnessed a mass disconnection of water in Mlungisi. Yet the result, by January 1998, was a decline in Mlungisi's payments rate.

Neglect of demand-side management

A large amount of time and energy was paid by Stutterheim officials and Councilors in trying to make people pay, in a context in which most could not, objectively, afford to. The main reasons higher levels of payment were required, were to increase the amount available for capital expenditure (and hence, potentially, new connections) and to fund the recurrent (operating and maintenance) costs of the services. Some such capital expenditure would not be required, however, if conservation were to take place. And payment requirements for recurrent costs could also have been mitigated by cross-subsidization through a socially just progressive block tariff with lifeline service. Such outcomes, which were not considered by the Stutterheim Council or its officials, would depend upon an effective "demand-side management" strategy.

Demand-side management was by the late 1990s an emerging subdiscipline of resource economics that drew attention not just to building supply-side capital projects (water works and other bulk infrastructure) to quench an unsatiable thirst for water and other services, but attempted to better distribute those resources so that basic consumption norms were met and other socio-economic and ecological goals, especially conservation, were achieved. Demand management techniques included repairing leaky pipes; changing water usage patterns through progressive block tariffs; embarking upon water conservation education; imposing regulations prohibiting excessive watering of gardens; and applying a variety of physical interventions. Amongst the latter were the replacement or installation of low-flow showerheads, dual-flush toilets, and similar mechanical interventions, as well as saving more water through clearing invasive alien trees and vegetation.

For example, the extent to which Mlungisi's water losses could be attributed to leaky pipes (or washers) and faulty infrastructure was unknown to officials. Investigating was, the treasurer conceded, "the most difficult task," for "Line losses do occur, but is very time-consuming" to calculate (Stutterheim TLC 1998:4). No attempt was made to bring community organizations into the process of monitoring water use and leakage. Yet Mlungisi's outdated apartheid infrastructure was a well-known problem, and the following comment appears in the October 1997 *Draft Structure Plan*: "The major problem with water supply in Stutterheim is that of water losses through old and inadequate water mains. There is thus a need to investigate costs of replacing many of the internal pipelines to limit losses" (Makalima Johnston Associates 1997:18). Under a system of fully privatized water provision, it would have been reasonable to expect the privatized water supply company, WSSA, to repair the Mlungisi pipes. But due to "cherry-picking"--the tendency of firms to avoid doing business in low-income areas--WSSA only provided service to Stutterheim and Amatolaville. (WSSA did make proposals to serve Mlungisi, but these were considered financially disadvantageous, according to Councillor Anna-Marie Mayekiso [interview 1998]).

That delegation of management for water provision, to WSSA, was to cost R753,575 in 1997/98. (The second largest expense in the water budget was R290 265 in interest payments on previous capital expenditure.) The "delegated management" line item began in the 1994/95 budget, and led to an increase from 1993/94 of 12 percent (R60,000) for salaries/wages/allowances, general expenses, repairs/maintenance and contribution to capital outlay associated with water. In addition, Stutterheim municipality took responsibility for covering R100,000 in additional interest and redemption charges on capital that year (a 130 percent increase on 1993/94), for water works now run by WSSA. To pay for this, the fees paid by water consumers were increased from R492,250 to R657,000.

However, notwithstanding the poor payments record and the additional costs associated with the privatization of water, the municipal water budget had a projected surplus of R136,825 for 1997/98. In addition, the sewerage budget included privatized services ("delegation of management") costing R439,446, also to WSSA, with high sewerage fees anticipated to generate a surplus of R164,782. Those surpluses were redirected into other aspects of the budget, rather than to expanding basic provision of services in Stutterheim's townships.

At the same time, Stutterheim dramatically increased its capital expenditure on the bulk water works, raising the capacity by 67 percent, from 1.5 ml/day to 2.5 ml/day, in the process incurring extremely expensive debt-servicing obligations. Apparently there was little or no attention in the Council or in the Stutterheim budget to demand-side management. The irony was that retail services were desperately necessary and were not being adequately funded, while expensive bulk water supply could have been mitigated through conservation on the demand side.

A small program to clear invasive aliens was funded through the national Working for Water scheme. But even this could have been expanded dramatically, given that, according to the *Stutterheim Draft Structure Plan*, "Invasion by black wattle and other alien species is a serious problem in Stutterheim, leading to a reduction in stream flow and diminution of wildlife habitat" (Makalima Johnston Associates 1997:12).

How much water could have been saved through such measures? Preston and Davies (1994) estimated 30 percent in typical South African conditions, hence reducing the need for large capital projects while at the same time assuring all residents a fair share of access to water--not through an open-ended and ultimately unsustainable indigents' fund (i.e., remissions on 61 percent of Mlungisi accounts and 44 percent of Amatolaville accounts) but instead through socially just tariff pricing.

Much the same principles applied to electricity pricing, which in Stutterheim was based on a regressive (not progressive) block tariff with an incentive to higher usage. Electricity fees generated a substantial anticipated income of R3,794,380 for 1997/98, permitting a surplus on the electricity account of R998,344. The main expenditures were R1,440,312 on raw electricity from Eskom and another R1.5 million on administration, salary, and other costs. Repairs and maintenance only accounted for R129,900, and capital charges (interest and redemption) for another R225,057. Connection and reconnection fees brought in only R96,000 for the 1997/98 year, indicating that fewer than 50 new accounts were supplied, notwithstanding the tens of thousands of residents in the greater Stutterheim area without electricity.

Unfortunately, the *Draft Structure Plan* did not set out demand management techniques such as cross-subsidization as options for infrastructure and services delivery. After making many observations about needs in this area, including detailed suggestions on projects, the authors proceeded to reiterate "Development Principles" which were originally "drawn up during the previous Framework Plan process" (Makalima Johnston Associates 1997:31). The last three (classically neoliberal formulations) are worth repeating *verbatim* [italics added, with commentary in brackets]:

- *As far as possible, decision-making should be consensus-based.* [Power relations surrounding the various stakeholders were hence ignored, permitting those with greater vested interests and ability to articulate these to dominate, as they did in relation to distribution of services.]
- *The principle of paying for services received must be respected.* [The possibility of a lifeline service was hence discounted from the outset.]
- *The upgrading of existing facilities and services, as well as new projects, servicing, housing and community developments, should be done in such a way that choice is maximized: people should not be forced into options which they do not want and particularly, that they cannot afford.* [If "choice" was based mainly on affordability, this left little or no choice, regarding development, to those who were poor.]

Finally, none of the extensive economic multipliers and other benefits of better demand management--including direct economic benefits (employment, SMME creation, productivity enhancements, smallholder irrigation, etc) and indirect public health, environmental, and gender benefits--were factored into Stutterheim's municipal services. Nor did such considerations apparently inform the town's broader budget.

Unreconstructed budget

Stutterheim's late 1990s budget expenditures for water, sanitation, and electricity were carefully considered in the previous section. There are a variety of other areas of the annual budget--in 1997/98, amounting to R11.4 million--that reflected a lack of transformation. Most importantly, the municipality cut back substantially on its capital spending, from 1996/97 levels of R1,706,645. That year, major expenses included upgrading the electricity network (R298,000) and installing the Lower Kologha Waterline (R232,100), the Mlungisi Main Water Supply (R219,750), public toilets in Stutterheim (R186,800) and a computer network for the town treasurer (R128,000). In 1997/98, the anticipated total capital spending slipped to R1,336,022, with the only major expenditures accounted for in the form of a new grader (R350,000) and an electricity ring connection to Lower Kologha (R140,000). Water reticulation spending fell from R67,500 to R50,000.

Amongst general expenditures, public health spending rose from 1996/97 to 1997/98 due to a 20 percent salary increase and a dramatic increase in medicines (from R60,000 to R248,928). However, public health income also increased, from R678,008 in 1996/97 to an anticipated R1,018,746 in 1997/98, largely due to a near doubling of the provincial government's health subsidy. The public health budget was targeted for a tiny surplus for 1997/98 after suffering a R40,915 deficit in 1996/97. The requirement that the municipality shoulder a greater healthcare budgetary requirement should have sensitized Councilors to the implications of service cuts for public health, but apparently did not.

Aside from public works (R964,092 deficit), the biggest single deficit item in the budget was for Parks, Gardens and Sportfields (R372,457, which included in 1997/98 a 40 percent increase for salaries/wages and allowances, to R303,204, in comparison to 1993/94, in which of R143,840 in spending less than R100,000 was for salaries and wages). Most of the public recreational facilities in Stutterheim--including the town park--were still located in the immediate vicinity of the wealthier residential areas. In any event, according to the *Draft Structure Plan*, Stutterheim's other recreational facilities were "generally of a private nature (e.g. the Country Club and Golf Course, as well as the swimming pool at Stutterheim High School). There is a need for public facilities such as sports fields both in the central part of town and Mlungisi" (Makalima Johnston Associates 1997:20).

Other aspects of the 1997/98 budget that bear mentioning included the 33 percent increase in Councilors' salaries (to R221,760); the housing budget which in 1997/98 was limited entirely to paying off the capital charges (R386,308) and associated expenses for the Cumukala housing loans (there were more tens of thousands of rands allocated to housing allowances and subsidies for Council officials); large maintenance expenses (R130,000) on regravelling instead of tarring roads; declining expenditure on refuse removal (yet a budgeted R43,254 surplus); a deficit on the cemetery--still geographically segregated by income class--of R28,149; and the continuation of small donations (of R13,000) to organizations that did not explicitly include community groups from the black townships (but that did include the Amateur Dramatic Society).

Could the budget have been transformed during the 1993/94-1997/98 period? Perhaps, but to be fair it must be pointed out that fiscal constraints associated with government's macroeconomic policy may also have played a role in locking in existing spending. The total government subsidy for Stutterheim in 1995/96 was R899,433. That was anticipated to rise to R1,003,262 in 1996/97 but, in reality, instead fell to R515,797 (the shortfall was covered by increased fee income). For 1997/98, the government subsidy fell further still, to R165,425. In real (after-inflation) terms, this 90 percent decline in central to local spending represented one of the most important constraints to Stutterheim's future transformation.

Growing housing backlogs

According to Stutterheim's *Draft Structure Plan*, "In the lower income residential areas, there is a great need for the upgrading of both services and housing. There is a need to expand the existing residential development in Stutterheim, as the future demand has been estimated to be in excess of 2,000 stands" (Makalima Johnston Associates 1997:19). This is an understatement, of course, given that the housing shortage legitimately extends to many tens of thousands of greater Stutterheim residents who live in impermanent, substandard housing. Indeed, according to the Plan, "The highest priority identified in the majority of the community workshops was that of the need to develop additional residential land" (Makalima Johnston Associates 1997:32).

Yet the "to do" list of development proposals in the October 1997 *Draft Structure Plan* gives some indication of just how little success has been witnessed in housing delivery since 1990. The following were fairly rudimentary steps associated with low-cost housing delivery, but had apparently not been undertaken by October 1997: verify and finalize housing waiting lists in Kologha, Ohlsen, Amatolaville, and Mlungisi; identify best suitable land; workshop desirable stand sizes with community; formation of social compact; prepare application for housing subsidy; access all available sources of additional funding; secure bridging finance; workshop land ownership/tenure options with community; implement housing delivery scheme; and establish participants for land transactions and costs.

What this list of "necessary actions" disguised, however, was a crucial housing policy prerequisite. Stutterheim essentially agreed to forfeit its responsibility to provide and maintain any form of public housing when in 1991 the Independent Development Trust's site-and-service model was adopted. Nel (1994:374) aptly described the function of housing privatization, as facilitated by the IDT in Stutterheim: "The injection of finance into the town has assisted the municipality through the removal of responsibility for providing housing sites." According to Max July (interview, 1998), the IDT funding did not pay for electricity, nor was there a top-up due according to the new 1994 national housing policy. Moreover, according to July, "There was protest over the small size of houses" built using the IDT subsidy.

The removal of municipal responsibility was marginally reversed after the 1995 local government elections, when the Council gradually began to take on responsibilities, no longer as a municipal developer of housing but instead as facilitator. Yet even this role was constrained by the difficulties presented by the developer-driven character of the national housing policy. For in undertaking Stutterheim's main housing project--500 units in Mlungisi, proposed initially in 1993--the two firms involved, Grinaker Construction and Ove Arup, spent an excessive amount (R9,000 per unit) on the provision of services during construction in 1997, leaving an insufficient amount for the top structure. Then, in December 1997, the Council realized that they had little room to maneuver when "Grinaker indicated that they were not in a position to continue with the project until they have received financial details" (MoS 1997g), presumably about how the Council wanted to proceed with funding house construction. Less than a year earlier, Grinaker had entered the Eastern Cape with the claim that it would generate 20,000 houses if given the opportunity to utilize their "bottoms up (*sic*) people driven" process (MoS 1997a:4), which indeed was the basis for the Council transferring the long-delayed construction of the 500 units (interview, Anna-Marie Mayekiso, 1998).

One of the core functions of post-apartheid municipal government is identifying Land Development Objectives. The Development Facilitation Act mandates that these integrate social, economic, institutional, and physical aspects of land development; integrate rural and urban areas in support of each other; assure optimal use of resources such as agriculture, land, minerals, bulk infrastructure, roads, transportation, and social facilities; discourage urban sprawl; and correct historically distorted spatial patterns while utilizing existing infrastructure. (There were other objectives, but those above were most directly relevant to the problem of post-apartheid municipal integration.) A coherent urban-rural form was a theme repeated in the development plan mooted by Dewar (cited in Nussbaum 1997:78), who noted that, as central pillars of the "developmental philosophy,"

> Small towns and settlements such as Stutterheim are an integral part of rural South Africa. Their future is tied to the future of their rural hinterlands. A crucial part of the development process, therefore, must be integrating urban and rural functions so that each complements and supplements the other.... Greater Stutterheim, though spatially divided, is one community: the interests and futures of sub-communities are inextricably interrelated. Both the problems and solutions of sub-communities, therefore, must be owned by all.

These were excellent ambitions for overturning the inherited apartheid settlement form. But here not only were the contradictions between theory and reality revealed in the decision to omit most of Greater Stutterheim from municipal service delivery, as discussed above. In addition, Stutterheim's East London planners also endorsed, in practice, contrary residential development objectives that exacerbated the tendency of class segregation to replace racial segregation. While denying this in principle--lip service was paid to establishing a single town "integrated physically, fiscally, administratively and politically"--Makalima Johnstone Associates gave this tendency full momentum by evoking "density" as a euphemism for class.

Thus, although demand for "medium to low density housing" was "limited," Makalima Johnston Associates (1997:34-35) set out several exclusive areas for development, including in-fill housing in the center of town. Moreover, high-density, high-cost housing should also be constructed in geographically-favorable areas: "Based on discussions with residents and local estate agents, there appears to be a need for additional flats and townhouses. These should be developed close to town around the Central Business District, where land and services are available." High-cost housing should also be located on 20 hectares of suitable commonage land immediately to the north and south of town, according to Makalima Johnston Associates (the low-income townships of Mlungisi, Cenyu, and Cenyulands are due east, and Kubusie is southwest of Stutterheim, so this trajectory of housing development for high cost housing would utilize land that could otherwise have been allocated to lower-income people desiring closer proximity to amenities).

In contrast, Makalima Johnston Associates (1997:32-34) observed, there were four options for high-density, low-cost housing to serve the 2,600 households (from Mlungisi, Kologha and Amatolaville) who were on formal housing waiting lists in 1997. Tellingly, even though land directly adjacent to Kubusie was cited for development, no Kubusie (or Cenyu or Cenyulands) residents were considered in need of Stutterheim housing.

Indeed, where there existed a (single) low-cost housing development option that had the potential to border wealthier neighborhoods near the golf course, the Makalima Johnston Associates (1997:33) planners were quick to point out that "Previous discussion that this portion of commonage should be set aside for future low-density residential usage is recorded. Many residents regard the area as prime land and if utilized for high-density housing will lead to depreciation of adjoining properties" (*sic*). The potential class bias of the "many residents" referred to was not recorded. Of the other three options, two included extending and amplifying the inherited apartheid geography of Stutterheim, by building on the southeast end of Mlungisi or west of Amatolaville, while the last option was a small piece of land around Amatolaville.

Most importantly, low-income residents were implicitly excluded from potentially well-located developments on in-fill spaces within Stutterheim, on nearby buffer land such as between Kubusie and Stutterheim, or just north of Stutterheim. In sum, the Makalima Johnston Associates' *Draft Structure Plan* dispensed with the early 1990s attempt to reinforce a physical buffer zone separating the white residential area from the African township, but its income-related planning had much the same effect.

These observations are made not to deny that very gradual racial desegregation was taking place. With one exception, the key Mlungisi leaders active in the SDF from 1990 moved to Stutterheim; several earned sufficient incomes from well-paying Bisho jobs to afford bond payments. The one SDF leader who didn't move by 1998 was Max July, who in an interview confirmed he stayed in his (unserviced) Mlungisi residence "to promote self-help."

Small business cul-de-sacs

The pride of Stutterheim's LED efforts is entrepreneurial training and small business promotion. Yet in the most important respects--retention of trained people in the community through local job creation, and enterprise sustainability--the SDF and its two main education/training and advice center offshoots were not successful.

The Business Advice Center provided support to entrepreneurs in the form of skills development (geared to local resources such as wood and sewing); assistance in the location of raw materials; facilitation of premises such as a hand weavers' workshop and rural market workshops; and marketing assistance. There was an attempt to establish six periodic markets (for sales of locally-grown agricultural products) linked to pension payouts, but these "never worked," according to Max July (interview, 1998).

Addressing the perennial problem of access to credit, the Advice Center and Eastern Cape Development Agency (ECDA) established a group credit scheme that replaced what Dewar (1997:82) had described as a "not particularly successful" small loan scheme of the Kei Development Trust. Writing in October 1994, Dewar (1997:83) found the new ECDA scheme was "particularly successful," yet after a facilitator--an American citizen--left, the scheme collapsed, according to Max July (interview, 1998).

More generally, bank credit for small entrepreneurs was unavailable in Stutterheim (interviews, 1998). There was allegedly no local decision-making power on the part of the town's bank branch managers, and although Stutterheim municipality possessed R5.3 million in four bank accounts (R3 million with First National Bank and R2.3 million with Unibank) in 1998, it had never enquired about the possibility of linking such deposits to lending relationships (Stutterheim TLC 1998:7; interview, Ferreira, 1998).

Thus, without credit, the Stutterheim entrepreneurial projects most often celebrated had a built-in ceiling on growth, leaving most beneficiaries of programs stuck in the cul-de-sacs of hawking and sewing, according to Councillor and entrepreneur Anna-Marie Mayekiso (interview, 1998). Moreover, she continued, of the ten sewing ventures begun during the early 1990s, only three still existed in 1998. Although pottery and shoe-making enterprises were still in business, there was nothing like the growth required to catalyze employment generation on anything more than a token scale.

Reflecting the limits of the entrepreneurial strategy, the other area of Stutterheim's community upliftment most often praised is privatized educational and child-care support. Yet here too the famous Amakhaya home-based educare creche program ran into difficulties associated with a neoliberal conception of the daycare problem and its self-help solution. Instead of receiving generous municipal funding, as would be a reasonable demand by residents, the creche scheme was based on a discrete intervention to rationalize child care, but with as little involvement as possible by the state. Ironically, the founder of the scheme (Nosimo Balindlela) went on to become the MEC for Education in the first post-apartheid Eastern Cape provincial cabinet (although she was dismissed from this position in early 1998). "In the initial conception," according to Dewar,

> the Amakhaya mothers were appointed by, and were accountable to parent groups, which in turn were responsible for collecting contributions from parents. The Foundation, in all good faith and with the best of intentions, raised some finance to supplement the "pocket money" of the mothers and paid this to them directly. This created the perception that the mothers were "employed" by the Foundation: this led to reduced contributions by parents and discontent over "levels of pay" on the part of the mothers. (1997:89)

For Dewar (1997:89), this problem reflected merely "confusion" in "lines of accountability," rather than a misguided structural relationship of workers to employers, and of citizens to their local state.

Land reform paralysis

"Land reform is failing here," commented Stutterheim Councillor Anna-Marie Mayekiso (interview, 1998). The main evidence of land reform in the Stutterheim area in the late 1990s was the 1995 demarcation of an additional 1,031 plots on the Mgwali commonage, which codified existing arrangements but which also exacerbated legal conflicts over control of the commonage land and social conflicts between long-term quitrent tenure holders and those without tenure security. The divisions generated by differential tenure, and the overall paralysis in redistributing the Stutterheim area's rural land, are the main reflections of ongoing rural development crisis. But the complete lack of access to water and any other municipal services also serves as a warning for the time in the near future when Mgwali and other peripheral--though densely-populated--rural areas will fall under Stutterheim municipal rule.

In 1995, 65 holders of quitrent tenure who were dispossessed during the betterment-era demarcation of sites, filed a Land Claims Court claim in 1995. The 1993 Upgrading of Land Tenure Rights Act allowed quitrent tenure to convert automatically, upon application, to freehold status. But to access the sites on the commonage from which the quitrent holders were dispossessed during the 1960s-70s reversion back to tribal and then homeland rule, requires the powers of the Restitution of Land Rights Act of 1994.

According to the quitrent holders' claim, the homes of subsequent settlers on the commonage land resembled "a rural slum and it is almost impossible for quitrents to continue with successful farming. Our main aim is to recapture the agricultural environment we once enjoyed before betterment took control of the commonage." Under these conditions, class differentiation between quitrent holders and other residents intensified, such that 14 Mgwali families owned more than one quitrent plot, and only 30 of the original 152 quitrent plot title deeds were considered legally valid. Moreover, according to the Border Rural Committee (1997:20), "There are class stratifications among the quitrenters themselves.... There is a tendency by original quitrenters to exclude the new owners in decision-making on the issues that affect all quitrenters, especially when a difference of opinion is anticipated."

Although in this uncertain tenure context, "The internal market for land in Mgwali appears to be very limited," as the Border Rural Committee (1997:20) put it, the estimated value of plots was R30,000. One form of return on such a substantial investment is cash rental (since labor tenancy on black-owned farms was prohibited by the Bantu Laws Amendment Act of 1964). But as the Border Rural Committee (1997:24) continued, "The uncertainty of land reform has resulted in the escalation of evictions of tenants, by landowners forcing tenants to move to their newly demarcated sites. This is attributed to a sense of fear and anxiety regarding the possibility of losing their land to the tenant occupants." Theft of agricultural implements, livestock, and fencing was also common.

In sum, a variety of informal tenancy arrangements had emerged in the 1980s and 1990s, some of which were formalized by post-1994 legislation. But strong class and patriarchal social residues hindered progressive changes in rural social relations. This was not because civil society was non-existent. Organizations in Mgwali that were involved in settling disputes over land included the SANCO Village and Central committees, the ANC, ANC Women's League, ANC Youth League, Community Policing Forum, the Farmers Association, and the church. But reporting on its role in mediating the land issue, the Border Rural Committee (1997:4) observed "serious tensions within the community, particularly between the youth who are active in local structures and a small group of the elderly who are quitrenters."

To illustrate, some quitrenters refused to sign a Code of Conduct proposed by government officials and the Border Rural Committee for the purposes, apparently, of codifying an initial consultation. "In the past," noted the Committee (1997:6), "signing government documents had resulted in loss of land. They suggested that the team continues with its work and finds land for the landless without their signing the Code of Conduct." Indeed, without good faith efforts to open up new land for the landless, conceded the Border Rural Committee (1997:7), "It was unrealistic to have expected the quitrenters, in particular, to sign a Code of Conduct. A second criticism is that it is arguable whether a signed Code of Conduct would have ensured community commitment in any case."

Women residents of Mgwali were particularly harmed by the process. In general terms, rural women played a vastly important but rarely recognized role in the formal South African economy by ensuring that their fathers, brothers and sons were born, raised, healed when sick, and cared for in retirement--so that employers in distant cities did not have to pay wages sufficient to cover such costs. The unpaid role of women in the reproduction of the male work force was particularly poignant in rural areas of the Eastern Cape, for it was only the women's extraordinary rural tenacity--on overgrazed land in areas fraught with social tensions--that ensured not only survival under difficult conditions, but the cross-subsidization of costs (rearing, caring, and retirement) that normally would be built into the wages and salaries of urban men, in societies not burdened by inherited bantustan-type rural-urban relations.

And yet the progressive denuding of women's rights to land--which existed, *de facto*, in customary arrangements but were removed in the 1927 Native Affairs Administration Act in favor of male primogeniture--were cemented, not overturned, by the introduction of an imperfect land market, which added a pecuniary incentive for men to retain control and effective ownership. Mgwali women saw "widows in this community being driven away from their homes by sons who claim to be owners" (Border Rural Committee 1997:29) and were further disadvantaged by illiteracy and lack of resources to transfer land into their own names. Although the Equality Clause of the Constitution provided equal rights to women, the failure to overturn sexist laws, and *de facto* discrimination--such as the requirement that a husband's signature accompany a bank loan application--together meant that by the late 1990s, very little had changed for the women of Mgwali (and most other rural areas) (Border Rural Committee 1997:27-28).

An additional set of Mgwali residents attempted in 1995 to gain transfer of the land and arable fields presently owned by the church (which has 210 hectares under freehold ownership). Provincial government replied to their request, "The Department advises tenants to negotiate with the church as there are property rights of the church to consider." However, attempts to do so were consistently blocked by the church Board of Trustees until November 1997, when an in-principle agreement was reached provided that compensation would be provided (Border Rural Committee 1997:15-16). Although a recent law--the 1997 Extension of Security of Tenure Act--had increased the tenure security of Mgwali and other rural residents, there were also constitutional issues at stake, for as the Border Rural Committee (1997:18) remarked, "Freedom of association is enshrined in the Constitution. It can be argued that the Church in Mgwali deprives people of this right by forcing them to be members of the church in exchange for occupational rights."

What must also be questioned in all of this relatively micro-level contestation of land rights--while the Stutterheim district's large tracts of white-owned commercial farmland remained untouched by distributional challenge--is whether the outcome envisaged by the Department of Land Affairs, namely a growing class of small-scale entrepreneurs, was realistic. According to the Border Rural Committee (1997:31, 33), "For an individual to cultivate the 10 acres of land [in Mgwali] it costs him/her approximately R1,000 and only a small proportion of the households can afford to pay this.... [Instead,] households do maintain small gardens where vegetables are grown for subsistence."

Perhaps most disturbingly, any vision of more thorough-going transformation--more aggressive land reform activity in white farming areas, government intervention in agricultural markets (including inputs such as seed, fertilizer, credit, and irrigation systems, such as those which white farmers depended on), much more technical assistance, a much larger grant from central government to buy land and own it, perhaps communally, or the opportunity to farm state-owned land (with security of tenure)--seems to have been lost in the process. Even the Border Rural Committee's (1997:39) recommendations to the Department of Land Affairs assumed that "Mgwali will never again be a thriving agricultural settlement, but with an integrated approach, it could develop into an economically viable and socially stable peri-urban area," all evidence to the contrary notwithstanding.

Conclusion: Crisis resolution or prolongation?

Stutterheim's local economic development crisis had the potential to be resolved only if there were enormous changes to power relations, institutional forms, planning and consultation processes, municipal budgeting, and ideological vision. None of these were on the agenda, and as a result Stutterheim suffered the prolongation of development crisis, as even activities considered viable at one stage were unveiled as unsustainable when donor funding was withdrawn.

Some observers would not approve of the pessimism implicit in this analysis of Stutterheim. At the other end of the spectrum, Nussbaum (1997:55), for example, remarked that

> If Stutterheim is a microcosm of what a reconstruction and development program in South Africa can be, may all communities be inspired by its example and its people! May all communities discover their own particular magical rainbow that is created by their own particular chemistry, skills, talents and vision in order to create a prosperous future and to inspire people to better serve their communities.

Yet criticizing Stutterheim for relying on an excessively ideological brand of local boosterism was not particularly controversial. As Nel (1994:374) remarked at a relatively early stage,

> This raises the question whether the initiative is replicable in other towns or even sustainable in Stutterheim in the long term without continued financial support. Most of the finance does not appear to have come from the private sector and a negligible amount was raised locally.... The limited private sector investment in the town and in major forum projects is a matter for attention in the future.

Tandy (1992:20) flagged the problem even earlier, commenting that "it is not clear that the Stutterheim funding is available for similar projects on a similar scale." For Nel (1994:374), "The effects in Stutterheim of the external financing and entrepreneurial development can only be assessed when current funding runs out and the town has to rely on its own resources and skills."

But already in the late 1990s, well before Stutterheim lost its appeal to external donors, it was feasible to assess the general results of the model adopted since 1990. Those results reflected the acceptance of a wretched *status quo* by Stutterheim's mass base, largely, it appears, because a small group of township leaders pacted with Stutterheim's *verligte* white elite, and demobilized popular protest. While Stutterheim was, in the process, highly celebrated by the intellectual and policy wings of big business--including Barlow Rand, a major conglomerate with a long track record of promoting neoliberal public policy--its premature local social contract conclusively failed in nearly every material respect in which it could be judged.

Yet the vexed problem of "sustainability" does not even begin to capture the scope of Stutterheim's deficiency. In his study of *The Rise and Fall of the South African Peasantry*, based on evidence from Stutterheim and similar settings, Colin Bundy (1988:243) asserted that "The underdeveloped sector of the South African economy is not 'separate' from the developed sector: the economy of the former is firmly integrated with that of the latter." This theme emerged repeatedly in historical and geographical ways throughout this chapter.

Indeed "uneven development"--differential growth of sectors, geographical processes, classes and regions at the global, regional, national, sub-national, and local level (Bond 1998a)--was readily observed as a continually evolving process that ties Greater Stutterheim residents to their fate in the local, national, and increasingly international divisions of labor. It is true that most people in the area were, historically, "surplus" to the formal capitalist economy, as witnessed by the high and rising rate of unemployment. But the informal ties to capitalism as a system binded residents very closely nevertheless, for rural women in Greater Stutterheim continued to surrender their unpaid labor to reproduce a male labor force in distant urban areas, a fact not in the least changed by the post-1990 "Stutterheim Experience" or by post-1994 democracy.

The phenomenon of uneven development in peripheral settings has, thus, been explained as a process of "articulations of modes of production" in which the capitalist mode of production depends upon earlier modes of production for an additional "superexploitative" subsidy by virtue of reducing the costs of labor power reproduction (Wolpe 1980). Smith (1990:156, 141) insists, however, that "it is the logic of uneven development which structures the context for this articulation," rather than the reverse. This observation appears valid in Stutterheim, for it was necessary to trace the historical unevenness of settlement in the area to understand how forcibly African people were thrown off their land, in efforts by missionaries and mercenaries to draw them into the formal capitalist relations that led to a century and a half of systematic underdevelopment.

It is in this broader context that the rationale for the Stutterheim Experience becomes clearer. Stutterheim was, after all, only an emblem--albeit a particularly impressive one--of the problems that South Africa's white elites faced during the 1980s. The solution to both the specific 1989-90 boycott and to the more general radicalization of Stutterheim's township conforms to the problem faced by what Ferguson (1994) has called "The Anti-Politics Machine" in a book subtitled "'Development,' Depoliticization and Bureaucratic Power in Lesotho." That important work calls our attention, as students of depoliticized development, to the fact that failure--in Stutterheim represented by multiple objectives set having not been reached, and instead an observable deterioration of living conditions--does not necessarily represent cause to change course. Ferguson (1994:19-20) cited the French theorist Michel Foucault to help deconstruct development discourse:

> Perhaps the best example of this kind of analysis is Foucault's "genealogy" of the prison.... By differentiating illegalities, and by turning one uniquely well-supervised and controlling class of violators against the others, the prison did end up serving as part of a system of social control, but in a very different way than its planners had envisioned. "If this is the case," Foucault (1979:276-77) writes, "the prison, apparently 'failing,' does not miss its target; on the contrary, it reaches it.... For the observation that the prison fails to eliminate crime, one should perhaps substitute the hypothesis that the prison has succeeded extremely well in producing delinquency, a specific type, a politically and economically less dangerous--and, on occasion, usable--form of illegality; in producing delinquents, in an apparently marginal, but in fact centrally supervised milieu; in producing the delinquent as a pathologized subject.... So successful has the prison been that, after a century and a half of 'failures,' the prison still exists, producing the same results, and there is the greatest reluctance to dispense with it."
> The point to be taken from the above argument is only that planned interventions may produce unintended outcomes that end up, all the

> same, incorporated into anonymous constellations of control--authorless "strategies," in Foucault's sense--that turn out in the end to have a kind of political intelligibility.

Of importance to concede is the undisputable evidence that in Stutterheim the issue was not an expansion of the state (as Ferguson observed in Lesotho) but rather its contraction and replacement by an unelected, elite-controlled development agency whose relations with external agencies--the Independent Development Trust, Development Bank of Southern Africa and a host of supporters in major foundations, corporations, allied think-tanks and periodicals--appeared far more successful than Stutterheim's own development trajectory. But to borrow Foucault's words, "after a century and a half of 'failures,' the prison still exists, producing the same results," just as after a century and a half of failures, so too did the metaphorical "delinquency" of systematically generated underdevelopment of people who come into contact with increasingly more sophisticated missionaries and mercenaries of capitalism. Likewise, the last decade of development and underdevelopment in Stutterheim bears all the scars of misapplied physical force, divide-and-rule strategies, cooptation, and indirect rule--all with the overriding objective of combining legitimation of the system with increasingly sophisticated efforts at drawing surplus from the victims of "development"--that were evident in the town's first decade or two.

The "political intelligibility" of all of this does not need much clarification, for it is Stutterheim's role as a poster child of LED and local social contracts ("reconciliation") that helps us understand the very limits of such concepts. Unless LED breaks loose from association with the set of discrete, unconnected (though often mislabeled "holistic"), marginal, and demonstrably ineffectual interventions that characterize the Stutterheim Experience, it is doomed as a strategy, either for local-level growth or for addressing poverty in South Africa, or anywhere else for that matter.

The alternatives to the kinds of depoliticized LED initiatives found in Stutterheim are many (Ecsecc 1998) and follow very closely the strategy proposed in the conclusion to the most serious analysis of the South African economy yet produced, Fine and Rustomjee's (1996:252) *The Political Economy of South Africa*: "We place considerable emphasis upon a state program of public expenditure to provide social and economic infrastructure. This forms part of a strategy to provide for basic needs. The problem of how to finance such a program is less acute than the formation of the political, social, and institutional capacity to carry it out."

The lack of apparent political, social and institutional *will* to attempt anything much more than the ineffectual initiatives associated with the Stutterheim Experience was not the subject of this research, though certainly deserves study. Instead, in this evaluation, a prerequisite understanding has been established. For writing somewhat myopically in the early days of the Stutterheim Experience, Tandy (1992:21) found that "The lesson of Stutterheim is that much can be done during this interim period without doing violence to the political objectives, short and long term, set by progressives." No one could deny the general logic of this comment--i.e., mass organizations' continually maturing engagement with the development industry, and potential for progressive outcomes. But the particular myth of Stutterheim as a developmental success story--for progressives and neoliberals alike--is certainly open to revision.

PART THREE

THE HOUSING QUESTION

chapter six

1980s Township Housing Boom

This chapter, written in mid-1990, reflected the need to identify what was already a clear process of financial expansion under conditions of overaccumulation, and its implications for urban development. At this early stage the vitality of finance appeared unstoppable, which perhaps explains why in retrospect I mistakenly overemphasized and extrapolated the late 1980s trends associated with township commodification via housing finance, as well as the possibility for further speculative activity in the Johannesburg city center. Indeed, just at the point at which the spatial fix associated with the financial explosion appeared decisive, it evaporated, nearly overnight, under the weight of neoliberal development contradictions: the banks retreated from the townships just after this article originally went to press, and elsewhere in Johannesburg, property prices peaked shortly thereafter. The chapter nevertheless draws our attention to the extraordinary flows of capital into financial-speculative outlets (including real estate), even within a strife-torn township like Alexandra. My colleague Mzwanele Mayekiso (1996:chs.9-10) picked up the story from here in *Township Politics*, a book which shows how many of the core contradictions noted in the pages below later flowered into full-fledged civic conflict over the character of housing development in Old Alexandra, the East Bank, and later the Far East Bank. Meanwhile, attempts to discipline commercial bankers were only fleeting as democracy dawned in mid-1994. The financial explosion continued, working its way out of property and into the local (and after 1995, international) stock and bond markets, where rates of return were extremely high in relation to real production. Thus the concerns expressed in this chapter about financial dominance in an era of desperate need for basic needs, are vindicated not only by the financiers, but by the subsequent void of state regulation.

[This chapter was originally published as "Township Housing and South Africa's 'Financial Explosion': The Theory and Practice of Financial Capital in Alexandra," in *Urban Forum* 1, 2 (1990).]

Introduction

Arising from South Africa's economic stagnation, the recent spectacular dynamism of the country's financial sector could not but have profoundly affected the post-Riekert Commission urban transformation of apartheid townships into free market investment arenas. This transformation represents a gruelling challenge for the many poor and working people who are likely to be displaced in the process (Swilling 1990). But consider two other risks: the unsustainability of financial speculation (including real estate speculation) in the larger economic environment; and the township tensions created by the uneven allocation of housing finance. Housing finance is becoming probably the single most important component in the development of townships at precisely the same time that financial capital is, ironically, both propping up and undermining the rest of the economy. These phenomena are not unrelated, and are not fundamentally different from processes under way in most countries, from America (Bond 1990a-c) to Zimbabwe (Bond 1990d).

This chapter begins by outlining the dramatic shift from productive to financial assets under way in the South African economy, a shift that for stagnant economies (of which even Japan appears now to fit the model) has been aptly characterized by Magdoff and Sweezy (1987) as "the financial explosion." There is a particular set of urban correlates to the financial explosion, and to review these also calls attention to the complex role of housing finance in uneven urban--particularly residential--development, for which Alexandra Township offers a useful case study. The conclusion reiterates a central theme: the unfettered freedom of market mechanisms in townships, given the broader processes of the South African economy, will constrain rather than catalyze sustainable, popular development.

South Africa's financial explosion

Speculation and debt

If there is a single fundamental barrier to the COSATU/ANC program of "growth through redistribution," or to the state's pre-De Klerk "inward industrialization" strategy, or to the current push for manufacturing export-based accumulation, it must be the overwhelming attractiveness of speculative financial assets by comparison to reinvestment in production. Even South African Reserve Bank Deputy Governor Jan Lombard--considered among those most responsible for infusing free market values into apartheid planning (McCarthy 1986)--has decried South Africa's financial explosion in no uncertain terms (Lombard 1988:9):

> As is typical of a stagnating economy, employment has hardly increased over the past decade except in government and in finance, where job opportunities for people with the appropriate skills in law, accounting, economics, public administration and so on, rose rapidly. Young upward mobile professionals (yuppies), able and interested in making money out of restructuring existing financial empires, are in great demand. But blue collar work has been expanding very little. For long periods the yields available from investing in rising stocks and shares remained more attractive than the expectations about new real capital formation. According to Reserve Bank calculations, the profitability ratio in practically all industries (including primary and tertiary industries) showed a markedly declining trend aver the past 12 years. In the sector "finance, insurance, real estate and business services," however, the ratio fully recovered its lost ground since 1981.

This passage outlines the broad economic trajectory represented by South Africa's financial explosion. The trend, as Lombard sees it, is that South African corporate management is "chiefly interested in maintaining net profits by replacing labor, avoiding taxation and financing lucrative investment opportunities in other countries in so far as exchange control does not prevent it" (1988:8). In fact, forex fraud has become endemic in the financial sector, running at R100 million a month and involving dozens of highly placed bankers (*Business Day* 22/5/90; *Financial Mail* 1/6/90)--and tax avoidance schemes involving "'respectable' and large companies and financial institutions" capture hundreds of millions of rand as well (*Financial Mail* 21/4/89). But where exchange controls and tougher enforcement do stifle capital's geographic mobility, liquid funds have flowed rapidly into several local speculative outlets--real estate, art, the stock market, and new financial instruments--while leaving the productive base of the economy (Black and Stanwix 1987) to wither.

Consider as one example the Johannesburg Stock Exchange (JSE), the nominal value of which (in terms of total shares represented) rose by a factor of eight from 1982 to early 1990 (approximately R400 billion), while reinvestment in plant and equipment stagnated over the period (Bond 1990e). As Kaplan (1987:526) explains,

> The booming stock exchange was not an indicator of business confidence but rather the reverse. The rise in share prices was principally a consequence of investors' reluctance to undertake productive investments given their lack of confidence in the longer-term prospects for the economy. Short-term liquid financial investments were preferred to longer-term fixed investments and resulted in booming financial markets but a diminishing capital stock.

Apart from the JSE's rise (and subsequent tumble in 1990 based on Japanese and Middle-Eastern gold sales due to liquidity problems), substantial international capital flight from South Africa, and real estate speculation in particular markets, another integral aspect of South Africa's financial explosion is the tendency for debt ratios--of corporations, consumers and the state--to rise as a consequence of declining internally-generated rates of revenue (that is, real profits, wages, and taxes). While political factors ultimately limited the exposure of corporate and state debt to foreign lenders after 1985, domestic debt ratios have risen steadily with only a minor downward blip during the 1985-86 credit crunch. By September 1989 the entire private sector debt held by the "banking sector" (including some consumer debt but not including building societies' advances) totalled R109 billion as against annualized GDP of R232 billion--a ratio of 47 percent; while a decade earlier, bank credit was R16 billion as against GDP of R61 billion (26 percent). Indeed, for many years, the domestic private sector debt to banks had hovered in the region of 28 to 30 percent of GDP (*South African Reserve Bank Quarterly,* December 1989). Even the sharp series of interest rate hikes from 12.5 percent in February 1988 to 21 percent by October 1989 did not prevent annual bank credit increases of 35 percent in 1988 and 31 percent in 1989 (*Standard Bank Economic Review* April 1990).

It is not surprising, then, that many creditor institutions are already looking over the edge of the debt abyss. Repayment problems are cropping up for farmers, small businesses, and some large businesses, and for record numbers of lower-middle-income whites (*Financial Mail* 3/11/89; *Star* 5/6/90). Even traditionally stable home loans, while issued at a breakneck pace, have created unprecedented risk. As an executive of the Perm building society commented in late 1989, "For the last six or seven years, losses and risk have been a fact of the mortgage lending business. When [interest] rates came off after 1984/85, there was an improvement but we have never returned to the risk patterns that existed before" (*Business Day* 13/10/89). And the Trust Bank recently pulled out of another popular line of business, long-dated bonds (in which the bank had lost R30 million in late 1989 as a result of an options fiasco), since, "We came to the conclusion that the potential rewards from an exposure in the market do not justify the risk, especially in view of the unpredictable nature of current market conditions" (*Business Day* 22/5/90).

Deregulation and cut-throat competition

In spite of the clear dangers associated with speculation, rising debt ratios, financial innovation, exploding interest rates, and increased borrower risk during a period of economic stagnation, the response of the Reserve Bank and Finance Ministry authorities has generally been to deregulate the financial system further. For example, minimum requirements for financial institutions to invest in government securities were scrapped in late 1989 (*Business Day* 11/12/89); sophisticated lending and saving products (some linked to JSE performance) are being made available to wealthy consumers by banks and trust companies (*Business Day* 20/9/89, 9/11/89, 22/11/89); new financial instruments--especially securitized mortgages--are popping up in investors' portfolios; and a 1989 Financial Markets Control Act helps create futures, options, and bond markets, and actually allows the financial industry to self- regulate in these new areas. According to the Friedmanite logic of Reserve Bank Senior Deputy Governor Japie Jacobs, these new markets "obviously do provide opportunities for speculation--and speculation can actually inject greater stability into a market [sic]" (*Financial Mail* 1/9/89). Although a Deposit-Taking Institutions Bill tabled in mid-1990 attempts to regulate and to increase disclosure of excessive credit exposures, it does so only because a *quid pro quo* allows concentration of bank ownership to increase dramatically (*Financial Mail* 1/6/90). Even the Reserve Bank's efforts to stem the worrisome R12 billion in banks' and building societies' repurchase agreements--assets that are kept "off balance sheet" so that the institution can avoid the costs of holding reserves against them--were weakened by a bond traders' protest last April. And other such off-balance-sheet items--widespread use of agency business (brokering other creditors' loans for a commission), cash management accounts, and options and futures--have seemed to escape notice. Besides, pronounced the *Financial Mail* (27/4/90), "bank supervision has been so slipshod for so long that conditions were created--and tacitly acknowledged by Church Square [i.e., the Reserve Bank]--which encourage this type of financing."

Deregulation of building societies, begun in 1986, is also likely to continue apace, in order to allow greater flexibility in several areas: a smaller proportion of the societies' assets could consist of relatively stable mortgage loans; a larger amount of their deposits could be short-term (hence violating the fundamental banking rule, "take long-term deposits, make short-term loans"); and the maximum ratio of the value of each mortgage loan to the price of the property could increase from 90 percent to 100 percent, thus adding greater risk in the event of a default (*Financial Mail* 10/11/89). As Morris and Padayachee (1988:6) note, such deregulatory trends, dating back to the De Kock Commission, were no accident: "In SA, local finance capital appeared to have a lot to do with shaping the local monetarist initiative, including the removal of interest rate ceilings and foreign exchange controls."

With the financial sector increasingly attractive since the early 1980s, thanks to deregulation, monetarist Reserve Bank policies, product innovations, and the broad decline in South Africa's productive base, competition has heated up dramatically. This has been especially true in the credit markets and has inexorably led to profit declines in the banking subsector. Rationalization of the major players is one result, as the already highly concentrated financial system recently lost one large building society and one major bank to mergers. But in the nooks and crannies of high finance, "boutique banking" for the rich is providing new institutions a toehold; thanks to much looser requirements, fifteen new banks were formally or provisionally licensed during the thirty-month period that closed the decade of the 1980s (*Financial Mail* 2/2/90). That decade had also witnessed a banking invasion of building societies' once sacred residential mortgage bond turf, leading in mid-1989 to "a major counter-offensive" as societies began purchasing estate agent firms, a strategy that proved to be of high risk in Britain (*Financial Mail* 13/10/89). Also in the early 1980s, relatively unregulated life insurance companies had begun taking substantial deposit market (that is, savings) shares from both banks and building societies, complained Reserve Bank General Manager for Supervision Chris de Swardt in a *Financial Mail* interview (1/9/89), "through offering insurance products with a minimal life assurance element." Major insurance firms Old Mutual and Sanlam could also dig into deep pockets to buy huge banks (Nedbank and Trust) that were on the verge of failing during the go-go 1980s. Pension funds, too, made important inroads into personal savings, and trusts are increasingly playing the role of the banks through participation mortgage bond schemes. Under such conditions of deregulation and ruinous competition, redirecting capital flows back to the real, productive sectors of the economy will be no small feat. "To my mind," warns Lombard, "such a trend for an economy in the position of South Africa is not a healthy one" (1988:9). The effects all of this have had on South African urban development will be taken up next.

Financial capital and urban housing

Cities, the financial explosion, and uneven development

According to the geographer David Harvey (1985a:73),

> Urbanism has been transformed from an expression of the production needs of the industrialist to an expression of the controlled power of finance capital, backed by the power of the state, over the totality of the production process.

Harvey's words are increasingly true--in South Africa as well as in the advanced industrialized countries--as the financial explosion that began a decade or more ago runs its course. Cities are more affected by the broad macroeconomic shift from production towards financial speculation than are any other spaces. The result is a diverse set of symptoms of a rather depraved urbanization process during a financial explosion, which include:

- the general flow of funds into ever more expensive real estate, because of its role as a hedge against inflation or, if the location is optimal, as a speculative investment vehicle;
- the consequent deterioration of the urban small and medium-sized business sector as rent costs become prohibitive;
- the general rise in housing prices, and the simultaneous intensification of processes of uneven urban development--gentrification of close-in slums on the one hand, and the ghettoization of working-class neighborhoods,is a counterbalance--as the use values of residential real estate are increasingly transformed by financial capital into exchange values;
- the increased concentration of corporate and financial command and control functions in city centers, and the

restructuring of regions around financial sector growth poles, concomitant with the broader process of the centralization of capital;
- the transformation of urban space and infrastructure away from industrial forms, and towards meeting the transport, communication, and recreational requirements of financial-administrative capital; and
- postmodern urban cultural attributes "irreducibly specific to the reckless overbuilding of commercial space" which arises from the "hypertrophic expansion of the financial service sector" (Davis 1985a:103).

All of these are notable tendencies, and they appear to be the logical outcomes of the 1980s rise of finance in most urban centers across the globe. Traditionally, before the advent of the financial explosion, finance played an accommodating role in development, lubricating the payments system and providing funds for productive investment. Yet housing finance in particular has always contributed substantially to unevenness in urban development, and still does so in remarkably variegated ways: housing finance can often enhance the stability of the entire financial system, since housing is among its best sources of collateral; it allows the housing market to be used as a site of commodity production and disinvestment, which are both crucial to the profitability of neighborhood change (Smith 1979); it contributes to class and community formation by imposing residential differentiation through different qualities of credit (Harvey and Chatterjee 1974); and it spreads the time horizon of investment significantly by allowing consumers of housing to service their housing bonds over the long term (usually 20 to 30 years). Such factors allow finance to act as a nerve center for urban capital flows, and this is not necessarily conducive to a rational allocation of housing resources.

Housing finance and residential differentiation

Consider race, class, and community differentiation more closely, for here unfettered housing finance can be particularly pernicious. In the United States, what may appear as contingencies of race and ethnicity have become cemented as patterns of geographic maldistribution of credit, patterns observable in most cities. Hundreds of studies of the theory and practice of bank "redlining" (lending (discrimination based, in the original formulation, on the 1930s Federal Housing Administration's red lines encircling undesirable residential locations) suggest that housing finance can play a significant role in fostering and perpetuating racism in communities. If, as is the case throughout the United States, African-American borrowers are overwhelmingly denied credit for homes in certain areas by financial institutions whose policy-makers are white, this suggests that simple institutional race discrimination is at work (Dedman 1989).

But there is far more to this than the outcome describes. The location of many urban African-American homes coincides with the trajectory of central business district expansion, since for historical reasons relating to labor markets and deindustrialization, ghettos are located near the Central Business District (CBD) core in most North American cities. Thus financial institutions and developers have a material interest in destabilizing the housing capital of African-Americans, since this will enable investor-speculators to purchase their residences --especially if they are just abandoned shells at that point--at very low prices; the next step, of course, is transforming block after block of dilapidated buildings into attractive gentrified homes to house the increasing numbers of young urban professional employees of the finance, insurance, and real estate industries who wish to reside close to their workplace. Hence the flip side of redlining is gentrification, and in nearly every United States city the worst slums can be found side by side with the newest gentrified neighborhoods, in a process that is continually and systematically reproduced.

This, of course, is antithetical to the Urban Foundation's (1990b:23) naive view that "*the best examples of residential integration and neighborhood stabilization in the United States have been those in which neighborhood revitalization and inner city redevelopment have accompanied such integration*" (original emphasis), since it is on just this turf that the most intense community-based struggles have been fought in recent years. Gentrification, largely the product of housing finance penetration after a period of intensive redlining (Smith 1979), is among the leading causes of displacement and homelessness in the United States (Bratt, Hartman, and Meyerson 1986), and it is safe to predict the emergence of such systemic unevenness for deracialised South African central cities if the Urban Foundation program is successful.

While residential differentiation through differential access to housing finance has been a factor in advanced capitalist urbanization for some time, the particular conditions of the financial explosion of the 1980s intensified the pace of housing valorization and devalorization considerably (Leitner and Sheppard 1989:73-74). And again, a resurgence of institutional race discrimination by the landed-financial capital nexus was one result of vast increases in interest rates, beginning in 1979. In addition to redlining and gentrification, there continue the practices of "blockbusting" and "blow-out" by many urban real estate agents who introduce African-American buyers to lily-white working-class neighborhoods, thus prompting massive sales (and hence commissions) and "white flight" (Harvey 1973). As the Institute for Policy Studies' Working Group on Housing has found (1989:15), "blockbusting tactics enable real estate speculators to buy cheap and sell dear, while banks convert their old, lower-interest mortgages to higher-yield loans made to new minority homebuyers." Again, contrary to the Urban Foundation's (1990b:17) impression that these processes are not operating in South Africa at present, there are revealing signs of blockbusting in Boksburg's Windmill Park, as well as in a few other white lower-middle-class semi-urban and suburban neighborhoods in the context of struggles over the demise of the Group Areas Act (*Financial Mail* 8/12/89). As with gentrification, it is safe to predict that blockbusting will become a much more widespread phenomenon in lower-middle-class areas in coming years, and hence the United States case offers a likely--and disturbing--scenario of how South African neighborhood development might proceed under a free market regime. And already there are other indications of the impact of finance-driven urban development patterns in contemporary South Africa that shed light on the future of the post-apartheid central city and black townships.

Finance and South African real estate

The most significant way in which financial capital is currently shaping South African urban development is through its strategic flooding of real estate markets in a process that looks very much like pure speculation. As the Venter Commission (1984:8,9) noted,

> The role of the building societies is of decisive importance in determining the effective demand for housing.... The building society movement made a mistake in 1979, 1980 and 1981. They overlent money on existing loans and did not increase the financing of new homes substantially. The result was demand inflation. Too much

> money chasing too few homes. The end result was spiralling home prices in some cases from R30,000 to R90,000 within 12 months.

Today the amounts of money involved are enormous and rapidly increasing. So far it is paying off, as home-buyers of all races seem content to pay ever greater percentages of their disposable income for housing, under the expectation, of course, that the price (if not value) of their investment will always escalate. With some hot suburban areas seeing price increases of up to fifty percent in 1989, one leading property developer conveyed shock that "the rise in interest rates has been almost totally ignored. In my 26 years in the property business I have never seen prices rise so steeply while mortgage rates are rising" (*Business Day* 21/12/89). Dangerous as the bubble might be, the process has by no means peaked; following consultations with international bankers in late 1989, a building society general manager expressed the expectation that, concomitant with political reform, the South African property market would be a leading beneficiary of new foreign investment (*Business Day* 21/12/89). For top city-center office space, prices could easily go much higher. Prime space in Johannesburg in mid-1989 fetched R28 per square meter, which did not even rank in the top fifty cities in the world (*Financial Mail* 30/6/89). "While there are anomalies resulting from SA's exclusion from world property, the similarities in development, investment and performance patterns are also remarkable," observed the *Financial Mail* (27/4/90). "Cash-rich institutions in SA, freed from the constraints of prescribed assets and concerned about the short-term volatility of equity, are queuing up to buy into hedges such as prime property investment."

Financial capitalists do more than pump money into land, though. They also strive to transform the land into a built environment suitable for further speculation. This is true in places as predictable as the Johannesburg central business district (the eastern half of which, said a city councillor, might attract "thousands of middle and upper income earners into flats east of Eloff Street. They would mostly be employed in the high-rise banking complex taking shape in the west of the city" (*Star* 22/4/90); as obscure as Port Elizabeth's Greenacres shopping mall (the location of one of South Africa's most sophisticated postmodern buildings, which is home to an insurance company); or as portentous as Durban's South Beach area (where the enormous R90-million "Wheel" shopping and entertainment center--ninety percent owned by Momentum Life and First National Bank Pension Fund--will play several functions, according to a booster: "In addition to serving as a tourist attraction, The Wheel will boost the confidence of other investors. The area will be transformed from a seedy, depressed part of town into an up-market area"--*Finance Week* 25/10/89).

Such transformation in the value of properties is the key, and the ebb and flow of financial capital is both driven by, and drives, this valorization process. During the 1980s, value increases and rental returns on the basket of three hundred properties which make up the influential Richard Ellis Property Index outpaced even the JSE industrial index. The most attractive properties over the entire 1979-88 period, according to the Property Index, were decentralized offices (430 percent increase), followed by shopping (400 percent) and city center (330 percent) real estate (*Financial Mail* 21/4/89). Following a politically induced downturn in 1984-86, much of the white residential property market has recovered, and there are even signs that gentrification is taking off in Johannesburg for black yuppies (*Financial Mail* 20/6/89).

As a result, total sales of real estate, commercial and residential, have increased explosively since late 1986, from around R12 billion per year to R20 billion in 1989 (*South African Reserve Bank Quarterly* December 1989). Along with financial capital's (led by insurance companies') equity investments in commercial real estate, the easy accessibility of mortgage bonds--especially in residential markets--has also driven property sales. The largest commercial banks began expanding their direct residential bond lending dramatically in 1979, and by late 1988 had over R10 billion of housing loans on their books as a result of a 180 percent increase that year. Other financial institutions carried another R30 billion in home loans (*Business Day* 13/10/89). With all the activity in the bond market, all sorts of new lending products were introduced in the late 1980s and a secondary market for securitized mortgages opened up (*Business Day* 9/11/89, 22/11/89, 11/12/89).

The harsh competition and new sophisticated products are harming old-fashioned building societies, especially in the wake of increased interest rates and the approach of white borrowers' debt threshold. Although the societies granted many more loans than ever before in 1988 and 1989, there were many redemptions by borrowers who switched their debt to banks or other financiers (*South African Reserve Bank Quarterly* March 1989). Subsequently, the societies' reflexive move to gain an edge by buying estate agent subsidiaries (*Financial Mail* 13/10/89, 20/10/89) has only intensified the competition. On top of that, some major building society clients are shifting their operations: "The growth of the building industry," says John Kane-Berman of the Institute of Race Relations, "now depends largely on home building for blacks" (*Financial Mail* 10/11/89). These are some of the reasons that prompted the building societies to play an increasingly aggressive role in providing housing bonds in black townships during the last couple of years.

Township housing finance, social control, and greed

Following the 1975 decision by the Vorster administration to promote leasehold housing in steps, potential black (here, "African") home-buyers finally regained formal legal access to building society bonds in 1978 when the Financial Institutions Act was amended. (Prior to that, a few government housing loans for blacks were granted at a 9.25 percent interest rate.) Still, by 1982, there were only 1,324 bonds registered by societies under the 99-year leasehold system (Hendler 1986:88). In 1983 the Steyn Committee (1985:27) forecast,

> The success of the [council housing] sales campaign will depend on the willingness of building societies and other financial institutions to make the necessary amendments to their policy in respect of the standard of housing which is acceptable as the collateral for bonds as well as the payment of market related interest rates on all bond loans. The Committee therefore charges financial institutions to give their immediate attention to the changing of their existing policy with regard to the granting of loans to more humble homes.

Without those changes, by the end of the 1980s the limits of the private black housing market had nearly been reached. According to an estimate by housing developers at Rabie Investments, the top five percent of township residents could afford R30,000 houses and thus gain access to formal housing finance, and another twenty percent could afford houses between R25,000 and R30,000, which "leaves 75 percent for which solutions have to be found" (*Finance Week* 25/10/89). Clearly, solutions will not be found without massive state investment by a democratic regime (not merely promises of providing all citizens a site-and-service subsidy far from their places of employment or traditional homes), but that does not mean that limited strategic deployment of housing resources will not produce results desired by the current state and capital. "When people are housed--more especially when they are home-owners--they are not only less likely to be troublesome," comments

Zach de Beer (1988). "They are also likely to feel they have a stake in the society and an interest in its stability."

Supplying a young black revolutionary with a housing bond through the disciplinarian private market (perhaps with some form of mortgage insurance program to spread the risk) is one way of tying her or him down to stable labor and community behavior. (This was certainly proved by the creators of the United States Federal Housing Administration loan guarantee program in the 1930s.) Here is not the place for a comprehensive review of 1980s state urban policies aimed, ultimately, at this sort of result (Mabin 1989; Sutcliffe *et al* 1989; see also Morris and Padayachee 1988 and Hindson 1987 for political economic context). But fiscal constraints are real, and so, along with the dramatically fluctuating interest rate, it is fair to say that *the decline of central state involvement in housing provision* in favor of the private market must be considered one of the main factors exacerbating the South African housing crisis (as is the case elsewhere across the globe). And the new R2 billion "Steyn Fund" is in its initial formulation so heavily orientated to the private sector--with its emphasis on loans, not grants; its need to grow, not dissipate; and its leveraging through private financial institutions--that it cannot seriously play the role of proxy democratic state. Yet through the army's capacity to quell township unrest by brute force; through the development projects of various semi-autonomous agents (for example, the South African Housing Trust and the Development Bank of Southern Africa); and through indirect means--mainly subsidies on financing schemes--the state continues to play a particular type of role in township housing.

What should be most evident is the enthusiasm the state has for the township accumulation strategy of financial capital. It took a good few years and plenty of state incentives, but eventually in October 1989 the Perm's influential managing director Bob Tucker and the Urban Foundation fashioned the policy changes in township bond lending that Steyn had called for in 1983 and persuaded the bulk of the major housing finance institutions to come aboard. This required amending the Usury Act to allow higher administrative costs for small loans to be passed to borrowers. It also spurred the creation of an insurance scheme--largely subsidized by foreign governments but with rather high 7.5 percent premiums charged to borrowers--designed to reduce lenders' collateral risk to as little as 60 percent, which "makes it possible, probably desirable, for financial institutions to enter this market" (*Finance Week* 18/10/89).

But the key factor in the Urban Foundation scheme appears to be an innovative and potentially risky downgrading of banks' and building societies' capital ratios (that is, the percentage of owners' capital an institution must maintain against assets), a factor Tucker himself designed (*Finance Week* 18/10/89) and one which, said an Urban Foundation spokesperson, "we hope will make low-cost housing just as profitable to banks as Hire Purchase business" (*Financial Mail* 8/12/89). The downgrade further weakens South Africa's capacity to withstand its financial explosion, and it also contradicts the Bank for International Settlements' current efforts to raise banks' capital ratios. South Africa's requirement (around 5 percent for banks and 4 percent for building societies) is already far below the 8 percent international standard, notwithstanding somewhat half-hearted recent moves to strengthen capital requirements (*Financial Mail* 2/6/90). In 1989, *The Banker* magazine (July) noted that South Africa's largest banks--Standard, First National, Bankorp, Nedcor, and Volkskas--ranked 290, 303, 412, 439, and 503 in the world in terms of assets, but their capital ratio rankings ranked a dismal 482, 774, 743, 540, and 451, respectively. And following that survey, South African banks' ratios actually declined (*Financial Mail* 2/2/90). While the Reserve bank's concern that repurchase agreements might threaten capital ratios was well noted by the financial press in April 1990, its prior concession that billions of rands' worth of township housing bonds could be carried on the books of financial institutions with no capital backing attracted little critical notice (the idea that ten-year debentures which will fund the housing bonds can partially substitute for capital is yet another accounting trick to hide what are in reality "liabilities" in the "owners' capital" accounts--*Financial Mail* 8/12/89).

The costs of insufficient capital ratios will in future very likely be borne by ratepayers or depositors--"If it comes to a real crunch," the *Financial Mail* (1/9/89) observes, "the Reserve Bank doubts whether any major [bank] shareholder would rescue a banking affiliate at great cost to its own pocket"--but that is not the end of it. The Urban Foundation loan guarantee fund and general rush of capital into township housing finance will produce other victims as well. There will be a significant multiplier effect on black consumer debt as credit histories are established and houses are now used for collateral (*Finance Week*

18/10/89) and, come a recession, it is this sector that will be hardest hit by a wave of defaults and foreclosures. Worse, the door is now wide open and beckoning for fast-buck lenders; an official of Durban-based Finhouse in early 1990 thus announced a township housing development financing scheme which commands a 2.5 percent to 20 percent underwriter's fee:

> We don't believe affordability has ever been the major constraint in low-cost housing--getting the finance is.... People want houses. Our research has shown an urgent need for a package like ours and if the finance can be attracted, I believe the possible extra costs will be met. (*Financial Mail* 18/1/90).

Add to this the Urban Foundation scheme's presumption of "normal business parameters of profitability and risk" (Tucker 1989:2), and one can envisage all manner of formal and informal racketeering practices emerging. As the Johannesburg Legal Aid Bureau's Brian Leveson insists, "The [Urban Foundation] scheme will unwittingly expose thousands of people to being taken advantage of by unscrupulous building contractors and credit brokers who will prey on those who desperately seek low cost housing" (*Star* 20/10/89). Already Tucker has been quoted as blaming the rapidly increasing rate of foreclosures upon homeowners (of all races) on "the greed of institutions who lent the money" (*Business Day* 31/7/89). He should know, because even the Perm has recently been accused of malfeasance in widespread cases where the house of an unwitting borrower is purchased from township councils by an unethical developer. The entire house is then used by the lender as collateral when even a small loan for an addition is granted to the resident. In such cases, the addition is constructed by the developer under no-deposit arrangements and the borrower is not aware that the ownership of the house has changed, so that if a default upon the small loan occurs, the house is foreclosed upon (*Weekly Mail* 7/12/89).

Most of the themes of this section--from real estate speculation to valorization and devalorization of housing to residential differentiation to credit scams--are returned to in the Alexandra case study. Note, however, that the guideposts are rather weak--most of South Africa's urban analysts have subordinated study of the institutional capital accumulation strategies of various fractions of capital in townships to a broader analysis of township development as "the sphere of collective consumption." In studies based on themes developed by Manuel Castells in the 1970s, South African scholars considered housing and the urban question as primarily one of class reproduction (see the debate between Hendler 1987 and McCarthy 1987b). In contrast, Paul Hendler's pioneering study of capital accumulation in South African townships from 1980 to 1985 drew attention to the theoretical and empirical basis for "connections between official [state] practices and business activities--links which were not merely conceptual, but were also a lived reality for the personnel of several firms" (1986:15). The most visible and active businesspeople in the townships were employees of construction, retail, and financing firms, many of whom "were at some stage obliged to lobby and exert pressure on personnel in the organs of state regulation of the provision of African housing." It is not difficult to identify these actors in Alexandra Township in the late 1980s and to trace their recent spectacular success to the repressive power of the state and the subsequent penetration of housing finance into the township.

The penetration of housing finance in Alexandra

Alexandra as a case study

Alexandra, Johannesburg's closest African township, is undergoing a dramatic change in landscape, as both physical terrain and class relations are being torn asunder by the state, financial capital and their allies. To dig beneath the surface and understand the processes--and the environment in which they unfold--requires a certain amount of background contextualizing. Future historians of Alexandra will cite 1979, the year the township won a reprieve from Pretoria's forced removal axe, as the crucial moment in its history. Alexandra at that point represented, as much as any township, the momentous transition in state thinking towards urbanizing capitalist relations. (An earlier version of this process, also influenced profoundly by financial capital, can be traced back half a century, and is worth some initial consideration.) Following the 1979 reprieve, the state encountered severe resistance, as the Alexandra Action Committee played a leading role in the national political unrest of 1984-86 and thereby rendered the state's initial development plans futile. When, in the wake of extremely heavy repression in 1986, capital in various guises saw an opening in Alexandra, its unequivocal entry signalled, to Alexandra activists, a whole new set of problems.

For both historical and contemporary reasons, Alexandra offers a particularly good case study of the penetration of housing finance as a means of institutionalizing capitalist social relations and transforming "use-values" into "exchange-values." Alexandra was chosen not because it is typical of South African urbanization, but because it represents the cutting edge of state repression, of capital's strategy, and of militant, sophisticated, community resistance. Within the township's 1.6 square kilometers and among its estimated 200,000 residents, it is possible to identify many of the class tensions that will haunt black South Africa in coming decades.

An historical precedent for housing finance penetration

Throughout its history, Alexandra had been a site for various processes of capital accumulation, most of them bound up with the metropolitan labor market, petty local racial domination, and formal apartheid legislation (Tourikis 1981; Ditshwantsho tsa Rona Study Group 1982; Sarakinsky 1984). What is most striking, though, is how during the two periods of greatest economic dynamism--the 1940s and 1950s, and the late 1980s--the rhythm of accumulation in Alexandra was timed according to the local practices of financial capital, especially in the housing market.

"The greatest weakness of the Township, apart from the poverty of the inhabitants, is the exploitation of many of its stand-holders by European individuals and organizations, who hold bonds on terms so onerous that they constitute a 'racket'--and a very profitable one to this kind of bond-holder," commented Professor Hoernle, Alexandra's administrator, in 1942 (Tourikis 1981; most of the following historical citations are drawn from Tourikis's excellent thesis). By then, as many as 85 percent of the three-quarters of Alexandra's stands which had freehold status carried mortgage bonds; by 1952 there were at least four dozen different mortgage lenders operating in Alexandra, both small institutions and individuals. This period is appropriate for comparison to the present day, because it was a time when the early gestations and subsequent maturing of a local housing finance market wrought unmistakable changes on the Alexandra built environment. Before underlining the similarities between the urbanization of capital through housing finance in the early 1940s and late 1980s, it is important to make note of the differences in order that this limited window on the history of Alexandra be placed in proper context.

Tourikis argues convincingly that in its early years, "the 'global' structure within which Alexandra Township was located--that is, the form that the capitalist mode of production had taken in South Africa--had the effect of *uniting* the African petit-bourgeoisie with the working class." In the 1980s, in contrast, the state and enlightened capital developed a much different vision of "global" processes, since it had become clear to them by the time the current economic crisis set in during the mid-1970s--that some major social restructuring to split off a black middle class was an absolutely necessary component of the general political-economic fix.

Another crucial "global" difference is that while from 1930 to 1953 there was a fairly steady decline in the real cost of rental housing in South Africa (taken as a whole) (McCarthy and Smit 1984:92), the more recent spectacular upswing of returns from the real estate market--indeed the switch from productive to financial-speculative circuits of capital more generally--had given financial capital a broader incentive to consider investments in sites like Alexandra. In contrast, major building societies did not stray far from the white communities in the 1940s; the building societies and individual loan sharks that Hoernle complained of were small and adventurous--definitely not the major institutions--and so could get away with lending at an interest rate of close to 10 percent (as against the 5 percent rate charged by major building societies). Indeed, the effective interest rate on housing loans in Alexandra sometimes reached 17 percent in the 1940s.

But today, major building society prejudices--on grounds of race, class, geography, or technical barriers (for example, related to foreclosures in the context of the Group Areas Act)--have been pretty much *submerged* as larger forces (credit Keynesianism, the limits to South African corporate and white consumer indebtedness, the political pacification program, the fiscal crisis of the central state, and, hence, housing privatization) have become overwhelming. What comes through perfectly clearly, though, is that the type of lender--in a sense, that is, the quality of the credit--was a key variable in Alexandra's development (as it was in the 1974 Harvey-Chatterjee study of Baltimore). In the Alexandra of the 1940s, Hoernle's administrative duty, in the face of dramatic bus boycotts and increasing ANC organizing, was primarily to maintain law and order (and only secondly to ensure health and welfare), a task made nearly impossible by the township's extreme residential density and the demoralizing housing conditions. Hoernle easily recognized the structural impediments responsible for the housing crisis; he bitterly criticized the unscrupulous lenders

> who get individual standholders into their clutches. A typical method, not to say trick, is, when a standholder finds difficulty in maintaining his payments, to suggest to him an additional loan for the purpose of building additional rooms on his property, from the rent of which, so it is represented to him, he will find it easier to pay the interest and redemption charges on the higher loan.

The result included foreclosures and hence uneven urban development: the devalorization of capital that set the stage for its revalorization in the next purchase cycle. This, it was suggested earlier, is a universal process in capitalist cities, and although there is as yet little evidence of this process in present-day Alexandra, it is only a matter of time before a housing resale market develops and deeds office records begin to unveil charlatan lenders who grant bonds in order to foreclose on unsuspecting borrowers and then resell their property, perhaps in the context of the wider upgrading schemes. The implications for the future of Alexandra are important, for if working-class home-owners are overindebted and the unethical lender is well equipped--even anxious--to push the debt ever higher and to then foreclose (rather than giving some forbearance to the struggling debtor), this will considerably hasten the ghetto's class segregation and residential differentiation, its physical dilapidation, and its lower-income residents' displacement.

The historical evidence is revealing, because although the political-economic context is different now, the processes set in motion by low-quality housing finance in the 1940s had much to do with the genesis of the housing squalor which exists in Alexandra to this day. Added to this legacy, there were also some striking similarities between the two periods (with the historical examples in parentheses):

- *very high land prices* (£100 per one-eighth acre stand in 1942--"higher than in swagger Houghton," according to a shocked legislator--with some prime Alexandra land even selling at £1,500 per acre); yet simultaneously, *the age-old difficulty in acquiring relatively small bonds* (Alexandra bonds were typically between £150 and £450 in the early 1940s, as opposed to a minimum bond in a white area--which, of course, paid for a much higher quality house--of £1,000);

- *pleas for state intervention to lower interest rates* (these had come mainly from the standowners' solicitors);
- *efforts by enlightened capital to end racial restrictions on land ownership* (from the Board of Directors of the Johannesburg Building Society in 1942, with reference to lending in Alexandra, "proposals to be laid before [the Minister of the Interior] will include a suggestion for an alteration of the law, by which the existing title deeds can be so amended that the Society can take possession of the land and buildings of a defaulting Native or Coloured borrower");
- the fact that *the default rate for blacks was lower than that for whites* ("The African will treasure his freehold property in an Urban area more than a European and will use every endeavor to retain such property," said the standowners' solicitors);
- yet simultaneously the unavoidable truth that for many blacks, "*loans are often the first step to losing the property*" (as the Alexandra Medical Officer wrote in 1941); and most importantly,
- the temptation for overindebted home-owners to *transfer interest payment costs to their tenants* through overcrowding, over-building, and high rental charges. ("The whole economic position in the Township would be greatly eased if the burden of debt were to be removed from the standholders," said Hoernle. "For, then they could reduce the rent of their tenants.")

What the historical evidence suggests, most of all, is that housing as a commodity (financed by private bonds) was a key factor in the class configuration of Alexandra. And although Alexandra was relatively unusual in having freehold status (which dated as far back as 1912), it did indeed, then and now, serve as a kind of model for developments elsewhere. As one study of the earlier period found, "Johannesburg property speculators, estate agents, building societies and construction firms had mobilized and were lobbying for a policy of home ownership and massive state financed building programs" (Wilkinson 1981, cited in Hendler 1986:45). Even as the major financial and landed capitalists had feared Alexandra as a site for investment in the 1940s and 1950s (its status was highly uncertain as a result of Johannesburg Council efforts to have the township removed), they were following their class interests in attempting to construct the conditions there and elsewhere for long-term accumulation through the commodification of township housing.

The efforts of the established building societies to change the underlying legal and environmental conditions in Alexandra failed. Subsequently, the state's decision in 1963 to transform Alexandra into a hostel city for twenty thousand male and five thousand female workers--and the concomitant mass expropriation of homes--replaced ownership with rental status, thus deeply affecting the politics of subsequent township protest. Although thousands of Alexandra residents were displaced between the 1960s and 1979 (the population dipped to forty thousand in 1973), urbanization pressures intensified in the Transvaal such that the illegal squatter sector of the population generally increased steadily from the mid-1970s, and shack dwellings sprouted in most backyards. In 1974, with just 950 freehold properties in black hands (down from a peak of 2,500), Reverend Sam Buti founded the Alexandra Township Residents Liaison Committee, which later became the Save Alexandra Party. Though Buti claimed responsibility for Pretoria's 1979 reprieve--which allowed Alexandra to maintain itself as a part-family-based, part-migrant-labor-based township--the decision probably had more to do with the problems of building hostels in Alexandra and with the shift in state strategies towards urbanization more generally as signified by the acceptance of the Riekert and Wiehahn Commissions. Buti co-operated in the West Rand Administration Board's development of a master plan for Alexandra in 1980, one which involved large-scale supposedly temporary displacement of residents. Intense community resistance developed over the next few years--initially from the Alexandra Residents Association and subsequently from the Alexandra Youth Congress and Alexandra Action Committee (AAC)--finally forcing the then-mayor, Buti, to resign in 1986.

Preparing the ground for housing finance

Despite the intense community pressure on local administration and the illegitimacy of the central state's strategy, both quite obvious from the early days of Alexandra's redevelopment, certain elements of private capital had begun some tentative steps towards Alexandra in the early 1980s. Their efforts were, it must be said, puny in comparison to the flood of capital that inundated Alexandra at the end of the decade, but ideologically they were not insignificant. Some initial charitable efforts must have appeared to the donors as merely that (for example, the *Star* newspaper's "Uplift in Alexandra" campaign which gathered private and corporate funds for building housing and amenities), while other endeavors were clearly geared to the long-term development of Alexandra as a site for capital accumulation. More serious in this respect was the non-profit Alexandra Development Fund (ADF), which gathered together companies whose interests in Alexandra ranged from contracting work to new retail markets. Among the ADF'S thirty major corporate supporters were the Perm, First National, and Nedbank. (The ADF has been a leading force in promoting middle-income housing for sale at cost or through small subsidies, and arranged the construction of 130 homes through a R1-million revolving fund in its first full year of operation.) Other huge corporations saw the importance of smothering Alexandra with monetary support. The Premier Group donated R100,000, and South African Breweries chipped In R55,000. Barlow Rand founded the Alexandra Enterprise Center as "a breeding ground for our future black manufacturers and industrialists" (Jochelson 1988:16). The "Progress through Employment" program of the Alexandra administrator and businesses aimed for a more realistic audience of future small business people, and was given support by First National Bank and other big companies. Earlier, First National (then Barclays) had provided a R500,000 loan for an old-age home (*Star* 4/8/82). Nedbank offered financing to Alexandra's creches (*Financial Mail* 20/5/88). All this was backed firmly by the state, which well understood the need to impose free enterprise values upon its subjects and also to back away from a direct role in housing development.

"In the past years," Nunka Mkhalipe and Buti observed in a 1985 newspaper column,

> the government has placed an increasing onus for black housing on the private sector. However, there are still many obstacles to be overcome before the private sector can participate meaningfully in this process. The availability of land, 99-year leasehold registration procedures and the surveying of plots have also hindered private sector involvement, but lack of finance is the hub of the problem. (*Alexandra Chronicle* December 1985)

It was not until after Buti's forced resignation as Alexandra mayor and after the state had smashed the AAC that private sector housing finance willingly entered the township. Not only had Alexandra been a most vivid example of political investment risk during the 1985-86

Witwatersrand uprisings, even the surrounding white areas were feeling the pinch. At the peak of unrest in April 1986, eighty percent of neighboring Marlboro's businesses (which employed many Alexandrians) were boarded up, and housing prices in white suburbs nearby began falling by as much as ten percent in a matter of weeks (*Financial Mail* 11/4/86; *Citizen* 8/5/86).

When the state reassembled its Alexandra forces following the May-July 1986 siege under the rubric of a mini-joint management center (JMC), it decided that alongside repression there must be a more focused effort to provide funds for upgrading Alexandra's existing legal residential base. The needs had become acute, for eighty percent of the township was without sewerage or electricity, only the main thoroughfare was tarred, and only ten percent of the streets were lit. Although two-thirds of Alexandra shack dwellers were born in the township or lived there more than two decades (Idasa "Factsheet on Alexandra," circa 1989), a September 1986 plan by Eskom engineers pointed out ways in which services for just 92,000 people (less than half the estimated population) could be provided. Eskom suggested maintaining the township's existing grid-block layout rather than continuing with the 1980 plan's complete overhaul (Halbig 1987), and on housing recommended, "Swift movement to private ownership on the basis of permanent title, so that owners can assist local authorities in creating order, promoting cleanliness, limiting crime and preventing squatting." In the words of a military officer on the Alexandra JMC, "We believe that if a person owns his own house, he will not tolerate stone-throwing or petrol-bombing in the vicinity" (*Guardian* 1/5/89).

With AAC leaders in jail on treason charges (which ultimately could not be successfully prosecuted, thanks in part to keen international attention), upgrading began in earnest, with three phases of infrastructure provision which was to cost R139 million. The new amenities include a post office, clinic, public phones, mast lighting, tarred roads, and some sewerage services, with plans for major recreational facilities (*Housing in Southern Africa* March 1990). According to Steve Burger, who managed the township following the 1986 army occupation,

> By the end of 1990, Alexandra will boast the completion of full services to the township. The transformation is unbelievable. Old houses are being refurbished and sold off, while brand-new houses are being built in the old Alexandra as well as on the new extension on the east of the

Jukskei River. Civic pride is also evident, as residents use the garbage cans that have been provided by the RSC. (*Financial Mail* 19/1/90)

For the state, Jochelson (1988:14) contends, "Alexandra's proximity to white areas, its symbolic value as an area of militant people's power, and international attention focused on the treason trials, [made] the township a particular challenge." And from the state's point of view, the new plan and its implementation were largely successful in meeting the challenge.

The private sector developers who moved in to take advantage of the redevelopment of Alexandra included SM Goldstein, Gough Cooper Homes, Tri-Time Housing, Alex Homes Forever, John Shaw Construction, and Rabie Property Developers. Stocks and Stocks had plans for shops, private offices and a municipal office in the town center of Old Alexandra. New land available on the east bank of the Jukskei River (East Bank) was quickly sought by Tri-Time, Rabie, LTA Comiat, Schachat Cullum, Basil Read, Habitech, Homes 2000, Minrav International (an Israeli firm), Permanent Development Corporation (of the Perm building society), and the Urban Foundation's FHA Homes. Ultimately, Rabie and its affiliates Murray and Roberts got the lion's share of East Bank, and did all the infrastructure provision. Murray and Roberts offered a "Learn While You Earn Homebuilding Course" for Alexandra residents. The 250-hectare Far East Bank was eyed hungrily by developers, with expectations that six thousand new units would be built by the private sector for low-, middle-, and high-income residents. Topping it all off, by mid-1990 construction on a R110 million "Alex City" shopping complex (with cinemas) was begun by the Logaro Group on a squatter settlement in Old Alexandra, though not without some community resistance. In the wake of winter demolitions of dozens of shacks, the company expressed somewhat misplaced concern "at the continuing influx of people into the already overcrowded township" (*Star* 6/6/90).

In this way the ground had been prepared for the penetration of financial capital in Alexandra Township. The value of residential building plans passed in 1986 was R601,000; R936,000 in 1987; and an extraordinary R19.6 million in 1988. The value of commercial plans went from R625,000 in 1986 to R372,000 in 1987 to R1.1 million in 1988 (Davies, Bristow, & Associates 1989:14). Financial institutions queued up to make loans in once-forbidden Alexandra.

The penetration of housing finance

Most of the Alexandra mortgage activity recorded at the Pretoria deeds office up to May 1989 (such records begin in early 1988) supported the R40 million housing development in East Bank. This reflects not only the capacity of developers to transform empty space into housing commodities--already occupied space requires displacement of existing residents, in many cases--but also the difficulty in formal surveying of the Old Alexandra stands. Most surveying of Old Alexandra took place through aerial photography, and this--plus the added filing costs passed on to buyers--made it difficult to transfer houses to freehold status. East Bank houses are freehold, while all the Old Alexandra house sales had leasehold status.

The leading issuer of mortgage bonds in Alexandra up to May 1989 was the combination of the Perm, Ned Perm, SA Perm, and Nedbank (Nedperm), with 262 loans. Allied had 198, nearly all of which were in East Bank. Of fifty-seven homes that had mortgages of more than R80,000, Nedperm accounted for forty-one, including the lion's share of residential loans greater than R100,000. But Nedperm also granted many mortgages of around R20,000, and even one as low as R10,000. The South Africa Housing Trust's Khayalethu Home Loan's loans were consistently in the R30,000 range, while most other lenders averaged R40,000 to R50,000.

Of about fifteen thousand dwellings in Old Alexandra, the Council still owned nine thousand or so in mid-1989, of which two thousand were structurally sound and three thousand could be made sound, according to Burger (*Weekly Mail* 6/8/89). While a February 1990 court decision against the Council temporarily halted home sales, and while Council negotiations with the Alexandra Civic Organization in May 1990 arrived at the position of sales only with full consultation and consensus by all parties affected, the effects of earlier housing privatization became acute. By September 1989, Budlender (1989:9-10) could report that "The most striking practical consequence of the sales has been a demand by the purchasers for sharply increased rent" from tenants; indeed, "in many cases the 'tenants' will in effect pay the full purchase price, and within a relatively short period." Budlender's Legal Resources Center documented a large number of enormous rent increases--from the R10-20 range to R50-150 range. Thus, says Mzwanele Mayekiso, "A class of petit bourgeois is being developed in Alex in the form of home-owners and stand-owners. These people in turn exploit their tenants. They charge high rentals and people are not happy with this situation" (*Work in Progress* 59, June/July 1989).

Apart from council house sales, private housing development in Alexandra is progressing rapidly, especially the construction and sales of flats in huge multi-floor apartment blocks. Sixty-four blocks were planned (*Housing in Southern Africa* December 1988), and by late 1988, 28 (housing 702 families) were under construction, supported by the National Housing Commission. (The R24-million construction contract went to SM Goldstein, with the mass production of construction materials such as wall panels moved from Alexandra itself to nearby Lombardy West--*Star* 17/11/88.) According to a Kaye-Eddie estate agent and developer, her company built and sold three blocks of 56-unit apartments in the center of Old Alexandra by January 1990 and four more blocks were planned. Financing for the flats was provided by the Allied Building Society, in whose nearby Orange Grove office Kaye-Eddie is located. The loans incorporate the state's first-time home-buyer subsidy, and in January 1990 carried a 17.5 percent interest rate. For R21,600 bachelor flats in the buildings, with a 10 percent deposit paid (some deposits were as low as 5 percent), the monthly bond payment was R223, and thus Allied and Kaye-Eddie required a minimum R800 per month family income. For two-bedroom R40,200 apartments, the monthly payment was R314 and R1,000-per-month income was required. For three-bedroom R55,500 apartments, R439 was the monthly payment and R1,200 the minimum monthly income. Yet market research data compiled by LHA Management Consultants suggest that only 20 percent of Alexandra residents earn the monthly income required by Allied for the bachelor flats; 10.5 percent the two-bedroom flats; and 4.3 percent the three-bedroom flats. Furthermore, after subtracting subsistence-level living costs and income tax, it is clear from LHA data that even this select group cannot really afford the Allied monthly bond payments.

Old Alexandra is also witnessing an increasing amount of private single-family housing construction and sales, which are again dependent upon housing finance. Johannesburg-based TIME Housing is one of the major developers. In a company brochure, TIME brags that "We work with all major Building Societies with particularly strong links with the SA Perm, NBS, Saambou and the Allied. We were also one of the first housing companies to offer Standard Bank bonds for the Coloured,

Asian and Black population groups." One TIME employee noted that individual financing for the company's range of R47,000 to R65,000 houses were typically 5 percent deposit bonds granted by NBS and the Perm (interview with author, 22/1/90). With its affiliate Tri-Time Housing (which includes black entrepreneurs), TIME worked on a joint venture to build fifty "quality" homes on 13th Street, half of which became the subject of a legal battle--over construction flaws--that in mid-1990 threatened to draw in the Perm for financing negligence. TIME aimed to move from its then upmarket client base to buyers of units worth less than R25,000. "In this range," said TIME managing director Mike Graham, "the SA Housing Trust offers substantial assistance in the form of serviced land" (*Sunday Times* 9/4/88). In addition to TIME, other Old Alexandra developers include Alex Homes Forever, Algemene Diensburo vir Kerlike Beplanning, Ontwikkeling en Bestuur, and John Shaw Construction. Gough Cooper (of SM Goldstein) began a 107-house complex named "Alexandra Mews" in Old Alexandra in March 1989, priced initially at R74,000 but repriced at R50,000 to R60,000.

In the Alexandra Council's attempt to impose new intratownship class relations, the East Bank was the first testing ground; 28 houses were constructed there in a 1986 pilot scheme. As early as March 1986 the far-sighted developers Murray and Roberts had gained East Bank development rights from the Johannesburg City Council (which then owned the land), so long as a "Millionaires' Row" buffer zone (and later, a golf course) would separate East Bank from neighboring white Lombardy. Murray and Roberts began developing 630 stands in April 1988 (with fourteen different house designs), of which 511 in the first phase cost an estimated R40 million (around R80,000 per house), for which the company received substantial infrastructural subsidies from the South African Housing Trust (SAHT). Another 334 sites were planned by the SAHT for "low-income" housing on 190-square-meter stands, a quarter of the size of the Millionaires' Row stands. The Housing Trust homes, just 40 square meters in size and built to very low standards, were priced at R20,000 in 1989 and financed by the Trust's Khayalethu Home Loans, while a relatively cheap Murray and Roberts house in East Bank was R45,000 (of which R12,000 was for the serviced plot) and financed by private financial institutions.

The East Bank's development offered the state and capital some particular lessons on what worked and what did not work in the township residential differentiation. According to Hendler (1989:108),

> The development of the private market [in East Bank] complemented the upgrading of the old section of the township, which formed part of the Joint Management Center strategy for the area. The creation of an up-market elite area would dovetail very neatly with the National Management Security System's strategy to defuse tension in Alexandra, and to create the basis for social stability there.

Fully two-thirds of East Bank's seven hundred houses were selling, in late 1988, for R50,000 or above, with a quarter higher than R80,000. "Although the top end is a little thin," Rabie Housing's managing director told *Business Day* (17/11/88), "sales have gone down extremely well with Alexandra residents." The newspaper also learned from Murray and Roberts's housing director that "Up-market projects will fulfil' a vital function of motivating township residents towards a better lifestyle," a view confirmed by an Alexandra home-owner: "Having something to strive for is going to change everything for us."

Such sentiments are the clarion call for a middle- and upper middle-class East Bank community that Alexandra resident Pascal Damoyi, in 1987, derisively labeled "a five star lokasie [location].... meant for the town clerks, cops and teachers. The project aims to create a population of active, employed and skilled people, afraid of losing their expensive houses, tamed, and effectively controlled" (*Work in Progress* 44). The largely upmarket East Bank was a launching pad from which a successful program of political pacification could begin.

Following the development of the entire East Bank, the next area for Alexandra's expansion would be the much larger 260-hectare strip known as Far East Bank. This area abuts the white area of Lombardy, hence the Johannesburg City Council's 1990 demand that any development there be buffered by a golf course and high-income housing. In addition to the obvious desire of Murray and Roberts to continue its East Bank building in consortium with several other developers, major players such as Eskom and the Development Bank of Southern Africa expressed an interest in the Transvaal Provincial Administration's Far East Bank tender proposal in mid-1990.

The ACO also submitted a Far East Bank tender document which called for development to be controlled by a non-profit "Community Trust" that would encompass a Land Trust, Loan Fund and Community Development Corporation. Only through such community-controlled vehicles outside the realm of the logic of capital, ACO argued, could the authorities' goal of housing even some of Alexandra's so-called "have-nots" be met, since land speculation would otherwise quickly make housing costs prohibitive for poor people. This project, along the lines of the community-controlled co-operative models of housing decommodification that Swilling (1990) promotes, offers perhaps the best hope for concrete popular opposition to the urbanization of capital through housing finance in Alexandra, and will serve as a national model for progressive development.

But in a more confrontational vein, there are other township challenges to financial capital emerging elsewhere in South Africa, even spurring the development of a housing bond insurance program for political risk (*Business Day* 7/6/90). In particular, "bond boycotts" arose from Blue Downs in the Western Cape in 1989 and spread ominously to other black townships like Old Crossroads and Khayelitsha, leading Planning and Provincial Affairs Minister Hernus Kriel to agonize to Parliament in mid-1990: "If bond repayments are not made, financial institutions involved in providing home loans will have no alternative but to refuse to finance black housing. I want to call on black leaders to stop these actions. Nobody, but nobody can benefit from such an attitude" (*Business Day* 22/5/90).

Conclusion

Whether grassroots resistance to financial capital's penetration of townships will stiffen in coming months and years, or--as in the United States--only after the full effect of housing valorization and devalorization and residential differentiation are felt, decades down the road, this issue is in the hands of the civic associations and mass democratic movement leaders who are presently gearing up for negotiations with the state (bringing with them a Freedom Charter whose demands include nationalization of banks). What can be learned from the preceding evidence?

If South Africa's financial explosion is, at some level, the driving force behind the penetration of housing finance into townships, this is extremely disturbing. Throughout history, the problem of a rising financial sector delinking from a shrinking productive base has been dealt with conclusively only one way: widespread defaults and general financial collapse (Clarke 1988). Black borrowers will be least able to withstand the severe shake-out and austerity that arises from the banks' frantic search for collateral. None the less, housing finance will provide the overriding logic for township development in the near future. The Alexandra experience suggests that state intervention--both through bald repression and "winning hearts and minds"--remains crucial to preparing the ground for housing finance; but it appears that this will generally proceed according to a public-private partnership model that subsidizes landed and financial capital (for example, the Steyn Fund). The issue then becomes to what degree the concomitant processes of class differentiation, rising land and housing costs, displacement of tenants, and community disintegration can be contained by progressive forces.

This chapter has merely outlined the problems of township housing within the context of the financial explosion. Before lasting solutions are found, popular struggle on the terrain of high finance must intensify, whether or not this conflicts with nationalist strategies of bringing on board all potential democratic allies (for example, liberal financiers). Here, United States civic associations, trade unions, students, and the anti-apartheid movement may have some lessons to impart (Bond 1987, 1990b-c). Failing this, it would be quite natural for the general pattern of United States urban development--with its systemic mix of postmodern fortresses for the rich surrounded by expanding slums and overpriced suburbs--to recur in an even more damaging and polarizing way in this country, as central business districts harbor uncontrolled financial speculation and as apartheid townships become free market free-for-all investment zones, the needs of the masses of poor and working people be damned.

chapter seven

1990s Gentrification Bust

with JOHNNY STEINBERG and PAUL VAN ZYL

Amidst the hype associated with finally making available middle-income housing finance to black South Africans was a perception that they would readily take up the slack in inner-city areas--from which large-scale property capital was, by the late 1980s, ready to disinvest. Our 1990 prediction of the difficulties associated with realizing this vision hinged on structural contradictions. But social struggle also played a key role, particularly steady (sometimes spectacular) resistance to evictions and rent increases by a myriad of community and even building-based organizations. Our analysis also failed to discern the generation of the new African humanity within inner-city Johannesburg's decaying physical infrastructure, which still makes this such an interesting, compelling place to visit and work (witness the stop-start Seven Buildings co-op housing project, which perseveres under very difficult conditions). But this chapter locates, nevertheless, the core economic processes which during the 1990s reduced Johannesburg's inner-city to a no-go zone both for capital and for many white-collar managers formerly comfortable in their cosmopolitan CBD offices. The corporate retreat north to Rosebank and Sandton appears permanent, in the wake of the late 1990s sell-off of much of the major institutional landlords' inner-city portfolios. While 15-year waves of property speculation are fairly permanent features of even the distorted South African version of capitalism, the investment flows probably won't return to the CBD. Perhaps the Johannesburg Council will one day find the resources (or tax rebates) to kickstart a few new investments in central Johannesburg, but unless social struggles are also revitalized, these would have more to do with the proclivities of developers than with meeting social needs.

[The chapter appeared as "Contradictions in the Transition from Urban Apartheid: Barriers to Gentrification in Johannesburg" in D.Smith, ed. *The Apartheid City and Beyond: Urbanization and Social Change in South Africa* (Routledge, London, 1992).]

Introduction

From the top of Africa's tallest building, the 50-floor Carlton Center in Johannesburg, the panoramic view is disquieting. The surrounding skyline began changing rapidly in the 1980s, in a dangerously uneven way. Now, while the western side of the central business district (CBD) is graced by ever more sophisticated, shiny, postmodern architectural gems housing mainly financial institutions, the eastern end remains clogged with dozens of overcrowded 1930s low-rise flats. On the rooftops of these buildings Carlton Center observers can see the cardboard shanties of poor and working families.

Hidden by the variegated surface-level mosaic of Johannesburg land-use patterns, extremely deep-rooted political and economic dynamics have spawned classic competitive struggles over urban space. The most contradictory of these are the seemingly irreconcilable encounters involving capitalists as individuals versus broader capitalist class interests.

The stakes are high, because half of all office space in South Africa is located in the Johannesburg CBD. (Threatening now to alter the balance of these forces, there is also to be found, competing for space on the east end of town, the militant tenant rights organization Actstop.)

From where did this struggle for the CBD of Johannesburg emerge, and what will result, especially in the portentous, so far relatively-untapped east end? We argue that the crusade for inner-city redevelopment has occurred in the context of a broader economic crisis; that it has been led by the structural rise of finance in the economy; and that it comes at a momentous time when urban desegregation permits the space of the city to play a greater role in the broader formation of class alliances.

Thus for the CBD's east end, the most coherent approach of the local state and capital is gentrification, but of a peculiar sort, aimed at an ascendant fraction of the black working class more than at traditional white yuppies. It is not, however, just the unusual target of this semi-gentrification project that creates the contradictions to which we refer. Instead the contradictions emanate from intercapitalist competition and the general tendency, deeply embedded in the South African economy, towards overindebtedness and untrammelled financial speculation.

It is in the struggle for this CBD space that some of the most glaring contradictions of South African urbanization in the 1990s can be readily observed. This chapter attempts to construct a broader political-economic framework that can shed light on the spatial fix to economic crisis in other South African settings, and on the social and political contradictions of post-apartheid urbanization.

Overaccumulation crisis

But what do we mean by crisis? It is widely accepted that South Africa has experienced a structural slowdown in economic growth since around 1974, the exact causes of which are subject to debate. Business economists (e.g. Dickman 1990) typically attribute the crisis to government policies ranging from apartheid to ineffectual monetary and fiscal policy and seek remedies in free markets and a non-interventionist state. Progressive economists point to increased labor militancy and wage struggles beginning in the early 1970s (Nattrass 1990); the transmission of international crisis (Moll 1990); or some combination of the two which served to undermine a previously stable racial Fordist regime of capital accumulation (Gelb 1991).

Meth (1990:33), however, is rightly opposed to arguments about the roots of crisis which "lay a large portion of the 'blame' on 'apartheid' and much of the rest of it on the 'unreasonable' (politically-motivated) wage claims of the workers." Many of the policy implications that stem from such analyses are objectionable to progressives and in any case could not be expected to resolve the crisis, as the failure of anti-labor, anti-government intervention programs of Reagan and Thatcher amply demonstrate (Clarke 1988). Yet, says Meth (1990:32), even Gelb "allows capital to slide too easily off the hook" of responsibility for the crisis. In contrast, Bond (1991a, 1991b) advances the proposition that South Africa's current economic crisis--like that, indeed, of the global system--is best described as one of overaccumulation of capital, a permanent tendency embedded in the normal operation of the system, at global, national, and even regional levels (Harvey 1982; Clarke 1988). From this starting point, the rise of finance and its simultaneous search for investment outlets in the built environment follow logically. The conditions in Johannesburg are very much related to these broader processes.

In South Africa's case, bottlenecks between investment for consumer goods and producer goods which emerged in the late 1960s were paramount to the particular form of the overaccumulation crisis (Clarke 1978). These were exacerbated by extensive multinational corporate direct investment in consumer goods industries; by aggressive import-substitution policies which gave enormous support to locally made consumer luxury goods; by enormously skewed distribution of income and wealth; and by South Africa's abundant mineral resource endowment, which promoted a lotus-eating effect--that is, it was easier to import producer goods than make them locally (Meth 1990).

The immediate results included a build-up of substantial retail and whole-sale inventories in the late 1960s; a "wild speculative boom" (Johannesburg Stock Exchange 1990) in the stock market from 1967 to 1969 (followed by collapse from mid-1969 to 1971); an intense but ruinous spurt of automation in private-sector manufacturing from 1971 to 1973; and the subsequent levelling off and decline of new private-sector manufacturing investment from 1973; all of which pointed to untenable structural bottlenecks and presaged a long economic slump. The 1980s witnessed negative per capita growth; negative growth rates in productive investment; and an absolute decline in the value of capital stock, especially in manufacturing.

The economic crisis directly affected the development of South Africa's built environment, especially cities, in a manner reminiscent of the spatial fix that Harvey (1982) theorizes. For example, one early state reaction to the slump in private-sector investment was a huge increase in parastatal spending on transport, storage, communications, and the like. As the crisis set in, state construction of electricity grids and water lines also rose dramatically by comparison with the boom years of the 1960s.

These built-environment investments mopped up some overaccumulated capital and helped overcome certain barriers to profitability that distance presented, but not enough to prepare the ground for renewed long-term private-sector investment and accumulation. And in any case the strategy was also built on an enormous foreign-debt build-up, which came home to roost with a vengeance from 1985. The debt facilitated intensive anti-apartheid financial sanctions pressure (a key reason for the political reforms described below); led to severe balance-of-payments constraints; forced the Reserve Bank to hike real interest rates; and caused a fiscal crisis from which the state attempted desperately and unsuccessfully to emerge through privatization of some key parastatal corporations.

In the 1980s the built environment continued to play a role in the way the crisis unfolded. The state led the spatial fix into the bantustans (homelands), partly to support the pre-De Klerk political vision of apartheid. Direct state investment in township housing declined after the 1970s, but there was a huge increase in bantustan development grants. In addition, massive state subsidies were provided to the private sector, from the early 1980s, for decentralized production in bantustan border regions.

In spite of shifting some 15 percent of manufacturing employment from urban areas to decentralization points during the mid-1980s, the strategy backfired when international anti-apartheid sanctions began to bite. Decentralized firms producing low-cost, low-technology, labor-intensive commodities had to turn from export to local markets in the late 1980s, thus squeezing metropolitan capital (Pickles 1991). Cities were by then already beginning to suffer from classic symptoms of deindustrialization, including vacant swaths of CBD manufacturing and warehousing space. The Urban Foundation, Development Bank of Southern Africa, South African Chamber of Business and Johannesburg City Council, among others, have since exerted pressure against Pretoria to cease subsidizing this temporary spatial resolution of overaccumulation, one beset in any case by rampant inefficiencies and corruption. (CBD warehousing districts also suffered due to the intensification of corporate vertical integration--hence less scope for merchant intermediaries--which accompanied South African monopoly capital's centralization and manufacturing diversification dating from the 1960s.)

This background is crucial to understanding the nature of the political-economic-spatial escape route favored by the state and big business in the late 1980s, a route which will be followed through to a waystation in the Johannesburg CBD in the pages below. The crisis and its initial bantustan spatial fix helped hollow out the core productive space in the CBD, and the subsequent financial fix helped fill the spatial vacuum. More so than mainstream investment theory or French regulation theory favored by COSATU's Economic Trends group (Gelb 1991), *the theory of overaccumulation captures the frantic if uneven search for profits in different sectors and circuits, different regions, and over different time horizons in the space economy.*

To make that clear, it is the financial fix--the creation of unprecedented amounts of fictitious capital to forestall the devaluation of overaccumulated capital--that we turn to in more detail in view of its assertive role in restructuring the South African city during a period of crisis in the productive economy. Fictitious capital refers simply to the paper representations of value, whether securities, debt instruments, real estate titles, etc. The concept is important because it allows researchers to link certain forms of spatial development directly to powerful financial markets (Harvey 1982: chs.9-10).

Finance and the city

In South Africa, the decline in the productive economy from the mid-1970s and the inability of the state's spatial fix to fully mop up overaccumulation, as summarized above, were the precursors to the enthusiastic flow of capital into financial markets in the early 1980s. Not long after the 1981 collapse in the gold price, the Johannesburg Stock Exchange began an eight-year upward spiral that outpaced investment in fixed capital stock by a factor of eight. In 1989 alone, the market rose by more than 50 percent in US-dollar terms, the highest increase in the world, while real economic growth was limited to 2 percent.

During the first nine months of 1991, amidst a 20-percent decline in average stock market value across the globe, the Johannesburg Stock Exchange industrial index ranked second best in the world, losing just 4 percent.

"It is a damning indictment of the economy," conceded Nedbank's chief economist, Edward Osborn,

> but we've also seen it in the States, in Japan, etc. This tremendous shift into simply pushing up values on the markets. So market values have risen extraordinarily, but the underpinning economic values have not been rising. So what we've really seen is financial inflation taking place at a horrendous rate. We haven't been immune from this international trend, in fact we've been one of the leading cases of this. (Interview, September 1990)

The financial rot has also extended deep into the credit system, not just the stock market. As a percentage of economic output, private-sector debt to banks doubled during the 1980s; personal and company foreclosures increased to record levels following the business cycle downturn in the late 1980s; and the fallout included severe banking collapses and a merger wave that left South African financial institutions entering the 1990s with far too many paper assets relative to their underlying capital (Bond 1990e). Worst of all, the debt was not, by and large, pumped into new productive investments. "A very large proportion of this has gone into bolstering the demand for financial assets," Osborn acknowledged. "So we've had the situation of a massive, exponential rise in financial flows, which are just swirling about, as it were, going into an inflation of values, financial assets, feeding a whole inflationary process in this country."

In short, capitalists facing the overaccumulation crisis examined their balance sheets following the 1981 gold bust, withdrew funds that might have otherwise gone into production and, with the help of the big institutional investors and new borrowings, funnelled the money instead into non-productive outlets. In addition to the stock market, real estate also became a major speculative investment arena, in spite of enormous interest rate hikes in the late 1980s, with turnover up 75 percent in nominal terms from 1986 to 1989 (*South African Reserve Bank Quarterly* December 1989).

Consider the scope for *residential* investments, organized by financial and landed capital, in inner-city Johannesburg. The target is the black market, which, after all, accounts for 70 percent of retail purchases in the CBD. White yuppies maintain stronger social connections to the northern suburbs and don't appear to fit into the plans of developers at this juncture. Illustrating the potential market in the black urban professional class, a 1990 brochure for the Anglo American Corporation's Inner-City Property Development Fund promotes a R16-million investment in Hillbrow; a six-block site with two dozen residential buildings and 1,500 units. The site, now occupied largely illegally by working-class blacks, and

> undoubtedly one of the primary residential hubs of South Africa, provides the investor with excellent potential in terms of both rentals and sales. Yet it should also be said that by giving residents a desirable place in which to live--and therefore a stake in the area's future--it will help to stabilise and renew one of the CBD's critical buffer zones. This important project should be seen as a vital first step in the urban renewal process.

Similarly, the Urban Foundation has targeted nearby Joubert Park for residential redevelopment, and for manufacturing revitalization based on the small-scale furniture industry and potential linkages into the broader export-orientation that the state and capital now favor so strongly.

Along with Hillbrow, the area has suffered severe devaluation, thanks in part to repossessions and redlining by financial institutions (Prinsloo 1988; *Weekly Mail* 25/10/90). Declines of up to a quarter in values of sectional title flats in repossession have been experienced by building societies. And the main drawback to the Urban Foundation's extensive redevelopment scheme, apparently, is that surveys conclude that current black residents are not interested in home-ownership, even though their incomes could support bond repayments. Inculcating home ownership values thus remains a strong theme of the Urban Foundation (interviews with the Foundation's staff and city planners, August 1990). As in the case of township social restructuring which proceeded largely according to the dictates of housing finance (see Chapter Six), the selected saturation of the inner city by capital took place within a broader context: the establishment of a post-apartheid social contract, of which top-level negotiations between Pretoria and the African National Congress are but a surface example.

A new political-economic dispensation?

As the 1990s begin, the broader avenue that the state and capital were paving to exit the economic crisis included the following byways: export-oriented manufacturing production; capital-intensive production processes; greater use of foreign debt to import the means of production; continued liberalization of domestic financial markets; privatization of state assets, and deregulation of commerce; differentiation of black workers into a 30-percent core of skilled workers and a 70-percent periphery of unskilled, self-exploited, informal sector labor; for the core workers, vast increases in consumer indebtedness, supported through the collateral provided by newly-privatized housing; relatively unhindered labor mobility and a commitment to urbanization, but both based on individuals' capacity to purchase urban exchange-values (like houses) organized increasingly by established capitalists; for the poor, one-off site-and-service grants of R6,000 which will locate them in controlled peri-urban dumping grounds a great geographical distance from the formal economy; and, to ease the tensions inherent in the package, a social contract and unprecedented access to development finance intended to coopt leading sectors of the progressive movement, especially urban civic associations and the ANC.

While the seeds of this approach to solving dilemmas raised by overaccumulation have been sown for some years (Morris and Padayachee 1988), it is only recently that coherence has emerged from the diverse set of programs within such powerful institutions as: the Urban Foundation, founded by Anglo American and other leading corporations to ameliorate social tensions and to carefully dismantle urban apartheid following the 1976 Soweto uprising; the R2.5-billion Development Bank of Southern Africa; and the Independent Development Trust, a R2-billion development initiative announced by President de Klerk in February 1990, run by Judge Jan Steyn, long-time chair of the Urban Foundation. These bodies have apparently assumed responsibility for guiding and grounding the overall political-economic strategy in the built environment, and for drawing into the package sufficient private capital and state resources and the appropriate political actors. Swilling (1990) labelled this aspect of the strategy--one constructed, he says, by the econocrats who replaced the P.W. Botha-era securocrats--"deracialized urbanization," although deracialized apartheid may be just as accurate to describe the likely spatial outcome of class differentiation, he suggests. "Coordinated by the Urban Foundation," the deracialized urbanization strategy "is the first time all the major private sector organizations linked together to tackle the challenge of formulating new policy directions for the country," the Urban Foundation itself testifies (*New African* 10/9/90).

Different corporate members of business organizations affiliated to the Urban Foundation have long tired of certain aspects of apartheid, including rigid labor markets, low cost and low quality consumption patterns, international isolation, and social and political instability. The constraints that apartheid urban land use impose on capital are damaging to capital's growth strategy for the 1990s, because, McCarthy and Smit (1987) argue, they even affect the capacity of manufacturers to expand their operations into international markets. Transport bottlenecks that accompany apartheid geography are an especially important barrier to profitability, and this provides at least some of the logic behind the Urban Foundation's compact city philosophy. And in any event, the population density of inner-city Johannesburg is remarkably low in comparison to both First World and Third World cities around the world. Tomlinson (1987, 1990) argues that Johannesburg could comfortably accommodate a 150-percent increase in population density, especially in such peripheral areas as the now sterile mining belt on the city's southern edge. Aside from Hillbrow, Joubert Park, and a few similar inner-city belt locations, the best indication of the success of the broader socio-spatial post-apartheid restructuring might be found in the east end of the Johannesburg CBD. It is there that the contradictions in the whole process are also evident.

The east end of the Johannesburg central business district

Originally, the built environment in east end of Johannesburg housed low-income whites as well as factory premises for small-scale manufacturing enterprises. In the early 1990s, the buildings were still predominantly owned by individuals and small firms, with financial and corporate capital only beginning to show noticeable interest at the margins of the district. Nearby, in Bertrams, 78 percent of property transactions involved investment companies, banks, building societies, and property developers in 1989, up from 28 percent in 1982 (Madisa *et al* 1990:49). Yet in the 1980s, a number of processes radically altered the character and property values of the east end.

With the *de facto* erosion of the Group Areas Act, residential buildings became occupied entirely by illegal black residents. One result is a marked decline in the value of housing stock, as unscrupulous landlords milk the properties, leaving widespread squalor, despair, and little legal recourse. However, due to the 330-percent rise in South African CBD real estate values since the early 1980s (*Financial Mail* 21/4/89), land prices in the east end are disproportionately high relative to the value of the buildings.

It is this zone of land which has been earmarked by the Johannesburg City Council for an ambitious redevelopment project. Local government would embark upon a substantial infrastructural upgrading scheme to improve not only services, facilities, and amenities, but also aesthetics. The Council then envisaged a process whereby *large corporations purchased the buildings in this zone of the CBD, restored them, and then sold them to employees.*

The prime targets were "thousands of middle and upper income earners.... mostly employed in the high-rise banking complex taking shape in the west of the city," according to one councillor (*Star* 22/4/90). Even the upper strata of the working class might qualify for sectional title ownership of flats in slightly refurbished tenements. "I'll be talking to the big boys [corporate capital]," said a leading city official.

"I'm sure they will jump at the opportunity. I can't even begin to describe what a problem it is for those chaps when their employees live in rented homes in Soweto" (Interview with Planning Department official, August 1990).

The Council's scheme would, if successful, result in the movement of formally employed black workers into the inner city, but would also intensify the spatial marginalization of the seasonally employed and structurally unemployed. The employee home ownership features established the conditions whereby the inner-city social structure would be regulated through a concrete relationship between monopoly capital and core workers. And the marginalization of excluded workers would occur in a *destatified* manner. "When people get evicted no one can lump the blame on the Council's shoulders. Market forces will dictate where people can and cannot live," said the city official, with some satisfaction:

> People complain that we are renovating theaters while people don't have roofs over their heads. But we cannot become a charity organization. It is not for us to mould this city's future. It is the role of the free market. We must leave the free market to its own devices. (Interview, 1990)

Thus the City Council's attempt to shape the east end of the CBD while remaining servile to the market would contribute, at a micro level, to a reorganization of the metropolitan region's class structure that corresponds to the larger political economic metamorphosis described in the previous section. But can the City Council's ambition be achieved?

At first blush, the eastern end of the CBD seems ideal for redevelopment based on classic gentrification processes (e.g., Smith 1979): disinvestment leading to the existence of a property (if not land) "rent gap"; willingness by the local state to play a catalytic role; sufficient liquidity of property investment capital; and the social pressure and conditions in the spatially-organized labor market that ensure a client base for redevelopment. Yet what is striking about this area, at the beginning of the 1990s, is that the opportunity to carry out the Council project successfully may well already be lost.

East end property market contradictions

Because of the high costs of underlying land, added to disproportionate new construction costs, investments in existing buildings are at optimum profitability in this area when directed to office, not residential, usage. The difference between building costs and yield for office space is now eight times higher than that for residential usage (interviews, August 1990). Furthermore, office blocks require less maintenance and do not carry with them the threat to the landlord of Group Areas Act violations and penalties. "People think residential rentals have gone through the roof, but they are still not enough to attract developers," says the financial director of Sable Holdings. "The returns on residential property are way below those of office or industrial property.... You have hundreds of tenants complaining about the plumbing and other stuff. Commercial property is a pleasure--you simply collect your cheque every month" (*Weekly Mail* 18/10/90).

Profitability calculations had become clear to the small property investors by mid-1990. At that time, in a 20-block area of the east end, no fewer than 33 buildings were, simultaneously, publicly advertised for sale, renovation, or offices to let. What was common to all the buildings was a unilateral move from residential and industrial usage into office usage.

An increase in evictions of poor tenants is one predictable outcome of this process. In one typical case in mid-1990, rents were raised for run-down single rooms in Polly Lodge [near Polly and Jeppe Streets] from R88 per month to R450 per month, leading Actstop members to construct tents outside for dislodged victims and to erect signs demanding, "Nationalize the buildings!" Adjacent to Polly Lodge stands Executive House, a one-way mirrored, upmarket office block boasting subdued hints of postmodern design. Home now to legal firms and government offices, Executive House was in 1985 an empty industrial building.

The trend emblematized by Polly Lodge and Executive House is clear. Lucrative small office development possibilities have fundamentally skewed the land-use patterns in the east end of the Johannesburg CBD. Both the capital investment in (and structural transformation of) buildings in this area will make the return to marginally-profitable residential usage virtually impossible.

What does this mean in theoretical terms? During an overaccumulation crisis, the logic of capital accumulation--which in early 1990s South Africa is based increasingly on the political-economic vision of high finance and its allies--confronts its own constraints simultaneously, as restructuring proceeds. The short-term investment strategies of individual capitalists, in the context of a CBD rife with land speculation, obstructs the realization of a new economic, social, and spatial order that would serve broader capitalist class interests.

Conclusion

We have argued that flows of capital through the built environment are a crucial ingredient in the way the state and capitalist class have addressed South Africa's overaccumulation crisis. When combined with the rise of debt and financial speculation within the South African economy--which are themselves logical outcomes of overaccumulation--the impact on the form and functions of the Johannesburg CBD, as one example, are conspicuous. Add to this the conjunctures of racial-residential change and the search for a political settlement to South Africa's problems, and the CBD appears as a key node for the contradictions wrought by the crises of both apartheid and South African capitalism.

The contradictions boil down to time-honored tensions and conflicts between individual capitalists and capitalist class interests. Because these do not appear anywhere near resolution at the urban scale, the attempt to redevelop the CBD through a limited gentrification project that simultaneously aims to support the broader restructuring of economy and society is likely to be futile.

The arguments presented in this chapter are best considered *suggestions*--not irrevocable conclusions--about the dynamics now operating on South African cities. It is entirely possible that the dire warnings implied by the analysis will prove to be groundless, if, somehow, the South African economy does manage to recover from structural stagnation. For example, a chaotic and perhaps depression-ridden 1990s global economic environment could conceivably allow gold to again assert its traditional role as ultimate store of value and, as in the 1930s, thereby help South Africa to play the role of "prosperous undertaker during the plague." Based on our analysis of the depth of South Africa's economic crisis, this seems, sadly, to be the country's best hope.

Or as another example, the state and capital's optimal political solution--a social contract with leading segments of the progressive opposition, but enmeshed in a fully capitalist post-apartheid society--may well be achieved elsewhere, if not through a stillborn vision of gentrification in the Johannesburg CBD'S east end. Joubert Park, the site of the Urban Foundation's ambitious redevelopment initiative, or Hillbrow, viewed with anticipation by Anglo American, are already undergoing a more thorough physical devaluation process that better sets the stage for the kind of financial and socio-economic restructuring which could, conceivably, overcome the contradictions faced in the east end of the CBD.

Only time and *praxis* will tell, as the inner-city poor, represented by Actstop, continue to show an extraordinary capacity to resist the mass evictions that will accompany either the gentrification or small corporate office strategy, not to mention the oppression they face in their current status (*Star* 26/8/90). This sort of resistance should come as no surprise, for, since the early 1970s, cities have been the sites of the main pressures for transformation of South African society. From early trade union organizing to the 1976 Soweto uprising to broad popular-front politics in the 1980s, South Africa's apartheid cities have hosted heroic resistance to both apartheid oppression and economic exploitation. And from rent strikes to bond boycotts to consumer boycotts to other forms of anti-apartheid and anti-capitalist organizing, this continues to be the case (Bond 1990f).

What is new and different about the recent rise of finance in the South African economy, though, is its totalizing capacity to both drive urban investment of a particular sort and, because real estate speculation has proceeded too far, to simultaneously block the urban political economic change necessary to stabilize a new social order. Hence the struggles for space in the CBD point to the acute need for further, deeper progressive analyses and political offensives against powerful--yet potentially vulnerable--financial peaks at the South African economy's commanding heights.

chapter eight

Transitional Housing Policy Discourses

The early 1990s were exceptionally confusing when it came to resolving South Africa's housing question. There was a clear crisis; there were extremely active participants, including formidable community activists; and housing continued its 1980s function as political lightning-rod. The Democratic Movement maintained tough rent boycotts to shake loose residual Black Local Authority officials (and bond boycotts also took on political overtones in mid-1992 when insurrection was in the air). The late-apartheid state used housing benefits as a means of delaying the inevitable transfer of power and trying to win a few black votes. And while construction and banking capital retreated, their policy advocates took center stage. By late 1994, it was possible to report, in retrospect, how the previous few years of housing policy discourses had evolved, culminating in the Botshabelo conference that laid the ground for the *Housing White Paper*. But to contextualise the deterioration of popular housing demands and social struggles also requires a return to some of the theoretical problems associated with "development discourses." Questioning assumptions implicit in policy and program frameworks became quite an academic fashion by the mid-1990s. But in contrast to many neo-Foucauldian accounts of the development industry emerging at the time, this chapter tackles the combined intellectual and material "development impasse" from a Marxian vantagepoint. At stake was how to explain a disjuncture between theory and experience. Social-contract centrism appeared, superficially, to win the day, against the more ambitious early 1990s civic agenda. But as subsequent chapters show, the neoliberal position was first dominant after 1994, but then suffered the hardest reality check.

[The chapter appeared as "Urban Social Movements, the Housing Question and Development Discourse in South Africa," in D.Moore and G.Schmitz, eds. *Debating Development Discourses: Institutional and Popular Perspectives* (London, Macmillan and New York, St.Martin's Press, 1995).]

Introduction

Urban South Africa offers fertile case study material in the application of political-economic theory to contemporary policy and practice, mediated by the twists and turns in the discourse which surrounds development. Political debate, policy analysis and contestation of development processes are all as advanced in South Africa's cities as in any present-day setting. The 1994 election of the African National Congress (ANC) to lead the first "Government of National Unity" was, in important respects, the culmination of the first round of debate over post-apartheid development discourse. In brief, the transition period witnessed a contest between proponents of three distinct policy ideologies--neoliberal, social democratic and radical--all of whom can claim to have won certain significant concessions.

A developmentalist, populist ANC-led regime is the apparent outcome: intent on putting down left-wing challenges (wildcat and public sector strikes, land invasions and the like); relatively protective of national sovereignty against Washington financial bureaucrats; logistically and ideologically uneven at the level of the nine new federal provinces (seven of which it controls); and throughout the country, never quite firm enough to hold together its multi-class coalition and achieve clear consensus, under increasingly difficult conditions of international economic integration. In these respects, proponents from all three camps may claim satisfaction from the please-all discourse of the ANC, yet each is likely to be dissatisfied with the new ruling party's practice. That practice will be particularly difficult in the context of a long-term structural downturn in the South African economy which has created a development impasse of grave proportions.

The conflicting discourses are more than evident in answers to the "housing question" provided by the market-oriented World Bank, the consensus-based National Housing Forum, and the more radical-popular urban social movements. But to judge the discourses and to draw out their implications for political-economic practice in the recent and coming periods, requires prior background deliberation--not of policy, but of theory. Of particularly interest is the Left's evolving perspective on race and class, which bequeaths future radical development strategists a strong but nonetheless contradictory intellectual legacy. Characteristic of high theory over the past couple of decades across the world, much of the South African analysis was rather disconnected from practice and was also questionable on its own terms.

Thus it is in the same critical spirit of David Moore's (1991) review of the disputed concepts "sustainability," "equity," and "participation" that South Africans must "link discourses emanating from the academic realm of development studies and the 'practical' development practice as articulated in the development agencies in the western world"--as well as those discourses articulated in the soot-filled matchbox houses in black townships where leaders of urban social movements strategize. Moore (1991) concludes that in part because of the failure of intellectuals to make these links, the analysis advanced by such "counter-hegemonic movements" has been "too easily co-opted into the dominant discourse" and that, as a result, "new delineations of terms and new strategies are required."

The development impasse

Moore's pessimistic assessment rings broadly true, but probably deserves reappraisal in South Africa based on the strength of 2,000 vibrant, counter-hegemonic, "civic associations" (community groups) organized under the rubric of the South African National Civic Organization (SANCO), which has generally taken a firm stance against conceptual and policy slippage on matters of basic need, particularly the struggle for access to housing as a fundamental human right. Consistent with Moore, I would argue that ultimately there is in fact no real crisis in the underlying concepts of sustainability, equity, and participation, merely a distraction in terms of the success of establishment development agencies--the World Bank, US AID, various UN bodies, international foundations and the like--in coopting progressive discourse while applying ineffectual policies inspired by neoliberal economic theory.

The far deeper crisis is to be found in the world capitalist economic system. Failing to achieve growth on even limited quantitative terms, the main agents of international economic integration--financial institutions and development agencies--have set impossible constraints on Third World developmental practice through structural adjustment and project conditionality. At the same time, largely through trade liberalization and financial deregulation, they push and pull speculative flows of capital into outlets which appear most profitable in the short term but which have a debilitating impact upon development.

These conditions fully pertain to South Africa. In the wake of several decades of apartheid planning, import-substitution industrialization, and state control of large sections of the economy, the ascendance of neoliberal thinking was unmistakable in the white government during the 1980s. Yet simultaneously the limits to the market as a force for development, and the danger of speculative, footloose finance (taking forms such as a volatile and vastly overvalued stock market, inordinate corporate and consumer debt, hugely overbuilt commercial property markets, massive capital flight), emerged to bedevil the transition from apartheid. The objective of South Africa's ruling *verligte* (enlightened) Afrikaners, backed by key corporate and military forces, was to move from race-based socio-economic segregation to class-based segregation. In local parlance, the "securocrats" gave way to the "econocrats." But what seemed a clear-cut strategy at the time the ANC and other political parties were unbanned in early 1990 quickly disintegrated.

Aside from two major trade union strike waves (1990 and 1994) and "Third Force"-related violence involving state surrogates such as the Inkatha Freedom Party, perhaps the most obvious terrain of conflict during the early 1990s was housing. Rent boycotts were the norm for township public housing, reflecting the challenge to apartheid-puppet local authorities. In the private market, only 10 percent of the black population could afford to acquire homes (which for middle-income workers able to raise credit bear a minimum price of roughly $12,000 per house), while at the same time housing finance brimmed over in the white suburbs and massive inflows of funds to banks and institutional investors generated speculative investment pools that in turn could find few productive outlets.

To illustrate the scale of the contradictions, South Africa is second in the world (to the United States) in the percentage of bank assets held in the form of mortgage credit (39 percent). Yet of $15 billion in total "housing bonds" (mortgage loans) on the banks' books in the early 1990s, just $2.3 billion (15 percent) was invested in the township market (blacks make up three-quarters of the population). Black people were allowed to own homes beginning in the late 1970s, and the state phased out new public housing construction and brutally repressed civic associations in 1985-1986.

Thus most of the bank loans were granted over just four years, until mid-1990, when a variety of factors--market saturation, an increase in nominal interest rates from 12.5 percent (minus 6 percent in real terms) to 21 percent (+10 percent), poor construction and lack of community facilities, a massive retrenchment wave, an upsurge of political violence in key areas, a decline in township housing values leading to widespread "negative equity" (in which bond value exceeds house price)--converged to end the flow of new loans and to reduce repayment rates on outstanding loans to as low as 67 percent. In sum, housing finance flowed in and then ebbed out of the black townships in a manner devoid of sustainability, equity, or community participation.

Meanwhile, capital market funds continued to swell by $10 billion per year, thanks in large part to billions of dollars in black worker pension contributions and insurance premiums. During the 1980s, the Johannesburg Stock Exchange share value rose by a factor of ten to in excess of $150 billion, and indeed was for several years the fastest-growing major stock market in the world. Speculative construction of commercial property also exploded, leaving 20 percent vacancy rates and artificially high land prices in central business districts by the early 1990s. Then, during the late 1980s and early 1990s, real economic activity dwindled, as South Africa suffered through the longest depression in its history. The official unemployment rate climbed above 50 percent, and net fixed capital investment dropped to just 1 percent of GDP in 1992 (in contrast to 16 percent per year during the 1970s). The apartheid state's response was to deregulate and privatize, run real interest rates of approximately 7 percent, and introduce a regressive Value Added Tax while lowering corporate taxes. The banks' response was to open more branches in the Cayman Islands, Panama, the Isle of Man, Guernsey, Jersey, Zurich, and other hot money centers than in all South Africa's black townships combined.

In short, the country's economy has faced an accumulation crisis of serious proportions, characterized by productive sector stagnation and untenable financial speculation, under conditions of state-led monetarist austerity, rapidly-growing official corruption and substantial capital flight--conditions not terribly dissimilar to so many other semi-peripheral national economies in recent years. The one widely-acclaimed social democratic route out of the impasse, a housing and basic needs economic kick-start, was barricaded by the failure of the state to apply its inordinately large budget ($40 billion in 1993, amounting to 35 percent of GDP) to housing, which received just $0.5 billion in 1993, far short of the $1.5 billion required for a Housing for All subsidy system.

An emerging development cottage industry, which was in deep remission during the apartheid era, adapted to such contradictions in various ways. Progressive forces were initially led into the *cul de sacs* of negotiating fora and sectoral social contracts (such as the National Economic Forum), most of which were soon unveiled as business-dominated experiments in low-grade corporatism, exonerating top-down neoliberal policies (such as the endorsement by even trade unionists, through the Economic Forum, of GATT--which will cost South Africa an extra $400 million per year by 1992, according to the OECD--and of an onerous IMF loan). The National Housing Forum falls into this category, as noted below. A national-scale social democratic deal, which might have been expected from such an unstable capitalist class, was dashed by the parameters of "macroeconomic stability" advanced by the orthodox development agencies. Such parameters would, if not rejected, exacerbate already acute processes of uneven development.

Yet the shallowness of the recent social democratic thrust, following the conspicuous failure of the neoliberal approach in the late 1980s and the inability of business elites to convincingly win ANC hearts and minds in the early 1990s, created the conditions by 1994 for a renewed round of more radical developmental discourse which submerges respect for the market by stressing the urgent provision of basic need goods (not commodities) for all. (This is witnessed by a largely-successful backlash against neoliberal ideas in the formulation of the ANC *Reconstruction and Development Program* in the months prior to the first democratic election.)

Across the world, just this sort of broad development impasse--characterized by continually intensifying uneven development in the economic sphere, "low intensity democracy" in the political sphere, and "global apartheid" (as some have termed it) in the socio-spatial sphere--must be addressed with far more gravity and strategic coherence by social movements. Here South Africa can perhaps convey lessons in ideologies, strategies and tactics. The first phase of the civic movement's national-level activity--a relentless critique of the apartheid-capitalist social reality during the 1980s through an "ungovernability" strategy, and tactics such as rent boycotts and mass stayaways--has moved to a second phase: bottom-up construction of a development discourse capable of winning over wary ANC policymakers. A third phase, namely the implementation of the radical policy during the 1994-1999 period of the first ANC government, will be less a problem of establishing the new hegemonic discourse of development, and more a function of two overriding constraints: external pressures and limited local-level delivery capacity. The latter cannot be addressed here; the former is taken up below. But in exploring the potentials and possible pitfalls of the radical project, the chapter moves next to a theoretical commentary which sets the stage for a discussion of selected developmental discourse in South Africa.

The race-class debate

The "crisis in developmental discourse" at the international scale stems from disjunctures between theory and recent development experience which have called into question the modernization and dependency theories, as well as their descendants.[1] Some influential critiques of structuralist theory have drawn sustenance from the excesses of Marxism[2] (and from some straw Marxist arguments).[3] This is not the place to review the theoretical impasse in international development theory; the purpose of revisiting the South African race-class debate is, instead, to draw parallels which may shed some light on the problems of historical materialism and developmental discourse.

To begin, there is much to be said for a dependency analysis of South Africa in the world economy, based upon the high-growth era of the relatively autarchic 1930s-1940s (Martin 1990)[4] and upon structural changes which occurred in the post-war years. Indeed it was the post-war reintegration of South Africa into international capitalist circuits which fostered the crisis conditions that are so overwhelming today: a near-exhausted raw materials export sector; an overproductive luxury goods sector hosting overprotected local monopoly capital and multinational corporations; an inadequate capital goods sector; and a hopelessly under-resourced basic needs sector. As in many semi-peripheral countries, import-substitution industrialization was geared to the desires of the local bourgeoisie and ended up generating serious balance-of-payments tensions. Under such structural conditions, as rising levels of class struggle combined with local processes of uneven development, an accumulation crisis surfaced during the 1970s and became acute during the late 1980s.

But South Africa's own development debate was consumed nearly entirely by the internal question of race/class conflict, as opposed to either issues of international economic relations posed by dependency theory, or classical Marxist concerns with accumulation crisis. The well-known South African equivalent of modernization theory was the traditional 1960s liberal thesis that racially-inscribed underdevelopment would succumb to the market's incessant drive to growth and progress. Radical social scientists contested this vigorously during the 1970s, arguing that the evolutionary paths of apartheid and capitalism were interwoven, and to break from one required breaking from the other. In retrospect it appears neither was correct.

From the late 1970s, leading elements of the ruling bloc made clear their desire to jettison apartheid. But, as this was occurring in a slow and extremely painful way, it also became evident that the condition for reform was not capitalist *growth*, but rather *stagnation* (and hence the need for capitalists to explore a new export-oriented route to accumulation unhindered by political unrest and their global pariah status). Hence it is ironic that while the strategic orientation of the ANC--weakening the economy through international sanctions (especially financial) as one pillar of the national democratic struggle--appears to have been correct, for many radical intellectuals the combination of state reforms and repression in the 1980s represented a debilitating paradox.

The strengths and weaknesses of the legacy of historical materialism in South Africa may explain the present ambivalence many feel towards an older, more explicitly Marxist discourse. South African Communist Party (SACP) cadres had, since the early 1960s, based their call for a "two-stage revolution" (bourgeois democracy followed by socialism) on the idea that the South African social formation represented "colonialism of a special type" (CST) (South African Communist Party 1989). But the CST framework, which was essentially an internal form of dependency theory, came under repeated questioning from Left intellectuals (e.g., Callinicos 1988) over a period of two decades, through several intellectual stages. A version of CST was rescued by Wolpe's (1980) application of "articulations of mode of production" theory in the early 1970s, with the conclusion that South African capitalism required the superexploitation that was available by harnessing colonial-style dominance of pre-capitalist modes of production.[5] Subsequent research and theoretical argumentation suggested there was ample room for contesting Wolpe's chronology and understanding of the dynamics of capitalism (see the review in Bond 1991b).

Meanwhile, international trends in historical materialism--especially the success of Althusserian and Poulantzian structuralism--were by the mid-1970s making a decisive impact on South African development debates. From articulations of modes of production emerged a fascination with which "fractions of capital" controlled the state at particular moments of political change. Although the various fractions had become increasingly blurred, as South Africa's big mining finance houses diversified into manufacturing several leading neo-Marxist researchers identified earlier distinctions between capitals in terms of their sector of production (mining, manufacturing or agricultural), their location within the circulation of capital (industrial, financial, commercial, landed), or their "nationality" (Afrikaner, English-speaking, British, other European, or US) (see, e.g., Davies, O'Meara, and Dlamini 1986).

The Poulantzian analysis itself came under sharp attack. Whereas focusing on fractions of capital highlighted questions of power, the costs of this single-minded focus were excessive: the capital accumulation *process* was downplayed, capital-labor conflicts dismissed, and thus any sense of necessity and contingency in the development of the social and economic formation lost (see, e.g., Clarke 1978). In any event, very little further work was done in this tradition during the 1980s. Part of the reason was a frontal attack on the fractions perspective from a new school of South African social history which prided itself for looking at society and economy not from the top (state and capital), but from the very lowest levels of the voiceless majority. As rich and interesting as the particularities of the social history case studies proved, however, they added up to very little that was generalizable as development theory. The broader theoretical discourse about race and class in South Africa seemed to peak in the 1970s and, with rigorous detailed probing underway in the 1980s in the context of the search for specificity, tailed off markedly.[6]

In the late 1980s the larger questions were again placed on the agenda. It was a time when South Africa's capitalist class demanded, more sincerely and energetically than ever before, an end to formal apartheid. The reasons for this are relatively clear (again, related directly to capitalist stagnation and financial crisis), but what was disconcerting was how dramatically this shook many Marxist theorists who, earlier, so profoundly rejected the liberal thesis that apartheid and capitalism were incompatible. As Gelb (1987) put it, radicals would have to "develop a substantial and consistent analysis of capital accumulation which preserves their view of the earlier relationship between apartheid and capitalism, explains the transformation from long run apartheid boom to economic crisis and then analyses the crisis itself." To support such an intellectual project, Gelb introduced French "regulation theory" to dissect the relative stability of South African capitalism from 1948 through the early 1970s. South African "racial Fordism," as Gelb termed it, captures the post-war combination of formal apartheid with import-substitution industrialization: "As with Fordism in the advanced countries, accumulation in South Africa during this period involved the linking of the extension of mass production with the extension of mass consumption, but in a manner that was restricted on both sides of the equation, as is very familiar."[7]

With the crisis in racial Fordism understood as a breakdown in the institutional apparatus that regulated capitalism and limited structural instability--a breakdown witnessed by 1970s strikes and social unrest, the import of international inflation, and the oscillating gold price--the key practical task for regulationists now becomes how to stitch together a new set of "post-Fordist" norms, practices, and institutions within a social democratic political framework. Wage restraint, productivity *quid pro quos*, and even Taiwan-style export-orientation have, since the late 1980s, been advocated by a grouping in the Congress of South African Trade Union who gain inspiration from this particular discourse. Enormous controversies over trade union policy--particularly social contracts and shopfloor flexibility--have begun to emerge.[8] But, reminiscent of some earlier neo-Marxist analyses which were ultimately discredited, regulation theory has subsequently come under attack by historical materialists aiming to debunk heuristic concepts which lead to false hopes of capitalist competitiveness, and to recover an analysis of more durable aspects of capitalist development which elude the easy French typologies.[9] Meanwhile the earlier critical mass of Marxist scholars all but gave up on class analysis by the early 1990s, favoring instead policy analysis, a dash of post-Marxist (especially Laclauian) theory, and the politics of (generally mythical) social contracts.

What, then, is a more appropriate framework for capturing the development processes which have deradicalized so many erstwhile South African Leftists? If we seek to understand why the condition for political reform was not capitalist growth, but rather stagnation (and hence the need for capitalists to explore a new export-oriented route to accumulation), a classical Marxist approach to *cycles of capital accumulation* may be more helpful. Cycles of accumulation are the waves of investment and growth which are invariably followed by periods of excess capacity and stagnation, often referred to as "overaccumulation crisis." (South Africa experienced such cycles throughout its modern history and has suffered persistent, worsening symptoms of overaccumulation since the late 1960s.)

Under such conditions, crisis displacement occurs to a large degree through intensified uneven development. This is because overaccumulated capital in its most liquid form, finance, flows easily across space in search of more profitable outlets. The advent of overaccumulation crisis across the world in the early 1970s was, not uncoincidentally, the same point at which the Bretton Woods institutions (the World Bank and IMF) assumed added global economic management power. Conditions of uneven development already underway between different regions of the world economy rapidly sharpened under the dominance of neoliberal policy, in a process not restricted to any particular national balance of forces. Instead, there is a deeper underlying meaning. In his authoritative study of the topic, Neil Smith (1990:141, 156) concludes that while uneven development dates to the time of "primitive accumulation and the opposition of capital against pre-capitalist societies," modern-day global capitalism retains a "dichotomous form. But today it is less an issue of the 'articulation of different modes of production,' more an issue of development at one pole and development of underdevelopment at the other." If true, then uneven development is not likely to be overcome through application of market mechanisms, which are at the root of the overaccumulation problem, nor through social democratic promises of a new, supposedly more harmonious regime of post-Fordist accumulation.

Of course, neither neoliberalism nor social democracy have patience for such analysis. Instead, according to Moore (1991), "If capitalism was not 'spontaneous,' it was felt [by development agency officials] that it could be implemented through bureaucratic reform, acculturation and even co-optation." The next two sections provide pointers as to how this was meant to be accomplished in post-apartheid South Africa through township housing, based on strategies geared to the market and to a social compact.

Homage to the South African township housing market: The World Bank

From the late 1970s, the South African state set in motion a series of programs aimed at inserting market rationality into apartheid residential location. As noted above, the lamentable results of a market-led development strategy were already clear a decade later. To a significant degree the state's new-found commitment to the market was based on prodding by the parastatal Development Bank of Southern Africa (DBSA) and by the Urban Foundation (UF). In turn UF strategists were inspired by the World Bank, especially during the late 1980s/early 1990s drafting of the UF *Urban Futures* policy series. One direct result of their lobbying was a $200 million site-and-service program implemented by the Independent Development Trust (IDT), a parastatal-cum-QUANGO itself founded in early 1990 (by the then-UF chairperson) to channel funds into townships and rural areas to foster social contracts, concomitant with the rapid political liberalization then underway.

The practical results of these and numerous other township housing initiatives conformed, however, far less to a social contract aimed at achieving political stability and kick-starting the economy, and far more to a market-mediated transition from apartheid race segregation to neoliberal class segregation. This was obvious not merely in the housing field (where "toilet policy"--the widely-derided site-and-service developments--replaced traditional state housing policy), but in related areas: the phasing out of economic decentralization subsidies for outlying small towns (at the behest of the DBSA and UF); DBSA market-aided land reform proposals aimed at fostering a black small commercial farming class; the IDT's university loan (not bursary) scheme; and a variety of other substantial attempts to channel grassroots demands into individualized commodities that would soon split the market achievers from those losers who ultimately would drop into the huge lumpenproletariat, living far from the cities in, at best, serviced shack-slums.

Definitive statements concerning the role of the market in township housing allocation can be found in the World Bank's first two "Urban Sector Aides Memoire" (May and December 1991).[10] The documents engender social-democratic sentiments and are reminiscent of classic discourse co-option on various fronts. Illustrating how far the Bank (1991d:5,7) can bend over to please, rhetorically, the second "Aide Memoire" carries the following philosophical commentary:

> [Housing sector intervention] will involve more than just changing the overt mechanisms of apartheid and then "letting the market work." It requires an active role for government to help markets to work in the interests of all citizens and when, as is likely to be the case for some time, markets are unable to provide for the needs and best interests of the most disadvantaged, it requires active intervention in the form of well-designed systems of transfers.

Such rhetoric was initially treated with misgivings by both oppressed civic associations and the oppressive white local authorities (see Chapter Eleven). "We are trying to enter the debate in South Africa with a full awareness that virtually anything that we do will have an unhappy outcome for one side or the other," noted Bank urban development division chief Michael Cohen (1992:59) at an international conference in 1991. "There are some important ways of demonstrating that reform and changes are to be to everyone's advantage, but politically this is going to be difficult. I do not have any difficulty in being regarded with suspicion--that's the way it goes."

Many civic leaders sensed that "participation," in the Bank's practice, was really a vulgar co-option process innocent of historical social struggles, community-oriented planning, gender-sensitive design, affordability for all community residents, relationship to surrounding economic, social, and cultural facilities, and other areas where real consultation would end up increasing delivery costs. One illustration of the one-sided approach to community participation the Bank envisaged is the proposal that housing finance "risks must be mitigated through agreements between lending institutions and community members of the townships" which would stress greater "provision of collateral services to borrowers than is now the case, in exchange for banks being able to enforce provisions of lending agreements" (Mayo 1994:9). The collateral envisaged as the basis for community participation is group credit based on joint borrower liability, an approach attempted by the IDT in 1991-92 but rejected quickly when the loans were still not being repaid.[11]

If participation on World Bank terms (commercial bank risk-reduction) was not achieved with township activists, though, the Urban Missions' research program design during the transition period nevertheless succeeded in attracting progressive intellectuals into a working alliance, which was considered an "essential condition" of policy formation (World Bank 1991c:2). Urban technical experts affiliated to the ANC and SACP accompanied Bank Urban Mission staff in their travels between 1991 and the 1994 election, providing legitimacy and contacts. As a result, even radical civic associations were ultimately drawn into the Bank's didactic briefing sessions, though not without occasional disruptions and challenges. (The country's most powerful metropolitan civic federation set out a "Protocol" to control Bank activity in Johannesburg--including an exhaustive list of conditions with respect to sharing of data, commitment to redistribution of wealth, and a non-racial, non-sexist philosophy — which the Bank promptly rejected.)

But while the Bank was as transparent and open to debate in South Africa as it has been anywhere, a closer look at its framework for analysis and ultimately for sectoral lending reveals many orthodox features. For while on the one hand there is talk of social contracts and participation in research, on the other hand the overall Bank analysis and agenda remains wedded to neoliberal principles. Bank reports continually stress the point that "effective demand is low for the black population because of the effects of apartheid," and never because of the exercise of class power. So central was market dogma to the World Bank's leading housing expert (Steven Mayo) that the consequence was a failure to distinguish between rather different forms of non-market determinations of housing:

> The legacy of apartheid policies is felt in terms of both macroeconomic distortions, similar to those experienced in a number of Eastern European countries, and in underperformance of the housing sector.... One of the most evident features of housing policies for non-whites in South Africa has been their resemblance to the housing policies of the command economies of Eastern Europe and other socialist countries. In such countries, an ironic consequence of the determination that housing was a "right" rather than a commodity, and, as such, a product confined to the "non-material" and "non-productive" sphere of economic activity was that housing markets were not permitted to develop. (World Bank 1991c:CC,11)

To solve this problem--namely that apartheid was functionally equivalent to socialism--the Bank's first "Aide Memoire" advocated "greater efforts to persuade the private financial community to extend mortgage financing to well-located housing for the upper end of the black market, with which the private financial community, and especially the Perm [Bank], has had genuine success in mortgage lending" (World Bank 1991c:CC,26). Similar faith was expressed in the second "Aide Memoire," to the extent of claiming that "both the Perm and the South African Housing Trust appear to have been more responsive than most other mortgage granting institutions to interacting on the ground with black township borrowers" (World Bank 1991d:II,8).

In reality the SA Housing Trust (a parastatal backed by market-rate investments from several of the country's largest corporations) was at that very time facing fifteen separate township "bond boycotts" (collective community refusal to repay mortgages), while suffering a 50+ percent arrears rate due in large part to the institution's well-known *lack* of credibility. The Perm was at the same time losing tens of millions of rands to township foreclosures which could not be consummated due to refusal of the defaulting borrowers (supported by the community) to vacate their houses, and the Perm's $700 million black housing bond exposure in September 1992 was the reason that its holding company (Nedcor) lost 20 percent of its Johannesburg Stock Exchange share value (in excess of $150 million lost) in a single week following a threat of a national bond boycott from SANCO. (A subsequent social contract with SANCO reduced the Perm's troubles, with very little payoff, however, to the civic movement.)

That the market so blatantly failed on its own terms somehow did not deter Mayo (1993:16) from further praise at a 1993 international housing conference: "The South African housing finance system clearly represents a world-class system, which is capable of providing for the needs of the vast majority of the population, if conditions are put in place which provide for secure tenure, reasonable standards, a housing delivery system that provides well-located and sound quality housing, and a regulatory framework which protects the interests of both housing purchasers and financial institutions."[12] Note the one crucial variable consistently omitted in Mayo's calculus: borrower affordability. With monetarist-determined interest rates for housing bonds remaining at 16 percent (7 percent in real terms) even during the fragile transition, South African practitioners tried and failed so many times to overcome the limits to the market through financial engineering that even lenders themselves (such as the chief housing officer for the country's largest bank) were finally willing to accept the obvious: "Banks are able and prepared to provide finance to those who receive a regular income and enjoy stable employment" (Marais 1994:4). Such clients represent at best only 35 percent of those families in need of housing, a far cry from Mayo's "vast majority."

For the Bank to accept the fact that the threshold to engage in purchase of formal housing is too high for most South Africans, would be to confess a profound flaw of capitalism. One solution is simply to define shacks as houses, which Mayo did, arguing that South Africa ranks quite respectably in comparison to other countries in the "production of houses" (with its increase of 3.6 percent per annum). In reality, according to Mayo's own data, a third of such "houses" are made of "temporary materials" such as straw, cardboard, or cloth (most of the balance are of more "permanent" substances like plywood and zinc sheets). Moreover, 89 percent of the new homes are "unauthorized" (illegal shacks subject to demolition at any time). In other words, faced with overwhelming contradictions between what the market promises and what it can deliver, the neoliberal discourse resorts to semantics to define away the problem. The problem, in short, is that the Bank is fundamentally opposed to societies determining that a sufficient share of their social surplus should be dedicated to ensuring that all citizens are provided minimal decent shelter. Mayo's conclusion from Bank policy experience is that housing finance "should complement user charges and other cost-recovery mechanisms in mobilizing private savings, thereby contributing to reducing the overall role of government in the sector" (World Bank 1991b:65).[13]

Will such advice find its way into loan conditionality in South Africa? Such conditionality by the Bank, US AID, and similar institutions is the preferred back-door way to policy and has been extremely effective in settings (such as neighboring Zimbabwe) in undermining, without even lip-service to transparency, socialist-sounding government philosophy (Bond 1992a:ch.10). But even setting aside the dangers of conditionality, it is difficult to understand why Pretoria would, in the mid and late 1990s, borrow dollars from the Bank in order to finance low-cost housing at a time of excessive domestic financial system liquidity. The import costs of housing are near 0 percent, while the effective interest rate on a foreign loan (once likely inflation-linked devaluation is accounted) is 83 percent higher than a domestic South African loan (Bond and Swilling 1992). Such arguments meant that the most recent ANC policy statement (the *Reconstruction and Development Program*, or *RDP*), influenced by trade union and urban social movements, took an extremely strong stance against the Bank:

> The *RDP* must use foreign debt financing only for those elements of the program that can potentially increase our capacity for earning foreign exchange. Relationships with international financial institutions such as the World Bank and International Monetary Fund must be conducted in such a way as to protect the integrity of domestic policy formulation and promote the interests of the South African population and the economy. Above all, we must pursue policies that enhance national self-sufficiency and enable us to reduce dependence on international financial institutions. (ANC 1994:145,146)

If, through such policy struggles, neoliberalism can be kept somewhat at bay, is social democracy ready to fill the void?

In search of social democracy: The National Housing Forum

Since political parties were unbanned in 1990, South Africa has been overwhelmed with rhetoric promoting the role of social contracts in fostering a political spirit of social democracy (here meaning a market-oriented system tempered by state social welfare support) (Bond 1993a). Emblematic was the formation of the National Housing Forum in mid-1992, encompassing a range of stakeholders including civics, the ANC and other political parties, trade unions, NGOs, developers, materials-suppliers, bankers, and parastatal agencies. By far the greatest influence was that of the UF, whose technical experts dominated most of the proceedings. The NHF experienced numerous conflicts with the conservative government housing minister, Louis Shill (who had been seconded to the National Party government from the large insurance company he had founded), but the forum generally backed down when the confrontations appeared debilitating.

Typical of the circumscribed nature of such forums for the Left was the agreement on housing subsidy policy reached just weeks prior to the 1994 election between the NHF and a campaigning Shill. Heralded by the government as a $26 billion, ten-year housing plan, the developer-led site-and-service policy lacked a number of aspects which had been raised by the Left as issues: no explicit commitment to eliminating gender bias; no support for squatters' rights; no commitment on ending bank loan discrimination; no assurance of end-user and bridging finance availability; no protection against downward-raiding of subsidies; no possibility of land banking for future development; no means of developing higher-cost inner-city areas; no attention to pricing of building materials.

The main problem, however, continued to be the size of the NHF-Shill subsidy itself. For those earning below $430 per month (roughly 75 percent of all South Africans), the state provides a maximum $3,600 capital grant which apply to individually-titled sites, as opposed to what is actually required: low-interest rate loans of a larger amount (say, $7,500) for full-fledged dwelling units. Hence, in the name of sustainability, transparency, and efficiency (i.e., not interfering in market determinations of interest rates and hence avoiding financial market distortions), the capital subsidy approach to serviced sites fills various market-related functions, not least of which is limiting fiscal outlays on housing subsidies.[14]

The NHF's insistence upon once-off grants makes it difficult to raise recurrent flexible interest rate funding for housing that would match recipient affordability. Once-off capital grants--as opposed to long-term loan commitments--also reduce popular pressure on subsequent government budgets to sustain sufficient subsidies (Bond 1993b). In sum, the NHF's application of the notion of "sustainability" mainly means sufficiently market-oriented and insufficiently threatening to the government budget so that the subsidy system is replicable.

"Equity" has also been the subject of inordinate debates surrounding housing subsidy policy, in which the NHF promotes both "vertical equity" (relatively wealthier households get a lower subsidy than the very poor) and "horizontal equity" (households of the same income group get the same subsidy). Although the NHF-Shill agreement was far more generous to the upper five percent of the black market than is warranted (a $1,400 housing grant is provided those earning as high as $1,000 per month), in practice the mobilization of the concepts of vertical and horizontal equity has led to a "width versus depth" debate in the NHF. This has the effect of emphasizing supply of massive numbers of serviced sites, especially to the very poor, rather than embarking upon a Housing for All program.[15]

Thus the NHF-brokered compromise, and the discourse underlying it, was subject to extensive criticism by former SANCO president Moses Mayekiso:

> It is a major scam. In my view, the whole subsidy scheme must be reworked, because the $3,600 maximum that is offered is just not sufficient to pay for anything more than a plot, a toilet and some few building materials. We say the subsidy must include a core house with full services and infrastructure. It must be at least 40 square meters in size, with good quality construction. There must be community facilities such as schools, clinics and creches. We have had to compromise, and we are getting far less than that. But we feel this is a temporary arrangement, until we have a humane government policy in place.
>
> There are other problems with the interim scheme. We don't want those subsidies to encourage speculation and immediate sale of the plot. Our country must not be left bankrupt by people selling their plots to the middle-class, leaving us with a low-income housing crisis. The subsidy should not be meant to enrich individuals, but to solve the homelessness crisis.[16]

As the new government was installed, a debate emerged as to whether to respect the NHF agreement or instead rapidly develop a more generous, appropriate housing policy. Key provincial leaders in the new federal structure began to recognize the weakness of the compromise, given ANC election promises for a much more substantive housing program. With the failure of social democratic precepts, a new discourse--based on the principle that housing is a right, delivered through highly-subsidized but community-controlled forms of social housing (community land trusts, housing associations and cooperatives)--proved to be the only viable approach. SANCO was its primary advocate prior to democratic government, and would continue to be in coming years.

A radical housing program: The civic movement

It was not only top-down market failure and the limits to social democratic compromises that forced SANCO to engage in housing policy debates. Grassroots struggle--especially resistance to the broader financial crisis--also began to play a significant role in the township housing market and added to already growing dissatisfaction that an individual ownership model, backed by bank credit, should be the basis of housing policy. The civic movement began to experiment in selected locales with the bond boycott tactic. The first such boycott was in the Port Elizabeth area in 1988 during a union struggle against Volkswagen, on grounds striking workers could not reasonably be expected to make monthly bond payments. Subsequently the strategy was adopted by civic associations in struggles over the quality of housing in townships near Cape Town, Bloemfontein, Johannesburg, and several other cities. In spite of appeals by politicians as diverse as (then housing minister) Hernus Kriel and (ANC leader) Thabo Mbeki that such actions were irresponsible, they continued, and in several cases resulted in substantial concessions by banks, developers, and parastatal agencies.

The bond boycott must be understood against the backdrop of militant township strategies which continued into the early 1990s. During the previous decade, the civic movement had used the philosophy of "ungovernability" to cripple, politically and financially, illegitimate black local governments. Residents' refusal to pay rent on township houses also conformed to local grievances and waning household economics. Such struggles played a large role in forcing the Botha and De Klerk regimes to contemplate power-sharing and by 1991 had resulted in the resignation of most of the apartheid township councils. Then in mid-1992, attempts by SANCO to channel the bond boycott threat into national political gains--by demanding banks cease funding homeland dictators, in much the same spirit as the ANC's financial sanctions campaign--met with firm opposition from ANC moderates. Nevertheless, through bond boycotts and rent boycotts, as well as land invasions on apartheid buffer zones, the civic movement established a capacity to utilize mass protest actions of various sorts to advance residents' interests (Bond 1994a).

This history of adapting local grievances to highly visible political campaigning gave the civic movement an important stake in the Mass Democratic Movement alliance of ANC, SACP, trade unions, and other anti-apartheid groupings within civil society. In turn this led to an invitation in late 1993 for SANCO to join the *RDP* policy-drafting process, which set the framework for subsequent ANC policy. The *RDP* housing program, in particular, was based on SANCO policy nearly word-for-word, which in turn was based on a year-long workshopping process. Thus housing is deemed a "human right" and one million low-cost homes are expected to be built over the first five years of ANC rule, with 300,000 houses a year thereafter. These houses, complete with a full set of internal services, would carry sufficient state subsidies (more than three times the amount budgeted by the last National Party government) so as to be affordable to even the poorest residents. A few clauses of the *RDP* make clear the scope of the new, more radical discourse:

> The housing problems created by apartheid and by the limited range of the capitalist housing markets have been aggravated by the absence of a coherent national housing policy.... Although housing may be provided by a range of parties, the democratic government is ultimately responsible for ensuring that housing is provided to all. It must create a policy framework and legislative support so that this is possible, and it must allocate subsidy funds from the budget--to reach a goal of not less than five percent of the budget by the end of the five-year *RDP*--so that housing is affordable to even the poorest South Africans. The approach to housing, infrastructure and services must involve and empower communities; be affordable, developmental and sustainable; take account of funding and resource constraints, and support gender equality.

The *RDP* continues with attacks on land speculation and on the construction and building materials industry, with a pledge to support "public, worker and community-based ownership where the market fails to provide a reasonably priced product." But it is in contesting housing finance that the *RDP* makes its most serious inroads against market determinations of basic needs goods. Thus, rather than a nuclear-family subsidy arrangement, as with the Housing Forum model, the *RDP* insists that "Mechanisms (such as time limits on resale, or compulsory repayment of subsidies upon transfer of property) must be introduced to prevent speculation and downward raiding." Moreover, quite contrary to the deregulatory spirit of the World Bank, the *RDP* determined that "A national housing bank and national home loan guarantee fund must be initiated to coordinate subsidies and financing most efficiently." And the existing financial sector requires state intervention:

> "Redlining" and other forms of discrimination by banks must be prohibited. Community-controlled financing vehicles must be established with both private sector and government support where necessary. Locally controlled Housing Associations or cooperatives must be supported, in part to take over properties in possession of banks due to foreclosure. Unemployment bond insurance packages and guarantee schemes with a demand-side orientation must be devised. Interest rates must be kept as low as possible.

If we are to understand the profound challenge that such development discourse presents to orthodox practice, housing is a good case study. Why, then, the demands (successfully advanced in the *RDP*) for community-control of housing and capacity-building financial resources for community-based organizations? It is not merely for the obvious reason alluded to above: the failure of private sector developers and financiers, or parastatals working to the World Bank model, to establish a truly sustainable, equitable, and participatory model for delivery. There is also, here, a distrust of the new government, a sense of a future "watchdog" role for the civic movement, as part of a vibrant, post-apartheid civil society.

The civic movement and "working-class civil society"

The civic movement is a highly political movement, but not tied to party-politics. It is as capable of working with the Pan Africanist Congress and the Azanian People's Organization, as it is with the ANC. Yet it also recognizes intrinsically the class character of Third World nationalism: all too often comprador, petit-bourgeois. Thus it continually re-establishes its footing in civil society and takes care to remain representative of working-class and poor peoples' interests, capable of withstanding neoliberal processes aimed at dividing and conquering a privileged fraction of workers from the masses.

The primary organizer of the Alexandra civic movement, Mzwanele Mayekiso, has long advocated "organs of *working-class civil society* which both serve the oft-discussed 'watchdog' function and provide the raw material and energy from which to construct socialist building blocks." In particular, Mayekiso (1992) argues,

> The examples of Africa and elsewhere tell us that simply because nationalist organizations like the ANC are apparently progressive today, does not mean they will remain so. The fact that there are, within the ANC, numerous class forces is a reason in itself for strengthening independent organs of working-class civil society. Class struggle will continue into the post-apartheid era. The ANC will lead a so-called "mixed economy," and if that means supporting private property rights, then there will necessarily be conflict with the working-class. On the other hand, an ANC government that in principle is strongly supportive of working-class interests will, in turn, need a strong working-class civil society to safeguard a progressive approach.

This sort of analysis, based not on a harmony model of social democratic modernization but on a street-smart historical materialism, is not uncontroversial. Such an approach, which stresses the continuities between urban social movement struggles from past to future, has come under considerable attack from orthodox observers who explain the post-1990 carnage in many townships in South Africa's industrial heartland by reference to the legacy of 1980s "politics of protest" (in contrast to the 1990s "politics of development" which ostensibly involves no protest). Mayekiso (1993) defends the earlier strategy of ungovernability:

> Within the decay of the old apartheid order, we knew that there were opportunities to plant the seeds of a new approach. We would seek out, through discipline, democracy and accountability, concrete alternatives to apartheid rule. Ungovernability led to the vision of building "organs of people's power" in townships. This required us to carefully assess how much power we had to challenge the very basis of the regime, and how to develop community-controlled organs of power such as the embryonic structures of the Alexandra Action Committee, People's Courts, and economic, developmental and cultural institutions.

It is in this context that the attempt to establish a radical development discourse has so many implications for grassroots political practice. The awesome ideological vacuum on the Left, in a country like South Africa which has paid so many unnecessary intellectuals debts to Third International Stalinism, may well be filled now by a truly internationalist, non party-political civic ideology. When translated into development discourse such as a Housing for All campaign, this could well offer the best means of challenging the hegemony of the orthodox agencies, which can provide no convincing answer to the housing question in either political or practical terms.

Conclusion

If SANCO remains a vibrant, community-oriented national coalition, even while many of its leaders are drawn into the new governments, and if the traditional South African civic perspective is maintained even under conditions of corporatism elsewhere in the polity, the movement will remain relatively inaccessible to co-optation. Indeed, this chapter has argued that the "sustainability" required to provide basic needs goods to all South Africans must entail a strengthening of civics and other organs of working-class civil society. "Equity" is an unstated, enduring premise, but one which requires further work to assure that "width versus depth" debates do not sidetrack progress. The notion of "participation" has recently been elevated by the civic movement to "community control." In each of these areas, it should be clear that the radical project is to continually strive for non-reformist reforms that reward the efforts of organized communities to fight market forces.

None of this is terribly new--what continually needs reminding, however, is the nature of the intellectual challenge: naming capitalism as the principal barrier to development. Remaining with housing, the same underlying analysis can, in fact, be traced to Engels (1935):

> In reality the bourgeoisie has only one method of solving the housing question after *its* fashion--that is to say, of solving it in such a way that the solution continually reproduces the question anew.... No matter how different the reasons may be, the result is everywhere the same; the scandalous alleys disappear to the accompaniment of lavish self-praise from the bourgeoisie on account of this tremendous success, but they appear again immediately somewhere else and often in the immediate neighborhood!.... The breeding places of disease, the infamous holes and cellars in which the capitalist mode of production confines our workers night after night, are not abolished; they are merely *shifted elsewhere*! The same economic necessity which produced them in the first place, produces them in the next place also.

In translating this analysis to contemporary policy debates, David Harvey (1973:144) makes clear the direction in which development discourse must go:

> Although all serious analysts concede the seriousness of the ghetto problem, few call into question the forces which rule the very heart of our economic system. Thus we discuss everything except the basic characteristics of a capitalist market economy. We devise all manner of solutions except those which might challenge the continuance of that economy. Such discussions and solutions serve only to make us look foolish, since they eventually lead us to discover what Engels was only too aware of in 1872--that capitalist solutions provide no foundation for dealing with deteriorated social conditions.

New discussions and new solutions are part, it would seem, of a radical development discourse which urban social movements across the world may be ready to grapple with at last, not merely through "IMF Riots" but through more sustained strategies (see, e.g., Schuurman and van Naerssen 1989 and Walton and Seddon 1994). And it is in South Africa during the portentous mid and late 1990s--with well-tested social movements demanding Housing for All (and other such) programs on the basis of well-considered policy inputs drawn directly from grassroots struggle--that many radical intellectuals may find a means to overcome their own development impasse and re-link theory and practice. If so, their/our challenge remains, as ever, to explore and to publicize the ideological and practical vulnerabilities of state, capital, and development agencies; to carefully track the surfacing of crisis tendencies and adapt analysis and strategy accordingly; and to be prepared to internationalize the most effective new principles and programs of social movements (such as the South African civic movement's ideology and strategies). For nothing less than a unified internationalist effort, based on strong national-scale movements grounded in grassroots organization in urban and rural centers of resistance, can end the tyranny of both the hegemonic developmental discourse and uneven capitalist development.

Postscript (November 1994)

This chapter was rewritten several times during a turbulent period, sent to the editors just after the April 1994 election, and should now be rewritten again. Regrettably, the subsequent six months of policy-making confirm the most pessimistic of perspectives on the South African transition, namely, that negotiations politics would take on a life of their own and that radical perspectives drawing even on ANC Freedom Charter traditions would soon be marginalised. Notwithstanding the fact that the best *RDP* discourse--which stresses the drive to meet basic needs through "people-driven development"--rapidly became hegemonic in South Africa (endorsed even by big business), the politicians and bureaucrats abandoned even the most feasible and urgent of radical proposals.

Predictably,, then, the World Bank moved quickly in August 1994 to promote market-oriented housing finance and discourage a national housing bank and loan guarantee plan for pension investments in housing (in both cases, the models selected had strayed far from *RDP* guidelines anyhow). Predictably too, the National Housing Forum's social contract model--including the insufficient subsidy inherited from the previous government--was advocated very strongly by the UF and by many (though not all) of its capitalist allies.

Unpredictably, the social democratic approach to policy-making was considered most appropriate by the new Department of National Housing, which ignored the *RDP* and instead sponsored an all-in "Housing Accord" conference at Botshabelo in October 1994. Perhaps more unpredictably, the vanguard for the rightward turn was Housing Minister (and SACP chair) Joe Slovo, who at Botshabelo resorted to a demagogic discourse against ongoing rent and bond boycotts: "It's clear who the boycotters are knocking: Nelson Mandela." Most unpredictably, one of the highest-profile individuals to endorse what became known as the "toilet-and-a-small-pile-of-bricks" policy was Moses Mayekiso (now a backbench ANC Member of Parliament), reflecting the depth of the descent into social contract politics and the separation of movement leaders from their base. Many in SANCO and the trade unions were shocked by such developments, and vowed to campaign for the original *RDP* housing program.

It all goes to show that, contrary to some faddish academic views, winning a debate over development discourse--in this case the *RDP*'s housing promises--is a far cry from victory in the material world. Attaining a true "Affordable Housing for All" policy from the new government will require from SANCO and its allies a quantum leap in pressure strategy and tactics.... perhaps leading to that second stage of the revolution that Engels also considered a prerequisite for an answer to the housing question?

Notes

1. The seminal paper was Booth (1985) and was followed by important works such as Corbridge (1986, 1989), Sklair (1988), Mouzelis (1988), Vandergeest and Buttel (1988), Edwards (1989), Stauffer (1990), and Schuurman (1993).

2. Of greatest importance was the switch by Laclau from Marxist critic of dependency theory (1971) to leading post-Marxist, as well as the oft-cited reversal from Althusserianism performed by Hindess and Hirst (1977).

3. Some of the more effective rebuttals include Wood (1986), Geras (1990), and Peet (1991). At least one defense of dependency theory can be found in Munck (1993).

4. Simply stated, as South Africa delinked from the world economy from roughly 1933 to 1945, its secondary manufacturing industry (beyond the traditionally-strong mining equipment sector) burgeoned. Moreover, the rate of growth of the black wage share rose more than 50 percent during this period (from 11 percent to 17 percent--the black share had reached only 21 percent by 1970). And the overall GDP growth rate (8 percent) was the fastest recorded in modern times (Nattrass 1981:Appendix 1).

5. Wolpe's (1988) more recent *Race, Class and the Apartheid State* backtracks substantially from the earlier position that apartheid was *necessary* to capitalist development; instead, aspects of their mutual evolution were contingent.

6. A notable contribution was an approach to understanding the social formation known as "racial capitalism," in Saul and Gelb (1986).

7. In "Making Sense of the Crisis" and his 1991 edited collection, Gelb explained that expensive imported machinery was paid for by a relatively stable flow of foreign currency provided by mineral exports. Although political turmoil disturbed the economic boom in 1960, growth was relatively secure for at least two decades after apartheid was introduced, and this qualifies as the longest uninterrupted period of prosperity that the country's entire white population had ever had. Even short-term business cycle downturns helped correct imbalances in the system, says Gelb, in a "reproductive" rather than destructive way. But white mass consumption only goes so far--an entire industrialized economy with South Africa's aspirations could not build on so small a base.

8. This is best documented in issues of the *South African Labor Bulletin* and the Toronto-based *Southern Africa Report*.

9. A thorough critique of the theory is to be found in Brenner and Glick (1991), as well as in Clarke (1988). For Marxist critiques of South African regulation theory, see Meth (1990), Bond (1991a), and Callinicos (1992).

10. See World Bank (1991c and 1991d), and for a full critique see Bond and Swilling (1992).

11. Mayo noted that the IDT group credit approach "should be encouraged" two years after it was abandoned. This lapse, and others in Mayo's recent work (such as the incomprehensible remark in the same paper that "at the present time," banks have had "a generally favorable lending experience with borrowers in black townships") reflects the enormous distance between H Street in Washington, DC and South Africa.

12. The reference to the world-class nature of white housing finance reflects the influence of "dualism," which allows Mayo to posit that by bringing the existing white suburban market institutions into the institution-less black townships, underdevelopment can be resolved. But the Bank's internal lack of coherency is revealed in Cohen's (1992:59) comment, consistent with the political project noted earlier, that "One of my colleagues [Mayo] has managed to desegregate housing indicators by race, and one of the conclusions being brought out is that the white sector is not doing very well either, because of the results of apartheid policy as it operates in housing and urban services."

13. A full statement of such principles is in World Bank (1993b), which was based on the United Nations Centre for Human Settlements (1988). For a summary of the emerging urban management approach to market-oriented housing and finance, see Urban Institute (1990).

14. In the process the site-and-service approach lowers the reproductive costs of labor power through self-help construction, and hence diminishes the wage bill (Burgess 1978, 1985).

15. In contrast, the two leading practical applications of *collective* community-controlled subsidies in South Africa--a land invasion in Wattville-Tamboville to the east of Johannesburg which led to the formation of a community land trust serving 700 households; and an inner-city Johannesburg "Seven Buildings Project" slum tenement

purchase, upgrade, and co-operative housing conversion of 460 apartment units--violated both types of equity. In each case the subsidy applied to the working-classes as well as the very poor within the community, and in each case the fact that the community was well-organized meant that they received a subsidy beyond that of their income-peers. In each case both types of violations were the result of extensive community mobilization following a rigorous education process which considered a variety of available housing tenure and financing options.

16. *Cross Sections* interview with Moses Mayekiso, June 1994, Toronto.

chapter nine

Do "Blacks like Shacks"?

Upon Joe Slovo's death in early 1995, his replacement as Minister of Housing, Sankie Mthembi-Mahanyele, soon realized that the inheritance amounted to what she scathingly termed a "toilets-in-the-veld" approach based on site-and-service schemes originally introduced by the stingy late-apartheid regime during the late 1980s. With delivery of even this rudimentary "product" far behind schedule, promoters of shack housing policy felt it crucial to justify their work. This required delving into a variety of subsidiary benefits alleged to accompany an incremental, "self-help" strategy for managing informal urbanization. When the Urban Foundation closed down, part of its portfolio moved to the new National Business Initiative, which hired former leftist researchers to argue in late 1995 that shack housing projects were not only acceptable but somehow pleasing to their "beneficiaries." At least one of the researchers was, in fact, a central strategist of site-and-service schemes for the Urban Foundation and Independent Development Trust. He and his colleagues discovered, in their evaluation of several upgrading projects, "a minor revolution in social relations, forms of financing, institutional development, capacity building and managerial practice." But in reality, this amounted--upon a second glance--to very little. Yet the media hype associated with the researchers' findings was itself revealing. As one of a series of neoliberal versions of post-apartheid social policy--amongst others were infrastructure, public works, land reform, education, welfare and arts/culture--the housing strategy had amongst the highest visibility. It was also an extremely politicized field of development. To show that the policy approach was working, notwithstanding conspicuous failure on its own terms and widespread community dissatisfaction with the tiny, poor quality houses, required an enormous intellectual leap. Such a leap deserves, in turn, an extended critique.

[Written mainly in early 1996, this chapter was published as "The Housing Question Revisited: 'Blacks like Shacks,' say South Africa's Corporate Liberal Intelligentsia" in *debate* 3 (1997).]

Introduction

The May 1997 departure of the Department of Housing Director-General, Billy Cobbett, was unfortunate in that it followed Cobbett's laudable whistle-blowing role regarding an irregular R185-million subsidy allocation to an old friend of Minister Sankie Mthembi-Mahanyele. Thus with a few minor exceptions, commentary focused entirely on apparent corruption and the well-documented personality clash between the two. Cobbett's neoliberal policy orientation and the potential for its replacement were essentially ignored as matters worthy of public concern, except insofar as one commentator warned to *Business Day* readers that now "it will surely be easier for those who favor a populist housing policy to have their way."[1] Regrets were expressed in particular that just as the oft-criticized policy now finally seemed to be "working"--with "housing starts" (note the new terminology) projected to reach one million by the year 2000--its architect was banished.

That is why it is all the more important to revisit hegemonic discourse concerning "incremental housing," that deft phrase adopted by Cobbett in 1994 to justify breaking *RDP* promises of Affordable Housing for All while instead marginally expanding upon existing late-apartheid programs that themselves originated at the World Bank during the 1970s. Those site-and-service programs generated poorly serviced sites at medium scale (never reaching more than 50,000 sites per year). More to the point, for reasons we explore below, the actual delivery of formal housing--at a minimum being well-constructed with permanent building materials, cement foundations, and internal wet core--on these sites never broached more than 20 percent. Thus from March 1994 through October 1996, of 130,000 subsidies granted (with an average value of less than R12,500) only 21,000 received credit so as to construct an actual house. Notwithstanding periodic announcements beginning in 1996 of huge "allocations" of funds devoted to servicing sites, and hence a public perception that housing policy was coming right, the banks continued to lend to just 16 percent of subsidy recipients, and in any case (as the notorious delivery overestimations of 1994-95 had shown), large allocations of subsidies to developers were no guarantee that even the serviced sites would actually materialize.

Clearly a set of minor policy amendments, excuses (such as the alleged lack of building artisans) and other distractions were required, and in December 1995 and October 1996 two reports of the Ministerial

"Task Team on Short Term Housing Delivery" were generated to reinforce the false sense of unity between Cobbett and Mthembi-Mahanyele while very slightly modifying policy, still never coming anywhere close to revisiting the bank-centered, developer-driven character of the policy, the paltry size of the subsidies (maximum value R17,500 in special cases) or the policy's consistent bias towards nuclear family home-ownership (social or cooperative housing was neglected, and municipal or national rental housing was rejected outright).

But with housing policy the subject of growing ridicule beginning in 1995, the neoliberal Department of Housing desperately required allies and endorsement from big business, particularly experts based at the Urban Foundation, who after all were responsible for the policy in the first place. A seminal document to this end was produced at the end of 1995. Three intellectuals serving big capital's "National Business Initiative" (NBI) issued, with great fanfare, a major report--*Evaluation of Informal Settlement Upgrading and Consolidation Projects*--celebrating incremental housing projects and policy.

The main purpose of this chapter is to dissect that report. The fact that two of the authors--Professors Jeff McCarthy and Doug Hindson[2]--were formerly leading Marxist scholars in the fields of South African geography and sociology allows us to document the degeneration of a thread of scholarship and political commitment that in turn underlies and amplifies the need for the journal *debate*. For in a climate in which invitations to do high-paying consultancies for corporations and the state easily smother rigorous intellectual work and unpaid gigs for social movements, there seems very little other opportunity than such an analytical exercise to raise issues of intellectual accountability, integrity, and political allegiance.

Behind the "incremental housing" philosophy

Incremental housing[3] and the upgrading and consolidation of informal settlements together refer to

> the provision of infrastructure and services such as roads, water and sanitation, and also, in principle, improvements in dwellings (sometimes called the top structure) on sites that have already been settled.... [or] the provision of infrastructure and services to [unoccupied, greenfield] sites.... The basic idea in developing incremental housing is that additions and improvements to this top structure can be made gradually over time as the household gains the means to do so. (p.2)[4]

The importance of the NBI report was reflected in banner headlines in the daily press.[5] The one-sidedly favorable coverage stressed both the report's finding that "the incremental approach is being widely supported by those who have benefitted from it so far" (*Star* 15/11/95)--i.e., in our more cynical wording, "blacks like shacks"[6]--as well as the (undocumented, incorrect) allegation that "conventional housing solutions are beyond the means of the state." As a *Star* editorial (20/11/95) continued, "All the more welcome, therefore is new research released by the NBI which proposes that informal settlements should be seen as part of an overall solution to the housing crisis rather than as such a large part of the problem."

A critical reading of the NBI report, as a good example of the discourse of big business liberalism, should unveil at least some aspects of the corporate intelligentsia's approach to policy argumentation and to the production of popular and technical developmental knowledge. Prior to interrogating the report itself, however, a few questions are in order:

- What is the NBI?
- What is its interest in incremental housing?
- What is the tradition of debate on incremental housing from which this report emanates?
- How are the NBI researchers implicated in such traditions, and what are their interests--intellectual and professional--in arguments surrounding incremental housing today?

Once such questions are posed and answered, it becomes easier to locate the premises, argumentation, methodology, and conclusions of the report, and to consider the strategies and tactics that may be required to offer real alternatives to both its concrete and its ideological findings.

The NBI was formed in early 1995 when the Consultative Business Movement (CBM) and the Urban Foundation (UF) were closed down and their projects and assets shared. The UF consistently advocated a larger role for markets in shaping South Africa's turbulent cities. The CBM was formed during the late 1980s to assist enlightened business visionaries to interact with the African National Congress and its allies.

The incremental housing report under review should be seen as the latest in a long-standing offensive, dating to the late 1970s, by ideologues of large corporations and the increasingly neoliberal apartheid state. The aim was relatively straightforward: *shifting both existing state-*

centered low-income housing policy and the Democratic Movement's housing policy discourse toward more conservative premises, in the process lowering the expectations of South Africa's homeless and poorly-housed populations.[7] Although the UF was only part of this offensive (other major forces have included the Development Bank of Southern Africa, the Independent Development Trust, the South African Housing Trust, the World Bank, and numerous private consultancies), it was usually the most vocal. For a time, the UF also put its money where its mouth was, by implementing incremental housing projects consistent with its political vision.

The incremental housing approach was adopted not only by apartheid state-related agencies like the old Department of Development Aid, homeland development corporations, and the Independent Development Trust (IDT) (which committed more than R800 million to incremental housing projects beginning in 1991), but also, beginning in 1992, by the National Housing Forum--the equivalent of a multi-party bargaining forum (excluding the government)--in the course of negotiations with the last apartheid housing minister, Louis Shill. One discursive accomplishment of the Housing Forum was the introduction of the "width versus depth" false dichotomy which implicitly rules out the possibility of achieving *both* width (many recipients) and depth (a full-fledged house, not merely site-and-service).[8] Subsequently, as discussed in more detail below, incremental housing was adopted by Housing Minister Joe Slovo and the Department of Housing.[9]

As is commonly pointed out, the housing market ("formal financial institutions and the property development industry") works, more or less, for the highest-earning 10 percent or so of the black population ("the top end"). For the poor, incremental housing "is only one of a suite of policies that is needed to meet the broader needs of a complex society. *It is nevertheless a very important option for the poor that we are evaluating here*" (original emphasis) (Executive Summary, p.3). As noted below, incremental housing is seen by the NBI researchers as practically the only option (not even another option--well-constructed, highly-subsidized social housing--located in the immediate vicinity of at least one of the eight case study areas was deemed worthy of mention).

Incremental housing was not, in fact, the only approach to housing policy under consideration during the 1980s and 1990s. Important "stakeholders" such as the South African National Civic

Organization (SANCO) and a coalition of progressive urban service organizations (the Urban Sector Network) had insisted at the outset that housing (not incremental housing) be considered a human right, and that the state provide sufficient funds in the form of subsidies and capacity-building support so as to make this financially and technically feasible. Extensive policy, program, and project work was conducted by these organizations, culminating in the adoption of a mass housing program as one of the centerpieces of the ANC's 1994 *Reconstruction and Development Program* (*RDP*).

At this point, it may be useful to locate the NBI researchers' own positionality, for in view of the hotly-contested nature of the housing policy debate, authorial conflicts of interest should probably have been forthrightly recorded: McCarthy's role as designer of one of the first major initiatives in incremental housing, as an IDT consultant in 1990;[10] McCarthy's and Oelofse's roles as defenders of incremental housing policy, in numerous articles and documents, as Urban Foundation staff during the early 1990s; all three researchers' roles as consultants to the National Housing Forum; and the Urban Foundation's role as developer of incremental housing.[11] If indeed there exists what might metaphorically be termed an incremental housing cottage industry, the NBI researchers qualify as some of its leading architects.[12] This fact places the NBI researchers in the position of rule-makers, players, and now referees in the evaluation of incremental housing projects.[13] Such conflicts of interest can sometimes (though not always) lead to shoddy analysis. In this case, the NBI report illustrates the danger of being active proponents of a particular policy approach, for the inherent bias has apparently clouded the analytical judgement of the NBI researchers.

After the UF's 1994 collapse, its staff migrated into the private sector, public sector, and independent consultancies. But what is important for our purposes is the residue of UF arguments and ideology for urban policy-making in South Africa. The report in question is a useful case study of the production and marketing of an ideological position on the hotly-debated housing question, dressed up as social science research. In turn, this response does not pretend to be anything other than an ideological critique and rebuttal, but is backed by argumentation, logic and facts that the reader will hopefully find more convincing than the pseudo-science presented by the NBI researchers.

"There Is No Alternative" to incremental housing policy?

Of greatest importance in this report is, right from the outset, the willful neglect of policy options aside from incremental housing, and hence the report's subsequent need to adopt a blinkered surveying methodology and to propose conceptually-limited argumentation on behalf of the incremental policy. To illustrate, Brian Whittaker, the development director of the NBI, opens his Foreword to the report with the statement: "An essential component of housing policy must be the upgrading of informal settlements and the large-scale introduction of incremental housing schemes."

The NBI researchers argue, in effect, "There Is No Alternative" (TINA): "[Incremental housing policy] assumes that conventional housing cannot be provided for the poor immediately" (p.2).[14] Indeed, "There is little alternative to the upgrading of informal settlements, if major health and environmental problems are to be averted" (p.84). As the "NBI Research in Brief" summary of the report baldly reiterates, "The researchers reach the conclusion that there is little alternative to large-scale upgrading programs in South Africa's teeming informal settlements" (p.2). And the *Sunday Times* (7/1/96) concluded its generous coverage of the NBI report with the penultimate paragraph of its Executive Summary (p.8): "There is little option for South Africa other than a modified incremental housing approach if we are to upgrade the living conditions of the two-thirds of South Africans who earn less than R1,000 a month."[15]

The "large-scale introduction of incremental housing schemes" is in direct contradiction to the housing policy advocated in the *RDP*, which specifies "housing standards" that must be adhered to (2.5.7):

> As a minimum, all housing must provide protection from weather, a durable structure, and reasonable living space and privacy. A house must include sanitary facilities, storm-water drainage, a household energy supply (whether linked to grid electricity supply or derived from other sources, such as solar energy), and convenient access to clean water. Moreover, it must provide for secure tenure in a variety of forms. Upgrading of existing housing must be accomplished with these minimum standards in mind.

From this statement of what was, at the time of the April 1994 election, the African National Congress' overall policy orientation (subsequently endorsed by the ANC's partners in the Government of National Unity), it is obvious that incremental housing policy was not considered a humane or viable option for providing shelter to the poor. Instead, a mass housing program aiming to build one million houses (not incremental houses) over five years was promised in the *RDP*, and extensive consultation and debate occurred in early 1994 surrounding the fiscal and technical feasibility of such promises. At the time, the *RDP* promises were considered viable.[16]

Subsequently, however, at the October 1994 Botshabelo conference organized by the Department of Housing, the incremental policy was adopted in the course of what has been described as a "social contract" which brought together all actors in the housing field. Indeed it was apparently decided by the Department of Housing even prior to the Botshabelo conference that any such policy would be reliant on bankers and developers, who would control the bulk of state subsidy funds; moreover, state resources would also be applied to providing guarantees to banks (in exchange for a promise that this would generate 50,000 new bonds a year, for people whose incomes had not previously allowed them access to housing credit). Regrettably, it was not contemplated at that stage that the banks would continue redlining many areas and on top of that raise interest rates by several percentage points for low-income borrowers, or that developers given commitments and contracts worth hundreds of billions of rands were to have these taken away for failure to perform.[17]

What are the research implications of this confusion between the housing mandate and the actual policy? Simply that in any evaluation of incremental housing policy or projects, an objective researcher should also evaluate other options (such as the *RDP* vision of a mass housing program) before blithely concluding that incremental housing is the only option. As a corollary, the NBI researchers' assumption that "conventional housing cannot be provided for the poor immediately" poisons the report's subsequent methodology, because when enquiring of residents of upgrading projects whether they are satisfied with their upgraded informal settlement, no obvious comparison point is offered.[18] It is true that the NBI researchers concede, quietly, that

> It should be understood of course that not all informally housed families would necessarily choose the upgrading of their settlement over other housing alternatives if these were available.... What is examined here, therefore, is how people have interpreted their recent upgrading experiences in a context of relatively limited housing alternatives.... (pp.13-14)

Yet not only was the caveat ("not all informally housed families would necessarily choose the upgrading") ignored in the NBI report's executive summary ("NBI Research in Brief") and its extensive publicity campaign; the fact is that other alternatives are indeed available for comparison. There are two simple points to make here.

First, it is critical that every time South Africans are told, "TINA," regarding some broad aspect of social policy (usually with the effect of restricting redistribution, choice, and the elimination of social ills), objective policy researchers should be capable of responding, "THEMBA!" (There Must Be an Alternative!), and show precisely how such alternative policies can be designed, financed, implemented, evaluated, etc. There must, in other words, be provided to the South African polity a set of policy options that allow society to publicly compare and evaluate costs and benefits, as is the case in many other democracies.

Second, there must be concrete alternatives in the form of *projects* which researchers bring to bear in their consideration of what is and what is not possible. In the case of housing, there must be full-fledged low-cost housing projects with which incremental housing projects can be compared. The NBI researchers, however, ignore such a possibility.[19]

This is particularly galling given the proximity of at least one potential case study (Wattville Tamboville 2) that had been established on the basis of the crucial *RDP* provision (s2.5.14) that subsidies be provided on a non-speculative basis, hence contributing to the "decommodification" of housing: "Mechanisms (such as time limits on resale, or compulsory repayment of subsidies upon transfer of property) must be introduced to prevent speculation and downward raiding." Throughout their report, the NBI researchers completely ignore the non-speculative subsidy provision of the *RDP*, and hence fail to truly grapple with the well-known "downward raiding" problem--as even the World Bank (1991b:65) has recognized (in the wake of countless failed low-cost site-and-service projects)--that "In cases where very poor families obtained plots, they frequently sold them to middle-income people to gain a windfall."[20]

In its single mention by the NBI researchers, downward raiding is blamed on the victim--"Those with low levels of education appear to underestimate the value of their properties" (Executive Summary, p.4)--instead of on the market. Indeed the NBI researchers appear to welcome the very process of property market formation that leads directly to such outcomes, by their conclusion that "anecdotal evidence indicates that some people have already sold their properties informally. Certainly, between 80 and 90 percent of residents are comfortable in the knowledge that they *own* their plot" (original emphasis) (p.27).[21]

In all these respects, the NBI researchers' insistence that "conventional housing cannot be provided for the poor immediately" cripples any general policy value of the report. It may have been true that, as the title of the NBI report suggests, the point was not to generate a policy *options* paper. And yet the extensive policy suggestions in the report, and consciously generated pro-incremental housing policy hype, may well have been meant to leave the impression that this is a well-balanced policy analysis.[22]

Incremental housing services--affordable and acceptable?

In juxtaposing the merits of incremental housing against the allegedly unsustainable expense of a mass housing program, it is apparently essential for the NBI researchers to ignore the variable common to both approaches: the affordability crisis regarding ongoing, monthly payments ("recurrent costs").[23] For if such a link were to be made, a substantial rationale for adopting incremental housing instead of a mass housing program, namely the ability of individual households to make monthly payments, would evaporate. As the "NBI Research in Brief" summary argues (p.1), "While...more than two thirds of black urban dwellers are in most need of housing solutions, they find themselves out of reach of formal finance institutions and the property development industry. They simply don't earn enough to qualify for loans."

By implication, it would seem, the poorest two-thirds of black urban residents *can* afford to pay for municipal services supplied in incremental housing projects. This argument sinks into the report not as something that must be proved, but as an assumption. Hence, in the report's very brief section on rates and service charges (p.48), the NBI researchers fail to ask the obvious question: are residents of the informal settlements studied really capable of paying for the services now offered (water, water-borne sewage, rubbish-removal, roads and stormwater drainage, perhaps electricity where it is supplied, rental of post boxes, access to telephones, recreational fees, and other repairs or services)? (Indeed, the researchers also failed to ask, how much is the monthly bill for such services?) This is a crucial oversight on the NBI researchers' part, for at least four reasons:

1) There is, it is often alleged, an ongoing "rent and service charge boycott" that has left cost-recovery for municipal services typically below 50 percent in black townships (and much lower for informal settlements, where services are often acquired through illegal access to pipes and wires).[24]

2) As it stands at present, residents of black townships pay much higher average amounts per unit of service than do residents of traditionally white areas. Reasons include the fact that long-established suburbanites paid off capital investments, but for black residents these were internalized in contemporary rates and charges (since services were more recently installed); the higher cost of installation of Eskom's racialized, individualized, pre-paid metering points; the fact that Eskom earns interest on the pre-paid funds; and the greater expense of infrastructure provision in peripheral areas where most black people reside.

3) Due to South Africa's polarizing income distribution (which has lowered the absolute standard of living of low-income black families since the late 1980s) and to levels of unemployment that in many townships exceed 50 percent, the affordability levels of township residents (including formal townships) are very low.[25]

4) Due to limited affordability of municipal services, many low-income people are ultimately compelled to sell their serviced sites (to downward raiders), hence negating the whole point of the incremental approach and intensifying homelessness.

The NBI researchers fail to grapple with the issue of service costs, although they do concede that incremental housing upgrading projects are sometimes bedeviled by poor quality of services.[26]

From incremental housing to top structures to sustainable communities?

The critique leveled at the NBI report thus far has concentrated on its blatant rejection of the possibility that government housing policy can ultimately adhere to *RDP* promises of a mass housing program, and on the implicit argument that (good quality) services can be afforded by recipients of incremental housing. But the NBI researchers would likely respond that the incremental housing policy is meant to generate not only affordable and good quality services, but also, eventually, full-fledged houses (sometimes termed "consolidation"). As the Executive Summary (p.5) insists, "In respect of changes in an area following on infrastructural upgrading, it is interesting that housing improvements emerge as the main factor...housing improvements are a direct outcome of infrastructural upgrading programs."

Are such improvements being made? The NBI researchers claim that a minimum of R2,000 to R3,000 has been invested in top structures in all of the case study areas (Executive Summary, p.4). Indeed, according to the "NBI Research in Brief" summary (p.2),

> Perhaps the most startling discovery made by the researchers was the level of personal investment which had gone into individual properties.... This appears to be a solid vote of confidence for the incremental housing philosophy--and by the very people it is designed to assist.

Yet the NBI evidence provided regarding personal investment in the top structure is highly variable and also highly questionable.[27] Tellingly, the possibility of the investor achieving a positive real return on the investment (a key ingredient of the "value" of an investment) is not even considered. In fact, the NBI researchers did nothing more than ask respondents to self-assess the presumed value of their houses and land. This is an unscientific means of determining investment value given several factors:

1) for nearly all residents of informal settlements, the "use-value" character of their investments in the top structure far outweighs any "exchange-value" considerations (i.e., the investments were not made for the sake of investing), and hence (as the NBI researchers concede) "It is likely that the lower estimated values result from the respondents neglecting to take into account the subsidized component of their property" (p.27);

2) the land and housing markets in both informal settlements and formal black townships have been relatively non-existent,[28] and the respondents lack experience in assessing underlying asset values (which makes comparisons and estimations virtually impossible);

3) there exist substantial externalities (typically environmental, but also relating to spatial location) that lower the intrinsic value of most informal settlements;

4) there is a high degree of informality--and hence difficulty in measuring value-added--in the labor input (which tends to be either personal/family sweat equity or informally hired labor);
5) distortions and wide variations characterize the prices of building materials (given extremely high transport costs, local supplier monopolies and cartels, and the impermanent nature of most materials used in shack settlements);[29]
6) it is impossible to extrapolate individual room/shack rental prices (typically, R50-120 per month in an informal settlement) to underlying asset values (through internal rate-of-return calculations), as would otherwise be feasible in formal sector rental projects; and
7) any individual typically invokes excessive value when assessing their personal assets.

Consistent with the ideological function of the NBI report, the researchers made no comment on or concession to these logical caveats regarding their "most startling discovery" of high personal investments in top structures.[30]

Aside from encouraging personal investments in top structures, the "challenge" of policy-making and implementation, according to NBI researchers, is to "ensure that the settlement is further developed over time until it is integrated with surrounding formal settlements, and acquires all the public goods and services that any conventional township[31] enjoys, and attracts the necessary private investment to create jobs, develop a commercial sector, etc" (p.3).[32] Yet the report provides no details on the sources and amounts of funds required to produce, maintain, and manage community facilities, nor specifics regarding the degree to which residents themselves contributed to public goods through either financial or sweat equity. Nor does the report provide any concrete evidence regarding other aspects of sustainable development in the case studies (or more generally), such as access to health care, nutrition, educational facilities, creches, the local environment, parks and recreation, libraries, gender and generational power relations and resources, and the like. Instead, vague, complaisant generalities abound.

A minor revolution in social relations?

The various shortcomings in the NBI report described thus far make it difficult to assess the Executive Summary claim (p.6) that "The research reveals a minor revolution in social relations, forms of financing, institutional development, capacity building and managerial practice." But the report does take up numerous issues relating to social processes that flow from incremental housing projects, and it may be worthwhile examining these in some detail.

For instance, the NBI researchers do pose "the profound question of the possibility of integrating in a successful new combination the power relations, networks and value systems of the informal settlement with those of planners schooled to service the needs of affluent white communities" (p.32). The possibility of choosing or schooling planners in the establishment of different power relations, networks and value systems that would service the needs of low-income black communities was apparently not considered worthwhile.[33]

Similarly, the NBI researchers appear to believe firmly in community participation, and not merely as a public relations gimmick. The reasons, however, may be self-interested from the standpoint of corporate interests, for it is largely because of "the legacies of the past, exclusion, suspicion, etc" that "a great deal of community consultation is required to make upgrade projects work" (p.38). Moreover, community leadership brings "the capacity to mobilize support and involvement of members of the community in the program" (p.63), without which, often, profits cannot be efficiently extracted from the development process.[34]

The difference between community participation and control is vast, however, and the NBI researchers stake a clear position in this scathing critique of participatory democracy:

> In some areas, notably, Soweto-on-Sea, there was a reluctance to entertain any housing option apart from the construction of formal dwellings on the already serviced sites in the area. The reason for this was that there was apparent virtual unanimity that there should be no upgrade of housing. One of our interviewees on Soweto-on-Sea commented that as far as the settlement was concerned "There is no man in the street. People can't give a private opinion. They have to go through the structures." It is possible that in this instance community organization was too restrictive and papered over the diversity of need and opinion that actually exists within the community (p.35).

It is also possible, however, that the community-based organization active in Soweto-on-Sea was acting with a mandate that did indeed represent "virtual unanimity" and that this mandate may have been developed with two (or more) rationales in mind: first, that the ANC-led Government of National Unity would indeed deliver promises made in the Reconstruction and Development Program for formal houses not incremental housing, and second that the construction of shacks on the serviced sites would have the effect of dramatically reducing anticipated social benefits of the Soweto-on-Sea project. In this latter case, it may be the case that much of the rest of the Soweto-on-Sea shack settlement offers such degrading living conditions that leaders of the beneficiary community for the project in question wanted to guard against the unfortunate physical, psychological and security conditions that will likely emerge from incremental housing. If either rationale were indeed true, this would not be unusual in highly-politicized urban South Africa.

As is the case so often in the report, the difficult issue here is that apparently no effort was made by the NBI researchers to determine the rationale for the community's "virtually unanimous" opposition to incremental housing. Instead, the NBI researchers' preference is apparently to ignore any such rationales and to proceed instead on the basis of market-oriented individualism whereby "more open and pragmatic" (p.35) processes generate a resigned acceptance of shack settlements.

Regarding the role of civic associations, the NBI researchers' comments are occasionally perceptive (identifying durable patterns of patriarchy, for instance), but are more often simply cruel and misinformed.[35] The NBI researchers employ a false dichotomy in this comment: "It is likely that civics will continue to stand midway between protest and development organizations for some time to come, and certainly during the phase when housing and development programs are still underway in their areas" (p.36). Implicit in this is the view that housing development is a smooth, consensual, largely technocratic process, a view denounced by Mzwanele Mayekiso (1996:168): "Hucksters of the development industry continued to try hard to convince us that we were moving from 'protest' to 'development,' as if serious development does not require active protest now and again." In other words, effective civics do not see the two approaches as mutually exclusive, and hence do not stand "midway" between what in reality represents an organic unity.

The NBI researchers do not hesitate to impose their own views of the natural township division of labor onto the communities under study: "....in general it seems that what is needed is a separation of roles and functions with community representatives not being able to obtain employment within the project" (pp.35-36), and furthermore, "Essentially civics need to withdraw from the managerial and financial aspects of the development process" (p.69). Justifications for such arrogant recommendations are either non-existent or unconvincing, and remain at the immature level that McCarthy (and former UF colleague Ann Bernstein) demonstrated in a *Business Day* article (4/11/94) just prior to the UF's collapse--entitled, with no obvious irony, "High time for some soul searching by civic organizations"--which effectively called for the liquidation of any kind of national civic movement.[36]

Ultimately, many civics believe that "community control" is the objective. The NBI researchers apparently do not, as witnessed by their comment, "There is a point at which the negotiation process can go too far towards community involvement" (p.38). The argument that community consultation, participation, and (ultimately) control are values to be pursued in their own right, as essential to participatory democracy, is not considered worthwhile even mentioning.[37] To the contrary, the NBI researchers seem to endorse the extraordinary proposition that "community" can be "created" in a top-down manner by "projects" (usually meaning development agencies or for-profit construction companies): "More recently upgrade projects have sought to tackle these problems at various levels by creating beneficiary groups of a manageable size" (p.38). The NBI researchers also note "an obvious need for training programs for communities to cover a whole range of civic rights and responsibilities" including "rights and obligations relating to ownership through to service/payments rights and obligations" (p.39). Implicit in this comment is the view that flagrant political ignorance is widespread among residents of informal settlements.[38]

Regarding progressive development NGOs, the NBI researchers appear confused when they argue, "A number of other non-governmental organizations initiated smaller scale upgrade programs, for example, the Built Environment Support Group (BESG) in Luganda and Planact in Tamboville" (p.4). In reality, the two NGOs mentioned have had a long-standing policy of taking direction *from* local community organizations like civic associations, not "initiating" programs on their own.[39] A more accurate reflection of these roles would stress how community-based organizations (especially civic associations), assisted by politically-allied non-governmental service organizations, initiated land invasions and defended residents of informal settlements as a response to the apartheid state's refusal to supply sufficient amounts of public housing and its continuing attempts to regulate urban residents. These initiatives were, unfortunately, nearly always limited to the establishment or defence of informal settlements (instead of building well-housed communities) because, as the *RDP* notes (s2.5.3), of the "problems created by apartheid and by the limited range of the capitalist housing markets." In short, affordable housing was not available to low-income South Africans from the state, the private sector, or the parastatal development agencies that were mandated to meet basic needs. The same conditions remain today, but the NBI researchers welcome the migration of development professionals from progressive service organizations to either government or business as "both inevitable and desirable" (p.77), for obvious reasons.

With regard to community-based development institutions, the NBI researchers argue, incorrectly, that development trusts "emerged to fill the gap created by the breakdown of local authority and were conceived as transitional phenomena" (p.40) and that they "are a form of institutionalized social compact" involving not only community representatives but business (p.41). In fact, beginning in 1990, development trusts (as well as "community development forums") were conceived by leading civic associations as permanent, independent, community-based institutions that would bring together stakeholders *internal* to a community along with democratically elected representatives of local government.[40]

Although the NBI researchers later suggest, correctly, that trusts "should not be seen as purely transitional phenomena" (p.45), they do seem, incorrectly, to endorse the conclusion (drawn from UF-related development projects) that

> the balance of power and expertise at first lies with the developers and the white professionals. With the experience gained in the development process and with the growing confidence and skill of community representatives, the balance shifts in favor of the community. It would greatly facilitate the staging of the development process if there was a deeper understanding amongst all actors of the likelihood of these shifts occurring.... (p.43)

But in stressing three subjective factors--experience, growing confidence and skill--the NBI researchers mainly ignore the crucial factor determining balance of power in such trusts: control of funding.[41] In the process, the NBI researchers implicitly dismiss the possibility that power might or should rest *initially* with community representatives, in the critical early design stages of local projects and programs (via community-based institutions having access to funds through which professionals might be hired to do work, rather than share or control power within the trust board). The NBI researchers thus dismiss the spirit of "people-centered" or "people-driven" development in favor of a model which gives excessive power to developers and white professionals.[42] If developers and white professionals had performed adequately in recent times, this might be a valid model; but they haven't, hence the model requires thorough revision.

With the advent of local government democratization, the NBI researchers confidently recognize municipalities' "development ambitions...which are also the sources of much hope" (p.83). The NBI researchers conspicuously miss, however, another factor that is sure to feature in local government development processes: growing popular resentment generated by the heavy white weighting in the 1995-96 local elections (thanks to 60 percent of local council seats being reserved for wards) and by white veto power--covering potentially redistributive budgets, zoning and other critical matters--which can be invoked with merely one third of local council seats.

With respect to class relations in informal settlements, the NBI researchers again demonstrate an ideological commitment consistent with the interests of large corporations in their hoary, predictable discussions of banks, emergent construction firms, and organized labor. Banks will need to make "major adaptations," it is conceded, but the only one mentioned is "to cater for the relatively small amounts [of township savers] entailed compared to their existing clientele. A potential fruitful area for innovative banking is in the support of informal savings and loans schemes designed for home construction."[43] Otherwise, "entry of the private sector into the upgrade market is probably also dependent on the development of a viable market in housing within the informal settlements" (p.56). The NBI researchers do not appear to even notice the Catch-22 involved here.[44]

Emergent black builders are treated by the NBI researchers with glowing admiration, as has traditionally been the case in corporate ideology. Hence the NBI researchers anticipate "The success of both the micro- and small scale enterprise economy, upon which so many hopes are currently pinned...." Moreover, the "emergence of a home-building contractor sector as a direct consequence of upgrading initiatives is cause for great optimism. This organic, grassroots economic development may be more sustainable in the long term than any self-conscious job creation programs" (p.83). Again, there is no mention of the notorious problems of overtrading, superexploitation of labor, or poor quality work that have bedeviled the small-scale construction industry. Nor is there consideration of the government support that will be required to bring black builders up to scale so as to compete in price and quality terms with extremely oligopolistic white-owned development and construction materials corporations.[45] Aside from conceding that exclusive arrangements with black builders from settlements undergoing upgrading "worked satisfactorily" (p.59), the NBI researchers apparently believe that a *laisser-faire* approach is satisfactory.

As for organized labor, the only mention of its role in the whole incremental housing process is, predictably, negative: in Soweto-on-Sea, the unions created "a serious problem" because they

> objected to the wage rates being paid to community labor on the grounds that they undercut workers within the formal sector. The intervention of the unions also made it difficult for local business to gain a foothold as it appears that labor on this scheme did not want to be employed by (black) subcontractors but rather by the (white) main contractor because this would mean that they would come under the mainstream labor legislation and thus have to be paid higher wages (p.58).

In just two sentences, the NBI researchers neatly combine a set of old (racial) and new (class divisive) prejudices via an anecdote that was obviously not replicated in the other seven case studies (otherwise we would have been piously informed). In reality, organized labor has been playing an important unifying role, both in broad social terms (generally fighting attempts to split the formally-employed from the unemployed across a wide range of social policies) and in microeconomic terms, whereby individual trade unionists are typically responsible for the survival of a large extended family. Such a role is not only beyond the experience of the NBI researchers, but would not be in keeping with the ideological mission of the report.

It appears, thus, that for the NBI researchers, the "minor revolution in social relations" represented by incremental housing is only worth discussing if it is basically consistent with a corporate agenda: "The formal private sector will only play a role in the upgrading and consolidation of informal settlements where it perceives involvement to be in its own *interest*" (original emphasis) (p.77). Some "revolution." The NBI researchers list several areas where self-interest may potentially come into play--"huge consumer markets.... better living conditions for many of the employees.... an investment in long-term political stability" (pp.77-78), and the (slightly exaggerated) threat that "the large land holdings of the mining houses, for example, are vulnerable to land invasions and could even be targeted for expropriation by the state" (p.80)--while explicitly ignoring the concept of market failure which would explain very clearly why the private sector is not nearly so active in incremental housing as corporate ideologues had originally hoped.[46] The NBI researchers conclude their discussion of corporate interests with this self-evident remark: "Finally, there is also the need for the private sector to lobby government to ensure that private enterprise can flourish" (p.81).[47]

Conclusion: Do blacks like shacks?

Should anyone pay attention to the ruminations of NBI's corporate ideologues, given the flaws we have uncovered in their report? The answer must be in the affirmative, not only because of the hype the NBI report generated in the corporate-owned press and its consequent effect of dulling thought processes and stifling what otherwise should have been a vibrant policy debate. There is also, we would argue, a self-destructive component in the NBI report's policy analysis and advice, consistent with the contradictory role of those corporate think-tanks and their organic intellectuals who have, over the past three decades or so, applied themselves to solving urban problems.

The contradiction lies in the fact that since liberals began more strenuously arguing the need for market processes to replace the apartheid social and economic order, higher expectations have been placed on the market than it can possibly meet. Thus, while capitalism, thanks to its intrinsic capacity to generate prosperity in great creative bursts (perpetually accompanied of course by what Schumpeter called creative destruction), was considered capable of gradually supplanting the inefficient, racist, and excessively authoritarian South African state, precisely the opposite happened in the 1970s and 1980s: the deep-rooted *crisis* of South African capitalism forced state managers to think twice about the isolation and high security costs of apartheid, and finally in the late 1980s move conclusively toward a neoliberal, "low-intensity democracy" (as such transitions are termed internationally).

But this relationship never truly sank in. Instead, those forces who have shaped and reshaped the liberal corporate agenda seemed to have gained increasing confidence as it became clear that the ANC would be called upon to manage an economy characterized by trade and labor liberalization, business deregulation, high interest rates, a far smaller state, far weaker state controls, and a pro-market ideology rigorously enforced on a daily basis by the mainstream press. Moreover, while the corporate sector may have seemingly lost a battle of position over the ANC's representation of social policy (the *RDP*), at least in the sphere of housing, banks and developers clearly won the war of manoeuvre.

But what has that accomplished for corporate South Africa? Here arises the contradiction. Whereas in the early 1980s, corporate ideologues would have spoken earnestly of the need for full-fledged commodification to transform township life (taxi transport, homeownership, electrification, legalization of spaza shops and hawking, consumer credit, and so forth), the actual experience of markets in townships has been nearly uniformly disastrous. Housing is a case in point, given the R8 billion invested by financial institutions in (an estimated 200,000) developer-built township houses during roughly 1986-90, which resulted in badly-constructed homes, negative equity, and ultimately defaults on an estimated 50,000 housing bonds.

Yet notwithstanding the failed experience of the late 1980s, market mechanisms were again, in negotiations between the Department of Housing and the Association of Mortgage Lenders in October 1994, expected to supply the bulk of township houses. Even those low-income people who would not ordinarily have qualified for bank loans were told that using a combination of (bank-distributed) subsidies and a mortgage guarantee scheme, the banks would rapidly gear up their financing of housing to at least 50,000 units per year. Even small loans (as low as R10,000) would be provided, consistent with the incremental housing philosophy. But it is all too clear that hype and self-interest characterized the banks' claims, and the production of only a few thousand formal low-cost houses over the period leading to the NBI report should have offered striking evidence of the deal's failure.

One might have expected that at least a degree of embarrassment would accompany the market's total mishandling of numerous opportunities to take advantage of state incremental housing policy since the early 1990s. Instead, if the NBI report is any indication, the intellectuals and ideologues of corporate South Africa have refused to go on the defensive and instead moved quickly to the offensive again. Not content with having won the incremental housing policy instead of the *RDP*'s mass housing program, the strategy appeared to be based on simple misinformation: the need to systematically disguise and reinterpret the concrete failures of that policy. Hence the NBI report is advertised as proving, in the words of the *Star*, that "informal settlements should be seen as part of an overall solution to the housing crisis rather than as such a large part of the problem." They are part of the solution, simply said, because blacks like shacks.

In short, the NBI report is a reasonably well-written, though methodologically flawed, poorly argued, error-ridden, demonstrably misleading, conveniently neglectful, self-interested, inconsistent, and essentially inhumane piece of conservative social policy advocacy. But the fact that well-qualified intellectuals generated the NBI report should, again, deter its readers from simply writing it off as mere corporate ideology. It is that, to be sure, but it is more. At a time of perceived fiscal crisis, when corporations and financiers (domestic and international) are mounting an intense attack on the state budget deficit, the aim of interventions in the housing sphere noted above still stands: shifting policy and policy discourse toward more conservative premises, in the process lowering the expectations of South Africa's homeless and poorly housed populations. What the NBI report does that is new and different is argue forcefully that blacks like shacks.

Many of the NBI researchers' technical shortcomings have been exposed in this critique. Further steps must be political. It should not be impossible, at this stage when housing policy can again potentially be called into question, for labor and social movements and those political parties which represent poor and working people to do the rest: prove through mass action, negotiations, and a radical reworking of policy that middle-income South Africa can do better than provide shacks and pit latrines to two-thirds of its population and pretend that this is a satisfactory outcome to all concerned.

Notes

1. Thus Centre for Policy Studies senior researcher Tomlinson (1997), South Africa's preeminent housing policy analyst, reiterated a variety of inaccurate claims about the merits of Cobbett's policy and the danger of a progressive alternative. But she conceded that the neoliberal housing policy had not been an easy sell: "Several provincial MECs for housing, and many MPs, rejected the policy outright, demanding that government fulfill its electoral promise to build four-roomed houses. On taking over from the late Joe Slovo, even the housing minister [Mthembi-Mahanyele] called the standards introduced by the policy into question. As one of the key participants in the formulation of the policy, the director-general became the target of much of this criticism." For alternative evaluations of the policy (and Cobbett's firing), see Chapter Ten of this volume, as well as Mayekiso (1997) and Tweedie (1997).

2. The two are based at the University of Durban-Westville's Institute for Social and Economic Research while the third (former Urban Foundation strategist Mike Oelofse) is an independent consultant. The NBI researchers are well-respected commentators on housing and urban development, and claim numerous consultancies, research reports, academic papers, and highly-regarded books between them. It is useful to examine their work because it normally represents some of the highest-quality research capacity in the housing field, as well as because all three are veritable housing policy opinion-makers.

3. In earlier times, the "incremental" approach would have (mainly disparagingly) been termed "site-and-service," "shack settlement," or even "toilets-in-the-veld" (the latter was the choice of Housing Minister Sankie Mthembi-Mahanyele when describing the housing policy she inherited from Slovo; see *Business Day* 21/7/95). However, "incremental housing" is now the preferred official term and will be used in the pages below, notwithstanding its obfuscating character. The NBI is somewhat embarrassed about the legacy of the term, however, for it notes that incremental housing has included "anonymous areas with rudimentary services but no houses, often at great distances from work opportunities and related facilities.... Such morbid environments are an aberration of the incremental housing philosophy...." (Executive Summary [ES], p.2). Moreover, the NBI researchers worry, "Unless the poor can see the longer-term benefits of such an approach, it will be politically unpopular, and unless the state can ensure that programs for sustainable development are set in motion, it will yield little but vast 'slums of despair'" (p.70).

4. Note, in this list of services, the absence of electricity (although it is buried later in the paper, nearly as an afterthought, along with telephone services, on p.72). The omission of electricity provision was one of the most heavily-criticized aspects of the Independent Development Trust site-and-service scheme, which one of the NBI researchers (McCarthy) was instrumental in designing. While the Department of Housing has more recently specified that its incremental housing program should include the installation of electricity, the Department of Constitutional Development initially planned for no electricity for those urban households with below R800 per month, and only after pressure agreed to install 8 Amp meters (not enough power for cooking or heating), and indeed continues to

insist on mass provision of pit latrine settlements. Reflecting this trend, the NBI researchers conclude their report with the stingy assertion that "Upgrading informal settlements at scale will require the acceptance by local and metropolitan authorities of *less than conventional servicing standards in these areas in the medium term*...." (emphasis added) (p.75). No mention, of course, of public health, environmental, labor productivity, SMME, gender time availability, and desegregation benefits to society as a whole if there were higher standards. Thus because of the failure of the corporate intelligentsia--in this case including World Bank and Constitutional Development consultants who planned the *Municipal Infrastructure Investment Framework*--to carry out rudimentary cost-benefit analysis, we have degenerated to the point that "toilets-in-the-veld" has become a revolutionary demand.

5. Sven Lunsche, "Housing drive gets off the ground slowly but surely," *Sunday Business Times* 7/1/96; "Housing pragmatics" (editorial), *Star* 20/11/95; Joshua Raboroko, "8-million do not afford housing," *Sowetan* 15/11/95; "Upgrading of settlements 'essential'," *Citizen* 15/11/95; David Robbins, "Upgrade settlements to solve housing crisis: 'Unrealistic' to think that more than 7 million people in settlements can be accommodated in conventional housing," *Star* 15/11/95; David Robbins, "New housing policy empowers," *Star*, 15/11/95; "Opknapping van informele huise kan huisnood verlig," *Beeld* 15/11/95.

6. A closer read quickly throws the conclusion that "the impacts upon infrastructure were widely noted with appreciation" (p.20) into question. As the report concedes, "The average evaluation attributed to changes in each of the settlements fell somewhere between 'good' and 'okay'" (p.21) (on a five-tier scale ranging from 'very good' to 'very bad'). To describe such a mediocre rating as "evaluated positively" is to resort to very low standards indeed. (Moreover, the report contains no detailed table outlining which settlements received which scores, standard deviations, and other elementary aspects of survey presentation.) In addition, the upgrading did not inspire further investment at anything like the rate suggested by supporters of incremental housing. A surprisingly small proportion (ranging from 2 percent to 50 percent, with the median at "around 20 percent") told the NBI surveyors that they "improved their housing conditions as a direct result of the upgrading initiative" (p.26).

Even if resident satisfaction instead of mediocrity had characterized the informal settlements studied by the NBI researchers, what difference would this make to housing policy for South Africa as a whole? Again, the NBI researchers offer a near-hidden concession: "The generalizations that arise from the study are applicable mainly to reasonably well-located settlements on the peripheries of the major urban centres" (p.13). Aside from the fact that this represents an internal contradiction ("reasonably well-located.... on the peripheries"), it is noteworthy that this extremely powerful reservation was omitted in both the report's Executive Summary and the media hype regarding the study.

7. In contrast, the NBI researchers offer a different explanation of why incremental housing was increasingly promoted during the 1980s: "....more than seven million people were living in informal settlements in and around South Africa's urban areas and clearly most of them could not be moved" (p.1). In point of fact, though, it is (and was) not

"clear" that shack-dwellers could not or cannot be moved. South Africa's tragic history includes the forced removal of millions of people from one place to another; the challenge, of course, is to help move people *voluntarily*, by dramatically improving their (and their communities') socio-economic status. Such dramatic improvement is not envisaged by the NBI researchers, who are instead committed to minor incremental reforms.

But if more radical policy options become logical for consideration as market-oriented policies continue to fail, and hence if, within five years, one million decent houses are rapidly built in well-located areas (as the *RDP* argues would be feasible [s2.5.2]), then several million shack-dwellers and other homeless people--such as hostel-dwellers or those occupying backrooms and forced into excessively cramped quarters--could indeed have a decent home to move into. And if appropriate social processes are launched to ensure choice, education, consultation, participation, and local control, then the homeless would logically want to move into proper houses.

The NBI researchers continue their historical explanation: "....the old government policy of delivering formal housing on a subsidized basis to the poor.... had proved expensive to implement and to administer, and forced some authorities to focus on the satisfaction of basic needs rather than on the delivery of high quality housing" (p.3). In reality, the old apartheid government switched its budgetary support for new housing to private housing bond subsidies and guarantees *not* because public housing was "expensive to implement or administer," but as part of a general strategy of privatizing state services and distracting the attention of growing urban protest movements away from apartheid targets. (Large corporations and the UF complied by lobbying for permanent residential rights for blacks, as well as for property ownership that in turn would support the expansion of the credit system into the townships. As Zach de Beer--both a businessperson and politician--put it in 1988, "When people are housed, more especially when they are home-owners, they are not only likely to be less troublesome. They are also likely to feel they have a stake in society and an interest in its stability.") A more accurate description of the history of state-oriented housing policy would acknowledge that the old apartheid government provided a mass supply of matchbox housing to working-class blacks in underdeveloped townships during the 1940s-60s, in order to assure a continuing supply of urban labor to local mines, corporations, and other businesses (notwithstanding that the workers remained "temporary sojourners" in the townships). As unequal, unfair, and racially-motivated as it was, the housing system for urban blacks was nevertheless inexpensive to construct and relatively easy to not only administer but to police (see Robinson 1996).

8. The NBI researchers illustrate the use of this red herring as follows (pp.4-5):

> ....arguments in favor of the incremental approach question the ability of the state to finance a program which aims at placing every eligible household in conventional housing at the rate and scale required. But the incremental housing approach is also not without controversy. As already indicated, the strategy hinges around the contention that by assisting households to access the most basic accommodation the state can do two things. It can spread available public resources as widely as possible rather than concentrating most of its resources on a limited number of beneficiaries. Secondly, and of particularly importance, it can engage the resources of a range of actors (individual households,

> non-governmental organizations, community-based organizations, the private sector, etc.) to improve the quality of this accommodation over time.

There is, looking more closely, no "controversy" within this paragraph, simply because the first sentence leaves no room for debate. The possibility that this initial statement may be "also not without controversy" is not even considered plausible. But in reality, the state has sufficient funds even in existing budgets to increase subsidy levels to the point at which real houses, not incremental housing, can be built to scale. The problem is that policy mechanisms to make this translation of state resources possible have not been adopted. As the *RDP* states (s2.5.3, s2.5.4, s2.5.5), in contrast,

> A mass housing program can help generate employment, skills and economic activity, both directly and indirectly, and should help ensure peace and stability....
>
> The *RDP* endorses the principle that all South Africans have a right to a secure place in which to live in peace and dignity....
>
> Although housing may be provided by a range of parties, the democratic government is ultimately responsible for ensuring that housing is provided to all. It must create a policy framework and legislative support so that this is possible, and it must allocate subsidy funds from the budget--to reach a goal of not less than 5 percent of the budget by the end of the five-year *RDP*--so that housing is affordable to even the poorest South Africans.

9. The primary reason for adoption of the incremental policy was the alleged "fiscal constraint," a widely-repeated (but never documented) argument that the South African budget could not possibly afford the subsidy levels required to ensure that all homeless or poorly-housed South Africans would have access to houses of the standards promised in the *RDP*. As stated in the Department of Housing's *Housing White Paper* (HWP): "The required annual delivery rate...., relatively high proportion of poor households and budgetary constraints do not allow sufficient subsidy money per household to enable the construction, at State expense, of a minimum standard complete house for each household not able to afford such a house."

This argument is, in fact, groundless. If one assumes (as was the case in October 1994) that a minimally decent house costs approximately R25,000, and that SA's income distribution requires an average of 50 percent subsidy, there was sufficient funding in even the first budget of the Government of National Unity to launch the *RDP* housing program. The HWP both failed to acknowledge the *RDP*'s call for *blending* government and private sector resources (i.e., housing constructed *not* entirely "at State expense"), and to consider the actual cost to the budget of meeting the *RDP* goal of one million new low-income houses built over five years (an average of 200,000 per year). At an average cost to the state of R12,500 per unit -- not including the other R12,500 per unit, which would come from private sector resources via the proposed national housing bank and would be repaid at the market rate of interest -- the *RDP* housing program would cost the government just R2,5 billion per year. Consistent with the *RDP*, the HWP's stated goal for resource allocation is to acquire 5 percent of the budget by the year 1998, which in the 1994/95 budget would have been roughly R6,5 billion (i.e., far in excess of R2,5 billion). This is obviously sufficient to meet not only the *RDP* goal, but to go far beyond that goal, even reaching 350,000 houses per year by 1998. Simple mathematics shows the inaccuracy of the fiscal constraint argument.

What is actually at stake here is whether the government budget can be sustained at the level of R3 billion or so (or perhaps even increased) over the coming years, in the face of enormous pressures to cut the budget deficit (partly through the emerging argument that in any case the Department of Housing is rolling over approximately 90 percent of its budget due to spending bottlenecks). Hence Whittaker was quoted in the *Star* (15/11/95) as alleging: "In countries with limited resources--and South Africa is certainly one of them--policy-makers must make do with what they've got." For Whittaker and the NBI, it goes without saying that a major redistribution of wealth in order to increase "what [policy-makers] have got" is simply out of the question.

10. McCarthy was central in justifying the IDT capital subsidy, which was the basis for several of the projects reviewed in the NBI report. That capital subsidy, which financed the construction of merely a toilet on a serviced site (with no building materials or electricity hook-up provided) was introduced as "a beacon of hope" by IDT director (and former UF director) Jan Steyn; it is eerie, hence, to read the NBI researchers' concluding argument that thanks to its incremental housing policy, "South Africa is widely regarded as the beacon of hope in a gloomy area" because "A recent international conference [in Abidjan, Ivory Coast, in March 1995; the sponsors are conspicuously omitted] on urban land management and informal settlements concluded that South Africa may well provide the world's best example of how to respond to the informal housing challenge "(p.81). Hence the NBI report has self-described international implications, and are all the more important to contest.

11. The story of the Urban Foundation (UF) role in incremental housing policy-making and projects is a long and sordid one and beyond the scope of this paper. Some of the aspects of incremental housing policy formulation initiated and advanced by the UF are discussed in Chapter Eight.

Regarding the UF's many incremental housing projects, such as several of those covered by the NBI researchers, there are aspects of organizational self-interest that must be remarked upon. In brief, during the late 1980s the UF gambled enormously on acquisition of land (often on the far, poorly located side of townships); in mid-1990, when township land and housing development ground to a halt, the UF began to have major cash-flow problems; in 1991, the UF recorded a loss of R17 million (on turnover of just R11 million) due primarily to the holding costs associated with the land, and to failed development projects by UF "utility company" subsidiaries; by 1992, IDT chief executive Jan Steyn, who was also the UF's former chief executive during the 1980s (and hence responsible for the land acquisition strategy), advanced a R70 million loan to the UF's new "Land Investment Trust" (LIT) at 5 percent interest, which had the effect of bailing out the UF by allowing the LIT to advance bridging finance to developers (including former UF utility companies) so as to develop the land and get it off the UF's books.

12. This is not to say that the NBI researchers do not engage in occasional auto-critique, such as their concession that the IDT capital subsidy was "rigid" (p.57) and that "The whole idea of consolidation appears to have emerged from the UF/IDT as a way of addressing the very serious conflict that arose out of lack of deep community involvement

in planning and decision-taking.... The capital subsidy schemes in most cases have been heavily product and delivery oriented" (p.60).

But just when self-criticism is most welcome, the NBI researchers spoil matters by shifting blame elsewhere (essentially to the victim), as in this example:

> It is necessary to record that the researchers were not at first welcomed in all the areas and that considerable time and effort was put into reassuring especially the community leadership of the integrity and value of the study. In two instances similar problems of initial distrust were encountered with development professionals associated with the NGOs involved in the upgrading project. The reasons given for the initial distrust were the perceived association of the ISER researchers with the Urban Foundation and the fact that community leadership in many of the areas had been engaged in a struggle with staff employed by or linked with the Urban Foundation over decision-making powers within the upgrade programs. (p.12)

The NBI report does not provide any evidence of the "similar problems" that NGOs faced, which is telling. In any event it would, however, be unlikely that these would be "similar" in view of the fact that NGOs retained no "decision-making powers" within upgrading project and were instead merely advisory (quite unlike the UF, which played the role of developer). Requesting information from four leading staffpersons from BESG and Planact (the only NGOs mentioned by name in the NBI report) who worked extensively at the St.Wendolin's and Tamboville projects, we could discern no such instances of "initial distrust." Hence while the UF may have had numerous problems in not only pushing the incremental housing philosophy, but in carrying it out on the ground, in contrast, NGOs like BESG and Planact, which opposed incremental housing but nevertheless worked with civic associations to make the best of a bad situation, quickly earned and retained the trust of community leaders.

13. This bias is all the more blatant in view of the fact that the NBI researchers conspicuously failed to investigate any control group case studies, either of communities that did not receive incremental upgrading assistance or of communities that received sufficient subsidies to have a true housing program.

14. This position is rebutted convincingly in SANCO 1994:34-38,79-92.

15. The usual disguise for advocating such a limited vision of housing policy is that, as the NBI researchers put it, "housing is not merely a product but also a process" (p.2). The assumption here--often repeated but rarely interrogated--is that "housing" is not actually the product being delivered; instead, a serviced site (misnamed "incremental housing") is the product. The "process" entails convincing potential beneficiaries that they will only be supplied with an inadequate product, and that if they want a real house they must build it themselves. Instead, housing is a *both* a "product" and a "process," in that, as the *RDP* puts it (s2.5.21):

> Beneficiary communities should be involved at all levels of decision-making and in the implementation of their projects. Communities should benefit directly from programs in matters such as employment, training and award of contracts. Key to such participation is capacity

building, and funds for community-based organizations must be made available.

Such arguments run against the grain of the NBI researchers' conclusions on community participation and organization, as shown below.

16. Although banks and mining companies vocally criticized provisions in the *RDP* relating to small business lending and ownership of minerals, there was no such public concern expressed by any of the actors in the field of housing.

17. The failure of the housing market is such a mundane observation at this stage that even the NBI researchers concede that "all informal settlements as well as the majority of neighboring townships were 'redlined' by the financial institutions on the grounds of political and financial risk" (p.56) (as if, perhaps, alleged but unproven concerns about risk justify redlining), even though the banks were given a Mortgage Indemnity Fund in October 1994 to lower their actual exposure dramatically in cases of politically-motivated bond boycotts. The fact that there were no withdrawals from the Fund as of May 1997 demonstrates the banks' ingenuity during the early 1990s in using the bond boycott threat as a red herring to justify not lending in townships, now that the emerging black middle class could migrate to formerly white areas.

18. Given that no comparative questions were apparently posed--such as, "Would you rather the *RDP* mass housing program be implemented so that you would ultimately have access to a house, or would you rather the *RDP* program be forever shelved such that you continue to stay in an informal settlement which has been or is being incrementally upgraded?"--the only way in which the NBI researchers feigned objectivity was by "providing respondents with opportunities for both negative and positive assessments against neutral criteria" (Executive Summary, p.4). Intellectually, this is a most unsatisfying means of dealing with the problem of comparability.

19. The NBI researchers' incompetence (or, alternatively, ideological bias) is highlighted by the fact that bordering one of the eight case study areas, Tamboville (a section of Wattville Township near Benoni on the East Rand), there is indeed an alternative to incremental housing: the Wattville Housing Association (WHA). Through the initiative of the Wattville Concerned Residents Committee and with the financial assistance of the French government, the WHA has built cooperatively-owned houses in the "Tamboville 2" section of Wattville. At the time of the NBI report, four dozen two-bedroomed houses with lounge, kitchen, and full internal services had been constructed at a cost of R25,000 each, including land acquisition and servicing; although local petit-bourgeois political squabbles have tarnished the project, it remains an appropriate alternative approach (see Matlala 1995).

20. The problem is, of course, even deeper than merely middle-income people "gaining a windfall." For when downward raiding occurs, individual subsidies or entire housing developments originally targeted to the poor are lost to middle-income households, while the poor again become homeless, contributing to the intensification of the housing crisis. This may or may not occur at prices that are below the level of state subsidy plus capital investment, but, in all cases, they entail market processes subverting social policy.

21. In reality, there is no property market to speak of in most townships, due to the combination of widespread negative equity (by which an owner owes more on the bond than the house is actually worth) and the failure of banks to make loans available again; such problems were not considered worthy of mention or discussion by the NBI researchers in their brief, inadequate, and over-optimistic three paragraphs on "the emergence of property markets" (p.27).

22. As the *Sunday Times* (7/1/96) put it, "The NBI says the study has important implications for government housing policy, particularly since the incremental approach does not have the full backing of many provincial governments and even Housing Minister Sankie Nkondo."

23. Only in the conclusion do the NBI researchers remark that "The capital subsidy program has offered important new services to the poor, yet the recurrent cost implications have not always been explained to them" (p.74). The NBI report does not otherwise mention (much less explain or analyze) affordability, other than to suggest, in passing, "less than conventional servicing standards in these areas in the medium term, and the promotion of service charge payments (i.e. an end to payment boycotts) and a degree of cross-subsidization *within* urban areas to help cover the costs of such items as bulk infrastructure, township management and administration" (emphasis added) (p.75). Consistent with large corporate interests, the NBI researchers here specifically reject the *RDP*'s argument that tariffs on water (s2.6.10), electricity (s2.7.8), and transport (s2.9.9), for example, should be determined at national level so as to promote a deeper national redistribution of wealth. Instead, the NBI researchers recommend a local government financing system sponsored by the sugar-based conglomerate Tongaat Hulett (p.75).

24. In August 1996, the total monthly bank balances of municipalities would cover only four months of the employee salary bill, with 77 local authorities unable to access resources to pay even one month's salary bill. Moreover, by mid-1996 37 percent of local authorities had not even finalized their financial statements for the previous year (Department of Constitutional Development 1996). Although this low payment rate is sometimes said to be the result of actual formal boycotts or to a "culture of non-payment," in reality, non-payment is due instead to a combination of factors including lack of billing, the generally degraded state of most townships, residual anger at the historical subsidy that blacks provided white residents (due to not having a tax base internal to the black townships), the extremely high cost of transport (which is often the largest component of the household budget), broken promises of service improvements, alienation from white (or often black) local government officials, and so on.

25. That only 20 percent of residents in the eight case studies are unemployed stretches credulity (p.18). If true, it suggests that the case studies have very little relation to most South African settlements, where unemployment is conservatively estimated at well over 30 percent.

According to surveys cited recently in the *South African Housing Journal*, only one in five township households can afford non-subsidized service charges (see *Business Day* 5/1/96). Moreover, subsidies are being phased out for many state services which face a variety of pressures--commercialization, privatization or simple municipal fiscal crisis--to recover costs.

The NBI researchers appear comfortable with this trend, arguing that "local authorities need to.... devolve functions to communities and to the private sector" (p.69) and that "private companies could be contracted to perform all or some of the tasks of local government.... through the full privatization of the service, or through some form of concession" (p.79).

26. Specifically, the report notes that sewage systems "topped the lists of 'things that have got worse' since the upgrade.... [W]hat appears to have happened is that quality or durability of the service provided did not match community expectations" (p.21). But the report gives no evidence to arrive at such a conclusion, which in any case implicitly blames the victims for having excessively elevated "expectations."

There may be other, just as likely reasons that residents are not happy with their sewage systems. First, installation of sewage lines in the context of in-situ upgrading is notoriously difficult, and some of the dissatisfaction may have resulted from temporary displacement, the digging of dangerous trenches, the dust and dirt (and possibly soil erosion) generated in the process, or other inconvenient features of sewage installation. Second, if *water-borne* sewage was not installed in the settlements, this should have been mentioned by the NBI researchers. Third, sewage systems may actually have physically broken down, generating unhygienic conditions and the risk of diseases such as cholera (as has been recorded in many South African informal settlements). Fourth, the sewage systems may have been designed for too few people due to inadequate subsidies or poor planning, with resulting back-ups and flow problems. Fifth, there may have been disputes with the developers about phasing, location, and other aspects of the sewage systems (given general unhappiness with the various incremental housing developers recorded by the NBI researchers, this is not unlikely). Sixth, there may not have been sufficient sewage intake facilities (e.g., toilets), or these may have to be shared by several households (as was the case in Tamboville, even with regard to water standpipes).

Any of these problems (or others) could easily have been investigated by the NBI researchers; instead, their report on services simply treats the residents' complaints as unmet "community expectations." Hence the report's "infrastructure" section is most unsatisfying, and indeed is useless for the purposes of policy-making or project-improvement. But the NBI report is not only incomplete and unconvincing in its treatment of the services component (affordability and quality) of incremental housing. In addition, the argument that communities can move easily from a serviced site to top structures to sustainable community facilities requires critical examination.

27. For example, St.Wendolin's is alleged to have an "average estimated home value" of nearly R40,000 (Executive Summary, p.4), which is contradicted by another statement in the NBI report that "The median respondent estimated value of house and plot ranges from R3,000 in Scenery Park to R20,000 in St.Wendolin's" (p.27), while a detailed accounting of other maximum, average or minimum figures is not provided for the other case studies.

28. In a bizarre conclusion contradicted by numerous far more cautious statements in the report--such as "it may be premature to make such an assessment [but] anecdotal evidence indicates that some people have already sold their properties informally" (p.27)--the NBI researchers claim that "There has already emerged *a vibrant housing market*.... within many of the upgraded settlements, and the key to this is the secure title and exchange value of the modest homes that have been secured" (emphasis added) (p.82).

29. Although it could easily have been gathered by surveyors on site visits, the NBI researchers failed to provide information as to whether top structure investments were made in what have been termed by World Bank housing expert Steven Mayo "temporary materials" (such as straw, cardboard or cloth), in "permanent" materials (zinc sheets and plywood, which are not in reality terribly permanent), in some combination of the two, or in formal brick-and-mortar-type construction that can last for decades. (Three sentences in the report [p.26] note that in five of the case studies, between 8 percent and "more than half of the houses" consist of "more permanent brick structures"--an excessively vague and incomplete analysis.) Mayo (1993:16) notes that even though 89 percent of new top structures erected in South Africa during the early 1990s were "unauthorized" (illegal shacks subject to demolition at any time), two-thirds of them were made with "permanent" (his definition) materials.

30. However, in a surprisingly honest revelation, the NBI researchers do acknowledge that "In every area studied, the need to pay more attention to houses.... emerged as the most commonly mentioned suggestion for the improvement of future upgrade efforts. Recent modifications to national housing policy appear to have anticipated this criticism" (p.21). This, of course, has been a consistent progressive criticism of incremental housing dating from the apartheid government's switch from public housing construction to incremental housing. As noted earlier, the UF, IDT and other agencies traditionally attempted to downplay the need for government to provide sufficient subsidy finance and to control the development process in order to assure construction of houses. (The NBI report is simply one more example of this.) Tragically, because such conservative forces have held sway over the Department of Housing, only minor modifications in policy have occurred to alter this fact: namely, the mid-1994 decision to increase the site-and-service subsidy to a maximum of R15,000. But because the minimal decent house on a serviced site costs increasingly more due to inflation in building materials and construction costs, the "new" policy's subsidy remains vastly inadequate. In short, the top structure investments will continue to largely consist of relatively impermanent building materials, and the actual value of such investments will be either impossible to determine or--depending upon whether low-cost formal housing production finally improves--will not achieve a reasonable return as the supply of similar informal settlement top structures continues mushrooming.

31. In this, however, the reader is left uninformed as to whether "any conventional township" refers to a conventional "white" township or "black" township; there are "conventional" public goods and services available to each, but they differ in quality and quantity dramatically.

32. The only public goods explicitly described in the NBI report, consisting of a full two sentences (hence perhaps insufficient to meet the policy "challenge"), are in Oukasie and Soweto-on-Sea (p.28).

33. What was more important, a footnote makes clear, was "the critical question" of how "to reconcile the tension between planning processes originating from, and designed for, and servicing the interests of the 'formal city,' versus planning processes grounded in an understanding of the nature and 'rules of the game' in the informal" (p.32). Again, the possibility of South Africa's transformation not hinging upon satisfying the "interests of the 'formal city'" (by which is usually meant the supply of a cheap labor force, the provision of demand for consumer goods, and safety/security for urban elites) is not considered.

34. With respect to community participation, at least one observation throws the NBI report's sampling and surveying methodology into question: "At the heart of the informal settlements was the attempt, sometimes abortive, to involve the communities. The interviews revealed that the personal involvement of respondents in the upgrading initiatives varied from project to project, with.... Tamboville showing the lowest rates of participation" at 1 percent (p.32). Yet in a more detailed review of Tamboville (relegated to the appendix), the report also states, in contrast, that "Under the auspices of the Wattville Association [*sic*; presumably meaning Wattville Concerned Residents Committee] and with the assistance of Planact, a careful process of planning of the settlement.... was undertaken.... The upgrade process was fairly participatory involving regular meetings to discuss various options and to familiarize residents with use of services" (p.92). Knowing, as we do (from personal experience), that *weekly* planning meetings for Tamboville regularly attracted 500-700 residents during the early 1990s, it is inconceivable that only 1 percent of the NBI researchers' respondents would have claimed to have been involved.

35. To illustrate, the NBI researchers ignored the gender component of policy and project evaluation throughout, which is striking given the traditional role of women in household labor (including shack construction). Only when it is convenient to attack the civic movement's patriarchy is gender analysis invoked (and only in a sentence or two) (pp.39, 57).

36. Related to the disrespect the NBI researchers show for the actual and potential roles of civics in township development is another extraordinary oversight: the "difficult question of how civic office bearers are paid for their services, given the extreme poverty of the communities and the difficulty of raising subscription fees adequate for the reasonable salaries" (p.36). Apparently the NBI researchers have read neither the *White Paper on Reconstruction and Development* (November 1994) nor SANCO's *Making People-Driven Development Work* (April 1994), both of which make suggestions as to the financing of civics either directly, in the case of the *White Paper* (s7.6.8)--"Government must therefore provide resources in an open and transparent manner and in compliance with clear and explicit criteria to mass organizations to ensure that they are able to develop or maintain the ability to effectively participate as negotiation partners of Government"--or indirectly, as in SANCO's case, as a percentage (5-10 percent) of each development project. The question is not terribly "difficult"; all that appears to be required

is the political will on the part of the Government of National Unity to fund what may be an increasingly hostile watchdog.

37. For more on this argument, see Mayekiso 1996:chs.8-15.

38. In contrast, specific training programs for white planners or developers in participatory democracy are not even considered by the NBI researchers. Instead, "The major challenge for development professionals is to acquire the skills to operate in the world of the informal settlement, to understand better its power relations and the needs, limitations and strengths of its residents" (p.40). Implicit here is the assumption that "development professionals" do not come from informal settlements, when in reality most of South Africa's progressive development NGOs are staffed by black South Africans, many of whom were raised in such communities and attained leadership positions.

For black "aspirant professionals" the NBI researchers offer this unsolicited advice: "abandon the ethos of entitlement and the aspiration to inflated wages and living styles adopted from their white predecessors and be willing both to acknowledge the considerable skills of white professionals and to accept that these can only be acquired over time" (p.40). The well-paid NBI researchers (each of whom have received generous consultancy salaries in the past) worry not only about "sometimes over-inflated salaries for young black professionals with potentially crippling effects in the longer term on community sustainability," but also that the strengthened "position of black professionals in project management and community leaders in the trusts" has as a consequence "the withdrawal of white expertise into consultancies which charge extremely high rates to do work that would have anyway been done under their management" (p.51). Unfortunately, these arguments rest at the level of allegations, for no documentary evidence is provided. If South Africa's white development professionals had actually performed their jobs effectively in black residential areas--by all accounts they have performed miserably, recently and in years past--such advice might conceivably be worth considering, but the NBI researchers' patronizing tone would make it difficult to determine whether such advice was truly being heard.

39. For example, the decision by Planact to support the Wattville Concerned Residents Committee in Tamboville was not, in any case, a matter of free choice (nor was it, technically, an "upgrade"). The greenfield development of Tamboville should really have been a housing project, but instead was reduced to a site-and-service project for two reasons alone: the private sector could not deliver low-cost housing, and the IDT provided an inadequate subsidy for a real house.

40. See, e.g., SANCO 1994 and Mayekiso 1996:chs.8-10.

41. This is mentioned only in passing (p.61), and merely as an allegation stemming from "an unhealthy competitive relationship" between black leadership and white professionals, not as a serious problem in its own right.

42. This is, however, slightly couched by the argument that "there is in reality a strong mutual dependency between skilled white professionals and skilled black leadership" (p.62).

43. Later, displaying a distinct lack of experience regarding microsavings and credit in both South African townships and the developing world, the NBI researchers claim that "There has already emerged a.... community savings and loans system.... within many of the upgraded settlements, and *the key to this* is the secure title and exchange value of the modest homes that have been secured" (emphasis added) (p.82). In reality, the operations of most stokvels, burial societies, and informal credit systems have no relation whatsoever to participants' ownership of housing.

44. Moreover, there is no mention in the NBI report of a Community Reinvestment Act or anti-discrimination legislation (as specified in the *RDP*), new branches or even Automatic Teller Machines in black residential areas, affirmative action in bank personnel policies, more appropriate marketing and product types, or more flexible credit criteria. In sum, it is business as usual for the banks, notwithstanding the NBI researchers' acknowledgement of their widespread practice of discriminatory "redlining" (p.56).

45. In contrast, the *RDP* (2.5.19, 2.5.20) is insistent here that "Special funds must be made available to support small and medium-sized enterprises [in the housing construction field]. Resources should be provided as loans for bridging finance, and grants for training and entrepreneurial development.... Support must be provided to black and, more generally, to small builders."

46. In contrast, the NBI researchers cheekily argue that "most countries relied on the public sector to upgrade informal settlements and provide for the poor. The failure of this approach has led to the search for alternatives" (p.79). Nowhere are experiences of mass public or social housing programs ranging from Colombia to Holland to Singapore (and many areas inbetween) considered.

47. This would mean, no doubt, for business lobbyists to ensure that a variety of *RDP* promises calling for profound state regulation of corporate activity in housing and related sectors (2.5.4, 2.5.9, 2.5.11, 2.5.14, 2.5.15, 2.5.19, 4.4.6.2, 4.7.3) never become formal policy. The NBI researchers make their contribution by failing to even mention, much less evaluate, whether these *RDP* policy proposals have any bearing whatsoever upon the potential success of incremental housing policy.

chapter ten

The Crash of Post-Apartheid Housing Policy

with ANGELA TAIT

The post-apartheid housing policy debacle was compounded by efforts to paper over the cracks through a series of "Ministerial Task Team" sessions convened by the director-general in 1996-97. It was like asking arsonists to advise on putting out the fire, although it had the desired effect of convincing many worried politicians, the press, and civil society organizations that "something was being done." The Task Teams generally codified the worst aspects of the policy and increasingly pushed the responsibility for implementation to local governments at a time of rapidly-worsening municipal fiscal crisis. By 1996, some housing advocates had grown weary of reminding government why the neoliberal approach had failed, technically, and instead turned to reminding the ANC of their political mandate, in the *Reconstruction and Development Program* (the purpose of this chapter). Neither approach had much influence, nor did the appointment of another housing director-general--another Planact graduate--make any difference to a demonstrably flawed housing policy. The institutions of capital kept up pressure to preserve the *status quo*, and the minister hurt her case by repeatedly claiming delivery on hundreds of thousands of houses (when in reality the number of subsidy recipients who received sufficient bank credit to build even a matchbox-grade house was far fewer than the apartheid regime had serviced in its dying years). By 1999, it was evident that most of the "houses" built since 1994 were substandard and located vast distances from urban opportunities. To blame are not only policy-makers, but also social movements which failed to galvanize protest against the neoliberal policy and, in turn, the ANC government for demobilizing those movements.

[The chapter was published as "The Failure of Housing Policy in Post-Apartheid South Africa" in *Urban Forum* 8, 1 (1997).]

Introduction

There are enormous implications to the failure of what can be accurately described as a "market-centered" approach to housing policy for public health, the environment, safety and security, the welfare of women and children, education, public hazards, urban planning, the labor market, and related economic sectors (building materials, manufacturing, etc). The failure of housing policy is also a cause of growing political alienation, which could see government undermined in coming elections and in its attempts to forge unity and reconciliation.

For these and many other reasons, it is critical to revisit housing policy. Although it is true that the so-called "incremental" policy--which derived directly from the National Housing Forum (which in turn was dominated by experts from the pro-business Urban Foundation)--was initially endorsed by a popular hero of the liberation struggle, the late Minister Joe Slovo, it is no secret that this endorsement occurred during a period of "unrealistic expectations": both that robust, durable, job-creating economic growth would ensue, and that reconciliation would be fully embraced by white business interests (particularly bankers and developers). Such expectations were subsequently dashed, as shown below, and by July 1995 a *Business Day* journalist described the incremental approach as "remarkably like the discredited site and service schemes advocated during the apartheid era," while at the same point Housing Minister Sankie Mthembi-Mahanyele labeled the policy she had inherited "toilets-in-the-veld" (*Business Day* 21/7/95). (The Minister subsequently retracted her criticisms and repeatedly provided assurances that the market-centered policy would not be challenged.)

In this context, the key policy documents--the Department of Housing's "Record of Understanding" with commercial banks, the *Housing White Paper* (*HWP*), the proposed Housing Bill, and two reports by the Department of Housing's "Task Team on Short Term Housing Delivery" (also known as the Ministerial Task Team)--together represent an uneven but sustained official commitment to the market.[1] Beginning with the most recent report, we consider the most important aspects of this policy, and explore how the policy has failed on its own terms and in terms of the mandate government was given to build one million houses within five years.

The analysis we offer is different from that provided recently by most other critics,[2] who have largely focused on institutional shortcomings (e.g., Tomlinson 1996),[3] government's failure to accurately understand household-scale dynamics (e.g., Spiegel, Watson, and Wilkinson 1996),[4] the "top-down" character of the policy and delivery process (e.g., South African Homeless People's Federation 1995),[5] or the Department of Housing's perceived anti-urban bias (e.g, Crankshaw and Parnell 1996).[6] It strikes us instead that the most extreme problems that characterize the housing policy adopted following the 1994 election are related to its various market-centered features, and that an alternative based on the *Reconstruction and Development Program* (*RDP*) would have solved many of these.

Will Ministerial Task Team recommendations make any difference?

In October 1996, the Ministerial Task Team released a document that, according to the accompanying press release, is well "within the framework of current housing policy" (as described originally in the *HWP* and codified in the Housing Bill), yet that nevertheless "identifies the need for a far greater and more proactive role for the state as being essential to speed up the delivery process of affordable housing" (Department of Housing 1996b). Given that the Task Team is headed by the Department of Housing's Director-General, it can be assumed that this report represents official thinking about the way forward for housing policy.

But contrary to relatively shallow interpretations in the media (e.g, *Star* 17/10/96), the Task Team's policy proposals *do not*, in reality, provide the means to truly empower the state--especially local government--to deliver housing. In particular, the notion that government has now adopted a state rental housing policy is extremely misleading, given the methods and parameters that are being applied. In reality, the rental policy appears to have been tacked onto existing policy primarily as a response to the delivery crisis. Instead, as shown below, the "new" housing policy amplifies many of the worst features of the existing approach, of which at least six critical shortcomings deserve mention at the outset.

First, the central intention remains that the state gradually withdraws entirely from housing provision.

Second, there is still no attention to limited consumer affordability--which remains the key problem preventing large-scale market delivery of township housing--and there is still no increase in the housing subsidy for those millions of South Africans who will be unable to afford the products of proposed public-private "joint ventures."

Third, the proposed joint venture delivery mechanisms put large corporate developers in the driver's seat, and neither provide sufficient new funding to build much-needed state and community capacity so as to ensure meaningful partnerships, nor require developers to construct inexpensive houses at the lower (approximately R20-30,000) end of the affordability scale.

Fourth, there is still no protection against "downward raiding" of low-income subsidy beneficiaries by higher-income groups (even as this phenomenon will become more important due to the promised improvement in location of housing projects).

Fifth, there are still no plans to creatively provide access to state-owned land or to otherwise intervene to make more land available, which would permit more of the subsidy to be spent on the actual house and services.

Sixth, likewise there is still no effort to intervene in the construction and building materials markets notwithstanding severe market imperfections.

Various other features reflect government's ongoing reliance upon a market-centered approach, which was adopted in 1994 in spite of the existence of what is generally considered the "people-driven" alternative spelled out in the *RDP*.[7] These include unnecessary constraints on the quantity and quality of subsidies and extremely generous incentives for banks. Together they help explain the failures of the market-centered housing program to date.

Following a critique of these components of market-centered housing policy, we can consider the "new" strategies--the devolution of responsibilities to local authorities without devolution of sufficient resources, and increased incentives for developers--in more detail, and ask whether they represent any real departure from the failed policy and whether they will deliver the goods. Finally, some truly different alternatives should be considered, particularly those that emanate from the *RDP*. The contrast between such alternatives and the failed policy (with its recent amendments) is clear, and will continue to provide South Africa's progressive labor and social movements with sufficient confidence to demand that the debate on housing policy be reopened.

Problems internal to market-centered policy

To begin, it is important to contest conventional wisdom regarding the financing of housing. As has often been remarked, housing policy is premised on an overall understanding of "fiscal constraints," which when considered carefully in fact appears as a *mis*understanding. Perhaps most importantly, the maximum R15,000 subsidy (for those households with less than R800 per month income) is not sufficient to build decent accommodation; hence the policy requires beneficiaries to also gain access to credit if they want a house (not merely a serviced site). The reason for this, the *HWP* argues, is that "The required annual delivery rate...., relatively high proportion of poor households and budgetary constraints do not allow sufficient subsidy money per household to enable the construction, at State expense, of a minimum standard complete house for each household not able to afford such a house."

In reality, *there is not a "fiscal constraint" to affordable housing for all in South Africa*. If we assume that a minimally decent house costs approximately R30,000, and that--using National Housing Forum calculations--the country's income distribution requires an average of 50 percent subsidy for urban housing, conventional wisdom is easily shown to be incorrect. The actual cost to the budget of meeting the *RDP* goal of one million new low-income houses built over five years (an average of 200,000 per year), at an average cost to the state of R15,000 per unit -- not including the other R15,000 per unit, which would come from private sector resources via the national housing bank, to be repaid at the market rate of interest -- would be just R3 billion per year.

Are sufficient funds available to meet this need? Consistent with the *RDP*, government's goal for resource allocation (as confirmed in the *RDP*, *HWP* and draft *Urban Development Strategy*) is to acquire 5 percent of the total budget for housing by the year 1998, which would exceed R9 billion. This is obviously sufficient to meet not only the *RDP* goal, but to go far beyond that goal, easily financing 350,000 houses per year by 1998.

Even if income distributions are more skewed than the National Housing Forum originally estimated, there remain sufficient funds budgeted for the state to afford the required subsidies to achieve Affordable Housing for All. Indeed, the 1995-96 budget alone contained more than R4 billion for housing (although more than R2 billion of this was rolled over, as was also the case in 1994-95, which again suggests that existing subsidy amounts have been excessively stringent). The 1996-97 budget was (including past rollovers) R4.6 billion. Simple mathematics shows the inaccuracy of the fiscal constraint argument about capital costs.

The argument that the subsidy is only the first step in an "incremental housing" system that will ultimately generate "top structures" is unrealistic given the lack of appropriate and affordable credit. The incremental housing strategy is further undermined by the likelihood--based on the *Municipal Infrastructure Investment Framework* under consideration by the Department of Constitutional Development--that future stands occupied by families earning under R800 per month *will not include water-borne sewage or a reliable supply of electricity*. The draft *Urban Development Strategy* (a document released in October 1995 which continued to reflect government thinking on service provision through 1996[8]) was based upon conventional fiscal-constraint wisdom: "Relative to the needs, the level of resources available from the Government is not sufficient to provide the necessary basic infrastructure in municipal areas." Yet in designing the infrastructure framework, the Department of Constitutional Development and its advisors (especially a World Bank team) had failed to factor in the additional benefits--including public health, environment, and macro- and micro-economic multipliers--gained from higher levels of services, and hence overplayed the net capital cost to the fiscus of providing high levels of infrastructure.[9]

Nor did government's infrastructure design team heed the *RDP* in its consideration of the recurrent (operating and maintenance) costs of water, sanitation and electricity services (see Part 2 of this book). In addition, the "upfront capital subsidy" approach to financing incremental housing inherited from the late-apartheid era is far less efficient than a flexible loan whose interest rate--a blend of a subsidy and market-rate borrowings from, for example, pension funds (backed by a state guarantee, as the *RDP* suggests)--could vary over time to reflect changing borrower affordability.

The fact that nearly all subsidies are geared to an individualized "nuclear family" model, will generate speculation, "downward raiding," and shacklordism. Due to the phenomenon of downward raiding (purchase of the subsidized plot by higher-income households for cash, typically at a large discount), it is very likely that subsidized properties will soon be in the hands of higher-income groups, as initial occupiers find if difficult to meet the range of ongoing water, electricity, and rates charges associated with the current "full cost recovery" policy approach. In this event, the subsidy program will have done little to solve the low-income housing crisis, and instead it may well raise the population of homeless people, who in turn will no longer be eligible for a future housing subsidy. As noted below, the *RDP* insists upon protections against subsidies being lost in this manner.

Access to housing subsidies remains largely dependent upon the actions of private sector developers, and in particular relies upon specific plans and the delivery of infrastructure. These technical requirements prevent communities from independently addressing their housing needs. In the absence of appropriately-skilled government personnel available to assist communities, beneficiaries of subsidies have few options but to turn to private sector developers. The housing NGOs that are able to provide these services are few and far between, and with rapidly declining funding for NGOs there seems little promise that they will play a significant role in the future (as do NGOs in many Latin American countries).

Existing private sector incentives

Generous incentives for banks and developers characterized the late apartheid era, as--at the same time the state retreated substantially from black "African" public housing provision--all manner of subsidies, financial engineering schemes, deregulatory changes and other measures were adopted to promote private sector housing. Those measures resulted in a burst of township housing construction and financing during the late 1980s, characterized by extremely poor quality construction practices (with no consumer recourse), poor or nonexistent consumer education, terrible location of housing (on the far sides of segregated townships), no protections against interest rate increases or against the emergence of "negative equity" (when due to various factors the value of most township bonds rose to levels higher than the value of the houses which served as their collateral), and an inability to sustain the building pace beyond mid-1990.

Nevertheless, notwithstanding the well-documented failure of the state's retreat from low-cost housing during the 1980s and the reliance upon the private sector, the new government's Department of Housing proceeded nearly immediately to reward financiers in a variety of ways--

using four new institutions that were allocated funding of more than R650 million during 1994-96--in exchange for delivery promises that were not fulfilled, as shown below. (When these measures failed, the Ministerial Task Team subsequently shifted financial support and incentives to developers.)

First, the Mortgage Indemnity Scheme announced in October 1994 guarantees banks against politically-related non-payment of new housing bonds in those areas covered by the scheme, up to 80 percent of the value of the bond. By September 1996, 113 areas of South Africa had been either denied cover by the scheme (i.e., formally redlined) or "deferred," leaving 437 areas covered (*Sunday Times* 22/9/96).

Second, Servcon is a joint venture established in 1994 in order to "rehabilitate" non-paying bonds and ultimately to "right-size" households to properties they can more easily afford. There are approximately 14,000 houses in technical default within Servcon's portfolio, of which half are being successfully brought to fruition in the form of a settlement with the existing residents. If the other 7,000--as well as another 26,000 low-cost bonds in arrears or default on the banks' books--are not resolved, the Mortgage Indemnity Fund will be utilized to refund the banks (*Sunday Times* 22/9/96). As proposed, government will capitalise Servcon with R50 million, but no details are available about the use of these funds or the ability of Servcon to raise other funds (thus far it has been supported entirely by the private sector).

Third, the National Housing Finance Corporation was established in early 1996 to provide wholesale funding to retail banks, to encourage banks to increase their low-income loan portfolios. The Corporation is meant to ultimately finance 700,000 houses, but this goal is seen as extremely unrealistic, especially in the wake of fatal problems experienced by one of the prime vehicles for the Corporation's funds, the Community Bank. The Corporation has also indicated its unwillingness to offer loans at below-market interest rates (notwithstanding a directive to do so in the *RDP*, by blending wholesale finance with subsidy funds).

Fourth, the National Urban Reconstruction and Housing Agency, another post-apartheid institution, guarantees bank-originated bridging finance for developers. The agency claims it will make available R2 billion in low-cost housing finance by the year 2000 (*SA Housing Scenario* 8/96). Aside from a R25-million state grant, much of the agency's funding is sourced internationally, by development foundations (e.g., Open Society) and governments (e.g., Swedish) which would otherwise be better occupied in funding actual housing.

In addition, one of the most generous incentives that government granted banks was to permit their imposition (in mid-1995) of a 4-5 percent interest rate premium on housing bonds to low-income borrowers. In view of the banks' 1 percent (and greater) discounts to many higher-income borrowers, this represents a substantial "reverse Robin Hood" mode of redistributing income from the poor to the rich. Further, government failed to promulgate legislation or policies aimed at reform of the financial sector (especially prohibitions on discrimination) called for in the *RDP*. Central government also took unusual steps--not even attempted by the apartheid regime--to support banks in their default proceedings against borrowers, even where non-payment was due to temporary involuntary unemployment or other conditions beyond the borrowers' control (the *RDP*, in contrast, insisted that demand-side guarantees be provided to support borrowers rather than bankers under such circumstances). In addition, government's market-centered housing policy was echoed by a variety of other incentives and sometimes hidden subsidies offered by different tiers of government (e.g., the Inner City Housing Upgrading Trust in Johannesburg) and international agencies (e.g., US AID guarantee and financing schemes).

Critique of bank incentives

The incentives enjoyed by the banks have thus far not succeeded in fostering--and in future are unlikely to significantly increase--low-income housing delivery. Indeed, the "Record of Understanding" in which banks committed to providing 50,000 bonds in their first year of activity, on the basis of the incentives, resulted in fewer than 20,000 bonds granted in applicable areas in the intended price range. There appear to be two main causes of this dramatic failure.

First, without any "stick," the hope that providing "carrots" will dramatically raise the level of bank low-cost home financing is unrealistic because of the costs to the banks of administering a large portfolio of small loans. It should not be surprising that banks do not favor low-income bonds. As profit-oriented companies their rate of return is much higher when they service fewer, larger loans. In light of this, either mechanisms such as a Community Reinvestment Act are needed to compel banks to make available loans (and savings products) to low-income customers--along with providing (presently nearly non-existent) township and rural branch, agency, or automatic teller facilities for payments and savings--and/or this function should be outside the retail commercial banking system (such as through a national housing bank or transformed Post Office Savings Bank system). Neither the old nor the new housing policy even considers either promulgation of a Community Reinvestment Act as mandated in the *RDP*, or the establishment of an effective state housing retail agency.

Second, low-income housing policy is based on the assumption that most people eligible for subsidies will be able to secure bond finance or other forms of credit to top up the housing subsidy. However, the poor can seldom afford bank loans or meet bank lending conditions (such as having secure regular employment), particularly at the present rate of interest (the highest, in real terms, in South Africa's history) and given the policy of permitting extremely high interest rates for low-income borrowers. Other forms of less formal credit have simply failed to materialize on the scale needed.

Thus despite the financial incentives directed at retail banks, during the period mid-1994 through mid-1996 only 18 percent of houses built under the subsidy scheme were linked to credit (a figure which actually began to decline in 1996) (*Housing Facts* 20/9/96). Put differently, 70 percent of the poor could not secure bank loans, yet 43 percent of the Housing Facilitation Fund was directed to those beneficiaries who, because they were in higher-income categories, were more likely to secure these loans.

The December 1995 report of the Ministerial Task Team itself acknowledged profound practical limitations to carrying out the market-centered housing finance policies, including "projects being delayed due to excuses put forward by banks.... the Mortgage Indemnity Fund being positioned as a red-lining process.... inadequate or inappropriate pressure being applied to banks to lend in areas where lending is most needed.... [and] additional (more onerous) barriers being perceived to be erected by banks to historically disadvantaged borrowers." Yet, as shown above, neither that report nor the subsequent Ministerial Task Team report of October 1996 provided any remedies. Instead, through the absence of strong countervailing policies or programs, these Task Team reports effectively endorse the *status quo*.

The consequences of market-centered policy

The consequences of a market-centered approach to low-income housing delivery are, in most respects, detrimental to the needs of South Africa to build houses for poor people and workers. These include:

- an *inequitable allocation of funding between different low-income groups* (favoring those with higher incomes because they have the capacity to gain access to credit and hence are the target of private sector developers' projects);
- an extremely *low rate of delivery*, witnessed by the fact that only 74 254 subsidies were delivered between March 1994 and July 1996, the vast majority providing little more than serviced sites, notwithstanding the expectation that more than 400,000 houses would be built by this stage to reach the figure of one million within the first five years of democracy;
- the *destruction of existing housing construction capacity* due to the failure to recognize contradictions within the market and provide a state-driven counter-cyclical construction boost, as 1994 witnessed the liquidation of 228 construction firms and 1995 witnessed 232 closures and the lay-off of more than 10,000 construction workers in 1995, thus reducing total industry employment to fewer than 200,000 workers;
- *communities being disempowered* in project planning as well as in their more general needs for capacity (given that many local leaders moved into government), which led to unwanted products as well as an increasing gap between developers' promises and community expectations, often resulting in intense conflict;
- a *reluctance on the part of the private sector developers* to be involved in conflict-ridden areas where the need for housing was often the greatest;
- *abuse of the scheme by local authorities and developers* (according to the Housing Director-General in September 1996), leading to a reduction in value of the subsidy by 50 percent in some cases;
- *the failure of the Mortgage Indemnity Scheme* (which is indirectly acting as a red-lining instrument) *and Servcon* (as there were practically no available low-cost properties for households to rightsize to);

- a *lack of success by the National Housing Finance Corporation* in reducing interest rates or increasing access to credit for low-income households (and indeed in keeping afloat the targeted intermediary lenders, such as the now-defunct Community Bank);
- the *demise of humane levels of service provision*--such as water-borne sanitation, a reliable supply of electricity, stormwater drains and tarred roads--as part of the vision of incremental housing, due to the fact that households with under R800-per-month income were not projected to afford the running costs of (mostly-unsubsidized) water/electricity; and
- the inevitability of *reproducing apartheid-style ghettoes*, although these in future will not be segregated along racial lines but in class terms, specifically whether the new slum settlements include--as a matter of public policy--sewage systems, electricity lines, stormwater drains, and tarred roads.

Just as importantly, the implications of a market-centered approach to housing include *the withering of state capacity* in fields as diverse as construction, building materials management, public works delivery, retail financing, and management. The ability of provincial and local governments to take up the additional responsibilities they are now being given appears severely limited.

New strategies to resolve policy failure

Ironically, perhaps, the second report of the Ministerial Task Team on Short-term Delivery (Department of Housing 1996a:1,2,7) identifies problems relating to the market-centered character of its policy:

> Large private sector developers and the banking industry remain largely uninvolved in the delivery of housing [in the R18-50,000] price range, often blaming each other and the state for their non-involvement.... It is clear that private capital is seeking alternative avenues where risk/reward relationships are more favorable.... The sterile and unimaginative products and processes being propagated by many private sector actors in the affordable housing market reinforces the marginalization and stigmatization of the poor.

Yet notwithstanding the Task Team's critique of present trends, its philosophical "points of departure" exacerbate the market-centered character of present housing policy: "The state's involvement should be structured to enable gradual withdrawal without disruption.... Measures introduced should not constitute an additional subsidy and the principle of full cost recovery should apply.... Measures introduced should entrench savings as the primary mechanism for prioritization of access to housing opportunities created" (Department of Housing 1996a:4). Although other principles are somewhat more flexible, such points of departure ensure that there will be no dramatic improvement of access to housing for South Africa's poor, and particularly, that apartheid's geographical legacy will ever be transformed.

Indeed, the primary objective of the Task Team, from its origins in 1995, appears to be improving private sector returns by further reducing risks. In the December 1995 report, the Task Team proposed that risks be reduced by enabling provincial MECs to override social compacts, thus allegedly reducing conflict and opposition to projects (although this provision does not address the underlying causes of problems); attempting to contain opposition to the policy (and/or the standards implicit in incremental housing) by requesting high level intervention to prevent dissent and ruling out major policy amendments; and allowing more rapid draw-downs of subsidies by developers so as to reduce their reliance on full bridging finance.

The Task Team's second report suggested that accredited local and provincial authorities should enter into joint ventures with private sector contractors so that housing can be delivered at scale. This will supposedly speed up the rate of delivery and--assuming cost savings with large-scale delivery--will increase the amount of money available for each unit. But not only does devolution of responsibilities conflict with the financially stricken state of most local authorities, the incentives to developers will pose additional costs that represent a redirection of subsidy funds towards the private sector. Both factors are considered next.

Devolution of responsibilities to financially impoverished local governments

Under the current legislation and the proposed Housing Bill (expected to pass through Parliament in 1997), accredited local authorities will be given the "power" and responsibility to administer the low-income housing policy. But insignificant resources and capacity--budgeted at merely R10 million for national, provincial, and local governments--are available through the Housing Facilitation Fund to exercise this power. The options available to them are to enter into joint ventures with private sector developers. Virtually all decision-making and quality control will be in the hands of these developers, while the local authority will be obliged to carry the risk and to provide finance, and little more. (This system quickly prompted at least one metropolitan council and at least one provincial government to decide not to take on such responsibilities, as they do not wish to be accountable for housing developments over which they had little control.)

Where local governments do not have the financial or administrative capacity to administer the housing program (as defined by the National Department), the provincial tier will act on its behalf until the lower tier is accredited. But provincial government capacity has been significantly undermined through public service rationalization policies. And where the provinces are not able to administer the housing program, there is no back-up (under the current policy) in the form of national-level intervention or even facilitation.

Incentives for private sector developers and managers

The new policy provides R100 million of central government funds for joint venture housing projects between provincial/local state housing departments and developers, a sum that is to be matched by the private sector. Furthermore, another R400 million in guaranteed housing sales financing is to be provided by central government through the National Housing Finance Corporation to underwrite the bulk purchase of property through proposed "Housing Corporations." Unspecified subsidies will go to support "professional" expertise related to management of rental housing (but not, apparently, to community- or tenant-managed housing corporations). Funding for various private sector incentives will be in excess of R510 million, not including the capital subsidies which already effectively entail permission for a substantial mark-up by private-sector developers.

Likely outcomes of the amended policies

Such proposals hold out little promise for a successful mass housing program, particularly regarding rental housing, because

- rents will probably increase if the private sector plays a major role in managing Housing Corporations (as the rents will be the only source from which profits can be accumulated);

- there will probably not be sufficient maintenance on properties (as the need to generate profits for the management institution will leave little money for maintenance costs);
- rental stock may well be sold as freehold housing (no protections have been introduced to ensure the housing stock continues, in perpetuity, to be available for rent to low-income people); and
- the most immediate problem is that rental housing (as a tenure system) will be jeopardized by the short-term delivery (not long-term residential) interests of private sector partners.

Notwithstanding the proposed amendments to the failed policy, there are no guarantees that the cost savings of delivery at scale will be passed to the beneficiary or that the increase in the subsidy (to R15,000 for all institutional projects) will go to increasing the size or quality of the housing unit. It is likely that in a market-centered joint venture program, much of the savings will be absorbed by the developer. While this approach does increase the probability of an increase in the rate of delivery of low-income housing (from an extremely low base level), it does little to solve the housing crisis of at least 40 percent of the poor who will not be able to afford units proposed under the scheme. Most importantly, perhaps, there is no target for the proportion of joint venture housing construction at the lower cost range of delivery.

Those households earning below R1,000 per month will have few options other than the self-build strategy, facilitated by government's new and as yet untested "People's Housing Process." Yet this strategy has long-term costs to poor households and represents a general decline in the social wage and in the state's capacity to meet its citizens' needs. Moreover, as a delivery system, self-building undermines society's broader attempts to spur macroeconomic growth, create formal sector jobs, and restructure apartheid urban geography, which have long-term economic costs not taken into account in current policy formulation.

Departure from government's mandate

At his victory speech on 2 May 1994, Nelson Mandela observed, "We have emerged as the majority party on the basis of the program which is contained in the *Reconstruction and Development* book. That is going to be the cornerstone, the foundation, upon which the Government of

National Unity is going to be based. I appeal to all leaders who are going to serve in this government to honor this program" (*Business Day* 3/5/94).

Previous pages have shown that the first democratic government's housing policy was based on market-centered principles and is failing on its own terms. One reflection of the frustration of attempting to reform the existing policy is witnessed in the contrast between the *HWP* (and subsequent policy amendments) and the mandate given to the Housing Ministry in section 2.5 of the *RDP* book. This is apparent regarding policy objectives, the roles of the market and of communities, the notion of the housing backlog, housing standards, cost recovery for services, the National Housing Finance Corporation, interest rates, savings, bond guarantees, construction regulation, building materials prices, emerging builders, tenure bias, and other aspects of the *RDP* mandate. Each is considered in turn.

Housing policy objectives

The *HWP* Preamble states the policy's objectives, namely that the approach adopted "aims to contribute to the certainty required by the market, as well as give the Provincial and Local Governments their capacity to fulfil their Constitutional obligations." Nowhere in the objectives is the *RDP*'s broad aim of fostering "people-centered development" mentioned (when finally referred to, much later in the *HWP*, it is only in passing). Only in the belated People's Housing Process--still being developed with only a few small pilot projects--is a system established to help people build their own houses (supported by training), but this is apparently limited to the very poor, in ghettoes segregated from formal township housing developments as well as from better-located settlements formerly reserved exclusively for whites, which together consolidate the geographical legacy of apartheid.

The role of the market

The *HWP* celebrates "the fundamental pre-condition for attracting [private] investment, which is that housing must be provided within a normalized market." (This is technically incorrect, since private capital could still be attracted into non-market housing, via state housing bank securities.) The Ministerial Task Team confirms that the withdrawal of the state from housing provision is a fundamental principle. In contrast, the *RDP* critique of "The housing problems created by apartheid and by the limited range of the capitalist housing markets" was based on the dismal recent experience in private sector township housing, namely, the approximately R10 billion in unsustainable, disastrously-implemented investments by developers and banks during the late 1980s. Hence the *RDP* concluded that a housing policy far beyond the realm of the market should be urgently implemented, including two crucial non-market mechanisms: a national housing bank (to provide borrowers with low-interest loans by blending subsidies with private financial resources such as pensions that can be attracted out of stock market and luxury real estate portfolios by virtue of market-returns plus government guarantees), and mechanisms that ensure state expenditures on housing take the form of "non-speculative" subsidies (that either must be repaid upon leaving or are passed through into the stock owned by housing cooperatives). Neither has been given serious consideration in the *HWP*. Indeed, the latest Ministerial Task Team report reinforces the downward raiding problem, particularly due to the attempt to build on better-located land in a manner that leaves the land without the necessary protections against speculation.

The role of communities

Civic associations and other community groups are completely ignored throughout the *HWP*, reflecting only the document's mere lip service to people-driven development. This is in glaring contrast to the *RDP*, which states: "Beneficiary communities should be involved at all levels of decision-making and in the implementation of their projects. Communities should benefit directly from programs in matters such as employment, training and award of contracts. Key to such participation is capacity building, and funds for community-based organizations must be made available." The Ministerial Task Team continues to ignore community organizations, with the exception of a vague proposal to "target community interests" on the boards of Housing Corporations.

The size of the housing backlog

After noting, correctly, that residents of hostels and rural areas are inadequately housed, the *HWP* defines the "present housing backlog" merely in terms of urban informal units not located on titled land (1.5 million). This is half the amount the *RDP* estimates as a backlog and implicitly signals an abdication of the *RDP*'s commitment to meet the housing needs of hostel-dwellers and rural residents as well as urban shackdwellers on registered plots.

Indeed the overall lack of attention to rural housing in the *HWP*, in the Ministerial Task Team reports, and especially in the draft *Rural Development Strategy* increases the likelihood of more rapid migration to the towns and cities.[10] The policy focus on private, individualized land tenure, as well as the orientation to avoid giving subsidies in outlying areas (such as former homelands), together mitigate against rural housing ever being delivered at scale and where it is most needed.

Inadequate standards

The *HWP*'s stated commitment to width over depth directly conflicts with the earlier *HWP* (and *RDP*) commitment that housing (not a shack) is considered a basic human right.[11] The apartheid regime also emphasized width over depth, hence the massive numbers of informal site-and-service programs built on cheap land a great distance from employment and commerce (which now are being revisited as "market anomalies"). As noted above, sufficient resources do exist to increase the subsidy to the amount required for all South Africans to eventually live in a decent house (with a commitment of 5 percent of budgetary expenditure as the basis for more generous subsidies), in other words to achieve both width and depth.

Cost-recovery for services

The *HWP* insistence upon cost-recovery on tariffs for basic services (water, electricity, rubbish removal, etc) ignores the huge subsidy that black township dwellers historically provided to white municipalities (by virtue of having no township tax base), as well as the failure to bill residents at local level and many other manifestations of systemic breakdown. In contrast, the *RDP* recognized such problems and hence advocated redistributive ("lifeline") tariffs established at national-level for services such as water and electricity. The *HWP* implicitly rejects the *RDP*'s commitment to more equitable, efficient national tariff structures based on cross-subsidization (see above, Chapters Three-Five).

In short, the *HWP*'s attempt to impose cost-recovered tariffs upon even the poor, who cannot afford to pay for ongoing water, water-borne sewage, and electricity, will likely result in continuing rent boycotts. Moreover, it suggests a lack of understanding of the township household budget. The Ministerial Task Team entrenches the problem by providing more responsibilities for local authorities, but no specific increase in resources.

Design of the National Housing Finance Corporation

As noted above, the *HWP* endorsement of a National Housing Finance Corporation ignores the crucial *RDP* provision that the housing bank must blend public and private funds to reduce the interest rate. And the *HWP*'s emphasis on mobilizing consumer savings (as opposed, for example, to pension funds presently wasting in the stock market and luxury real estate) is misplaced, given the very limited disposable income of poor people and the extremely high costs of housing.

Interest rate affordability

The single most crucial determinant of housing market affordability -- the interest rate -- is completely missing from the *HWP*'s list of "economic issues" which "militate against a massive increase in effective demand for" housing. The interest rate for housing bonds rose from 12.5 percent to 21 percent from early 1988 to late 1989, thereby causing an unprecedented affordability crisis and leading to massive numbers of involuntary defaults. With the Department of Housing permitting banks to discriminate against low-income borrowers by raising the rate to 23 percent (compared to 18.5 percent for high-income borrowers), affordability remains impossible to attain through the market. In real (after-inflation) terms, the low-income housing bond interest rate of roughly 15 percent is unprecedented in South African history.

What this omission suggests is that the *HWP* authors were either inexperienced at actually designing housing packages (where they would confront the interest rate constraint), philosophically opposed to blending subsidy and private funds to achieve a below-market interest rate, or anxious to avoid confrontation on the issue of monetary policy with the Reserve Bank. Whatever the reason, the *HWP* ignores the *RDP* suggestion that "Interest rates [on housing finance] must be kept as low as possible." Subsequent policy amendments ignore the issue entirely.

Moreover, the *HWP* commitment to the "up-front capital subsidy" approach (in contrast to lower interest rates spread over time) is a direct violation of the *RDP*, which insists that "Government funds and private sector funding must be blended in order to make housing finance affordable." Worse, the *HWP* endorses a bank plan to charge "a higher interest rate on [low-income] bonds than the prevailing bond rate," an unprecedented form of class discrimination. Moreover, the National Housing Finance Corporation confirmed in 1996 that below-market interest rates (based on blending subsidies) are not being considered.

Emphasis on personal savings

The *HWP* explains that declining rates of personal savings "reduced the availability of savings for investment in housing." This is highly questionable, given the massive increases in credit granted by the banks during the late 1980s (when savings rates were falling at their fastest levels). Indeed, the SA financial system has shown an impressive ability to disregard savings and instead to create housing credit (mainly for the white market) based on factors such as the property market cycle, the unusually high spread on interest rates (the difference between what banks pay savers and lend to borrowers) and inter-bank competition. The failure of the *HWP* drafters to recognize this reflects a conservative economic bias reminiscent of the Normative Economic Model, and bodes ill for future interventions in housing finance markets. The Ministerial Task Team is apparently considering a new study on savings, reflecting a continuing reliance upon market mechanisms and insensitivity to the plight of the very poor who cannot save.

Supply-side bond guarantees

The flaws in the October 1994 housing finance insurance deal (Mortgage Indemnity Fund) between the Department of Housing and the commercial banks are too numerous and serious to be discussed in depth here. In short, however, the Mortgage Indemnity Fund disempowers communities (by taking away their sole leverage to prevent foreclosure and occupation), ignores the underlying reasons for bond boycotts or defaults, gives too much leeway to banks, fails to prevent redlining (and even permits redlining), and hence will simply not make much of a difference to the availability of credit in areas where it is most needed. As a supply-side (pro-bank) scheme, the Mortgage Indemnity Fund also directly violates the *RDP* provision that "Unemployment bond insurance packages and guarantee schemes with a demand-side orientation must be devised." As noted earlier, the demand-side feature--which is common to housing guarantees in many other countries--would allow people who lose their jobs or other sources of income through no fault of their own to continue living there. The R400 million National Guarantee facility proposed by the Ministerial Task Team, to be administered by the National Housing Finance Corporation, will effectively underwrite future private-sector housing, again on the supply-side.

Regulation of the construction industry

The *HWP* suggests self-regulation for the construction and building-materials sectors. In contrast, the *RDP* states, "Cartels, price agreements and market share agreements must end, and consideration must be given to public, worker and community-based ownership where the market fails to provide a reasonably priced product. Community-controlled building-materials suppliers must be encouraged, possibly with government subsidies to enhance competitiveness. An enforceable Code of Conduct must be established to guide developers." The *HWP* falls far short in addressing the traditions of severe problems in these industries, which are known to be virtually impossible to self-regulate. Subsequent policy amendments continue to ignore this issue, and the National Home Builders Registration Council is applicable only to homes built with bank bonds.

Building-materials price inflation

The *HWP* notes that "it is necessary to determine whether a rapid increase in supply will lead to an increase in the price of housing" without also acknowledging the *RDP*'s demand that if inflation is generated artificially by highly concentrated building-materials suppliers (as has happened, by all accounts, in past years), the government should intervene to break down such cartels. Where there are supply bottlenecks, in short, government should ensure a smooth supply of inputs for housing construction. However, the Draft Housing Bill prevents the Department of Housing from making interventions in the construction and materials markets.

Emerging construction firms

Incredibly, the *HWP* comments, "the growth and support of the emerging (black) construction sector is not seen as a primary housing responsibility and therefore does not justify the allocation of housing funds" even though the *RDP* commits the opposite: "The development of small, medium- sized and micro enterprises owned and run by black people must be incorporated into the housing delivery program." The *RDP* further states, "Special funds must be made available to support small and medium-sized enterprises. Resources should be provided as loans for bridging finance, and grants for training and entrepreneurial development" and, furthermore, "If necessary, the democratic government must provide some subsidies as a catalyst for job-creation programs controlled by communities and/or workers, and target appropriate job creation and development programs in the most neglected and impoverished areas of our country." Housing is a particularly good example of such programs, yet the *HWP* only weakly commits to "proactively seek to facilitate the participation of this sector in the housing process" without any specific endorsement of financial support to emergent black businesses. The People's Housing Process and the Housing Support Centers (of which there are at present fewer than a handful) are apparently going to address this need, but it is likely that the clients will be individual self-builders rather than emerging contractors.

Bias in tenure

The *RDP* insists that "Sufficient affordable rental housing stock should be provided to low-income earners who choose this option." The *HWP* does not consider rental stock, and even leaves out public housing stock from a list of housing functions to be fulfilled by local government. And while the *RDP* suggests that "Locally controlled Housing Associations or cooperatives must be supported, in part to take over properties in possession of banks due to foreclosure," the *HWP* simply ignores such a solution to the properties-in-possession problem. Later, the *HWP* notes that "Government rejects the elevation of the individualized private homeownership above other forms of secure tenure," yet the *HWP* policies are nearly entirely geared to precisely this tenure form. As noted, subsidy policy encourages market transactions, speculation, and downward-raiding, not permanently affordable housing. The subsequent proposals made by the Ministerial Task Team are based on rental systems geared largely to the private sector, which are not likely to be affordable to the poor.

Other omissions from the RDP mandate

The *RDP* calls for legislation protecting tenants' rights, squatters' rights, and the rights of people living in informal settlements. The *RDP* also suggests the need for further legislation regarding evictions, exploitation in rentals, and many other housing-related problems, as well as interventions in the land market. The *RDP* notes that "All legislative obstacles and constraints to housing and credit for women must be removed." Elsewhere in the *RDP*, the rights and needs of disabled people are also cited. All of these are missing from the *HWP* and have been, at best, mentioned vaguely in subsequent legislation and Ministerial Task Team reports.

The time for policy debate has arrived

The *HWP* Preamble stated, "The time for policy debate is now past." While mass housing construction is already long overdue, this was an unnecessary closure of debate and threatened to shut out those social forces which had fundamental objections to the *HWP* approach. Moreover, this position has not proved durable over time, as land invasions, occupations of vacant buildings, rent strikes, and other forms of popular resistance have continued. Yet notwithstanding public pressure to revisit the policy, the December 1995 report of the Ministerial Task Team on Short-term Delivery categorically confirmed that "No review of the fundamental position of government in respect of [minimum standards and levels of housing subsidies] is on the table and will be on the table for some time to come."

However, due to the untenable character of market-centered housing policy, there have subsequently been heated official debates (though rarely in the public sphere) and some minor alterations to policy. But this has never occurred in a context of true public consultation and of participation on the part of those forces within society opposed to market-centered policy. In particular, key issues--the role of the state, the nature of rental policy, housing standards, worker and community participation and control, and the alleged "fiscal constraint" to higher subsidies, etc.--have not been convincingly addressed by government officials, leaving constituents and civil society organizations nearly uniformly angry and alienated.

Given the widely recognized failure of existing policy, there should be an intensified search for options that do not place as much reliance on the market as is currently the case. For example, housing strategies recommended by many progressive organizations at the March-April 1996 Parliamentary Public Hearings on the *HWP* are significantly different from those advocated by the Department of Housing and the Ministerial Task Team. The fact that the Hearings received so little attention from decision-making bodies and the media--and hence the difficulty of launching a fruitful public debate--is no doubt *because* the strategies are so different from those that seek to protect the interests of the private sector, even though these vested interests are usually in direct conflict with those of the poor and workers who most need housing.

Many of the alternative strategies center around ways to increase the size of a unit that can be built within the subsidy (by preventing leakage to profit-motivated institutions, for instance). Others address the "risk" problem by suggesting that the responsibility for implementing the housing program and managing rental stock be shifted to communities and/or to locally elected government. Yet even these limited recommendations become progressively less realizable as each new market-centered policy proposal is adopted and implemented by the Department of Housing.

Finally, the possibility of expanding state capacity to deliver and finance housing through rationalization of the central state's and other agency's housing capacity into a national housing agency has gone entirely unconsidered within official circles. Trade unions and some of their allies have advocated this route for more than a year, but society has for too long been lulled into thinking that a market-centered approach would finally deliver or that sufficient amendments are being made to make the failed policy work.

But given the continuing deficiencies of market-centered housing policy, and given the fact that an alternative policy framework achieved wide support (in Chapter Two of the *RDP*) yet was never applied, it is likely that more meaningful debate will emerge again, but catalyzed by civil society and progressive politicians rather than by government bureaucrats and policy drafters who avoid self-reflection even when confronted with glaring failure.

Notes

1. The same is true of the draft *Urban Development Strategy* of October 1995; see Chapter Thirteen.

2. An exception is the Congress of South African Trade Unions, which consistently has argued for a more state-centred approach and has advanced important critiques and policy options papers to this end.

3. Tomlinson's surveys and reports are of enormous value in documenting the roles and interests of particular actors, yet invariably fall short of asking and answering bigger questions about the capacity and appropriateness of the market as the central organizing vehicle for housing delivery, and what alternatives might be feasible.

4. It is useful, on the basis of case studies, that researchers "alert policy makers to what may be the unintended consequences" of trying to "reduce the complexities of the real world situations [that policy] seeks to address by standardizing or normalizing its objectives and its proposed outcomes." And yet there are universal basic needs, such as shelter; and universal dynamics associated with various types of policy (whether market-related or not); and especially in South Africa, a relatively universal popular demand that arose repeatedly over several decades and informed the first democratic election: affordable housing for all. It behooves students of the policy process to ask and answer how such a universal challenge, "extraordinary complexities" and all, can indeed be addressed in a systematic manner through advocacy of the "alternative policy framework" that Spiegel *et al* (1996:17-18) eschew.

5. There are, in such critiques, idealized notions of self-help alternatives which unfortunately tend to take the burden of establishing a system for housing provision from society as a whole and impose it upon "community" (with gender implications that are rarely acknowledged). Criticisms that have been leveled at this approach in historical and international contexts include Engels (1935ed) and Burgess (1978, 1985).

6. In particular, claiming (with only one piece of anecdotal evidence) that government has an "anti-urban attitude," Crankshaw and Parnell (1996:34) fail to realise that the Department of Housing has lacked a coherent rural housing policy, has put a tiny fraction of its subsidy funds into rural areas, and does not even count rural housing within the "backlog" to be addressed (notwithstanding an explicit directive on the rural backlog in the original *RDP*). Nor do they acknowledge the extraordinary failure of the land reform program, which in the *RDP* aimed at redistributing 30 percent of agricultural land within five years but which--due to the market-driven character of the policy (willing-buyer, willing-seller plus market-rate credit) adopted following the election--will be lucky to achieve 10 percent of that target. Crankshaw and Parnell's concerns about the durability of migrant labor, the cementing of peri-urban apartheid spatial relationships, and the gender bias intrinsic in tribal tenure forms are very well founded, yet arguments that lead to suggestions for tenure reform to facilitate "transferable assets" and access to collateral for credit hark back to old-fashioned modernization theory.

7. Notwithstanding the endorsement of the housing section of the *RDP* "Meeting Basic Needs" chapter by both the first housing minister and director-general, the detailed policy directives were largely ignored. This was not surprising given the dominance of pro-business policy advocates behind the scenes. Enormous power to decide and amend housing policy was vested in the private sector, either implicitly or explicitly, for various reasons: the dominance of the National Housing Board, which (although being replaced with a new--but not necessarily representative--advisory institution in 1997) effectively weights the interests of the private sector above all others; the secondment of key private sector personnel to national government to assist in policy formulation; growing ties between business lobbies and government (e.g., the National Business Initiative Task Team on "unblocking delivery"); and the national Department's almost exclusive reliance upon consultants drawn from the private sector (rather than Democratic Movement structures) to develop policy proposals. Under these circumstances, housing policies, programs and project decisions have largely been determined by the needs of the private sector. Provincial governments, in contrast, have little or no meaningful influence over such issues as policy development, minimum standards, etc. Local governments, community groups, and other NGOs were also disempowered in policy development, which led to regular eruptions, for example, between the South African National Civic Organization and the Department of Housing over the Record of Understanding (see, e.g., Mayekiso 1996:277-278).

8. See, e.g., *Business Day* 21/10/96, in which the Department of Constitutional Development's chief director of infrastructure defended the low levels of service provision.

9. A broader analysis of such costs and benefits has subsequently been generated by a team of independent academics and researchers on contract to the Department of Constitutional Development; it is unclear at this writing as to whether this will affect the level of services that the Department will ultimately propose. Preliminary indications are that the net benefits of on-site water and some electricity (8-Amp connections, which are too weak to run more than one appliance at a time) will be accepted, but that pit latrines will remain policy for those earning less than R800 per month in densely-populated urban areas outside the main metropolises, and that services will be provided on a relatively unsubsidized (not lifeline) basis to even the very poor. (See National Institute for Economic Policy 1996.)

10. There are, finally, informal policy statements on rural housing now beginning to emerge, as well as administrative capacity-building. But in the absence of broader policy debate, it is difficult to have confidence that rural systems will be an improvement on urban systems.

11. The *RDP* defines a house as follows: "As a minimum, all housing must provide protection from weather, a durable structure, and reasonable living space and privacy. A house must include sanitary facilities, storm-water drainage, a household energy supply (whether linked to grid electricity supply or derived from other sources, such as solar energy), and convenient access to clean water. Moreover, it must provide for secure tenure in a variety of forms. Upgrading of existing housing must be accomplished with these minimum standards in mind."

PART FOUR

POLICY RETREAT--
POLITICAL REVIVAL?

chapter eleven

The World Bank Urban Agenda

Taking a step back, both chronologically and to gain wider perspective--while still keeping housing and infrastructure issues in mind--a good way to understand the narrowing of urban policy options is by mapping the agenda of the most important international agency involved. The World Bank was welcomed to the townships during their early 1990s "reconnaissance missions"--warmly by the ANC, warily by civics, and with some measure of intellectual hostility by NGOs such as Planact. Central in the Bank's initial approach was Geoff Lamb, a former South African Communist Party member and neo-Marxist intellectual, who later became a key assistant to Bank president Barber Conable. In April 1990 Lamb persuaded his former Sussex friend Thabo Mbeki to open the way for a variety of social and economic sector studies. An attempt by my colleague Mark Swilling to get the ANC to funnel Bank research teams through what became the NGOs' Urban Sector Network failed, as Durban colleagues broke ranks to start an engagement process that had dreadful results. Civics put up some subsequent opposition, but overall, enormous damage was done. In 1992, an extensive critique of Bank-think was requested of Planact by the Johannesburg Metropolitan Chamber, which generated an inkling of the problems that lay ahead. Bank staff realized the need to co-opt Planact, but this was unsuccessful. The reconnaissance missions continued through the election, generating massive outputs on housing, infrastructure, urban economic processes and intergovernmental fiscal relations. An August 1994 housing mission was one reason for the housing policy retreat. And by November 1994 Bank staff could claim to have coauthored the first and most debilitating drafts of the post-apartheid government's infrastructure framework. Though the ANC refused loans from the Bank for urban development, the damage done was substantial.

(This chapter was published as "Bank Braves South Africa's Townships," in *BankCheck*, February 1994; for more details see Bond and Swilling 1992.)

Introduction

They are among the most violent places on earth. The black townships of South Africa have witnessed nearly 10,000 politically-related deaths since the reform process got underway in 1990. Many of the killing fields are in the eastern environs of Johannesburg, where migrant workers affiliated to the proto-fascist Inkatha organization have been manipulated by security agents and the white right-wing into wars with communities generally aligned to the African National Congress. But regardless of ANC-Inkatha clashes, most townships are hotbeds of crime, unemployment, poverty, overcrowding, domestic violence, sickness, extremely poor "bantu education," and a variety of social and gender tensions.

Can the World Bank go to work in this environment? After all, these are also amongst the most politicized cities in the world. The black liberation struggle was based in part within township "civics" (civic associations), which promoted successful rent and service charge boycotts, work stayaways, consumer boycotts, and the establishment of new "organs of people's power" to contest apartheid structures. The civics were generally democratic and developed a broadly left-wing mass-popular ideology.

When the ANC was unbanned in February 1990 in the wake of the collapse of East European Stalinism, civics endorsed the concept of an independent "civil society." This will assure that even the forthcoming ANC government is kept honest by community-based watchdogs. Populist statism is out. Community-controlled housing and upgrading programs, resourced by a "strong but slim state" and assisted by a developmental local government, are in.

Thanks largely to civics, well-organized townships are defended against criminals and security agents, since police are still not trusted. Demands for "affordable housing for all" are being seriously advanced at the highest policy-making circles. Local governments are being democratized from the bottom, not just reformed from the top down. Civics are trying to address some of the more serious flaws in township capitalism, such as badly-built housing, rip-off home loans, chaotic minibus-taxi transport. While it is true that civics remain patriarchal and that clientelism and corruption sometimes seep in where resources are scarce, all things considered, civics and their allies in trade unions, women's groups, youth organizations, churches, and other such like represent the best hope for taking the national democratic struggle forward to achieve social justice.

Into this maelstrom of activity and rising confidence enters the World Bank. Thus far the Bank's six Urban Missions to SA have been surprisingly forthcoming with data and with their analyses. This allows civics and NGOs to get a clear sense of how the Bank views reform of the apartheid city.

The urban missionaries

Urban Mission leaders have come under sufficient heat to make them sensitive about their role. After some false starts, Bank staff such as Jeff Racki began to consult widely, to draw in local sources of information and to adopt the anti-apartheid urban vocabulary. Most importantly, the Bank made an arrangement with the African National Congress in 1992 which allowed Bank personnel access to both municipal governments and the townships, accompanied by prominent ANC urban experts.

There is still, however, the occasional *faux pas*. Stereotypical Bank arrogance is not uncommon and, as a result, technocrats from both parastatal and NGO development agencies have been provoked into hammering away at Bank mistakes, from both the left and right. Local-level activists are still extremely suspicious of the Bank, generally stressing the need to influence its agenda. As Lechisa Tsenoli, the leader of the South African National Civic Organization (SANCO), commented in late 1993, "The World Bank and IMF already have a presence in SA. They are being challenged but there is still no systematic approach to dealing with them. It is vital for SANCO to develop such an overall approach so as to safeguard our objectives."

When the ANC chaperone team failed to accompany the Bank on a November 1993 trip to Bloemfontein (one of SA's most conservative white outposts), Racki and others went ahead anyway to meet the white National Party council. But two leaders of the township civic association and local ANC branch came to the meeting and promptly denounced the Bank team for engaging in important dialogue without their approval, and brought the proceedings to a halt.

Generally, though, Racki and his associate Juneid Ahmed have been humble, deliberately downplaying their future contributions. "South Africa is not Tanzania," says Racki when questioned about the Bank's ability to shape SA cities through loan conditionality. Indeed the

Bank will shy away from controversial project loans and focus instead on sector loans and on providing advice (especially on urban economic planning and intergovernmental fiscal transfers). Ahmed's recent report on the benefits of metropolitan government is viewed quite favorably by even leftist planners.

From apartheid township to neoliberal city

But notwithstanding such efforts to smooth the turbulent surface of urban transitional politics, the Bank's broad neoliberal agenda continually bubbles into view. In an important report last year, for example, Bank urban economist Kew Sik Lee concluded that "low income housing development in the 'available land' between the central city and townships should be avoided" in order to densify the townships--a position which undermines Civic Associations of Johannesburg efforts to force the local white city council to open up buffer-strip land once used to separate the races.

In general, urban apartheid (not racially biased *capitalism*) still gets most of the Bank's blame. Where market forces are the clear culprit--for example, Johannesburg inner city decay resulting from (among other factors) enforced tenant overcrowding due to unduly high rents, refusals by landlords to maintain buildings which are already fully paid off, and bank redlining (loan discrimination)--the Bank has little to say, notwithstanding major local policy debates now underway. To engage the *structural* causes of urban poverty, or even the simple civics demand that poor people have a right to live in the inner-city, would mean identifying problems that cannot be solved with market-oriented solutions. Thus no public housing investment by the state and no "social housing" (i.e., co-operatively owned) movement struggles will be examined, much less championed by the Bank.

On top of all of this is the international financial agencies' export-oriented macroeconomic vision, which nearly everywhere splits the urban working-class into a small fraction of "insiders" served by the market, and masses of peri-urban, slum-dwelling "outsiders." US AID consultant George Peterson explained just such a linkage between cities and macro-economic policy to a 1991 conference in Johannesburg:

> It aims to eliminate or reduce urban food subsidies and price controls, abolish requirements that part of export food production be diverted into the domestic market, reduce the urban wage structure in cases

where government pays or mandates above-market wage levels, and reallocate government capital investment away from subsidies for urban industrial production and public service provision.

Because this philosophy goes entirely against the grain of the long-standing progressive movement agenda here, the World Bank, US AID, and certain Northern governments have found a much greater need than in any other country on earth to co-opt local progressives in other ways (capacity-building assistance, for example, not related to policy formation). If the city is to be the new unit of macro-economic control, civics and their allies will continue to be given special attention. And that in turn requires two sorts of reactions by opponents: renewed emphasis on international solidarity aimed at learning lessons of urban battles against the Bank elsewhere, and new ventures into radical policy research which will allow urban activists and intellectuals to contend with the endless caravans of Bank missions.

chapter twelve

Municipal Crisis Premonitions

with GREG RUITERS

By early 1996, shortly after the first municipal elections, it became clear that the new government's half-hearted urban programs and stingy projects were not working, nor could municipal officials enforce cost-recovery on basic services. One classic response by economic elites, Old Guard bureaucrats, and even politicians who should have known better, was to blame the victim, using a "culture of non-payment" explanation for the growing municipal crisis. The local elections had assured a stalemate due to the veto power that white councilors--overrepresented due to ward-based voting--commanded over redistributive budgets if they mustered just a third of a council's seats (a compromise in the Interim Constitution of November 1993). Tragically, the result was fragmentation of organic alliances involving ANC councilors, municipal workers, and community organizations. In turn, the subsequent political strife in many townships across the country cemented the Interim Constitution's implicit premise for municipal governance: a distinct lack of possibilities for local transformation or even redistribution. Two questions that must be posed in retrospect are: a) whether cul-de-sac municipal government was part of the *quid pro quo* for the National Party giving up national power; and b) whether the ANC constitutional negotiators (led by Cyril Ramaphosa) who agreed to limitations on local democracy at Kempton Park realised the dangerous extent to which they were speculating, in their (vain) belief that such concessions would draw Conservative Party politicians into the election--on (also incorrect) grounds that if they boycotted, the Conservatives could have sabotaged the election's logistics (see Mayekiso 1996:226 for details). Councilors, municipal workers, and community leaders can be forgiven for serving as unwitting victims of the flawed elite-pacting exercise, whose legacy will be felt even after 2000 when the transitional restrictions fall away.

[The chapter was published as "The Development Bottleneck" in *Southern Africa Report*, April 1996.]

Introduction

"They make a path directly to my door, asking me for money, healthcare, jobs, housing," says Trevor Ngwane, a newly-elected local ANC councilor in Pimville, Soweto. "I don't sit on the committees where the big decisions are made. I earn R2,000 per month. And I don't have the power to do anything."

Like their apartheid predecessors, the ANC councilors of South Africa's impoverished, violent townships are beginning to bear the brunt of popular frustration. This is ironic perhaps, for one of the prime scapegoats for the lack of *Reconstruction and Development Program* delivery between May 1994 and November 1, 1995--the date of the country's local elections--was that previous municipal governments lacked legitimacy.

Today, if freshly-minted local councils are the *RDP*'s "hands and feet," in Minister Jay Naidoo's words, what are the prospects for breaking the so-called "culture of entitlement" and for the implementation of the expansive social policies promised by the ANC during its national campaign two years ago?

More broadly still, what are the prospects for building robust participatory democracy at the local level, revitalizing civil society, and ensuring that South Africa's political transition begins to make a socio-economic difference to the lives of at least twenty million still trapped in unemployment and the ghetto? Not good in the short term, we must conclude after reviewing the society's structural contradictions, political compromises, and mainstream ANC reactions to both.

Low-intensity local democracy

Consider first the highly-constrained ("low-intensity," as some call it) nature of South Africa's local democratic transition. We are all too familiar with the late 1992 "Sunset Clauses" that paved the way for a Government of National Unity, for an excessive degree of federalism (even big business now concedes), and for the absurd job guarantees that protect apartheid-era civil servants.

But there were also rather less-understood local-level corollaries as well, which together mean that the new-found legitimacy won't run terribly deep:

- the far higher voting weight accorded to whites in the recent election (30 percent of municipal seats were given to formerly white residential areas to start, on top of the proportion of their total vote);
- the extraordinary veto power that white councilors now enjoy (with just a third of the local council seats, they can prevent passage of local budgets and town planning bills);
- the persistence of white bureaucrats at many local government interfaces with the public;
- local government's intensifying budget constraints, accompanied by neoliberal cost-recovery principles and municipal privatization programs; and
- the sometimes undemocratic process by which local candidates had been chosen, which led to enormous acrimony and numerous independent candidacies (some by progressive local SA National Civic Organization leaders).

Add to this two somewhat more subjective political features:

- a surprisingly widespread corporatist commitment by national and provincial bureaucrats to the enforcement of "social contracts"--meant to involve all "stakeholders" (i.e., the state, local capital, and organs of civil society)--as a precondition to the project-level dispersal of housing and many other developmental goods and services; and
- a wariness by even ANC politicians regarding former allies in civil society that sometimes borders on paranoia.

These conditions are not universal throughout the country, and we don't mean to discount courageous efforts by sincere, competent, and sometimes radical politicians (like Ngwane) drawn from the rank-and-file of the ANC and SACP, the unions, civics, churches, women's groups, and the like. But these women and men are quickly learning the limits to their power, which are not only technical and political in character but also social (for they include a formal "code of conduct" prohibition against participation in mass action that all local councilors had to endorse).

In particular, there is danger that the best councilors will be split from their social base, as is evidently the case with nearly all national and provincial ANC politicians. Maintaining strong South African traditions of consultation and accountability will be no mean feat, for the local government elections failed to energize and mobilize the masses of township dwellers. Voter registration and turnout were less than reassuring, as no more than a third of potential voters bothered to vote. Far from greeting local government elections with enthusiasm, many expressed the view that if central government cannot deliver under conditions of the power-sharing compromise, how is local government going to.

The Masakhane mistake

The primary vehicle for restoring government's links to alienated township residents was meant to have been Operation Masakhane--"let us build"--which President Mandela and three key ministries (*RDP*, Constitutional Affairs and Housing) launched in February 1995. The R30-million campaign was aimed at reversing the "culture of non-payment" that was alleged to have emerged as a cancerous side-effect of the 1980s ungovernability struggle.

But while Masakhane was aimed at both improving services (through the injection of R700 million, a piddling amount, really) and goading larger percentages of residents into paying the rent/service bills (as well as, in the process, atomizing residents as consumers and deradicalizing township organizations), it was not to be. In August 1995, Tokyo Sexwale, the leader of Gauteng (Johannesburg-Pretoria-Vaal) province, proclaimed, "The people of Gauteng have rallied behind the call to implement the Masakhane campaign as a vital step in the reconstruction and development process." In reality, official statistics released a month later showed that Gauteng townships from Mamelodi outside Pretoria, to Ivory Park in northern Johannesburg, to Daveyton in eastern Johannesburg, to Sebokeng and Sharpeville in the Vaal Triangle, were all recording payment rates of less than 5 percent.

Masakhane actually seemed to be having the opposite effect of that desired, for in most townships the R10 million spent on publicity (via advertizing agencies) coincided with a 15 percent drop in rate payments. Following a crisis meeting in January 1996, Department of Housing director-general Billy Cobbett commented, "The campaign and the ideas behind it are correct but it needs to be politically reinvigorated. It's not just about getting people to pay for services but a social contract between government and the people in terms of rights and responsibilities on both sides."

But social contracts--which under South African conditions boil down to a weak appeal for corporatism--are not only untenable in townships, they have not succeeded in the boardrooms either. To illustrate, by all accounts government's housing program is a national tragedy. This is mainly the case, we argue, because the *RDP*'s more progressive, decommodified, "people-driven" policy framework was rejected in favor of an all-in attempt at a social contract in October 1994. The official policy relies entirely upon developers to provide serviced sites (i.e., put in pipes and toilets), and upon banks to hand out subsidies to low-income blacks who they really did not want to see in their branches.

Not surprisingly, the system crashed, and fewer than 15,000 houses were delivered during the national housing program's first 18 months. Most embarrassing was the grandiose mid-1994 claim by Sexwale that with the assistance of the developer Stocks & Stocks (garish builders of Sun City's R1 billion Lost City complex), Gauteng province would witness construction of 150,000 homes in the coming year. In reality, millions of rands in government subsidies earmarked for Stocks & Stocks were withdrawn in January 1996, as the developer had delivered only 1,000 of 10,000 serviced sites (not even full houses) that it had contracted for. Stocks & Stocks was also (temporarily) deemed ineligible for future funding as a result. Lost City indeed.

With what effect on local morale? Physically and psychologically, the housing crisis contributes to township degradation and continuing unwillingness to pay. And this is not merely due to fiscal constraints, as many policy wonks argue, as more than three quarters of the state housing budget goes unspent. Indeed, it remains eminently feasible to subsidize an Affordable Housing For All program within present budgetary limits. We would conclude, thus, that it is the philosophy of the social contract applied to housing--that is, the developer-driven, bank-centered, fully commodified, inadequately subsidized, gender-insensitive, geographically-segregated provision of sites, with the hope of "incremental" housing construction later--that constitutes the prime delivery bottleneck at this stage.

Rent boycott rationales

If you lived in a South African township during the 1980s and early 1990s, there were any number of compelling rationales--related (but not exclusive) to the legacy of undemocratic local government and the 1985 ANC campaign to "Make the Townships Ungovernable"--for not paying the monthly bill for rental or service (mainly electricity, water, sewage) charges.

Indeed, sporadic rent boycotts in the Western Cape, East Rand and other sites predate the 1983 launching of the United Democratic Front, and represented informal modes of struggle based on the survival mechanisms implicit in the township moral economy. This was logical given that the black township was, as Jeremy Cronin of the SACP once remarked, the "highest expression of Colonialism of a Special Type."

Although monthly charges are often less than R100, the majority of black South Africans today survive on less than R1,000 per month income, according to a recent World Bank study. Poverty and mass unemployment are the simplest and most durable rationales for not paying the bills. And if, then, individual accounts were cut, either a supply of electricity or water could simply be stolen (with the help of informal electricians and plumbers) or mass action by street committees would prevent evictions.

Moreover, the quality of the services--and of the matchbox houses for which residents paid rent without any secure urban tenure rights--was generally abominable. This was also the case for many of the 200,000 or so houses built by the private sector and financed by banks during the late 1980s, leaving homeowners little choice but to refuse to pay their loan ("bond boycotts"), so as to get the banks to force the developers to repair their shoddy work.

But aside from resistance politics, the waning household budget, and the poor quality homes and services, there were--and in many cases remain still today--other important structural contradictions contributed to the success of the rent and service boycotts. Today, it would not be surprising if these add, in many residents' minds, to their own justification for dissing Operation Masakhane:

- We must never forget that, not by choice, blacks historically subsidized white residents' rates, due to the fact that blacks worked and bought goods in white towns while those firms and retail outlets paid their rates to white town councils, thus generously supplementing residential rates (while black townships had only the beer hall for revenues). This reverse-Robin Hood phenomenon was well-understood in the townships, as it formed the basis for the civic movement's

"One City, One Tax Base" demand. But only a few municipalities--Johannesburg stands out--have begun to redress the black-white subsidy by introducing progressive tariffs that would allow redistribution to occur in the other direction.

- Due to the effectiveness of earlier boycotts, many local authorities simply neglected to even send township residents their accounts (published reports suggest billing rates in many large townships are still at just 50 percent). This is only beginning to change and naturally is a high priority for the new government, but it will require accurate township residents' rolls and the identification of addresses in informal settlements, which are not going to be easy.
- Those townships residents who received electricity accounts from the parastatal Eskom--which had simply left black townships powerless until the 1980s--were often most justified in boycotting. Their complaints about much higher average payments per unit of service than in white areas were based on the fact that whites had long ago paid off capital charges, but for blacks these were internalized because services were newer, and that infrastructure provision was far more costly in peripheral areas of the metropolis, where most blacks reside. Then, when Eskom began installing individual pre-paid metering points in an effort to break the payment boycotts, these also cost more than ordinary hook-ups, and the interest on the pre-paid funds went to Eskom. While some progress has been made in equalizing the unit rate of electricity in Johannesburg, this is not true in most other areas, and even Johannesburg has not begun to cross-subsidize from rich to poor consumers as is called for in the *RDP*.
- The state of a township's housing stock signals to residents the merits of paying the rent and service charges. During the 1980s, the apartheid state simply stopped building new township houses, instead turning to banks and developers to take over. Today, notwithstanding detailed policy attention to the housing crisis and huge increases in the state housing budget, fewer than 800 new low-cost houses are being built each month (4 percent of the rate the *RDP* promised). Government departments at all levels are failing to construct (or even facilitate construction of) proper houses, and instead--

in contradiction to *RDP* provisions--channel subsidies to for-profit developers.

- Government subsidies are insufficient to finance a house, and it is nearly impossible to build a solid structure on the serviced sites because of the lack of affordable credit. Commercial banks not only charge 22 percent for low-cost township housing loans (compared to 17.5 percent on home loans to the petit and haute bourgeoisie)--notwithstanding a new state mortgage insurance program which protects much of their investment--they also still formally "redline" more than a quarter of all townships. Both these practices ensue with the explicit approval of the government, whose timid goal is simply to have the banks involved at all.
- The long-awaited transfer of existing council houses to long-term residents has been extremely inefficient, with just over one-third completed to date in even the advanced, wealthier provinces.
- In addition to housing policy failures, most household investments in township homes (and hence greater willingness to pay for services in order to avoid cut-offs or eviction) will be financially fruitless because there is still nothing much of a secondary housing market to ultimately recoup the investments.
- Apartheid spatial location and the high cost of (extremely dangerous) transport--the single largest component of the urban black household budget--together have meant that the average township resident pays far more of her household budget on commuting than do whites (incredibly, most new developments are still being sited on the periphery of cities).
- Schools, clinics, creches, libraries, recreation and other publicly funded facilities are of very low quality in townships, if they exist at all, and the physical environment (air, water, hygiene, etc) is lamentable.
- Police are far worse at combatting township crime--which in any case is far more extensive and violent--than they are at tracking criminals in well-fortified white neighborhoods.
- Promises made by government to those community-based organizations (especially the civics) which were charged with implementing Operation Masakhane--promises ranging from

financial support for organizational capacity-building and basic infrastructure, to funding for explicit projects--were mainly broken, and most community organizations are still overlooked by the major non-governmental donors.

- Perceptions of racial, class, and gender injustices run very deep. Reports (and public perceptions) of increasing inequality between low-income blacks and upper-income whites contribute to these, and feed a general social alienation that is entirely understandable if one considers what hell it is to live in apartheid townships.

In many cases, such rationales for rent/services boycotts flow easily from the apartheid era to the present day. No amount of multimillion-rand Operation Masakhane advertizing campaigns (featuring the likes of Archbishop Tutu and former SANCO leader Moses Mayekiso) can change the material realities and the psychological aversion many township residents have to spending declining take-home pay on inferior services and rented matchbox homes.

To reverse these causes will require far more serious policy and financial commitments by the new government and by society at large than appears possible in the near term. A tough first question often posed by our own sources is this: In a middle-income country like SA, why should anyone pay anything to live in a typical township?

Reviewing a list of reasons for the legacy and durability of rent boycotts--or merely having a close look at one of South Africa's open township sores--makes it difficult to argue. Yet at this stage of the country's political development, to even pose such a question in policy circles is to run the risk of being labeled "dangerous ultra-leftist" by ANC politicians (as were your correspondents in *Business Day* in January).

Blame-shifting and buck-passing

In contrast to neoliberal policy and social contract practice, barriers identified by Cobbett and his colleagues in January 1996 included housing industry "perceptions" of differences between the Housing Department and the Housing Ministry. (In July 1995, Minister Sankie Mthembi-Nkondo had publicly criticized the program she had inherited from the late Joe Slovo as unacceptable "toilets-in-the-veld," generating much hand-wringing amongst fiscal conservatives, but she was brought back into line.)

Such symbolic blame-shifting aside, Cobbett also identified actual bottlenecks in the provincial housing boards. These multi-stakeholder boards, in turn, also reflected the social contract mentality brought from national to provincial level, and heightened conflicts of interest implicit when banks and developers play a deciding role in giving out the subsidies. Banks, for instance, were well-known opponents of low-cost developments in the apartheid-era buffer zones between black and white areas, for fear of dragging down property values (i.e., their collateral) in the latter.

The solution Cobbett has now chosen is to give more responsibility for housing facilitation to local government, an artful bit of buck-passing. Again, there is no chance for this incremental reform to a fundamentally flawed policy to deliver the goods, given enormous local-level fiscal constraints and imbalances of power, which is still largely held in the white bureaucracy, with white councilor vetos standing by.

In short, the real social problems--mass poverty, intensifying income inequality, and the ongoing cementing of apartheid geography--are simply not being recognized and grappled with. Hysterical demonization of those low-income South Africans allegedly suffering a "culture of non-payment"--coming as it usually does those from those white, petit-bourgeois and bourgeois South Africans who exhibit what Mzwanele Mayekiso has termed a "culture of privilege"--is no substitute, though we can expect the whinging to increase.

And for progressives committed to a sustained campaign for social justice, there is no substitute for the back-breaking work of rebuilding mass organizations. Now that official racial oppression is being supplanted by neoliberalism, those organizations will have to tackle South African capitalism head on.

chapter thirteen

A Strategy for the Development of Urban Underdevelopment

with MZWANELE MAYEKISO,
DARLENE MILLER, and MARK SWILLING

When in 1995, Jay Naidoo--the minister responsible for the *Reconstruction and Development Program*--authorized a bureaucrat to contract specialists from the Urban Foundation and Development Bank of Southern Africa to formulate South Africa's urban strategy, he effectively cemented apartheid. There were, to be sure, at least three different interpretations of the *RDP* mandate. A neoliberal version of the *RDP* was evident in the fiscal, monetary, and trade policy directives. Too, a centrist tone permeated, promoting social contracts and stakeholder forums. But overall, the essential characteristics of several decades worth of social struggles prevailed within the *RDP*'s chapter on Meeting Basic Needs. This was particularly true in relation to urban development--and it is here that the *RDP* was most decisively rejected in practice. Of course, one cannot argue that by itself, the draft *Urban Development Strategy* prevented change. Instead, it codified an incremental approach to changing the apartheid city that in reality amplified its worst characteristics. While our critique helped push the *UDS* to the back burner, in mid-1997 another, much more nuanced version (the *Urban Development Framework*) was issued. This time the consultants included ex-World Bank consultants from Canada, whose contributions appeared to mitigate but not in any way alter the neoliberal character of the overall approach to the apartheid city. This chapter recalls infrastructure and housing debates, but adds many other concerns that have not, subsequently, been resolved.

[The chapter originally appeared as a "Response to Government's Draft *Urban Development Strategy*" in *Urban Forum* 7, 1 (1996).]

Introduction

> **The overall direction and ideals contained within the document stem from a large body of work produced by the old Urban Foundation and the Private Sector Council on Urbanization, and now carried forward by the Center for Development and Enterprise. This is a heartening development for the private sector (which sponsored all this work) and for the country as a whole.**
>
> Ann Bernstein
> *Business Day*, 28 February 1996

Ann Bernstein of the Center for Development and Enterprise is honest, even if profoundly misguided in her assertion that the government's October 1995 *Urban Development Strategy* (*UDS*)--codrafted by a former Urban Foundation strategist and a Development Bank of Southern Africa staffperson--is good news for South Africa "as a whole." It is good news only for big business interests, whose despoilation of urban South Africa is well-documented and who had feared some retribution under the first democratic government. Luckily for them, but not for most urban residents, the job of transforming the many policy directions and ideals of the *Reconstruction and Development Program* (*RDP*) into an explicitly urban strategy was tackled by neoliberal consultants. Whether the document remains neoliberal will depend upon the Democratic Movement's desire and capacity to enter into struggle over the detailed form that the policy takes.

What would social movements argue when negotiating with government over the language, content, and process of urban strategy? Perhaps that it is time to revisit the *RDP* and implement its detailed policies and programs, rather than ignoring them. But, the drafters would probably rebut, the *UDS* is already "underpinned by the principles of the Reconstruction and Development Program" (p.1). Moreover, they would say, the *UDS* is "implementable within the social, fiscal and financial constraints marking South African society" (p.1).

And here we confront the basic flaw intrinsic to many such policy documents. As *Business Day* editorialists described the *Growth and Development Strategy*, "The correct marketing strategy is a difficult one, as government has to please the markets, the unemployed, foreign investors and organized labor--all at the same time. That makes for vague language and wish lists that no one will attack" (28/2/96). It also usually makes for failure of analytical nerve.

For between "the principles of the Reconstruction and Development Program" and "the social, fiscal and financial constraints marking South African society" lies a wide gulf of opinion about what can and should be done to remedy South Africa's urban slums. Supporters of the *RDP* argue that not only the basic principles, but the entire program is implementable, and that timid politicians, hostile bureaucrats, and unreliable private sector partners are delaying or sabotaging implementation. Others argue that the state is an extremely poor vehicle for changing the shape of apartheid cities, that delivery should be accomplished by the private sector wherever possible, that government subsidies should be minimized, and that low-income communities should largely be consumers (assuming they can afford to be) rather than planners or producers of their own development. Hence the often vitriolic debates between those arguing for dramatic, community-driven, state-supported urban transformation and those who support a more measured pace of market-oriented change.

Regrettably, the *UDS* consistently fails to openly acknowledge or to confront these two positions, even where the differences are most glaring. Yet because in its detailed policy positions the *UDS* consistently leans toward the latter view--that many constraints to people-centered, state-supported development cannot be overcome, and thus that "the incremental nature of the strategy must be emphasized" (p.14)--the draft document leaves itself open to the charge that in many crucial respects it steps backward from the *RDP*. Indeed, the repeated references to "global competitiveness" as a primary objective for South Africa's towns and cities--because "South Africa's cities are more than ever strategic sites in a transnationalized production system" (p.41)--reinforce the sense that the *UDS* is mainly geared to rearranging cities for the benefit of multinational corporations and export-oriented producers. (Interestingly, aside from numerous plant closings due to GATT, the main evidence thus far of the impact of globalization on South African cities--regional migration--is only mentioned once, in the context that immigrants cause "neglected residential neighborhoods" to "buckle" [p.10].)

The *status quo* (or "incremental") orientation of the *UDS* is also evident in two incompatible assertions regarding power and self-interest in South African cities: "To be practicable, the Urban Strategy addresses the real interests of those living and working in urban areas" (p.7); "Most key stakeholders now understand that townships cannot be insulated from higher-income suburbs, as in the past" (p.13). In reality, most powerful stakeholders remain intent on maintaining urban segregation. Nowhere in the *UDS* are the real interests of white suburbanites, bankers, developers, construction-material suppliers, industrial corporate polluters, estate agents, slum landlords, mining houses or other land speculators either addressed or even identified. Their interests are often presumed to be consistent with those of remaking towns and cities in a manner that "overcomes the legacy of urban apartheid" (p.7). They are generally assumed to agree that "The dormitory role of low-income areas must finally be terminated" (p.16).

But this assumption is belied by the respective roles of many suburbanites, bankers, developers, construction-material suppliers, industrial corporate polluters, estate agents, slum landlords, mining houses, and speculators in attacking the homeless, redlining townships and areas that are desegregating, directing excessive investment into high-priced commercial developments, raising prices of building materials inordinately through cartel power, polluting the urban air and water, steering clients on a racial basis (while ignoring the township real estate market), gouging desperate tenants, maintaining the migrant labor system, and warehousing vacant land, to name a few common practices. Few if any of these practices are explicitly addressed in the *UDS*, which by implication suggests that no government action should be taken against them.

A contemporary example of some urgency is the Gauteng Provincial Housing Board's consistent blockage of the progressive land release strategy promoted by the Johannesburg Planning and Urbanization Department and the Gauteng government. Banking and suburban interests aim to prevent property devaluation that they believe will result from low-income development being "too close" to middle-class residents (for the first time, the PHB insists on provision of "development impact assessments" geared to property values).

The neoliberal impression is reinforced when, across a variety of issues, including those just mentioned, one compares the *UDS* to the original *RDP*. The most important of these comparisons are in the nature of the *UDS* drafting process, the degree to which social resources can be marshalled to reshape our cities, the respective roles of the market, the state, and civil society, deconcentration policies, the quality and cost of housing and related services, reform of urban finance and transport, local economic development, and privatization. There are also omissions, of which the neglect of women, youth, and disabled people stands out. All these shortcomings are explored in the following pages.

The policy-formulation process

The *UDS* states that "The drafting process entailed months of consultation with national, provincial and local government departments and officials, urban policy makers and experts and other urban stakeholders" (p.5). In contrast, "The *RDP* has been drawn up by the ANC-led alliance in consultation with other key mass organizations.... This process of consultation and joint policy formation must continue as the *RDP* is developed into an effective program of government" (1.1.3, 1.1.4). Moreover, "The *RDP* requires fundamental changes in the way that policy is made and programs are implemented. Above all, the people affected must participate in decision-making" (1.3.7).

No attempt was made by the *UDS* drafters to consult with mass-based community organizations or urban social movement networks, such as (to name the three largest) SANCO, the National Homeless People's Federation, and the Trust for Christian Outreach and Education. No attempt was made to contact progressive urban development and environment NGOs.

Measuring society's contribution to basic needs

The authors' failure to consult with grassroots organizations helps to explain why basic progressive principles regarding the need to redistribute wealth are rapidly dispensed with. According to the *UDS*, "Relative to the needs, the level of resources available from the Government is not sufficient to provide the necessary basic infrastructure in municipal areas" (sidebar, p.25).

The *RDP* is rather more ambitious: "With a per capita gross national product (GNP) of more than R8,500 South Africa is classified as an upper middle income country. Given its resources, South Africa can afford to feed, house, educate and provide health care for all its citizens" (2.1.3). The *RDP* proceeds to list a number of specific areas (many related to the International Covenant on Economic, Cultural and Social Rights) in which South Africans can consider themselves *entitled* to an adequate consumption level of goods and services. The *RDP*'s approach, in short, is to ensure that basic needs are met through vast increases in government subsidies when the market fails, and by mobilizing additional resources through partnerships, more forcefully tapping capital markets, and via off-budget methods.

Even though the issue of directing social resources into urban development is highly contentious, the *UDS* makes no attempt to prove its point (there is no reference to fiscal reorganization, tax levels, private sector financing leverage, or other aspects of redistribution) or contribute to debate on this critical issue. Ironically, the *UDS* later states, "the government's aim is to increase housing's share of the budget to 5 percent and housing delivery to a sustained 350,000 units per annum within five years" (p.28) which repeats the *RDP* commitment (2.5.5). With that level of fiscal support--roughly R8 billion in public investment per annum (in present value rands)--devoted to the capital costs of housing, and with the sorts of cross-subsidies and lifeline service provision anticipated in the *RDP* to offset households' ongoing expenses, there is no question that the supply of services at full (not partial) levels is financially feasible for all South Africans.

What role for the market?

Partly reflecting its origins in private sector research and ideology (as Bernstein records), the *UDS* boldly states,

> The government has great confidence in the private sector's ability to identify opportunities and secure an efficient allocation of resources. The preconditions for this are a proper market environment and the necessary supporting mechanisms to address market failure (e.g., intergovernmental grants, public intermediaries like the Development Bank of Southern Africa, etc). If these preconditions are met, the private sector can invest significantly in urban areas of different sizes. Ongoing attention is being given to this matter. This is being done in close consultation with various sectors, notably financial and construction interests and public sector intermediaries like the Development Bank of Southern Africa. (p.22)

The DBSA co-author certainly earned his salary in this paragraph. But contrast this "great confidence" to the *RDP*'s doubts about the market:

> The South African economy is characterized by excessive concentration of economic power in the hands of a tiny minority of the population. Through the pyramid system and the resultant control over a vast network of subsidiary companies, a small number of very large conglomerates now dominate the production, distribution and financial sectors. In addition there is a high degree of monopolization and blatant anti-competitive tendencies such as predatory pricing and

> interlocking directorships in certain industries (4.1.5).... Exploitation in rentals charged and in quality of housing provided must be specifically legislated against (2.5.9).... Cartels, price agreements and market share agreements [in the supply of construction materials] must end, and consideration must be given to public, worker and community-based ownership where the market fails to provide a reasonably priced product. (2.5.19)

The *RDP* provides many other examples of skepticism regarding the private sector's ability to contribute to reconstruction and development without high levels of state regulation and intervention. The *UDS* is essentially uncritical, and this has important policy implications. After nearly two years of democratic government, very little has been and is being done at national level to fundamentally challenge the power of the private sector in urban development, even where the banks refuse to make home loans, developers fail to deliver on government contracts, construction-materials firms raise their prices unreasonably, polluters ruin the environment, landlords systematically run down properties, mining houses refuse to part with desperately needed land, etc. (Some provincial and local authorities are making progress, but with scarce support from national departments.) Moreover, the *UDS* posits as a logical corollary that not only should the private sector continue with business as usual, proactive state interventions to correct market failure should also be avoided at all cost.

Should the state address urbanization patterns?

According to the *UDS*, no major state intervention is required in South Africa's urbanization process: "The country's largest cities are not excessively large by international standards, and the rates of growth of the various tiers also appear to be normal. Hence there appears to be little reason to favor policies which may artificially induce or restrain growth in a particular center, region or tier" (p.9). Moreover, "the growth rate is sufficiently normal to suggest that effective urban management is possible and there is, therefore, no justification for interventionist policies which attempt to prevent urbanization" (p.9).

An alternative view is never mentioned, much less seriously considered: the megacities of the Third World and the large metropoles of South Africa (specifically, the five largest conurbations) are terribly overcrowded, dangerous, environmentally-unsustainable, unpleasant places that--even if growing at a "normal" rate--should undergo a fundamental transformation rather than be considered acceptable by international standards. In short, by downplaying problems associated with excessive concentration of population, and by focusing only on relative growth/size as the indicator for state intervention, the *UDS* ignores the numerous other reasons for the state to help shape urbanization patterns. The contrast between the *UDS* and *RDP* could not be clearer:

> Macro-economic policies must take into consideration their effect upon the geographic distribution of economic activity. Additional strategies must address the excessive growth of the largest urban centers, the skewed distribution of population within rural areas, the role of small and medium-sized towns, and the future of declining towns and regions, and the apartheid dumping grounds. (4.3.4)

By comparison to Third World cities, South African urbanization patterns are not awful, but is the ideal in this critical area merely the "international standard"? After all, it is clear that certain macro-economic policies (such as very high interest rates, or reduced tariff protection for agriculture) are intensifying the rural crisis and speeding the urbanization of laid-off farmworkers and evicted labor-tenants. Instead of the *laisser-faire UDS* (which promotes drift to the major cities), government support for village or small town economies would be closer to the spirit of the *RDP*. But such opportunities perhaps reminded the drafters of apartheid-era deconcentration policies.

What role for decentralization/deconcentration policies?

The *UDS* correctly notes that "the legacy of decentralization and deconcentration policies has left these cities and towns with industrial zones and townships far away from town centers" (p.13). As a result, "Costly and uneconomic subsidies will be phased out.... Public investment at all levels will be expected to relate to the economic or functional base and potential of an area" (p.22). The *RDP*'s perspective is not only more nuanced, it explicitly recognizes that tens of thousands of jobs and enormous amounts of fixed capital are still located in the deconcentration areas:

> The incentives for decentralization introduced under apartheid frequently proved excessively discretionary and open to misuse. Still, in many areas simply eliminating them would cause severe job losses. For this reason, the democratic government must establish clear-cut guidelines and procedures for reviewing decentralization incentives. Where communities and workers can certify that the subsidies are being

> utilized in a sustainable, non-exploitative manner, the democratic government must maintain the incentives. Otherwise, it must redirect subsidies to ventures that promote linkages within the local economy. (4.3.6)

The *UDS* not only ignores the progressive principles in the *RDP*'s discussion of the three dozen deconcentration points, it contains no explicit discussion of what will happen to the concentration of labor and capital that now exist there.

Related to this debate, one "urban reality" proposed by the *UDS* is that South Africa's small towns are incapable of growing into a useful, non-racial role as centers serving a transformed agriculture market: "The market dynamics around commercial agriculture have made it increasingly attractive to farmers to conduct their business in larger centers. Many small towns cannot meet the demands which might emanate from large-scale land reform programs in the rural areas" (p.17). Yet the "farmers" who conduct their business in larger centers are overwhelmingly white, upper-income commercial farmers, while those who will benefit from land reform are overwhelmingly black, low-income subsistence farmers. There is no basis to reject the possibility of towns meeting the needs of the latter group simply because they are less central to the economy of the former.

What quality of housing and services should be provided?

More specific policy arguments also deviate enormously from the *RDP*, particularly in the fields of housing and urban services. As opposed to the *RDP*'s generous promises of affordable housing and services to all within a reasonable time frame, the *UDS* offers a menu of substandard shelter and inadequate services. To get away with this requires the *UDS* to imply that shackdwellers live where they do as a matter of choice:

> The goal is to secure shelter and tenure for all South Africans, but it is fully acknowledged that the form this takes could vary sharply. Informal settlements, for example, have become part and parcel of the urban landscape and offer many people the most feasible option. Others attach greater value to formal structures and environments. Others do not with to own property and would rather rent. The government does not wish to prescribe and will continue to develop a range of options. (p.29)

From this, it is clear that an easy option for government is to provide "informal settlements." Indeed, most of central government's present housing policy is oriented to precisely this outcome, but the *UDS* does at least provide some specifics about how far below generally accepted standards neoliberal policy-makers are now willing to sink:

> An average national distribution of 55:25:20 between full, intermediate and basic levels of services in municipal areas is considered a realistic target for the infrastructure investment strategy over the next ten years.... "Basic services" means communal standpipes (water), on site sanitation, graded roads with gravel and open stormwater drains and streetlights (electricity). These services will be targeted at households with an income of less than R800 per month and charged for at between R35 and R50 per month. "Intermediate services" entail water provision through yard taps on site, simple water-borne sanitation, narrow paved roads with no curbs and open drains and 30 amps electricity with prepaid meters for households. These should be affordable to households which earn between R800 and R1,700 per month and will cost them between R100 and R130 per month. "Full services" mean house connected water supplies, full water-borne sanitation, paved roads with curbs and piped drains and 60 amps electricity provision. It is anticipated that households in the R1,700-R3,500 monthly income class could afford "low consumption" costing them between R180 and R220 per month. Households with monthly incomes of above R3,500 will be assumed able to pay for "full services at high consumption" at charges between R270 and R350 per month. (pp.24-25)

The *RDP*, in contrast, offers rather more hope for a decent residential existence: "As a minimum, all housing must provide protection from weather, a durable structure, and reasonable living space and privacy. A house must include sanitary facilities, storm-water drainage, a household energy supply (whether linked to grid electricity supply or derived from other sources, such as solar energy), and convenient access to clean water" (2.5.7).

Hence, in direct violation of the *RDP*, the *UDS* codifies apartheid shack settlements, and does so by implying that--in contrast to having a formal structure--these are the residential choice of their inhabitants. The *UDS* does not acknowledge that people live in shack settlements either because they cannot afford housing provided by the market, or because the construction of public rental housing ended nearly two decades ago. Moreover, the service levels envisaged by the *UDS* are, for nearly half the population, a dramatic step backward from the *RDP*.

Who should have access--and at what cost-- to services and infrastructure?

According to the *UDS* (drawing on a December 1994 World Bank report on urban infrastructure),

> Services and infrastructure will be introduced in line with the affordability levels of communities affected. The principle that people should pay for the services to which they have access is central. This means that the level of services in each area should relate to what the consumers there can afford and are willing to pay for. Where government support is needed to ensure basic service delivery, it will be provided transparently. Deliberate steps will be taken to remove any disguised subsidies. Limited cross-subsidies to enhance household affordability and secure "lifeline" consumption will be necessary. (p.22)

But what if South Africa's majority is so poor--especially in relation to the minority of luxury consumers--that "limited cross-subsidies" are insufficient? The *RDP* notes that enormous subsidies will be required, for instance, in the provision of housing and services:

> ....the democratic government is ultimately responsible for ensuring that housing is provided to all. It must create a policy framework and legislative support so that this is possible, and it must allocate subsidy funds from the budget--to reach a goal of not less than five percent of the budget by the end of the five-year *RDP*--so that housing is affordable to even the poorest South Africans. (2.5.5)

Consider just two other examples from the *RDP*: "The democratic government must upgrade hostels where residents cannot pay costs" (2.5.16); and

> ....the national (water) tariff structure must include.... a lifeline tariff to ensure that all South Africans are able to afford water services sufficient for health and hygiene requirements [and] in urban areas, a progressive block tariff to ensure that the long-term costs of supplying large-volume users are met and that there is a cross-subsidy to promote affordability for the poor. (2.6.10)

In short, the *UDS* leans heavily toward full cost recovery, and where this is not possible, advocates much lower service levels. The *RDP* leans heavily toward urban goods and services as entitlements, and hence where these cannot be afforded by poor households, it argues for state subsidy.

Finally, the *UDS* fails to mention that urban services in existing middle- and high-income areas are still heavily subsidized, and have been for decades, from surpluses generated through business levies (ultimately based on transfers from black workers and consumers whose employers and retail outlets were historically, by law, located in white areas). Why must the urban poor now accept that their position will improve without substantial subsidies?

In sum, the opportunity for the *UDS* to take forward debates on cross-subsidies, tariff structures, and social justice relating to particular services is missed. Similarly, an opportunity to help sort out malfunctioning urban finance systems is ignored.

Are banks a help or hindrance to urban development?

Among the supposed "Strengths of the Urban Sector" the *UDS* includes the banks: "A relatively sophisticated and effective banking system can finance much of the urban investment required and, with some innovation, will be able to explore new opportunities and serve the development market better" (p.13). The *RDP* is rather more critical:

> A handful of large financial institutions, all linked closely to the dominant conglomerates, centralize most of the country's financial assets. But they prove unable to serve most of the black community, especially women (4.7.1).... The democratic government must introduce measures to combat discrimination on the grounds of race, gender, location and other non-economic factors. The democratic government must, in consultation with financial institutions, establish prudent non-discriminatory lending criteria, especially in respect of creditworthiness and collateral; reform the laws on women and banking to ensure equality; forbid blanket bans on mortgage bonds to specific communities ("redlining"); require banks to give their reasons when turning down a loan application; establish community liaison boards; develop simpler forms for contracts and applications, and create an environment which reduces the risk profile of lending to small black-owned enterprises and requires banks to lend a rising share of their assets to small, black-owned enterprise. (4.7.3)

The *UDS* offers only this half-hearted, voluntary measure: "An agreed code of conduct for mortgage lending will require banks to apply credit criteria on a non-discriminatory basis" (p.29). The difference in assumptions about bank lending is clear, and so are the policy implications. The *UDS* promotes the Department of Housing plan to give banks additional positive incentives and support, including providing a generous subsidized guarantee program and intervening (against consumers) to end bond boycotts and evict defaulters. The *RDP* emphasizes regulation of the banks and "to enforce laws against discrimination.... financial ombuds structures must include community representatives" (4.7.3).

Moreover, the *UDS* does not admit the fact that the Department of Housing has formally approved the redlining of more than 200 townships that were not approved as boycott-free under the Mortgage Indemnity Scheme. Nor does it concede that low-income, mainly black applicants are being discriminated against through a far higher loan cost (22 percent on a bond at present, compared to 17.25 percent for higher-income white clients). Nor does it acknowledge the Department of Housing's explicit approval of such interest rate segmentation.

How should government relate to banks regarding housing defaults and guarantee schemes?

Consistent with its high regard for banks, the *UDS* offers three types of housing finance programs with a "supply-side" (pro-bank) orientation:

- Existing Properties in Possession: Where no payments are being made by occupants, and financiers are unable to obtain relief in accordance with court orders and contractual rights, actions taken will have to be consistent with those of the Mortgage Indemnity Scheme.
- Rightsizing: A service organization, SERVCON, has been established which will help borrowers to downsize/rightsize their accommodation to suit their affordability level.
- Mortgage Indemnity Scheme: Government is to indemnify financial institutions for losses within certain limits. This will apply where normal contractual rights to access and attached securities provided for mortgage loans cannot be exercised due to a breakdown in the due process of law (p.29).

The *RDP* argues that "Locally-controlled Housing Associations or cooperatives must be supported, in part to take over properties in possession of banks due to foreclosure" (2.5.15), a provision which apparently has been ignored in subsequent policy-making. The concept of rightsizing is not inconsistent with the *RDP*, but it is inconsistent with the availability of smaller, low-cost houses (as is widely recognized, there simply aren't any that people who have defaulted on larger houses can now move into). Rightsizing is the product of poor policy-making and evidence of a lack of familiarity with the nature of the housing market.

Finally, the Department of Housing's Mortgage Indemnity Scheme is "supply-side" in orientation in that it only assists the lender, not the borrower. There are no provisions to support those borrowers who, through no fault of their own (sudden unemployment, injury or illness, etc) are unable to make bond repayments. The *RDP*, in contrast, suggests that "Unemployment bond insurance packages and guarantee schemes with a demand-side orientation must be devised" (2.5.15). Moreover, the main political role of the Mortgage Indemnity Scheme is to remove the only tool--pressure not to foreclose--that communities had to negotiate better terms from banks.

How should urban transportation be organized and subsidized?

The *UDS* offers a long-overdue call for reviewing transport policy: "Policy towards the country's public passenger transportation system requires immediate reappraisal" (p.19). But one of the main *UDS* complaints is classically neoliberal in tone: "Transportation subsidies alone cost the fiscus in excess of R2 billion a year, and are particularly excessive in providing for the inhabitants of far-flung 'commuter townships'" (pp.18-19).

"Particularly *excessive*?" Most township residents who are forced into dangerous taxis, buses, and trains argue that present government subsidies to the collapsing transport system are particularly *insufficient*. Given that on average black urban residents pay more for transport than they do for housing, it would be unreasonable to request higher levels of cost recovery. The insufficient level of public transport subsidies can be raised, the *RDP* argues, by taxing private transport beneficiaries:

> All privately-controlled passenger transport must be effectively regulated and controlled (2.9.3).... Commuters should be encouraged to use public transport, and should be actively discouraged from using cars (via parking, access and fuel levies). The funds so raised must be used to directly benefit the provision of public transport. As a first priority, rail transport must be extended.... Rural areas require more frequent public transport and improved facilities, at affordable costs (2.9.5).... The needs of women and children for affordable and safe transport are important. Adequate public transport at off-peak hours, and security measures on late-night and isolated routes, must be provided. Additional subsidies for scholars, pensioners and others with limited incomes will be considered. (2.9.13)

While the *UDS* fails to take the transport debate forward from the *RDP*, it does hint that the *RDP*'s suggestions of much more generous transport subsidies--especially for residential (and other) victims of apartheid--should not be seriously considered.

How best to promote urban economic development?

The *UDS* makes general points in support of Local Economic Development:

> As a matter of urgency, government is resolved to establish a policy framework for Local Economic Development (LED); promote the concept of LED at national, provincial and, most importantly, at local government level; establish fiscal and regulatory mechanisms to support LED; assist relevant stakeholders in urban and rural areas to initiate LED ventures--effectively as pilot projects--and thereby gain experience in the utilization of LED techniques. (p.33)

But the *UDS* neglects to provide specific suggestions about what kind of LED, who benefits, and who drives the process. In contrast, the *RDP* has many more suggestions (including control by civil society as opposed to business and state interests), culminating in a pledge for government subsidy support (which is conspicuously absent from the *UDS*):

> In order to foster the growth of local economies, broadly representative institutions must be established to address local economic development needs. Their purpose would be to formulate strategies to address job creation and community development (for example, leveraging private sector funds for community development, investment strategies, training, small business and agricultural development, etc.). If necessary, the democratic government must provide some subsidies as a catalyst for job-creation programs controlled by communities and/or workers, and target appropriate job creation and development programs in the most neglected and impoverished areas of our country. Ultimately, all such projects should sustain themselves. (4.3.5)

What scope for privatization of local authority functions?

The *UDS* is cleverly worded to avoid controversy on the privatization issue, but it is not difficult to see where the "public-private partnership" policy is moving:

> Partnerships can be formed to manage and administer certain services on behalf of the Local Authority, to invest in service delivery companies (often jointly with overseas investors) or to finance infrastructure investments. Such arrangements could vary between corporatization of local government departments into independent business units, service contracts, lease arrangements, "build-operate-transfer," "build-operate-own" arrangements through to full-scale privatization. (p.36)

Although the *UDS* does not call explicitly for privatization, neither does it warn against this approach by referring to the damage done to goods and service delivery in South Africa by more than two decades of privatization, commercialization, and shrinkage of local government. The *RDP*, in contrast, is far more measured about privatization:

> In restructuring the public sector to carry out national goals, the balance of evidence will guide will guide the decision for or against various economic policy measures. The democratic government must therefore consider: increasing the public sector in strategic areas through, for example, nationalization, purchasing a shareholding in companies, establishing new public corporations or joint ventures with the private sector; and reducing the public sector in certain areas in ways that enhance efficiency, advance affirmative action and empower the historically disadvantaged, while ensuring the protection of both consumers and the rights and employment of workers (4.2.5). The democratic government will reverse privatization programs that are contrary to the public interest. (4.4.4.3)

More generally, in a discussion of institutions required for urban development, the role of local government is again poorly considered. In the wake of the November 1995 elections, local government is assumed to be "fully democratic" and "non-racial" (p.35). The *UDS* hence ignores the racial voting weight given to white-dominated wards (an automatic 30 percent of council seats) and the veto power over budgets and zoning that can be wielded by a small local council minority of 33 percent. The *UDS* also comments that "Where local authorities have a strong rates base, all efforts should be made to leverage finance from the capital markets for development initiatives" (p.36). No mention is made of the role of major capital market institutions (the life offices and banks) in discriminating against all of South Africa's local authorities in the early 1990s, as it became apparent that they would become integrated with black townships. No capital market interventions are contemplated other than "the use of public intermediaries and debt pooling" (p.36). In comparison, the *RDP* is much clearer: "If the major financial institutions do not take up socially desirable and economically targeted investments, the democratic government should consider some form of legislative compulsion such as prescribed assets" (6.5.17).

Finally, the *UDS* is inadequate when it comes to the institutional capacity of local government. As a result of the neoliberal approach to service delivery that is now gaining influence in many government departments, there are moves afoot to force local government to give up the right to supply services such as electricity and bulk water. This is coupled to various related measures that have had the effect of crippling local government across Africa and that may do the same in South Africa: decreasing intergovernmental grants, rate-capping, limiting planning powers, delivering from higher levels of government what can better be done at local levels, undermining community participation by relying on private sector expertise, and increasing direct political controls from the center in the name of efficiency. In short, more is expected of local government, but with fewer resources.

What will be the role of--and what level of assistance will be given to--urban social movements?

The *UDS* makes only the vaguest reference to social movements' capacity to "participate in planning and implementation and voice their concerns about service delivery" (p.42). Moreover, there is a sense that civil society is really only there to implement what the state deems necessary: "To implement the Urban Strategy successfully, it is essential to tap local initiative and to create local-level partnerships between public, private and community sectors. These partnerships will be actively supported by government" (p.39). The unasked question is, what happens if local stakeholders don't agree with the strategy?

The *RDP* was not only drawn up by democratic social and political movements, it reinforces the need to keep such movements active in the democratization and delivery process:

> A wide range of trade unions, mass organizations, other sectoral movements and community-based organizations (CBOs) such as civic associations developed in our country in opposition to apartheid oppression. These social movements and CBOs are a major asset in the effort to democratize and develop our society. Attention must be given to enhancing the capacity of such formations to adapt to partially changed roles. Attention must also be given to extending social-movement and CBO structures into areas and sectors where they are weak or non-existent. (5.2.7)

The *White Paper on Reconstruction and Development* (Chapter Seven) amplifies this argument considerably. The *UDS* is a step backward from the *RDP*, which specifies capacity-building support for community organizations, as well as support for their extension into areas not already covered. No details are provided in the *UDS* of the "active support" anticipated. And in its list of "Strategic Goals" (p.6) and analysis of "The Strengths of the Urban Sector" (p.13), social and community organizations are not included. Other major constituents are also neglected, particularly women, youth, and the disabled.

Distinctive needs of women, youth, the disabled

The *RDP* stresses that "A key focus throughout the *RDP* is on ensuring a full and equal role for women in every aspect of our economy and society" (1.4.6) because

> Women are the majority of the poor in South Africa. Mechanisms to address the disempowerment of women and boost their role within the development process and economy must be implemented. The *RDP* must recognize and address existing gender inequalities as they affect access to jobs, land, housing, etc. (2.2.7)

Similarly, the *UDS* makes the comment that it is "crucial to address the distinctive requirements of women, youths and other specific groups" (p.7) and that "Differential racial and gender impacts must be anticipated and planned for in every aspect of the implementation of urban development" (p.7). Yet in contrast to many detailed provisions in the *RDP*, no such distinctive requirements are ever mentioned in the *UDS*, and no differential impacts are anticipated anywhere in the strategy.

The same is true for youth. Because, as the *RDP* acknowledges, "Many youth are presently outside the socio-economic mainstream of the country" (3.1.4), there are numerous specific *RDP* programs to assist young people. Many have implications for urban development. For example,

> The national youth service program must better educate, develop, train and empower youth and enable them to participate in the reconstruction of society through involvement in service projects in the community such as literacy, welfare, and improving infrastructure. All development and job creation programs such as a national public works program must address the problem of youth alienation and unemployment. (3.6.3)

Specifically, the *RDP* calls for "environmental education programs to rekindle our people's love for the land, to increase environmental consciousness amongst our youth" (2.10.6.3); and notes that "Particular attention must be paid to the provision of [recreational] facilities at schools and in communities where there are large concentrations of unemployed youth" (3.5.4). No such provisions are included in the *UDS*.

Regarding South Africans with other special needs, the *RDP* also argues that "Although a much stronger welfare system is needed to support all the vulnerable, the old, the disabled and the sick who currently live in poverty, a system of 'handouts' for the unemployed should be avoided. All South Africans should have the opportunity to participate in the economic life of the country" (2.3.3). Specifically, the *RDP* insists that "The provision of appropriate housing for the elderly and the disabled is also an important priority" (2.5.9); that "a future transport policy must take into account the transport needs of disabled people" (2.9.3); and that "The *RDP* must seek to improve community care, rehabilitation and education for all disabled people, particularly the mentally disabled, and must support their families and care-givers. It must also increase access to relaxing environments such as recreational facilities" (2.12.7.3). Yet the distinctive urban design, employment, housing, transport, recreation, health care and other needs of the disabled are ignored in the *UDS*. Indeed, the *UDS* is characterized by important omissions in most of its key strategies.

Omissions from the *UDS*

Aside from the many stark differences in approach, there are other areas where the *UDS* disappoints the reader. Omitted from the strategy of "Integrating the Cities and Managing Urban Growth" is any specific consideration of suburban land markets, infrastructure for waste disposal, access to water, and the possibility of densifying large residential plots. Since excellent infrastructure exists in the largely-white, spacious, upper-income suburbs, this failure to specify how existing resources will be more efficiently used is inconsistent with the broader, market-oriented theme of the document. There is no mention of curbing land speculation, applying taxes to unutilized land, or land acquisition through rights of eminent domain (all of which are standard techniques for urban land management in other countries).

Omitted from the strategy of "Investing in Urban Development" is any concession that at least two of the three main programs--Masakhane, the Special Presidential Projects on Urban Renewal, and the National Housing Program--are widely considered to be failures. Because these failures are not acknowledged, there is no attempt to learn from past mistakes and correct these. (In contrast, the Department of Housing issued a major report in January 1996 acknowledging failures in the

National Housing Program.) Masakhane is considered "a joint initiative of the Government of National Unity, the major political parties and local government stakeholders" (no mention is made of community organizations, many of which are not by any stretch of the term "local government stakeholders") (pp.27-28).

There are other omissions in the strategies of "Building Habitable and Safe Communities" (such as community-based justice and policing); of "Promoting Urban Economic Development" (community-controlled and worker-owned initiatives); and of "Creating Institutions for Delivery" (a role for civil society, aside from government partnerships with businesses). In the latter case, a sidebar on "Community Involvement" notes only that this "will ensure greater accountability and integrity of local government, appropriate types and affordable levels of service, payment for services, and competitive pressure on service suppliers" (p.34), far short of the *RDP* vision of people-driven development.

From these standpoints, it is hard to see how the *UDS* can claim to be following *RDP* principles. Moreover, it is hard to see how apartheid urban planning can be reversed and apartheid cities dismantled. For while the *UDS* claims, "The intention is certainly not to reinforce the segregation between different parts of the city" (p.16), the document nevertheless also calls for development to "occur along already existing transportation corridors" (p.16).

Most importantly, whereas the *RDP* calls for many basic needs to be considered as entitlements, the *UDS* prefers that they take the form of commodities, to be provided only if the recipients can pay the full cost. Thus while the document promises urban residents they will be provided "affordable housing and shelter and greater security of tenure for urban residents within fiscal and other constraints" (p.1), the *UDS* suffers from treating those constraints as assumptions rather than political positions that must be interrogated. This allows *status quo* interests to enjoy the fruits of the apartheid city, without having to pay any price for the ongoing inefficiencies (aside from an anticipated rise of 2 to 3 percent in local rates and taxes).

Environmentally, the *UDS* provides substantial policy recommendations, yet omits leading arguments regarding urban sustainability. Indeed, despite its repeated insistence that South Africa's cities must come into line with global processes, the *UDS* is far out of line with progressive international urban environmental thinking. The

UDS does not address the relationship between cities and the sustainability of their ecological context in a way that goes beyond "impact analysis." It is now internationally recognized that the "ecological footsteps" of the world's cities now have global reach, and that they have become ecologically (and hence materially) unsustainable. Sustainability cannot be realized via the kind of neoliberal strategies that underpin the *UDS*. The approach of the city of Curitiba in Brazil is a living example of a progressive sustainable approach. In South Africa, sustainable urban development can only be achieved via the kinds of policies advocated in the original *RDP* and left out in the *UDS*.

Conclusion: A rewrite of the *UDS*?

Writing policy documents in the New South Africa is an exceptionally difficult exercise, given the contradictory interests and policies that have to be reconciled, at least on paper. It may be the case that many of the *UDS*'s key departures from the *RDP*--omission of community organizations, women, and other groups; lower service standards; emphasis on cost-recovery instead of subsidization; excessively pro-business orientation--can be changed through discussions, debates, and lobbying. On the other hand, given its origins and content, some might argue that the draft *Urban Development Strategy* is unfortunately not a document which can be amended or improved, and that government must go back to the drawing board and ensure that the process of drafting urban strategy involves a wider range of inputs and a return to both the principles and detailed policies of the *RDP*. Ultimately, the integrity of the *RDP* may well depend upon the capacity of urban movements to insist that South Africa adopt a genuinely sustainable Urban Reconstruction and Development Strategy instead of what now represents a neoliberal strategy for the development of urban *under*development.

chapter fourteen

The Final Nail in the Urban Coffin

with MZWANELE MAYEKISO

By the late 1990s, the most important reflection of urban crisis in South Africa was a version of the famous "IMF Riot," a spontaneous event in some areas but in others (such as Tembisa) the outcome of systematic organizing around municipal social justice issues. And yet, notwithstanding a modicum of progressive rhetoric in the *Local Government White Paper* (released in early 1998), the Departments of Constitutional Development and Finance continued with business as usual, which meant that early in the 21st century low-income South Africans would face an urban existence worse off in many ways than before 1994. Overwhelmed, too, by a "homegrown" macroeconomic structural adjustment program--including the highest interest rates ever, massive pressure to cut state spending, deregulation, privatization, trade and financial liberalization, and the deindustrialization of large parts of the manufacturing sector--South Africa's cities would take an ever-greater burden of the pain associated with the growing global economic crisis. Regrettably, this pessimistic account is an apt conclusion for a book that has documented a tragic betrayal--though not, I hope, without leaving some serious basis for hope. Virtually anyone who has worked in a South African township will have left with positive memories of the strength, humanity, and resilience of residents who struggle under conditions not of their own choosing. No doubt, poor and working-class people's own memories of recent campaigns for urban liberation still burn bright, and no doubt, they will again restore revolutionary spirit to mass-democratic organizational forms, and again direct these against an urban capitalism that continually reproduces cities of gold, townships of coal.

(The chapter was published as "Urban Betrayal: The ANC in the Townships," in *Southern Africa Report*, August 1998.)

Introduction: Municipal neoliberalism

The deterioration of municipal services and declining standards of infrastructure have become commonplace in post-apartheid South Africa. Housing has been a policy farce. Rising crime (especially in black townships), growing alienation, and political confusion mount.

All of this is not because South Africa is now under "black rule," as many conservatives would have it, but on the contrary because a combination of factors representing residual white power remain intact. These factors are evident in the profoundly anti-redistributive, market-oriented policies on municipal services designed in late 1994 by the World Bank and inexplicably adopted by the *RDP* Office in 1995 and Department of Constitutional Development (DCD) in 1996 once the *RDP* Office was closed and local infrastructure became DCD's responsibility.

Led by Minister Valli Moosa, a core United Democratic Front strategist during the 1980s, DCD had the misfortune of carrying over to the New South Africa some of the country's worst bureaucrats, the white men who designed the complex, surreal systems of racial segregation. But some of Moosa's new bureaucrats have decided to challenge the legacy of apartheid planning by invoking neo-liberal principles. Some are quite brazen about it.

In late 1996, for example, government's main infrastructure bureaucrat, Dr Crispian Olver--who during the 1980s was a leading white student activist and member of the ANC's underground armed forces--was challenged about his failure to adopt the *RDP* provision that services such as electricity and water should be cross-subsidized. Alusaf, the big aluminum plant in Richard's Bay, for instance, receives electricity at roughly R0.02 per kilowatt hour while rural consumers often pay as high as R0.48.

Olver's response, to the *Mail and Guardian*: "If we increase the price of electricity to users like Alusaf, their products will become uncompetitive and that will affect our balance of payments." More recently, in a Port Elizabeth seminar on municipal water, Olver blamed opposition to privatization by the trade unionists present for "the failure of the *RDP*."

In both cases, however, Olver was simply articulating principles established by World Bank teams who came not only to design national policy but also to invest in privatized municipal infrastructure (through a US$25 million equity stake made by their subsidiary, the International Finance Corporation, in a fund that promises a 28 percent US$ rate of return). This clearly generates conflicts of interest, as for instance when Bank staff went to Port Elizabeth in 1996 to study the capital expenditure on household water supply and after a week produced a plan with only one option: privatization. The tenders for establishing a formal privatization policy have just been reported back to the Port Elizabeth City Council, but the SA Municipal Workers Union vow to fight the plan.

Beyond the shrinkage of the state through privatization--ironically supported by former radical community activists of the SA National Civic Organization, whose near-bankrupt investment fund allied with the British water firm, Biwater, to bid for the first big municipal contract, in Nelspruit--another sign of declining standards suffered by low-income black South Africans is the level of essential services they can expect when new infrastructure is built in coming years.

Services surprises

For those with below a R800-per-month income who live in municipalities with no other means of topping up the subsidy, services will be reduced to a pit latrine (not flush toilet), low-voltage electricity (not enough to run a heater or hot plate), a yard tap (not even in an internal sink), high-mast lighting, and gravel roads.

Again, thank the World Bank for these declining standards, far lower than even the worst formal apartheid planning, which were established in a March 1995 infrastructure investment report and which are justified mainly by DCD's and the Department of Finance's refusal to cross-subsidize the provision of reticulated water and electricity. These services are now considered so expensive at non-subsidized costs, that low-income families will be denied the ability to flush their excrement or to turn on an appliance that requires more than 5 amps to run.

The excrement will often seep into ground water, however, through Johannesburg's dolomitic rock or down Durban's many hillsides or into Cape Town's and northern Pretoria's high water tables. Water purification costs will increase, diseases will multiply, and women will bear the brunt of the heaviest burdens. But these and many other socio-economic costs of the planned standards--as well as the countervailing benefits of the "alternative" *RDP* strategy--were never seriously factored in by Bank staff and DCD consultants.

The housing policy offers no relief, with official figures showing the construction of less than 50,000 units carrying the subsidy plus bank credit over four years notwithstanding nearly 300,000 subsidies granted (which at R15,000--and no inflation adjustment since 1994--are roughly half the amount required to build a proper house as mandated by the ANC campaign platform, the Reconstruction and Development Program, or *RDP*). Meanwhile at least 200,000 new families search for houses each year, as the backlog soars. The R15,000 subsidies provide enough shelter to qualify as "kennels," as recipients described them recently to Australian journalist John Pilger.

The ecological, public health, and gender-related problems associated with infrastructure and services will come to light in the future, once project developments are more advanced. But already South Africa has witnessed its share of urban protests since the November 1995 elections, not unlike the "IMF Riots" that have gripped so many Third World cities.

Urban protest

Most strife has come in the deregulated field of urban transport, where instead of massive provision of public transport as the *RDP* mandated, Minister Mac Maharaj expanded the neoliberal policies of the National Party regime, failing to stem the ubiquitous taxi violence and accidents bred by overtrading and an intense speed-up of drivers in search of profit. On public rail lines, as well, transport restrictions and higher commuter prices in Tembisa (just east of Johannesburg) sparked riots that left nearly a dozen people dead at the hands of a (privatized) security company in mid-1996.

In early 1997, even more intense riots broke out in El Dorado Park, the low-income coloured township of Johannesburg whose local political leaders have regularly taken up populist, ethnicist campaigns against the ANC. During a day-long protest, four people were killed over resident demands for lower municipal rates. In August 1997, several protests over service payments shook East Rand and Pretoria townships, the Mpumalanga town of Secunda, and even Butterworth in the distant ex-Transkei (where after three straight days of protest against municipal officials one resident was shot dead before crowds dispersed). In KwaThema, east of Johannesburg, the houses of three ANC councilors were, tragically, burned down by angry residents.

The protests were sometimes marked by a high level of sophistication. Thousands of residents of Tembisa went on a march that left R13 million worth of electricity meters destroyed one winter afternoon in August 1997, in anger about the installation of a "pre-payment" system that, in the words of local Communist Party leader Tebogo Phadu (writing in the journal *debate*), was "being pushed by transnational corporations--Siemens and Sony in particular.... [and that] would have a profound impact on our tradition of community organization/mobilization as it promotes 'everyone for him/herself' (i.e. individualizing payment), further marginalizing the working class, particularly the unwaged."

The last three months of 1997 witnessed an intensification, not amelioration, of local grievances. During that time the pace of water disconnections, on grounds of non-payment, soared--from 11,729 by just the 220 largest municipalities during the previous three months to 19,162--while the number of households in those cities and towns that could afford to reconnect rose only from 6,004 to 7,065. Electricity disconnections in late 1997 numbered 58,678 and reconnections just 35,113. The numbers of summonses issued--ultimately to kick defaulting consumers out of their houses--rose from 33,025 in mid-1997 to 55,234 during the last three months of the year. Tens of thousands more cut-offs occurred in the other 660 municipalities not recorded in surveys.

By mid-1998, the conflicts had reached even deeper into East Rand townships and smaller rural towns. In the townships of Witbank and Tsakane, municipal offices and a post office were burned after evictions and summonses stripped residents of their personal property. In Amersfoort, community residents kidnapped a leading councillor in anger over mass cut-offs of water which led directly to the death of an infant. Tembisa saw more strife over evictions from houses where commercial banks declared foreclosure. Everywhere, urban alienation and rural despondency were on the increase.

White Paper whitewash

At precisely the same time, a *Local Government White Paper* (*LGWP*) was being drafted by DCD consultants who managed to avoid any mention of these problems. Released in March 1998, the *LGWP* contains serious contradictions, omissions, and surrenders to neo-liberal orthodoxy.

Depoliticized analysis characterizes orthodox "developmental" white papers, and the *LGWP* is no exception. The numerous precedents for municipal social struggles prior to the early 1980s are ignored, and 1980s struggles are reduced to those questioning the legitimacy of apartheid political structures (not township socio-economic conditions). The theoretical approach underlying the ANC's "National Democratic Revolution" (the concepts of municipal dual power and organs of people's power, for instance) is evacuated. And the *LGWP* fails to recognize the subsequent inability of local negotiations processes to resolve deep-rooted municipal problems during the early 1990s, and why that might have been.

Yet the municipal quagmire, partly associated with the tragic inheritance of the Local Government Transition Act (LGTA), is at least conceded: "Real transformation has yet to occur.... The compromises reached during the negotiation of the LGTA, such as the delimitation of wards in a manner which skewed representation and the requirement that municipal budgets must be approved by a two-thirds majority, will remain in force until the final phase of the transition.... Huge infrastructural disparities and inequalities resulting from apartheid local government remain.... Delivery on new municipal mandates cannot be achieved within the existing institutional framework."

But having conceded the injustice (and practical failure) of this arrangement, the *LGWP* considers only a series of residual technical challenges: "skewed settlement patterns and extreme concentrations of taxable economic resources.... huge backlogs in service infrastructure.... great spatial separations and disparities betweens towns and townships and urban sprawl.... new municipal institutions which recognize linkages between urban and rural settlements.... entrenched modes of decision-making, administration and delivery.... inability to leverage private sector resources for development.... substantial variations in capacity.... need to rebuild relations between municipalities and communities."

These are vital challenges, to be sure, but only at the end of this list are readers informed, obliquely, that transitional municipal governance has had a deeply alienating affect on the ANC's local-level constituency. The next question is whether the kinds of provisions made in the *LGWP* begin to offer relief to "formerly disadvantaged" but still very much oppressed township residents.

Redistribution--from poor to rich

Our own sense of the neo-liberal formulations of municipal development policy leads us to the opposite conclusion: that the next period will see intensified alienation, largely because of the failure of DCD (as well as other departments) to decisively redistribute national and local-level resources to low-income people.

The *LGWP* offers at least lip-service to the idea of redistribution, as well as three specific (if relatively minor and localized) techniques: "service subsidies.... support to community organizations in the form of finances, technical skills or training.... linkage policies to directly link profitable growth or investment with redistribution and community development."

But in its dereliction, for example, in grappling with macroeconomic policy ("*GEAR*"), the *LGWP* implicitly toes the government line that trickle-down policies will ultimately benefit locales. The *LGWP* doesn't mention *GEAR*'s budget cuts, nor their implications for local-level service delivery. Nor is there a recognition that under the export-oriented logic of *GEAR*, competition between cities for new investors is likely to get out of hand.

More specifically, the *LGWP* fails miserably to prepare South Africans for the shock of receiving extremely low levels of infrastructure and services, as described above. There are, to be sure, vague promises that an "equitable share" of central government revenue will "enable municipalities to subsidize the operating costs of providing basic services to poor households"--without discussing the option of cross-subsidizing higher levels of services (rejected by the World Bank) or acknowledging the 85 percent real decline in such intergovernmental transfers since 1991. Here, in Finance Minister Trevor Manuel's office, lies the real "culture of non-payment."

Local democracy: Too expensive for SA

Likewise, there is no explicit mention of the bankruptcy or forced rationalizations of approximately half the 850 municipalities in South Africa, notwithstanding that this has often been mentioned by DCD officials in the press. The *LGWP* offers only a justification of "amalgamation" (and this based on a theoretical, harmonious relationship between urban and rural municipalities, not the reality of bantustan settlement patterns which have left most rural towns without recourse to a neighboring wealthy city).

The *LGWP* does acknowledge that income differences threaten to generate a neo-apartheid urban form, for "inadequate service levels may perpetuate stark spatial divisions between low, middle or high income users (particularly in urban areas) and jeopardize the socio-economic objectives of the Council." Yet there is no official recognition that precisely the DCD's low levels of service delivery--especially pit latrines which cannot be incrementally upgraded to water-borne sanitation--for low-income people will permanently relegate the poor to far-away ghettoes from which any upwardly mobile residents desiring higher infrastructure levels will have to emigrate.

Additionally, the chapter's various options for "approaches to service delivery" are highly biased in favor of privatization. None of the arguments for municipal transformation offered by the SA Municipal Workers Union, for example, are considered. The *LGWP* at least acknowledges that privatization carries risks of "cherry-picking" (refusal to provide services to low-income areas), poor quality services, and unfair labor practices. Notably, though, no warnings are made about excessive levels of profit (such as the 30+ percent in US$ terms demanded by the World Bank's privatization fund).

Fiscal crisis

The *LGWP* chapter on Municipal Finance fails to mention several indicators of fiscal stress:

- the country's very high--27 percent--rate of arrears on municipal rates and service charges;
- inadequate collection and billing procedures;
- increased "credit control" and service cut-offs across the country, without adequate safety nets or administrative arrangements for means-testing;
- default by 10 percent of municipal borrowers on the Local Authorities Loan Fund, and the dramatic decline in local authority bank accounts;

- more than a third of local authorities have difficulty finalizing financial statements for the previous year on time; and
- the systematic difficulty municipalities have in gaining access to credit.

In short, the *LGWP* neglects to divulge the conditions under which roughly half of all municipalities will be found to be financially insolvent. After failing to mention, much less resolve, these obvious problems, the chapter proceeds to take the most extreme, conservative interpretation of tariffs (price) policy for water, electricity, and other municipal services.

Cut off the communities

The *LGWP* provisions that a) there must be "payment in proportion to the amount consumed," b) there must be "full payment of service costs," and c) tariffs must "ensure local economies are competitive" by insulating businesses from cross- subsidies, together have the effect of preventing municipalities from adopting a) progressive block tariffs, b) a universal lifeline service to all consumers, and c) local level redistribution from often wasteful business users to low-income consumers. All these provisions directly violate the mandate DCD was given in the *RDP*, which explicitly calls for block tariffs, lifeline services, and redistribution from businesses to consumers.

The final chapter, on the Transformation Process, nearly entirely negates the roles of communities and municipal workers. Hence the document ends by appealing to citizens to trust a largely technocratic process. This may be entirely appropriate, for as an explicitly and implicitly neo-liberal policy document, the *LGWP* probably requires the demobilization of the two key constituencies (communities and labor) which would be capable of allying with the (unpredictable, petit-bourgeois) cadreship of ANC councilors to actually achieve transformation.

The transformation envisaged in the *LGWP* is essentially--in its key economic and development components--a neo-liberal amplification of local apartheid. The segregated city will now be cemented along class lines, with a small fraction of black South Africans expected to migrate into white suburbs which in all other respects will remain effectively intact. Township livelihoods and informal settlement survival strategies will decay. Gender and generational relations will become more tense under the pressure of municipal crisis. Unemployment will worsen as privatization takes hold, often entailing (as the World Bank predicted in the case of Port Elizabeth water) a 40 percent rationalization of municipal workers. People who once had access to close-by councilors in small towns will find their local councils many dozens of kilometers distant following amalgamation.

The DCD has many responsibilities and powers, and could have done far more in the *LGWP* to right historic wrongs than simply facilitate the free market. The question of achieving social and economic (and gender and ecological) justice, under these circumstances, moves decisively to civil society.

Watchdog--or watch the townships die

Who monitors the likely violation of constitutional rights when municipal water supplies are cut off completely? Who ensures comparability between white residential areas and black residential areas when vast distortions in standards of living become more not less pronounced? Who intervenes when national government has failed, in many of the most crucial categories, to provide municipalities with the leadership required to bring South African democracy to fruition?

If organizations of civil society do not urgently step forward to address the profound shortcomings of the *LGWP* and associated housing, infrastructure, water, energy and economic policies, then these questions will be merely be rhetorical. Evidence of the *LGWP*'s shortcomings will then continue to be in the fracturing of traditional alliances between community, labor and progressive political parties, which has been underway these past few years, not to mention the periodic riots of furious urban citizens and the denial of South Africans' rights to live in humane conditions.

Hope lies in the potential unification of two political trajectories now underway: one in the growing strength, militancy, and wisdom of the SA Municipal Workers Union in their anti-privatization struggles; and the other in the attempt, led by dissident progressive activists in the Alexandra and Soweto civic organizations, to establish an alternative community voice at national level. The latter has included a May 1998 launch of the new Association of Resident and Civic Organizations in Gauteng, that pulled many civics out of SANCO affiliations. The conditions for a community reassertion of independent civil society politics, working from the Left, are excellent, even if resources are extremely scarce for such a challenge to the Alliance power structure. Evidence of the potential for allying production and consumption struggles is found in the SAMWU bumper sticker that states, simply: "No to privatization! 50 liters of water per person per day free!" There will be more such issues where community and labor--and women, the youth, churches, and other social forces--will come together in unity against neo-liberal notions of development.

works cited

Abbott, J. (1996), *Sharing the City: Community Participation in Urban Management*, London, Earthscan.

African Development Bank (1997), "Investment Proposal: South Africa Infrastructure Investment Fund," ADB Private Sector Unit, Abidjan.

African National Congress (1994), *Reconstruction and Development Program*, Johannesburg, Umanyano Publishers.

_______ (1996), "The State and Social Transformation," Unpublished discussion document, Johannesburg.

Allanson, B. (1995), "An Introduction to the Management of Inland Water Ecosystems in South Africa," Report TT 72/95, Water Research Commission, Pretoria.

Alliance (1998), "The Global Economic Crisis and its Implications for South Africa," Paper presented to the ANC-SACP-COSATU Alliance Summit, 24 October, and reprinted in *The African Communist*, Fourth Quarter 1998.

Amin, S. (1990), *Delinking*, London, Zed.

Andoh, R. (1994), "Urban Drainage: The Alternative Approach," Paper presented at WEDC Conference, Colombo, Sri Lanka.

Angel, S. (1995), "The Future Lies in a Global System of Competitive Cities," *Countdown to Instanbul*, 1.

Armstrong, K., A. Glyn and J. Harrison (1991), *Capitalism Since 1945*, Oxford, Basil Blackwell.

Arrighi, G. and J. Saul (1973), "Nationalism and Revolution in Sub-Saharan Africa," in G. Arrighi and J. Saul (Eds), *Essays in the Political Economy of Africa*, New York, Monthly Review.

Backeburg, G.R. (1996), "Policy Proposal for Irrigated Agriculture in South Africa," Report KV 96/96, Water Research Commission, Pretoria.

Barchiesi, F. (1998), "Delivery from Below, Resistance from Above: Electricity and the Politics of Struggle over Basic Needs in Tembisa," *debate*, 4, 12-27.

Bassett, M., D. Sanders, C. Todd and S. Laver (1992), "Rural Water Supply and Sanitation Sector Review: A Study of the Health Aspects," Report prepared for the World Bank, Department of Community Medicine, University of Zimbabwe, Harare.

Benabou, R. (1993), "Workings of a City: Location, Education and Production," *Quarterly Journal of Economics*.

Benton, T. (1993), *Natural Relations: Ecology, Animal Rights and Social Justice*, London, Verso.

Black, A. and J. Stanwix (1987), "Manufacturing Development and the Economic Crisis: Restructuring in the Eighties," *Social Dynamics* 13, 1.

Blacklaws, G. (1991), "Leaders get Together to Talk over Town's Troubles," *Daily Dispatch*, 11 July.

Bond, P. (1987), "From Divestment to Reinvestment," *Dollars and Sense*, June.

_______ (1990a), "Speculation and Debt," *Multinational Monitor*, July/August.

_______ (1990b), "Alternative Politics in the Inner City: The Financial Explosion and the Campaign for Community Control of Capital in Baltimore," in M. Keith and A. Rogers (Eds), *Hollow Promises: Policy, Theory and Practice in the Inner City*, London, Mansfield.

_______ (1990c), "The New United States Class Struggle," *Capital and Class*, 40, Spring.

_______ (1990d), "Riding the Waves of Uneven Prosperity," *Africa South*, May/June.

_______ (1990e), "The Wild Card in the Economy," *Africa South*, March/April.

_______ (1990f), "The Struggle for the City is On," *Africa South*, September/October.

_______ (1990g), "The Battle for Township Housing," *Southern Africa Chronicle*, 3, 6.

_______ (1990h), "Deracialised Urbanization," *New African*, 10 September.

_______ (1991a), *Commanding Heights and Community Control*, Johannesburg, Ravan Press.

_______ (1991b), "The Theory of Economy," Johannesburg, Phambili Books Pamphlet Series.

_______ (1991c), "Possibly the City's Best Hope: Review of Richard Tomlinson, *Urbanization in Post-Apartheid South Africa*," *Weekly Mail*, 21 February.

_______ (1991d), "The Bare Backside of the 'New' South Africa: Many Thousands, Swamped by Violence, Still Live in Degradation"; "Black Polish and Balaclavas: Phola Violence Inquiry runs into a Brick Wall," *Africa South*, March-April.

_______ (1992a), "Finance and Uneven Development in Zimbabwe," Unpublished doctoral dissertation, Johns Hopkins University Department of Geography, Baltimore.

_______ (1992b), "Community Development Finance for Electrification Initiatives," Paper presented at the National Meeting on Electrification, Cape Town, 5 February 1992, and published in P. Theron (Ed), *Proceedings*, ANC Department of Economic Planning and Center for Development Studies, Cape Town.

_______ (1992c), "Facelift for Inner-City Slums," *Reconstruct 2, Work in Progress*, April.

_______ (1992d), "Redlining cuts off Jo'burg's Lifeblood"; "Just a Stroke from a Banker's Pen," *Weekly Mail*, 17 April.

_______ (1992e), "Alexandra Township Burning," *Financial Gazette*, 7 May.

_______ (1992f), "A Vision for Alexandra," *Financial Gazette*, 14 May.

_______ (1992g), "Urban Communities on the Brink: The Region's Citizens have to Live with a Cycle of Continuous Eruptions"; "Postmodern Mishaps: A Serious Case of the Po-Mo's in the Region," *Africa South*, June.

_______ (1993a), "Scenario Plundering," *Southern African Review of Books*, July-August.

_______ (1993b), "The World Bank Likes Capital Subsidies Too," *Work in Progress/Reconstruct*, December.

_______ (1993c), "The Fate of Hillbrow (Part One)," *Financial Gazette*, 8 April.

_______ (1993d), "The Fate of Hillbrow (Part Two)," *Financial Gazette*, 15 April.

_______ (1993e), "Housing Crisis Reveals Transitional Tension"; "When Housing Pressures Boil Over," *Financial Gazette*, 11 November.

_______ (1994a), "Money, Power and Social Movements: The Contested Geography of Finance in Southern Africa," in S. Corbridge, R. Martin and N. Thrift (Eds), *Money, Power and Space*, Oxford, Basil Blackwell.

_______ (1994b), "Who will Enforce a Redline Ban?," *Weekly Mail and Guardian*, 3 June.

_______ (1994c), "Huff and Puff and Blow the House Down," *Weekly Mail and Guardian*, 7 October.

_______ (1995), "Undermining the *RDP*," *Southern Africa Report*, July.

_______ (1997a), "Developmental Aspects of Municipal Infrastructure and Service Delivery," Paper presented to the *Local Government White Paper* Research Process, Johannesburg, August.

_______ (1997b), "Homegrown Structural Adjustment: Implications for Service Delivery and Public Health," in *The New World Order: A Challenge to Health for All by the Year 2000*, Proceedings of a Conference hosted by the International People's Health Council, National Progressive Primary Health Care Network and the South African Health and Social Services Organization, Cape Town.

_______ (1997c), "Infrastructure Plan Still a Disappointment," *South African Labor Bulletin*, 21, 2, March.

_______ (1997d), "Read the Fine Print," *Local Government Chronicle*, 3 October.

_______ (1997e), "Foreign Loans: No Free Lunch," *Local Government Chronicle*, 17 October.

_______ (1997f), "Will World Bank Reconsider," *Local Government Chronicle*, 31 October.

_______ (1997g), "Infrastructure Policy Flawed," *Local Government Chronicle*, 14 November.

_______ (1998a), "Uneven Development," in P. O'Hara (Ed), *The Encyclopaedia of Political Economy*, London, Routledge.

_______ (1998b), *Uneven Zimbabwe: A Study of Finance, Development and Underdevelopment*, Trenton, Africa World Press.

_______ (1998c), "A History of Finance and Uneven Geographical Development in South Africa," *South African Geographical Journal*, 80, 1.

_______ (1998d) "Review of Jennifer Robinson, *The Power of Apartheid*," *Journal of Southern African Studies.*

_______ (1999), *Elite Transition*, London, Pluto Press.

_______ and G. Ansell (1992), "The Crazy Pavement Wars go On," *Africa South*, November.

_______, S. Hosking and J. Robinson (1998), "Port Elizabeth," in E. Pieterse (Ed), *Studies in Local Economic Development, Job Creation and Poverty*, Pretoria, Department of Constitutional Development and British Department for International Development.

_______ and M. Mayekiso (1996), "Developing Resistance, Resisting 'Development': Reflections from the South African Struggle," in L. Panitch (Ed), *Socialist Register 1996: Are There Alternatives?*, London, Merlin Press.

_______, T. Mogale and D. Moellendorf (1997), Infrastructure investment and the integration of low-income people into the economy, Report prepared for the Development Bank of Southern Africa, Midrand.

_______ and Y. Pillay (1995), "Health and Social Policies in the New South Africa" (with Yogan Pillay) — *International Journal of Health Services*, 25, 4.

_______, Y. Pillay and D. Sanders (1997), "The Rise of Neoliberalism in South Africa: Developments in Economic, Social and Health Policy," *International Journal of Health Services*, 27, 1.

_______ and G. Ruiters (1996), "'Boycott Culture' could Worsen, not Abate," *Business Day*, 5 January.

_______ and M. Swilling (1991), "Scenario of an Unlikely Deal," *Work in Progress*, 73.

_______ and M. Swilling (1992), "World Bank Financing for Urban Development: Issues and Options for South Africa," *Urban Forum*, 3, 2.

Booth, D. (1985), "Marxism and Development Sociology: Interpreting the Impasse," *World Development*, 13, 7.

Border Rural Committee (1997), "Tenure Test Case Progress Report," Grahamstown.

Branford, S. and B. Kucinski (1995), *Brazil: Carnival of the Oppressed*, New York, Monthly Review.

Bratt, R., C. Hartman, and A. Meyerson (1986), *Critical Perspectives on Housing*, Philadelphia, Temple University Press.

Brenner, R. and M. Glick (1991), "The Regulation Approach: Theory and History," *New Left Review*, July-August.

Bryan, D. (1995), *The Chase Across the Globe: International Accumulation and the Contradictions for Nation States*, Boulder, Westview Press.

Budlender, G. (1989), "The Selling of Existing Properties in Alexandra," Unpublished mimeo, Johannesburg, Legal Resources Center, 4 September.

Building Industries Federation of South Africa (1995), "Analysis of Job Creation," Unpublished report, Johannesburg.

Bundy, C. (1977), "The Transkei Peasantry, c. 1890-1914: Passing through a Period of Stress,' in R. Palmer and N. Parsons (Eds), *The Roots of Rural Poverty in Central and Southern Africa*, Berkeley, University of California Press.

_______ (1988), *The Rise and Fall of the South African Peasantry* (Second Edition), London, James Currey.

Burgess, R. (1978), "Petty Commodity Housing or Dweller Control? A Critique of John Turner's Views on Housing Policy," *World Development*, 6, 9-10.

_______ (1985), "The Limits of State Self-Help Housing Programs," *Development and Change*, 16.

Cain, P.J. and A.G. Hopkins (1980), "The Political Economy of British Expansion Overseas," *Economic History Review*, 33, 4.

Callinicos, A. (1988), *South Africa Between Reform and Revolution*, London, Bookmarks.

_______ (1989), *Against Postmodernism*, Cambridge, Polity Press.

_______ (1992), *South Africa Between Apartheid and Capitalism*, London, Bookmarks.

Cape Town Metropolitan Non-natural Mortality Study Group and Health Consulting Office (1997), "Violence and Injury Mortality in the Cape Town Metropole," Report to the South African Medical Research Council, Johannesburg.

Carter, C. (1991), "Comrades and Community: Politics and the Construction of Hegemony in Alexandra Township, South Africa, 1984-1987," DPhil thesis, University of Oxford, Oxford.

Castells, M. (1983), *The City and the Grassroots: A Cross-Cultural Theory of Urban Social Movements*, Berkeley, University of California Press.

Chaturvedi, S. (1996), "Rural Enterprise Development: The Stutterheim Experience in South Africa," Manual prepared for the Stutterheim Development Foundation, Stutterheim.

Clarke, S. (1978), "Capital, Fractions of Capital and the State: 'Neo-Marxist' Analyses of the South African State," *Capital and Class*, 5.

_______ (1988), *Keynesianism, Monetarism and the Crisis of the State*, Aldershot, Edward Elgar.

Cohen, M. (1992), "Comment," in N. Harris (Ed), *Cities in the 1990s*, London, UCL Press.

Corbridge, S. (1986), *Capitalist World Development: A Critique of Radical Development Geography*, Totowa, NJ, Rowan & Littlefield.

_______ (1989), "Marxism, Post-Marxism and the Geography of Development," in R. Peet and N. Thrift (Eds), *New Models in Geography* (Volume 2), London, Unwin Hyman.

_______, R. Martin and N. Thrift (Eds)(1994), *Money, Power and Space*, Oxford, Basil Blackwell.

Cox, R. (1992), "Global Perestroika," in R. Miliband and L. Panitch (Eds), *The Socialist Register 1994*, London, Merlin.

Crankshaw, O. and S. Parnell (1996), "Housing Provision and the Need for an Urbanization Policy in the New South Africa," *Urban Forum*, 7, 2.

Davies, Bristow & Associates (1989), *Towns of South Africa: Black Towns of the PWV*, Durban.

Davies, R., D. O'Meara and S. Dlamini (1986), *The Struggle for South Africa*, London, Zed Press.

Davis, Mike (1985), "Urban Renaissance and the Spirit of Postmodernism," *New Left Review*, 151.

Davis, Mark (1996), "Financial Analysis of the Electrification Program," *Development Southern Africa.*

De Beer, Z. (1988), "Address to CSIR Conference: Finance--The Pathway to Housing," Council for Scientific and Industrial Research, Pretoria, 2 June.

debate (1997), "Editorial--Intellectuals in Retreat," #3.

Dedman, W. (1989), "Blacks Turned down for Home Loans from S&Ls Twice as Often as Whites," *Atlanta Journal and Constitution*, January 29.

Department of Constitutional Development (1996), "Project Liquidity Questionnaire 9," Unpublished paper, Pretoria, October.

_______ (1997a), *Municipal Infrastructure Investment Framework*, Pretoria.

_______ (1997b), "Project Viability--Questionnaire 14, Stutterheim," Unpublished Project Viability document, Port Elizabeth.

Department of Finance (1996), *Growth, Employment and Redistribution: A Macroeconomic Strategy*, Pretoria.

Department of Housing (1995), "Report of the Ministerial Task Team on Short-Term Delivery," Pretoria, December.

_______ (1996a), "Report of the Ministerial Task Team on Short-Term Delivery," Pretoria, October.

_______ (1996b), "Press Release: Measures to Enhance Scale Delivery of Affordable Housing," Pretoria, October.

Department of Public Works (1997), *Towards the 21st Century: White Paper on Public Works*, Pretoria.

Dewar, D. (1995), "The Stutterheim Experience: A Review and Appraisal," University of Cape Town, reprinted in B. Nussbaum (1997), *Making a Difference*, Florida Hills, Vivlia.

Dickman, A. (1990), "The Economic Debate," Speech to the South African Institute of Management, Johannesburg, 7 August.

Ditshwantsho tsa Rona Study Group (1982), "'They like our Hands, not Us': A Study of Policy Bearing on Alexandra from 1948 to 1963," *Africa Perspective*, 21.

Dunstan, J. (1991), "A Brick in the Wall," *Work in Progress*, 72.

Ecsecc (1998), "Local Economic Development in the Eastern Cape: A People-Driven Option," Discussion document.

Edwards, M. (1989), "The Irrelevance of Development Studies," *Third World Quarterly*, 11, 1.

Electricity Working Group (1996), "Report on Meeting South Africa's Electricity Distribution Challenges," Unpublished report, Johannesburg.

Engels, F. (1935ed), *The Housing Question*, New York, International Publishers.

Esrey S.A. (1996), "Water, Waste and Well-Being: A Multi-Country Study," *American Journal of Epidemiology* 143, 6.

Ferguson, J. (1994), *The Anti-Politics Machine: "Development," Depoliticization and Bureaucratic Power in Lesotho*, Minneapolis, University of Minnesota Press.

Financial and Fiscal Commission (1997), "Local Government in a System of Intergovernmental Fiscal Relations in South Africa: A Discussion Document," Midrand.

Fine, B. and Z. Rustomjee (1996), *The Political Economy of South Africa*, London, Hurst.

Foucault, M. (1979), *Discipline and Punish: The Birth of the Prison*, New York, Harvester.

Fourie, A. and M. van Ryneveld (1995), "The Fate in the Subsurface of Contaminants Associated with On-Site Sanitation: A Review," *Water SA* 21, 2.

Frank, A.G. (1967), *Capitalism and Underdevelopment in Latin America*, New York, Monthly Review.

Frankel, S.H. (1938), *Capital Investment in Africa*, Oxford, Oxford University Press.

Friedrich Ebert Stiftung (1996), "Stutterheim's BAC is now Independent," *Local Economic Development News*, December.

Friends of the Earth/Center of Concern (1995), "Open Letter to the G-7," Presented in Halifax, June.

Gelb, S. (1987), "Making Sense of the Crisis," *Transformation*, 5.

_______ (1990), "Economic Crisis and Growth Models for the Future," Speech to the South African Institute of Race Relations, 22 May.

_______ (Ed)(1991), *South Africa's Economic Crisis*, London, Zed Press.

Geras, N. (1990), *Discourses of Extremity*, London, Verso.

Ghirardo, D. (1984-85), "Past or Post Modern in Architectural Fashion," *Telos*, 62.

Goldstein, J. (1988), *Long Cycles: Prosperity and War in the Modern Age*, New Haven, Yale University Press.

Gordon, D. (1988), "The Global Economy: New Edifice or Crumbling Foundations?," *New Left Review*, March-April.

Greenberg, S. (1998), "Agrarian Reform in Perspective," *debate*, 4.

Greenfield, G. (1997), "Globalizing TQM: The World Bank's *The State in a Changing World*," unpublished, Hong Kong.

Grossmann, H. (1992)[1929], *The Law of Accumulation and Breakdown of the Capitalist System*, London, Pluto.

Halbig, G. (1987), "Alexandra: An Urban Renewal Project as Opposed to a Total Redevelopment Scheme," *Fidelitas*, April.

Harvey, D. (1973), *Social Justice and the City*, Baltimore, Johns Hopkins University Press.

_______ (1982), *The Limits to Capital*, Chicago, University of Chicago Press.

_______ (1985a), *The Urbanization of Capital*, Oxford, Basil Blackwell.

_______ (1985b), "The Geopolitics of Capitalism," in D. Gregory and J. Urry (Eds), *Social Relations and Spatial Structures*, London, Macmillan.

_______ (1987), "Flexible Accumulation through Urbanization: Reflections on 'Postmodernism' in the American City," *Antipode*, 19.

_______ (1989), *The Condition of Postmodernity*, Oxford, Basil Blackwell.

_______ (1996), *Justice, Nature and the Geography of Difference*, Oxford, Basil Blackwell.

_______ and Chatterjee, L. (1974), "Absolute Rent and the Structuring of Space by Financial Institutions," *Antipode* 6, 1.

Hemson, D. (1997), "Privatization, Public-Private Partnerships and Outsourcing: The Challenge to Local Governance," Paper presented to the *Local Government White Paper* Research Process, Johannesburg, August.

Hendler, P. (1986), "Capital Accumulation, the State and the Housing Question: The Private Allocation of Residences in African Townships on the Witwatersrand, 1980 to 1985," Master's Dissertation, University of the Witwatersrand.

_______ (1987), "Capital Accumulation and Conurbation: Rethinking the Social Geography of the 'Black' Townships," *South African Geographical Journal*, 69, 1.

_______ (1989), "Metal Box Provident Fund Housing Project 1988/1989, Final Report," Unpublished mimeo, Johannesburg, Metal Box South Africa Provident Fund.

_______ (1991), "The Regulation of Land Use Planning: African Residential Settlement in the PWV Region, 1970-1990," Unpublished paper, Department of Geography, University of the Witwatersrand, Johannesburg.

Henry, J.A. (1963), *The First Hundred Years of the Standard Bank*, London, Oxford University Press.

Himlin, B. (1997), "Some Environmental Cost Calculations Relating to Infrastructure," Unpublished report prepared by the Development Research Institute for the National Institute for Economic Policy, Johannesburg.

Hindess, B. and P. Hirst (1977), *Mode of Production and Social Formation: An Autocritique of Pre-Capitalist Modes of Production*, London, Macmillan.

Hinds, M. (1990), "Outwards vs. Inwards Development Strategy: Implications for the Financial Sector," Washington, DC, World Bank.

Hindson, D. (1987), *Pass Controls and the African Proletariat*, Johannesburg, Ravan Press.

Hollingworth, M. and M. Muller (1991), "Water Resources, Economics and the Future of Irrigation in Southern Africa," presented at Symposium of the Southern African Irrigation Institute, Durban.

Houghton, H. (1978), *The South African Economy*, Cape Town, Oxford University Press.

Imiesa (1993), "Umgeni Water Integrated Water Management Policy," Unpublished report, Johannesburg.

Institute for Policy Studies' Working Group on Housing (1989), *The Right to Housing: A Blueprint for Housing the Nation*, Washington DC, Institute for Policy Studies.

Jochelson, K. (1988), "People's Power and State Reform in Alexandra," *Work in Progress*, 56/57.

Johannesburg City Engineer's Department (1989), "Water Loss Analysis on Municipal Distribution Systems," Report 157 1/89, Water Research Commission, Pretoria.

Johannesburg Stock Exchange (1990), "South African Industrial Share Prices, 1920-89," Johannesburg.

Jones, G. and P. Ward (1994), "The World Bank's 'New' Urban Management Program: Paradigm Shift or Policy Continuity?," *Habitat International*, 18, 3.

Kane-Berman, J. (1990), *South Africa's Silent Revolution*, Johannesburg, Southern Book Publishers.

Kaplan, D. (1987), "Beyond the Indicators: A Perspective on the South African Economy," in G. Moss and I. Obery (Eds), *South African Review 4*, Johannesburg, Ravan Press.

Kaplinksy, R. (1990), "A Policy Agenda for Post-Apartheid South Africa," *Transformation*, 12.

Kendall, F. (1991), *The Heart of the Nation*, Johannesburg, Asagi Books.

Khosa, M. (1990), "The Black Taxi Revolution," in N. Nattrass and E. Ardington (Eds), *The Political Economy of South Africa*, Cape Town, Oxford University Press.

Kondratieff, N. (1979)[1926], "The Long Waves of Economic Life," *Review*, 2.

Korton, D. (1995), *When Corporations Control the World*, Connecticut, Kumarian Press.

Kowarick, L. (Ed)(1995), *Social Struggles and the City*, New York, Monthly Review.

Laclau, E. (1971), "Feudalism and Capitalism in Latin America," *New Left Review*, 166.

_______ and C. Mouffe (1985), *Hegemony and Socialist Strategy: Towards a Radical Democratic Politics*, London, Verso.

Leitner, H. and E. Sheppard (1989), "The City as a Locus of Production," in R. Peet and N. Thrift (Eds), *New Models in Geography*, London, Unwin Hyman.

Lewis, O. (1961), *The Children of Sanchez*, Secker & Warburg, London.

Lewthwaite, G. (1998), "Stutterheim Started its Reconciliation in 1990," *Baltimore Sun*, reprinted in *The Star* (Johannesburg), 4 May.

Lombard, J. (1988), "Housing Finance and the National Economic Scenario," Address to CSIR Conference: Finance--The Pathway to Housing, Council for Scientific and Industrial Research, Pretoria, 2 June.

Lupton, M. (1992), "Collective Consumption and Urban Segregation in South Africa," *Antipode*, 25, 1.

Mabin, A. (1985), "Concentration and Dispersion in the Banking System of the Cape Colony, 1837-1900," *South African Geographical Journal*, 67, 2, 141-159.

_______ (1989) "Struggle for the City: Urbanization and Political Strategies of the South African State," *Social Dynamics*, 15, 1.

_______ and B. Conradie (1987), *The Confidence of the Whole Country*, Johannesburg, Standard Bank Investment Corporation.

_______ and S. Parnell (1983), "Recommodification and Working-Class Homeownership: New Directions for South African Cities?," *South African Geographical Journal*, 65, 2.

Maclean, B. (1991), "A Commitment Built on Trust," *Daily Dispatch*, 11 July.

Madisa, E., P. Mason, S. Murphy and B. Payne (1990), "Berea Street Blues: A Study of Tenure in Relation to Attitudes and Experiences of Living in Bertrams," Unpublished Human Geography research project, Johannesburg, University of the Witwatersrand.

Magdoff, H. and P. Sweezy (1987), *Stagflation and the Financial Explosion*, New York, Monthly Review Press.

Makalima Johnston Associates (1997), *Stutterheim: Draft Structure Plan*, Unpublished document for the Stutterheim Transitional Local Council, East London, October.

Mandel, E. (1980), *Long Waves of Capitalist Development*, Cambridge, Cambridge University Press.

_______ (1989), "Theories of Crisis: An Explanation of the 1974-82 Cycle," in M. Gottdiener and N. Komninos (Eds), *Capitalist Development and Crisis Theory: Accumulation, Regulation and Spatial Restructuring*, London, Macmillan.

Marais, P. (1994), "The Latest Developments on Experiences in Making Available End-User Finance in the Affordable Housing Market," Paper presented to the *Euromoney* conference on "Financing Low Cost Housing," Midrand, 25-26 January.

Marks, S. and A. Atmore (Eds)(1980), *Economy and Society in Pre-Industrial South Africa*, London, Longman.

Martin, W.G. (1990), "From NIC to NUC: South Africa's Semiperipheral Regimes," in W.J. Martin (Ed), *Semiperhipheral States in the World-Economy*, New York, Greenwood Press.

Marx, K. and F. Engels (1848), *The Communist Manifesto*, Various publishers.

Matlala, M. (1995), "Wattville Housing Association: Lessons from a community-based development organization," *Planact Discussion Document*, Johannesburg.

Mayekiso, M. (1992), "Working Class Civil Society: Why we Need It and How we Get It," *African Communist*, Second Quarter.

_______ (1993) "The Legacy of Ungovernability," *Southern African Review of Books*, 5, 6, November-December.
_______ (1996), *Township Politics*, New York, Monthly Review.
_______ (1997), "Cobbett to Blame for Housing Shortfall," *Mail and Guardian*, 30 May.
_______ and M. Menu (1998), "Request for World Bank Inspection Panel claim against the Lesotho Highlands Water Project, Letter filed to the World Bank by the Alexandra Civic Organization and Soweto Civic Organization, Johannesburg, 3 March.
Mayo, S. (1993), "South African Housing Sector Performance in International Perspective," Paper presented to the 21st World Housing Congress, Cape Town, 10-14 May.
_______ (1994), "Housing Policy Reform in South Africa: International Perspectives and Domestic Imperatives," Paper presented to the *Euromoney* Financing Low Cost Housing conference, Midrand, 25-26 January.
McCarthy, J. (1986), "Contours of Capital's Negotiating Agenda," *Transformation*, 1.
_______ (1987a), "The Apartheid City and the Problem of Commercial and Industrial Location," Unpublished paper prepared for the Private Sector Council on Urbanization, Johannesburg.
_______ (1987b), "Paul Hendler's Rethinking of the Social Geography of Black Townships: A Brief Reply," *South African Geographical Journal*, 69, 1.
_______ and D. Smit (1984), *South African City: Theory, Analysis and Planning*, Cape Town, Juta.
_______ and D. Smit (1987), "The Internal Structure of the South African City," Unpublished commissioned research paper, Urban Foundation, Johannesburg.
Merrifield, A. (1996), "The Potential Construction Employment Opportunities Arising from the Government's Growth and Development Strategy," Unpublished report for the Department of Public Works, Pretoria.
Meth, C. (1990), "Productivity and the Economic Crisis in South Africa," Research monograph, Durban, University of Natal Economic Research Unit.
Ministry of Reconstruction and Development (1994-95), *Urban Infrastructure Investment Framework*, Pretoria.
_______ (1995), *Draft Urban Development Strategy*, Pretoria.
Moll, T. (1990), "From Booster to Brake? Apartheid and Economic Growth in Comparative Perspective," in N. Nattrass and E. Ardington (Eds), *The Political Economy of South Africa*, Cape Town, Oxford University Press.
Moore, D. (1991), "The Crisis in Development Discourse and the Concepts of Sustainability, Equity and Participation: A Way Out of the Impasse?," Paper presented to the Canadian Political Science Association Annual Meeting, June 2-4, Queen's University, Kingston, Ontario.
Morris, M. and D. Kaplan (1987), "The Implications of the New Technology for Industrial Location," Unpublished paper, Johannesburg, Urban Foundation.
_______ and V. Padayachee (1988), "State Reform Policy in South Africa," *Transformation*, 7.
Mostert, N. (1992), *Frontiers: The Epic of South Africa's Creation and the Tragedy of the Xhosa People*, London, Pimlico.
Mouzelis, N. (1988), "Sociology of Development: Reflections on the Present Crisis," *Sociology*, 22, 1.
Munck, R. (1993), "Political Programs and Development: The Transformative Potential of Social Democracy," in Schuurman, F. (Ed), *Beyond the Impasse*, London, Zed.

Municipality of Stutterheim (1990a), "Minutes of the Ordinary Monthly Meeting of the Stutterheim Town Council," 27 March.

_______ (1990b), "Minutes of the Ordinary Monthly Meeting of the STC," 11 April.

_______ (1990c), "Minutes of the Ordinary Monthly Meeting of the STC," 2 July.

_______ (1990d), "Minutes of the Ordinary Monthly Meeting of the STC," 31 July.

_______ (1990e), "Minutes of the Ordinary Monthly Meeting of the STC," 15 October.

_______ (1991a), "Minutes of the Ordinary Monthly Meeting of the STC," 7 May.

_______ (1991b), "Minutes of the Ordinary Monthly Meeting of the STC," 21 May.

_______ (1991c), "Minutes of the Ordinary Monthly Meeting of the STC," 4 June.

_______ (1991d), "Minutes of the Ordinary Monthly Meeting of the STC," 20 August.

_______ (1991e), "Minutes of the Ordinary Monthly Meeting of the STC," 5 November.

_______ (1992a), "Minutes of the Ordinary Monthly Meeting of the STC," 4 February.

_______ (1992b), "Minutes of the Ordinary Monthly Meeting of the STC," 7 April.

_______ (1993a), "Minutes of the Ordinary Monthly Meeting of the STC," 13 April.

_______ (1993b), "Minutes of the Ordinary Monthly Meeting of the STC," 18 May.

_______ (1996a), "Minutes of the Ordinary Monthly Meeting of the STC," 23 January.

_______ (1996b), "Minutes of the Ordinary Monthly Meeting of the STC," 20 February.

_______ (1996c), "Minutes of the Ordinary Monthly Meeting of the STC," 19 March.

_______ (1996d), "Minutes of the Ordinary Monthly Meeting of the STC," 21 May.

_______ (1997a), "Minutes of the Ordinary Monthly Meeting of the STC," 13 January.

_______ (1997b), "Minutes of the Ordinary Monthly Meeting of the STC," 26 February.

_______ (1997c), "Minutes of the Ordinary Monthly Meeting of the STC," 18 March.

_______ (1997d), "Minutes of the Ordinary Monthly Meeting of the STC," 24 June.

_______ (1997e), "Minutes of the Ordinary Monthly Meeting of the STC," 18 August.

_______ (1997f), "Minutes of the Ordinary Monthly Meeting of the STC," 21 October.

_______ (1997g), "Minutes of the Ordinary Monthly Meeting of the STC," 9 December.

National Business Initiative (1995), "Evaluation of Informal Settlement Upgrading and Consolidation Projects," Johannesburg.

_______ and International Republican Institute (1998), *The Local Authority's Role in Economic Development: A Handbook for Councilors and Officials*, Johannesburg.

National Institute for Economic Policy (1996), "Why Government's Plans for Service Provision must be Fundamentally Rethought," Briefing paper, Johannesburg.

Nattrass, J. (1981), *The South African Economy*, Cape Town, Oxford University Press.

Nattrass, N. (1990), "Economic Power and Profits in Post-War Manufacturing," in N. Nattrass and E. Ardington (Eds), *The Political Economy of South Africa*, Cape Town, Oxford University Press.

Navarro, V. (1980), "The Nature of Democracy in the Core Capitalist Countries: Meanings and Implications for Class Struggle," *The Insurgent Sociologist*, 10, 1.

Neckermann, K. and Kirschenmann, J. (1990), "Statistical Discrimination and Inner-City Workers: An Investigation of Employers' Hiring Decisions," Paper presented at the annual meeting of the American Sociological Association.

Nel, E. (1994), "Local Development Initiatives and Stutterheim," *Development Southern Africa*, 11, 3, 363-377.

Nel, E. and C. Rogerson (1996), "The Application of Local Economic Development Planning in East London, South Africa, 1927-1955," *Urban Forum*, 7, 1, 69-87.

Nelson, P. (1995), *The World Bank and Non-Governmental Organizations: The Limits of Apolitical Development*, London, Macmillan.

Nussbaum, B. (1997), *Making a Difference*, Florida Hills, Vivlia.

Palmer, I. and R. Eberhard (1994), "Evaluation of Water Supply to Developing Urban Communities in South Africa: Phase I--Overview," Report KV 49/94, Water Research Commission, Pretoria.

Palmer Development Group (1993a), "Urban Sanitation Evaluation," Report 385 1/93, Water Research Commission, Pretoria.

_______ (1993b), "Sanitation and the Environment," Urban Sanitation Evaluation Working Paper B5, Water Research Commission, Pretoria.

_______ (1993c), "Evaluation of 2 VIP Latrine Programs in Natal," Urban Sanitation Evaluation Working Paper B2, Water Research Commission, Pretoria.

_______ (1993d), "Simple Model Illustrating the Environmental Impact of Sanitation," Urban Sanitation Evaluation Working Paper B5. 1, Water Research Commission, Pretoria.

_______ (1994), "Botshabelo: Case Study of Water Supply and Sanitation Arrangements," Water Research Commission, Pretoria.

_______ (1995), "Winterveld: Case Study of Informal Water Supply Arrangements," Water Research Commission, Pretoria.

Panitch, L. (1994), "Globalization and the State," in R. Miliband and L. Panitch (Eds), *The Socialist Register 1994*, London, Merlin.

Peet, R. (1991), *Global Capitalism: Theories of Societal Development*, London, Routledge.

Peires, J.B. (1981), *The House of Phalo: A History of the Xhosa People in the Days of their Independence*, Johannesburg, Ravan Press.

Petras, J. and M. Morley (1990), *US Hegemony Under Siege: Class, Politics and Development in Latin America*, London, Verso.

Phadu, T. (1998), "An Inside View of the Tembisa Struggles," *debate*, 4.

Phimister, I. (1992), "Unscrambling the Scramble: Africa's Partition Reconsidered," Paper presented to the African Studies Institute, University of the Witwatersrand, Johannesburg, 17 August.

Pickles, J. (1991), "Industrial Restructuring, Peripheral Industrialization, and Rural Development in South Africa," *Antipode*, 23, 1.

Port Elizabeth Municipality (1997), "Public Private Partnerships for Municipal Services," Report by Director: Administration to the Executive Committee, 4 February.

Port Elizabeth Municipality (1998), "Report to the Management Team on Urban Water Demand Management," Report by the City Engineer, 11 March.

Pouris, A. (1986), "Price and Income Elasticities of Electricity Demand in South Africa," *South African Journal of Science*, 82.

Preston, G. and B. Davies (1994), "The Palmiet Phase 1 Scheme versus Water Demand Management & Water Catchment Management: A Case of Tunnel Vision?," Unpublished paper, University of Cape Town.

Prinsloo, D. (1988), "Die Afsaking van die Groepsgebiedewet en die Invloed daarvan op die Woonomgewing: 'n Leningstrategie vir Finanside Instdlilngs," MBL dissertation, University of South Africa, Pretoria.

Pye, L. (1965), *Aspects of Political Development*, Boston, Little, Brown.

Rakodi, C. (1994), "Poverty Lines or Household Strategies?: A Review of Conceptual and Methodological Issues in the Study of Urban Poverty," Unpublished paper, University College of Wales, Cardiff.

Ramos, M. and F. Cassim (1989), "Beyond Dependency: Peripheral Fordism in South Africa," Unpublished paper presented at University of the Western Cape Institute for Social Development "Lausanne Colloquium," 8-13 July.

Republic of South Africa (1996), *Constitution of the Republic of South Africa*, Act 108, 1996, Parliament, Cape Town.

Rencken, G. E. and D. A. Kerdachi (1991), "The Inadequacy of Conventional Water Treatment Processes to Cope with Future Poor Raw Water Quality," *Municipal Engineer*, July.

Robinson, J. (1991), "Post-Apartheid or Postmodernism? 'Progressive' Local Economic Development Initiatives in South Africa," Paper presented at conference of the American Association of Geographers, Miami, April.

_______ (1996), *The Power of Apartheid*, London, Heinemann.

Roome, J. (1995), "Water Pricing and Management: World Bank Presentation to the SA Water Conservation Conference," Unpublished paper, South Africa, 2 October.

St. Paul's Evangelical Lutheran Church (1989), "A Stutterheim Saga: 1864-89," Butterworth, Our Own Press.

Sanders, D. and P. Groenewald (1996), "Public Health and Infrastructure," Unpublished report to the National Institute for Economic Policy, Johannesburg.

Sarakinsky, M. (1984), "From 'Freehold Township' to 'Model Township'--A Political History of Alexandra: 1954-1983," BA (Hons) dissertation, University of the Witwatersrand, Johannesburg.

Saul, J. and S. Gelb (1986), *The Crisis in South Africa*, New York, Monthly Review Press.

Schapera, I. (1928), "Economic Changes in South African Native Life," *Africa*, 1.

Schumann, C.G.W. (1938), *Structural Changes and Business Cycles in South Africa, 1806-1936*, Staples, London.

Schuurman, F. (1989), "Urban Social Movements: Between Regressive Utopia and Socialist Panacea," in F. Schuurman and T. van Naerssen, *Urban Social Movements in the Third World*, London, Routledge, 1989.

_______ (Ed)(1993), *Beyond the Impasse: New Directions in Development Theory*, London, Zed.

_______ and T. van Naerssen (Eds)(1989), *Urban Social Movements in the Third World*, London, Routledge.

Simmonds, G. and N. Mammon (1996), "Energy Services in Low-Income Urban South Africa: A Quantitative Assessment," Unpublished report by the Energy and Development Research Center, University of Cape Town, Cape Town.

Sklair, L. (1988), "Transcending the Impasse: Metatheory, Theory and Empirical Research in the Sociology of Development and Underdevelopment," *World Development*, 16, 6.

Smith, N. (1979), "Gentrification and Ideology in Society Hill," *Antipode* 11, 3.

_______ (1990), *Uneven Development*, Oxford, Basil Blackwell.

Sogge, D. (Ed)(1996), *Compassion and Calculation*, London, Pluto Press.

South African Broadcasting Corporation (1993), *The Stutterheim Forum*, Video documentary, Johannesburg.

South African Communist Party (1989), *The Path to Power*, London.

South African Homeless People's Federation (1995), "Four Way Street," Cape Town, People's Dialogue.

South African National Civic Organization (1994), *Making People-Driven Development Work*, Johannesburg.

_______ (1995), "Strategies and Policies for Local Economic Development in the New South Africa," Johannesburg.

Spiegel, A., V. Watson and P. Wilkinson (1996), "Devaluing Diversity? National Housing Policy and African Household Dynamics in Cape Town," *Urban Forum*, 7, 1.
Stauffer, B. (1990), "After Socialism: Capitalism, Development, and the Search for Critical Alternatives," *Alternatives*, 15.
Stephenson, D. (1993), "Analysis of Effects of Urbanization on Runoff," Report 183 1/93, Water Research Commission, Pretoria.
Steyn Committee (1985), "Report of the Committee of Investigation into the Financing of Black Housing," Pretoria.
Stiglitz, J. (1998), "More Instruments and Broader Goals: Moving Toward the Post-Washington Consensus," WIDER Annual Lecture, Helsinki, Finland, 7 January.
Stutterheim Historical Society (1984), "Historical Stutterheim," Stutterheim.
Stutterheim Transitional Local Council (1998), "Town Treasurer's Report," Unpublished municipal document, January.
Sutcliffe, M., A. Todes, and N. Walker (1989), "Managing the Cities: An Examination of State Urban Policies since 1986," Paper presented at the Conference on Forced Removals and the Law in South Africa, Cape Town, 16-18 April.
Suter, C. (1992), *Debt Cycles in the World Economy*, Boulder, CO, Westview Press.
Swilling, M. (1990), "Deracialised Urbanization: A Critique of the New Urban Strategies and Some Policy Alternatives from a Democratic Perspective,' *Urban Forum*, 1, 2.
_______ (1997), "Inter-Governmental Institutional Arrangements for Fiscal Equivalence," Unpublished report for the National Institute for Economic Policy, Johannesburg.
Swilling, M. and T.Mashinini (1994), "South African Civics Meet the Bank," *BankCheck*, January.
Tandy, P. (1992), "Stutterheim Case Study," Corplan discussion document, East London.
Thorne, S. (1996), "Financial Costs of Energy Services in Four South African Cities," Unpublished report by the Energy and Development Research Center, University of Cape Town, Cape Town.
Ticktin, H. (1986), "The Transitional Epoch, Finance Capital and Britain: The Political Economy of Declining Capitalism," *Critique*, 16.
Tironi, E. (1987) "Pobladores e Integracion Social," *Proposiciones*, 14.
Tomlinson, M. (1996), "From Institution-Building to House-Building: The Second Year of the Government's Housing Subsidy Scheme," *Policy: Issues and Actors*, 9, 7.
_______ (1997), "Cobbett's Departure may mean Fewer Houses for the Poor," *Business Day*, 30 May.
Tomlinson, R. (1987), "The Year 2000: Possible Alternatives for the Physical Form and Structure of the Johannesburg Metropolitan Region," Unpublished commissioned research paper, Urban Foundation, Johannesburg.
_______ (1990), *Urbanization in Post-Apartheid South Africa*, London, Unwin Hyman.
Tourikis, P. (1981), "The 'Political Economy' of Alexandra Township: 1905-1958," BA (Hons) dissertation, University of the Witwatersrand, Johannesburg.
Tucker, R. (1989), "Housing for the Urban Low Income Population: A Strategy to Break the Finance Logjam," Memo to the Association of Mortgage Lenders, Johannesburg, 21 June.
_______ and B. Scott (1992), *South Africa*, Johannesburg, Juta.
Tweedie, D. (1997), "Bobbitting of Cobbett is not a bad thing," *Mail and Guardian*, 30 May.
United Nations Center for Human Settlements (1988), *A Global Shelter Strategy for the Year 2000*, Nairobi, UNHCR.

Urban Foundation (1990a), *Regional Development Reconsidered*, Policies for a New Urban Future Series, 3, Johannesburg.

_______ (1990b), *Tackling Group Areas Policy*, Policies for a New Urban Future Series, 4, Johannesburg.

Urban Institute (1991), *Urban Economies and National Development*, Report prepared for the US Agency for International Development, Washington, DC.

van der Pijl, K. (1984), *The Making of an Atlantic Ruling Class*, London, Verso.

van Horen, C. (1994), "Financing and Economic Implications of Household Energy Policies," Paper 18, South African Energy Policy Research and Training Project, Energy and Development Research Center, University of Cape Town, Cape Town.

_______ (1996a), "Eskom, its Finances and the National Electrification Program," *Development Southern Africa* 13, 2.

_______ (1996b), "The Cost of Power: Externalities in South Africa's Energy Sector," PhD thesis, School of Economics, University of Cape Town, Cape Town.

_______ and M. Davis (1996), "Raising Electricity Service Levels in the *Municipal Infrastructure Investment Framework*: Financial and Economic Implications," Unpublished report by the Energy and Development Research Center, University of Cape Town for the National Institute for Economic Policy, Johannesburg.

Vandergeest, P. and F. Buttel (1988), "Marx, Weber and Development Sociology: Beyond the Impasse," *World Development*, 16, 6.

Venter Commission (1984), "Summary of the First Report and Second Report of the Commission of Enquiry into Township Establishment and Related Matters," Pretoria.

Vivian, J. (1993), "Non-Governmental Organizations, Institutional Reform, and Rural Development: Findings from Zimbabwe," Unpublished PhD Dissertation, Cornell University Planning Department, Ithaca, NY.

Wagar, W. (1992), *A Short History of the Future*, Chicago, University of Chicago Press.

Wainwright, H. (1994), *Arguments for a New Left: Answering the Free Market Right*, Oxford, Basil Blackwell.

Wallerstein, I. (1979), *The Capitalist World Economy*, Cambridge, Cambridge University Press.

Walton, J. and D. Seddon (1994), *Free Markets and Food Riots*, Oxford, Basil Blackwell.

Wilkinson, P, (1981), "A Place to Live: The Resolution of the African Housing Crisis in Johannesburg, 1944-54," African Studies Seminar, University of the Witwatersrand, Johannesburg.

Wilson, W.J., (1987), *The Truly Disadvantaged: The Inner City, the Underclass, and Public Policy*, Chicago, University of Chicago Press.

Wolpe, H. (Ed)(1980), *The Articulations of Modes of Production*, London, Routledge and Kegan Paul.

_______ (1988), *Race, Class and the Apartheid State*, New York, UNESCO.

Wood, E.M. (1986), *The Retreat from Class*, London, Verso.

Wood, I. (1990), "The Compact City," Unpublished paper, Johannesburg, The Urban Foundation.

World Bank (1991a), "South Africa: Post-Apartheid Economic Options," Unpublished paper, Washington, DC, 27 March.

_______ (1991b), *Urban Policy and Economic Development: An Agenda for the 1990s*, Washington, DC.

_______ (1991c), "Urban Sector Aide Memoire," Southern Africa Department, Washington, DC, May.

_______ (1991d), "Urban Sector Aide Memoire," Southern Africa Department, Washington, DC, December.

_______ (1993a), *World Development Report 1993: Investing in Health*, New York, Oxford University Press.

_______ (1993b), *Housing: Enabling Markets to Work*, Washington, DC.

_______ (1994), *World Development Report 1994: Infrastructure for Development*, New York, Oxford University Press.

_______ (1996), *Global Economic Prospects and the Development Countries 1996*, Washington, DC.

_______ (1997), *World Development Report 1997: The State in a Changing World*, New York, Oxford University Press.

index